Cold War History Series

General Editor: **Saki Dockrill**, Senior Lecturer in War Studies, King's College, London

The new Cold War History Series aims to make available to scholars and students the results of advanced research on the origins and the development of the Cold War and its impact on nations, alliances and regions at various levels of statecraft, and in areas such as diplomacy, security, economy, military and society. Volumes in the series range from detailed and original specialised studies, proceedings of conferences, to broader and more comprehensive accounts. Each work deals with individual themes and periods of the Cold War and each author or editor approaches the Cold War with a variety of narrative, analysis, explanation, interpretation and reassessments of recent scholarship. These studies are designed to encourage investigation and debate on important themes and events in the Cold War, as seen from both East and West, in an effort to deepen our understanding of this phenomenon and place it in its context in world history.

Titles include:

Günter Bischof
AUSTRIA IN THE FIRST COLD WAR, 1945–55
The Leverage of the Weak

Dale Carter and Robin Clifton (*editors*)
WAR AND COLD WAR IN AMERICAN FOREIGN POLICY, 1942–62

Martin H. Folly
CHURCIIILL, WHITEHALL AND THE SOVIET UNION, 1940–45

Ian Jackson
THE ECONOMIC COLD WAR
America, Britain and East–West Trade, 1948–63

Saul Kelly
COLD WAR IN THE DESERT
Britain, the United States and the Italian Colonies, 1945–52

Wilfred Loth
OVERCOMING THE COLD WAR
A History of Détente, 1950–1991

Donette Murray
KENNEDY, MACMILLAN AND NUCLEAR WEAPONS

Kevin Ruane
THE RISE AND FALL OF THE EUROPEAN DEFENCE COMMUNITY
Anglo-American Relations and the Crisis of European Defence, 1950–55

Antonio Varsori and Elena Calandri (*editors*)
THE FAILURE OF PEACE IN EUROPE, 1943–48

Cold War History
Series Standing Order ISBN 0–333–79482–6
(*outside North America only*)

You can receive future titles in this series as they are published by placing a standing order. Please contact your bookseller or, in case of difficulty, write to us at the address below with your name and address, the title of the series and the ISBN quoted above.

Customer Services Department, Macmillan Distribution Ltd, Houndmills, Basingstoke, Hampshire RG21 6XS, England

The Failure of Peace in Europe, 1943–48

Edited by

Antonio Varsori
Full Professor of History of International Relations
Jean Monnet Professor of History of European Integration
University of Florence
Italy

and

Elena Calandri
Lecturer in History of International Relations
University of Florence
Italy

First published 2002 by
PALGRAVE
Houndmills, Basingstoke, Hampshire RG21 6XS and
175 Fifth Avenue, New York, N. Y. 10010
Companies and representatives throughout the world

PALGRAVE is the new global academic imprint of
St. Martin's Press LLC Scholarly and Reference Division and
Palgrave Publishers Ltd (formerly Macmillan Press Ltd).

ISBN 0–333–72338–4

This book is printed on paper suitable for recycling and
made from fully managed and sustained forest sources.

A catalogue record for this book is available
from the British Library.

Library of Congress Cataloging-in-Publication Data
The failure of peace in Europe, 1943–48 / edited by Antonio
Varsori and Elena Calandri.
      p. cm. — (Cold War history series)
   Includes bibliographical references and index.
   ISBN 0–333–72338–4 (cloth)
      1. World War, 1939–1945—Peace. 2. Europe—History—1945–
3. Cold War. 4. World politics—1945–1955. I. Varsori, Antonio,
1951– II. Calandri, Elena. III. Series.

   D816 .F35 2001
   940.53'14—dc21
                                                    2001035791

10   9   8   7   6   5   4   3   2   1
11   10   09   08   07   06   05   04   03   02

Printed and bound in Great Britain by
Antony Rowe Ltd, Chippenham, Wiltshire

Contents

Part III East–West European Relations in the Aftermath of the Second World War: the View from the East

Part IV The Partition of Europe 1947–48

Part V The Setting-In of the Cold War

Notes on the Contributors

Bruno Arcidiacono is Professor of History of International Relations at the Institut Universitaire de Hautes Etudes Internationales at the University of Geneva.

Stefano Bianchini teaches the history of Eastern Europe at the University of Bologna.

Jerzy W. Borejsza is Professor of History at the Historical Institute, Polish Academy of Sciences in Warsaw.

László Borhi is a Senior Research Fellow at the Institute of History of the Hungarian Academy of Sciences in Budapest.

Elena Calandri teaches the history of International Organization at the University of Florence.

Anna Di Biagio is Associate Professor of History of Eastern Europe at the University of Florence.

Ennio Di Nolfo is Professor of History of International Relations at the University of Florence and Deputy-Rector of the University of Florence.

Saki Dockrill is Senior Reader in International History at King's College, London.

René Girault was Emeritus Professor of History of International Relations at the University of Paris I Sorbonne.

Annie Guénard is agrégée d'histoire, gained her Ph.D. in history and is a member of the P. Renouvin Institute in Paris.

John Kent is Reader of International History at the London School of Economics and Political Science.

Martina Kessel is Professor of Modern History and Gender History at the University of Bielefeld in Germany.

Ann Lane is Reader of International History at the Queen's University, Belfast.

Wilfried Loth is Professor of Modern History at the University of Essen in Germany.

Vojtech Mastny is Fellow at the Woodrow Wilson International Center for Scholars in Washington, in charge of the Parallel History Project on NATO and the Warsaw Pact.

Antoine Marès is Director of the French Cultural Institute in Prague.

Svetla Moussakóva is maître de conférences at the University of Paris III Sorbonne Nouvelle.

Mikhail M. Narinskii is Professor of International Relations at the Moscow State Institute of International Relations (MGIMO).

Stevan K. Pavlowitch is Emeritus Professor of History of the Balkans at the University of Southampton.

Giorgio Petracchi is Professor of History of Eastern Europe at the University of Udine in Italy.

Ronald W. Pruessen is Professor of History at the University of Toronto, (Missisauga) in Canada.

Oliver Rathkolb is Research co-ordinator at the Bruno Kreisky Forum for International Dialogue in Vienna.

Klaus Schwabe is Emeritus Professor of Contemporary History at the University of Aachen.

Georges-Henri Soutou is Professor of Contemporary History at the University of Paris IV Panthéon Sorbonne.

Giampaolo Valdevit teaches International History at the University of Trieste.

Antonio Varsori is Professor of History of International Relations at the University of Florence.

General Editor's Foreword

We are living in an extraordinary situation. The Cold War is over. We are told that the world has now changed completely, though no one can tell us exactly what the Cold War was really about. Nevertheless, the bulk of historians and scholars, who used to write about the Cold War have now branched out into other subject areas, such as European integration, the sociological and cultural approaches to contemporary history, decolonization and imperialism.

This book is produced by historians who take the importance of the recent past seriously, and who feel that a study of the recent past, and especially an examination of the changes that took place *during* the Cold War, rather than emphasizing changes *after* the Cold War, will deepen our understanding of the present world. That is our *raison d'être* today.

For the last twenty years, a group of European scholars have advanced the revisionist view that the Cold War was not just a series of struggles between the two superpowers. They have successfully highlighted, for instance, the limits of the United States as a hegemonic power, by identifying the role of European states in shaping and directing the Cold War. They have also shown that Europeans had different interests and different priorities, which were not always in accordance with those of the United States. After the end of the Cold War, newly opened documents and other new research materials available in many former Soviet-bloc countries in central and eastern Europe have made it possible, as this volume shows, to reappraise comprehensively the evolution of pan-European history from the Second World War to the origins of the Cold War.

The Cold War was by no means a primary concern for European leaders until 1946–47. Although the Western powers understood Stalin's security needs for central and eastern Europe, they did not foresee that Europe would be divided by an iron curtain for several decades. The Cold War was born, grew and matured in Europe, but its end did not terminate, as some have asserted, the pan-European history of international relations. On the contrary, it has helped to resurrect it from the ashes of the Cold War. The war has influenced our way of thinking, values, and beliefs in varying degrees: some European countries felt that war in an immediate and brutal way, while other states escaped the worst by the skin of their teeth.

The volume is an informed account of pan-European history between 1943 and 1948, and it is about how and why Europe failed to secure a peaceful existence after having defeated Nazi Germany. I am sure that readers will learn a number of lessons from the recent past from this book, which they can pass on to future generations who will be responsible for determining the direction of the 21st century.

SAKI DOCKRILL
London

1
Introduction[*]

Antonio Varsori

More than ten years have elapsed since the fall of the Berlin Wall; the most important international leaders during the dramatic events which marked the last part of the 20th century are no longer in power. George Bush has seen the election of his son to the presidency of the United States; Margaret Thatcher is an elderly politician who is compelled to witness the achievements of the Blair Labour cabinet; François Mitterrand died of cancer a few years ago; Helmut Kohl is defending his image as a great statesman from the stain of serious financial scandals; Mikhail Gorbachev's political fortunes faded a long time ago; but perhaps the most tragic symbol of a past era is Ronald Reagan, who, struck by a terrible disease, is no longer able to remember anything about his presidential experience. The Cold War appears more and more a closed chapter in world history and the events which captured the front pages in the press for about half a century are now the topics for the cultural sections of newspapers and magazines and in order to raise some interest in the average reader those episodes have to compete fiercely with current affairs issues, which seem to be more relevant, such as globalization, the strength of the US economy and local conflicts from Kosovo to the Caucasus. Historians now show less interest in the Cold War and, in spite of the weakness of the euro or the difficulties raised by the enlargement of the EU to east central Europe – incidentally a consequence of the end of the Cold War – scholars of international history are focusing their attention on European integration, which is still in progress.

If the Cold War is becoming an out-of-date topic for everyday reading, its end has provided historians with precious opportunities. The opening of archives in former Communist countries in the early 1990s has made available important new evidence,[1] although in some cases

1

such opening has been rapidly closed down. However, the dialogue between western scholars and their colleagues from central and eastern Europe and, albeit to a lesser extent, China, no longer meets serious obstacles. The Cold War may now be interpreted with less political bias.[2]

The reassessment of the 'Cold War' has been one of the major goals of a research project, which was launched a few years ago by a group of international historians. Another important aim of this project is to examine Europe's role in the Cold War, as, on several occasions, this historical process has been portrayed as the contrast between the two superpowers – the United States and the Soviet Union – and Europe was perceived as the stage where the two international 'primadonnas' performed their roles.[3] But to contrast such a schematic view it would be enough to stress that the Cold War had both its origins and its end in Europe with the partition of Germany and the fall of the Berlin wall.[4] Furthermore most European nations were not passive elements in the East–West conflict: Britain, West Germany and Italy tried to develop autonomous foreign policies within the framework of a US-led western camp; France's ambition to develop an 'independent' foreign policy, from de Gaulle's Free France onwards, is almost a commonplace in the postwar historical scene.[5] As far as east central Europe is concerned, in 1948 Yugoslavia split from the Soviet bloc and in the mid 1950s it became the standard-bearer for 'non-alignment'; from the 1960s Romania played an autonomous role within the Warsaw Pact and, although for a long time the eastern bloc appeared to be more homogeneous than its western counterpart, the 1980s Hungarian 'goulash' communism was very different from the Polish military régime.[6]

It was an almost obvious choice that the first volume of the research project on 'Europe, East and West, in the Cold War' would deal with 'The failure of peace in Europe: 1943–48'. The chapters which form the present volume try to give an answer to questions which have haunted numerous historians.[7] Was the 'Cold War' unavoidable? Was it a consequence of the new balance which the Second World War had created in international relations? What was the role played by Europe and by European actors in such a phenomenon?

Most of the contributors share the conviction that during the final stage of the war both in the West and in the Soviet Union very few decision makers envisaged an open conflict between Moscow and the Western powers, at least in the immediate postwar period, and the victorious powers' postwar planning was based on the assumption that wartime co-operation would continue and would be the framework of a stable world settlement.[8] Furthermore Europe was regarded by the both the Western allies and the Soviet Union as the most important 'test case', which would confirm the anti-Fascist alliance in a postwar perspective. The United States – which came out of the war as the most powerful nation from both an economic and a military viewpoint – based its plans on a world-wide approach, stressing the roles the 'four policemen' would play in creating and policing a new world order.[9] Such a policy envisaged continuing co-operation with the Soviet Union, and Moscow had to be a fundamental partner. On the other hand the ideological characters of the Soviet state had been shelved and in the minds of politicians, opinion-leaders and propagandists Russia was the gallant wartime ally which had fiercely resisted Nazi aggression. In Roosevelt's view Europe was a test case in order to confirm allied co-operation, as all the major victorious powers, through their troops, were present in the European continent. Germany's defeat had been the main war goal and such an objective implied that Nazi-dominated Europe was the arena in which the anti-Fascist coalition had to create a new settlement; a model for other areas in the world. But the 'four policemen' theory which appeared to grant to the Soviet Union a leading role in postwar Europe, at least in east central Europe, conflicted with Roosevelt's increasing belief that the United States had to safeguard some role in the continent as a whole and the partition of Europe, as well as of Germany, into spheres of influence had to be avoided. Such an opinion was shared by Truman and was destined to clash with Stalin's eagerness to impose control on the European countries which had been liberated by the Red Army, so fuelling mutual disagreements and suspicions which in 1945–46 had already influenced the new administration's attitude towards the Soviet Union. However, the new Secretary of State James Byrnes still aimed at achieving some lasting compromise with Moscow, which would enable the signature of the peace treaties with Germany's minor allies.

In London, Europe was regarded as a key area in postwar planning and Britain's interests to favour a balance of power within the continent a traditional aspect of British foreign policy.[10] For some time British leaders tried to convince themselves that the Soviet Union had turned into Russia, a traditional competitor but a suitable ally too.[11] In 1943 the British Foreign Office suggested that liberated Europe could be ruled by the Big Three through common responsibilities.[12] Only in 1944 did Churchill begin to be seriously concerned about the Red Army's thrust towards central Europe and the power vacuum which would characterize the continent after Germany's defeat. The Prime Minister tried to create a new balance through the well-known Moscow percentages agreement and the creation of two spheres of influence. Later on Britain, which was aware of its military and economic weakness as well as of the need to face its worldwide imperial commitments, favoured the restoration of France as a European power which could counterbalance the Soviet Union's might.[13] But de Gaulle had no intention of being regarded as London's pawn on the European chessboard. After the end of the conflict, although the new Labour Cabinet, and in particular the Foreign Secretary nurtured growing suspicions about Stalin's ambitious plans, the British government appeared to stick to the principle of wartime co-operation, which did not contradict with the hard bargaining and local conflicts experienced with Moscow.[14] A total confrontation still seemed to be far off.

Only during the final stages of the conflict, France had been able to restore, albeit only in theory, the status of a great power and in spite of that the French authorities were not present at either Yalta or Potsdam. Nevertheless a French zone was carved out of the British and US zones of occupation in Germany. In fact Germany's fate was the main factor in de Gaulle's postwar opinions and plans.[15] The French wartime leader also was convinced that Moscow's goals could not be so different from the traditional objectives of Tsarist Russia. Therefore, France and the Soviet Union might share similar views about Europe's postwar settlement, above all the end of the German threat: the 1944 French–Russian alliance was the obvious consequence of de Gaulle's vision.[16] France's position was influenced by the fact that wartime co-operation with the Soviet Union was mirrorred by the internal situation whereby the French Communist Party played a paramount role in the coalition government in Paris. On the other hand numerous French diplomats and politicians remembered too well that both the United States and Britain had favoured Germany's rehabilitation in the 1920s and that British decision makers had been the advocates of appeasement in the 1930s. Last but not least the relationship between France and the Anglo-Saxon powers was negatively influenced by serious difficulties and suspicions: from Roosevelt's lack of confidence in de Gaulle to the rivalries which opposed Paris to London in the Middle East. It is not surprising that the Soviet Union could be regarded as a suitable partner, particularly in the European context.[17]

If the three major Western powers seemed to favour some long term agreement with Moscow about Europe's postwar settlement, at least until 1945 Stalin did not reject such an hypothesis. As some authors have argued, Moscow's postwar planning was very vague.[18] The Soviet leaders were mainly concerned with security and they advocated both the safeguarding of the territorial advantages achieved between 1939 and 1941 (part of Poland, the control of the Baltic States, Bessarabia) and the establishment of friendly régimes in the countries which bordered the Soviet Union. In Stalin's opinion such claims were substantiated by the triumphs of the Red Army, which in 1945 liberated most of east central Europe and defeated Nazi Germany. Furthermore, the Soviet leader favoured a three-power – later four-power – control of Germany. In fact it is very likely that 'influence' and 'control' had very different meanings in Moscow than in the Western capitals and Stalin was perhaps tempted to widen his aims as a consequence of the apparent weakness and the divisions showed by the Western powers. Furthermore, the Soviet Union could not forget that Communist leaders in east central Europe knew too well that they would maintain power only if they were able to destroy their opponents; on the other hand anti-Communist sentiment, as well as being hostile towards Russia, had been traditionally widespread in most of those countries and, with the exception of Czechoslovakia, local Communists enjoyed scant popular support. In fact in numerous eastern and central European nations, during the period between 1945 and 1946, the political balance appeared to be uncertain and if Poland, Romania and Bulgaria were under firm Communist control, in Hungary and Czechoslovakia the bourgeois parties still enjoyed some room for manoeuvre and their fate was not yet sealed.[19] Moreover, during the conflict the exiled governments of some Balkan nations cherished the hope that in the postwar years they could pursue independent foreign policies and in this connection they developed plans for the formation of federations, which found some support in London.[20]

If we take into consideration the characters of the Western powers' postwar planning, it is not surprising that they tried to renew fruitful relations with some countries of east central Europe. The British authorities made strenuous efforts to safeguard at least some of their interests in the Balkan area. Britain did not reject the hypothesis of Russia playing a leading role in this part of Europe, but it could not accept Communist rule, which would exclude other influences. On the other hand, the British cabinet could not ignore the development in Washington's policy which, at least in some interpretations, radically changed from an apparent lack of interest towards the fate of eastern Europe to a strong hostility to Moscow's goals.[21] However, by 1946, the Labour Cabinet had become convinced that Stalin nurtured definite expansionist intentions including the complete domination of east central

Europe. It was evident that the West could not do too much to change such a development.[22]

The aspiration to renew old bonds with the eastern half of Europe was shared by France too. From new archival sources it appears that the French authorities were very keen to strengthen their ties with a restored Czechoslovakia. In the interwar years Prague had been an important element of French foreign policy and, until the 1938 Munich conference, Czechoslovakia had been regarded as a faithful ally in the so-called Little Enténte; the Czechoslovak state could once again become a precious factor in a postwar settlement which would be characterized by Paris' will to curb German revanchism.[23] It is confirmation that in the immediate postwar years France appeared to be more concerned about Germany than about the Soviet Union.[24] The Paris–Prague relationship began to change only in 1947; in a few months French decision-makers became aware that Czechoslovakia was becoming more and more tied to Stalin's policy.

Although Italy was perceived as a defeated enemy, especially after the end of the hostilities, it hoped to enjoy some room for diplomatic manoeuvre. Rome's main goal was the restoration of both its independence and the status of a middle-rank power.[25] In this connection Italy's most important partners were the victorious powers, but Italy did not conceal its ambitions to exert some influence in eastern Europe; the Rome authorities did not ignore the political developments which were taking place in this part of the continent, especially the increasing Soviet influence, but they hoped to profit from the restoration of fruitful economic relations.[26] This is further evidence that past experiences shaped both the minds and the decisions of moderate politicians and diplomats who were unable to foresee the revolutionary changes which would characterize east central Europe, as well as the birth of an iron curtain which would divide the Old World.[27]

The hope of a renewed dialogue between the Communist movement and the representatives of democratic thought was a relevant feature in the attitude of most Western European socialists, as the common struggle against Fascism was often regarded as a factor which would shape the relationship among the European political forces which had defeated the Nazi threat. Such a view led the most important western European socialist parties to avoid an open confrontation with both the Communist movement and the socialists from east central Europe who were rallying themselves to the Communist-led governments. Only in 1948, mainly as a consequence of the Prague coup, did the Socialist International (at that time the COMISCO) openly condemn Soviet policy. If for some time in the immediate postwar years, most Western socialists had hoped to become a sort of 'bridge' between the Communist world and the West, from this moment onwards they were compelled to accept the existence of an iron curtain and they focused their attention on the European integration process which would, however, become a symbol of Europe's partition.[28]

The eagerness to restore fruitful bonds among European nations was shared also by numerous decision makers in east central Europe. For example Bulgarian archival sources demonstrate that members of the Bulgarian intelligentsia forcefully tried to renew their traditional contacts with Western culture, especially with France's intellectual milieu which had exerted influence on Bulgarian scholars and intellectuals before the Second World War. Such an attitude, which was nurtured in particular during the final stages of the conflict and the early postwar period, had political meaning too, as it showed that Western democracies, especially the European ones rather than the United States, were still a point of reference and a source of hope for bourgeois political forces in east central Europe.[29] Those hopes were quickly frustrated by the growing influence exerted by the Soviet Union and the local Communist parties and, although the Western powers were unable to counter the imposition of Communist régimes, they could not forget what was happening to east central European anti-Communist élites, and their longing for Western culture and models was further evidence of the totalitarian character of the 'friendly' régimes which were set up in the eastern half of the continent with Stalin's support.

Some of those aspects are confirmed by research in other eastern European archives. In Hungary's case the harsh economic exploitation pursued by the Soviet authorities has been stressed, an aspect usually neglected by the historiography on the process of Sovietization.[30] In fact to speak of the postwar situation in east central Europe as a coherent context would be misleading. The historical processes in this part of the continent were as complex as in the western half. As far as Yugoslavia is concerned – a significant test case – Tito's policy was shaped by the country's historical experience, especially the ethnic contrasts, which had characterized Yugoslavia's political life in the interwar period. Nationalism was an important feature in Tito's strategy as it could concur in overcoming the contradictions and struggles of the past which had severely hampered the structures of the state created at the end of the First World War. Communism, on the other hand, was the element, which could give substance to Yugoslavia's national identity. Those aspects would explain the patterns of Belgrade's foreign policy towards both the Western powers, especially on issues such as the Trieste question, and the relations with the Soviet Union.

But such internal factors seem to contrast with interpretations which stress the role played by the superpowers in shaping the path towards a divided Europe.[31] The influence exerted by the relationships among the Communist leaders in the Balkan area has been highlighted. Although their projects for dealing with a Balkan federation ended in complete failure, those plans were of significant importance in shaping the policies pursued by leaders such as Tito and Dimitrov and those events demonstrated that the heritage of well-rooted local historical processes had a significant impact on the settlements which characterized east central Europe in the postwar period.[32] Furthermore, Stalin's involvement in the Balkan federation issue seems to prove that the expansion of Communism was not Moscow's only goal and the ideological factor was sometimes exploited in order to avoid the surfacing of conflicts and ambitions which had few links, if any, with Lenin's and Stalin's ideals.[33]

In fact we may wonder whether the major Western powers were able to understand the complex character of east central Europe in the immediate postwar period. As far as the developments in British decision-makers' perceptions about east central Europe, some authors point out that by the second half of 1946 the reports which reached London convinced the Foreign Office that, in spite of different local situations, the future of half of the continent would be shaped by Stalin's expansionist ambitions. The Communist parties were regarded by British officials as a coherent movement skilfully led by the Russian dictator and east central Europe having lost its previously differing characteristics to become the mere European bulwark of a rising 'Soviet empire' – a platform from which the Soviet Union would try to expand its influence to the rest of Europe. It is very likely that such a perception was partially wrong, but such assumptions played some in role in Bevin's eagerness to face down what was perceived as a definite Communist threat to the West.[34] A development which was not too far from the one which took place in Britain, seemed to characterize Washington's attitude towards east central Europe.[35] In the period between 1945 and 1947 the US authorities began to be convinced that the events in this part of the Old World were the most obvious evidence of Stalin's expansionist intentions and from 1948 onwards the process of 'Sovietization' was a useful instrument to give substance to the policy of 'containment', which, however, mainly dealt with Western Europe. In fact it seems to be of some significance that in the analysis of what was happening in east central Europe the US administration focused its attention on

Soviet policy rather than on the various national situations and it is possible to state that while the eastern part of the European continent raised much interest in Washington it was not a priority on the US decision-makers' agenda.

Once again France's policy appeared to be partially different from the ones pursued in London and in Washington. As has already been stated, for some time after the end of the war Paris hoped that it would be possible to renew some traditional bonds in east central Europe. Obviously most French decision makers were aware of the relevant political and social changes caused by the growing Soviet influence, but, at least until late 1947/early 1948, they struggled to maintain some room for manoeuvre and, if Paris had few illusions about the chance to restore the kind of political leadership exerted in the 1920s, the French authorities took the view that culture could still provide France the means by which to spread her influence.[36] Only in 1948 did the French understand that the 'Iron Curtain' would become an almost insurmountable obstacle, not only to political decisions, but also to cultural influence.

If east central Europe played a relevant role in shaping Western perceptions about Soviet postwar goals (and this part of the continent was regarded as lost to Communism very early on), the German question was the most important issue at stake and Germany's future settlement strongly influenced the path which led to the outbreak of the 'cold war'. In the immediate postwar period the German question was a very complex issue; the Western powers could not forget that Germany had posed a deadly threat to both their interests and their very existence. The influence exerted by public opinion must also be acknowledged, which could not forget easily the sorrows and plights of the wartime experience and the ideals which had motivated the struggle against the Nazi régime. A future settlement would mean the possibility of dealing effectively with German revanchism in order to avoid what had happened in the interwar period. The year 1946 was the turning point. Also as a consequence of economic questions, from that period onwards London and Washington began to develop an autonomous policy towards Germany, which would lead to a serious conflict of interests with the Soviet Union. Although France's attitude would change only in 1947, in some author's interpretation at the time of the Moscow conference the fate of Germany was more or less sealed and both the Anglo-Saxon powers and France were aware that there would be no agreement with the Soviet Union.[37]

If in 1946 both in Washington and in London, the developments in the European continent (especially in Germany), the obstacles to the achievement of a sound postwar settlement, and the perceptions about

Soviet intentions towards east central Europe had convinced most decision makers that open conflict with the Soviet Union would be a very
likely event and in Moscow the suspicions about the Anglo-Saxon
powers' attitude were definitely increasing, the year 1947 saw the 'reve-
lation' of the 'cold war'. In this connection it is impossible to disregard
the role played by the Marshall Plan. It has been stressed how the
Marshall Plan strongly influenced Stalin's interpretation of Washington's policy and such a development quickly served to confirm the
Soviet dictator's usual fears about the capitalist powers' intentions.[38]

Such a view appears to be substantiated by the Soviet decision to
create the Cominform.[39] The creation of the new Communist organization in the autumn of 1947 was evidence that in the opinion of the
Soviet leaders there was no room for diplomatic manoeuvre in their
relations with the West: ideology was now a fundamental factor in the
interpretation of the Western powers' policies and motives. The Marshall Plan also played a significant role in postwar dynamics, serving not
only as a symbol of the unavoidable contrast between Moscow and
Washington, but as has been highlighted, rooting Washington economic policy and the US project in Western Europe.[40] If the 'cold war'
meant the partition of the continent into opposing and different
worlds, it may be wondered whether the western half became truly
'Americanized'.[41] It is very likely that the Western Europe, the object
of Washington policy, would remain a multifaceted reality and the
Western European system the outcome of the interaction among the
United States and their Western European partners. Europe's complex
reality, in spite of the 'cold war' and the tortuous path which led to its
partition, appear to be confirmed by the Austrian case. In this connection it has to be pointed out the role played both in the United States
and in the Soviet Union by plans and ideas which had their roots in
wartime planning. It is of particular significance that the interest which
Moscow had always showed towards the creation of a neutral 'belt' in
Europe was an hypothesis which would continue to explain the attitude
of the Soviet leadership into the mid-1950s.[42]

As a conclusion it would be possible to state that during the late stages
of the Second World War very few decision makers thought that partition of Europe and the outbreak of a 'cold war' would characterize the
postwar period. The leaders of the victorious powers aimed at creating a
lasting settlement which would guarantee a peaceful future. Most US
decision makers thought it was possible to reconcile ideology and 'Realpolitik', while in Moscow, in London and in Paris it was often hoped
that traditional interests and wartime co-operation would lead the 'Big

Three', later the 'Big Four', to work out useful compromises. Moreover, past experiences concurred in shaping the attitudes of numerous leaders in the minor European countries and their hopes in the recovery of an independent role. But the achievement of peace in Europe was a more complex a task than it was originally thought; the military developments which strongly influenced local political situations did not always suit the victorious powers' wartime planning. Furthermore the Second World War was a very different phenomenon as compared to the 'Great War'. The power vacuum – especially that created by the total defeat and occupation of Germany – created growing suspicions and conflicts further fuelled by deep mutual misperceptions. Early ideology, both in the East and in the West, surfaced once again; ideological schemes that had already shaped minds during the decades of the interwar period. It was not difficult to return to previous ideological frameworks, which had been widely accepted in the 1920s and in the 1930s, and to identify new enemies. Although the victorious powers were only partly European nations, Europe was the main stage of the new conflict and numerous European actors played relevant roles in shaping the postwar period and the path to the 'Cold War'. Nevertheless the European scene maintained its complex and multifaceted character which the East–West confrontation barely concealed behind the screen of a mere bilateral conflict. Such an evaluation is shared by René Girault[43] and in this connection it is of some significance that the initiative which led to the present volume may be regarded as a spillover from a project promoted by Girault himself which aimed at defining the character of Europe's changing role on the international scene between the Second World War and the postwar period.[44] It is to be hoped that this new scholarly endeavour may also pay homage to a truly European historian who unfortunately left us not too long ago.

Notes

* I would like to thank Dr Jennifer Greenleaves who carefully revised the translation of the chapters by non-English authors.

1 The most evident aspect of those opportunities has been offered by the 'Cold War International History Project' and its very useful Bulletin, which was launched in 1991 by the Woodrow Wilson International Center for Scholars.

2 See for example the conference proceedings edited by Odd Arne Westad *Reviewing the Cold War: Approaches, Interpretations, Theory*, (London: Frank Cass, 2000), organized in 1998 as a Nobel Symposium by the Norwegian Nobel Institute.

3   See for example J. P. Dunbabin, *The Cold War The Great Powers and Their Allies* (London and New York: Longman, 1994).
4   On Europe's role see for example A. DePorte, *Europe Between the Super-Powers The Enduring Balance* (New Haven and London: Yale University Press, 1979); W. Loth, *The Division of the World 1941–1955* (London: Routledge, 1988); C. S. Maier (ed.), *The Cold War in Europe. Era of a Divided Continent* (New York: Marcus Wiener, 1991); D. Reynolds (ed.), *The Origins of the Cold War in Europe International Perspectives* (New Haven/London: Yale University Press, 1994); and the more most recent M. Trachtenberg, *A Constructed Peace The Making of the European Settlement 1945–1963* (Princeton (NJ): Princeton University Press, 1999).
5   See J. Becker and F. Knipping (eds), *Power in Europe? Great Britain, France, Italy and Germany in a Post-war World 1945–1950* (Berlin and New York: de Gruyter, 1986); E. Di Nolfo, *Power in Europe? Great Britain, France, Germany and Italy and the Origins of the EEC 1952–1957* (Berlin and New York: de Gruyter, 1992).
6   See for Example Z. Brzezinski, *The Grand Failure. The Birth and Death of Communism in the Twentieth Century* (London: Macdonald & Co., 1990); C. Gati, *The Bloc That Failed Soviet–East European Relations in Transition* (Bloomington, Indianapolis: Indiana University Press, 1990); B. Fowkes, *The Rise and Fall of Communism in Eastern Europe* (London: Macmillan (– now Palgrave), 1993).
7   Among the numerous works that offer a reassessment of the Cold War as a consequence of its 'end' I recall J. L. Gaddis, *We Now Know. Rethinking Cold War History* (Oxford: Clarendon Press, 1998).
8   On wartime co-operation see for example R. Edmonds, *The Big Three Churchill, Roosevelt and Stalin in Peace and War* (London: Penguin Books, 1991).
9   See K. Schwabe's chapter 'The United States and Europe from Roosevelt to Truman'. On US foreign policy and the origins of the 'Cold War' see for example J. L. Gaddis, *The United States and the Origins of the Cold War 1941–1947* (New York: Columbia University Press, 1972); M. Leffler, *A Preponderance of Power. National Security, the Truman Administration and the Cold War* (Stanford, Ca.: Stanford University Press, 1992).
10   See J. Kent's chapter 'British Post-War Planning for Europe 1942–45'. For Britain's attitude see for example V. Rothwell, *Britain and the Cold War 1941–1947* (London: Jonathan Cape, 1982) and D. Reynolds 'Great Britain', in Reynolds op. cit. *The Origins of the Cold War* (ed.), pp. 77–95.
11   See D. Carlton, *Churchill and the Soviet Union* (Manchester: Manchester University Press, 2000).
12   See the interpretations in B. Arcidiacono, *Le 'précédent italien' et les origines de la guerre froide. Les Alliés et l'occupation de l'Italie 1943–1944* (Brussels: Bruylant, 1984).
13   See P. M. H. Bell, *France and Britain 1940–1994 The Long Separation* (London/ New York: Longman, 1998) pp. 47–67; see also F. Kersaudy, *De Gaulle et Churchill* (Paris: Plon, 1981).
14   For a comprehensive view of Bevin's attitude see A. Bullock, *Ernest Bevin Foreign Secretary 1945–1951* (London: Heinemann, 1983).
15   See for example G. H. Soutou's Chapter 4 in this volume, 'De Gaulle's Plan for Postwar Europe'.
16   G. H. Soutou, 'General de Gaulle and the Soviet Union, 1943–5: Ideology or European Equilibrium', in F. Gori and S. Pons (eds), *The Soviet Union and*

Europe in the Cold War, 1943–53 (London: Macmillan (– now Palgrave), 1996) pp. 310–33.

17 For a broad view of French foreign policy see P. Gerbet, *Politique étrangère de la France. Le relèvement 1944–1949* (Paris: Imprimerie Nationale, 1991).

18 V. Mastny, 'Soviet Plans for Post-War Europe'; see also Gori and Pons (eds), op. cit.; V. Mastny, *Russia's Road to the Cold War Diplomacy, Warfare and the Politics of Communism, 1941–1945* (New York: Columbia University Press, 1979); V. Mastny, *The Cold War and Soviet Insecurity The Stalin Years* (New York/Oxford: Oxford University Press, 1996); V. Zubok and C. Pleshakov, *Inside the Kremlin's Cold War From Stalin to Khrushchev* (Cambridge Mass.: Harvard University Press, 1996).

19 See for example Fowkes, *The Rise and Fall* op. cit., pp. 6–51.

20 See the chapter by S. K. Pavlowitch, 'The Balkan Union: an Instance in the Postwar Plans of Small Countries' in this volume.

21 B. Arcidiacono, 'Great Britain, the Balkans, and the Division of Europe, 1943–1945', Chapter 6, this volume. For a broader analysis see his *Alle origini della guerra fredda. Armistizi e Commissioni di controllo alleate in Europa orientale 1944–1946* (Florence: Ponte alle Grazie, 1993).

22 On the development of Britain's policy see for example G. Warner, 'From "Ally" to Enemy: Britain's Relations with the Soviet Union, 1941–48', in Gori and Pons (eds), *The Soviet Union and Europe*, op. cit. pp. 293–309.

23 A. Marès' chapter, 'Franco-Czechoslovak Relations from 1944 to 1948 or the Munich Syndrome'. On the Communist take-over in Czechoslovakia see for example K. Kaplan, *The Short March The Communist Takeover in Czechoslovakia 1945–1948* (London: Hurst & Co., 1981).

24 See for example C. Buffet, *Mourir pour Berlin. La France et l'Allemagne 1945–1949* (Paris, Colin, 1991).

25 See my interpretations in A. Varsori, *L'Italia nelle relazioni internazionali dal 1943 al 1992* (Rome: Laterza, 1998) pp. 3–42.

26 See G. Petracchi, 'Italy and Eastern Europe, 1943–1948' in this book. On the roots of Italy's policy towards the Soviet Union see, G. Petracchi *Da San Pietroburgo a Mosca. La diplomazia italiana in Russia 1861/1941* (Rome: Bonacci, 1993) and R. Quartararo, *Italia–URSS 1917–1941 I rapporti politici* (Naples: ESI, 1997). On the postwar period see R. Morozzo della Rocca, *La politica estera italiana e l'Unione Sovietica 1944–1949* (Rome: La Goliardica, 1985); E. Aga Rossi and V. Zaslavsky, *Togliatti e Stalin. Il PCI e la politica estera staliniana negli archivi di Mosca* (Bologna: il Mulino, 1997).

27 On the role played by past experiences and by myths see C. Buffet and B. Heuser (eds), *Haunted by History. Myths in International Relations* (Oxford: Berghahn Books, 1998).

28 See for example W. Loth, 'Socialist Parties between East and West'.

29 S. Moussakova, 'Bulgaria between East and West (1944–1948) Cultural Elite's perception of Europe'. For a broad analysis see the contributions by M. Pasztor and D. Jarosz, C. Vrain, S. Moussakova and A. Guénard in E. du Réau (ed.), *Europe des élites? Europe des peuples ? La construction de l'espace européen 1945–1960* (Paris: Presse de la Sorbonne Nouvelle, 1998).

30 L. Borhi, 'Soviet Economic Imperialism and the Sovietization of Hungary' in this book, and C. Gati, *Hungary and the Soviet Bloc* (Durham: Duke University Press, 1986).

31   See G. Valdevit's chapter, 'Yugoslavia between the Two Emerging Blocs 1943–48. a Reassessment'. On Yugoslavia and the Balkan area there is a growing historical and journalistic body of work see for example S. K. Pavlowitch, *A History of the Balkans 1804–1945* (London/New York: Longman, 1999) and M. Glenny, *The Balkans 1804–1999. Nationalism, War and the Great Powers* (London: Granta Books, 2000).

32   S. Bianchini, 'Relations between East European Countries: the Balkan Federation (1942–49)' in this book and also *Sarajevo le radici dell'odio. Identità e destino dei popoli balcanici* (Rome: Edizioni Associate, 1993) pp. 193–227.

33   On Stalin and the plan for a Balkan confederation see Mastny, *The Cold War* op. cit., pp. 20–39.

34   See A. Lane, 'British Perceptions of the Sovietization of Eastern Europe 1947–48' in this study.

35   R. W. Preussen, ' "Unpleasant Facts" and Conflicted Responses: US Interpretations of Soviet Policies in East Central Europe, 1943–48' in this book. On US policy see for example Leffler, *A Preponderance* op. cit., pp. 100–81; Trachtenberg, *A Constructed Peace* op. cit., pp. 34–65.

36   See A. Guénard's chapter, 'The Cultural Policy of France in Eastern Europe', in this volume.

37   M. Kessel, 'The Art of Failure. British and French Policy towards Germany and the Council of Foreign Ministers 1947' in this book. On this issue see Buffet, *Mourir pour Berlin*, and A. Deighton, *The Impossible Peace. Britain, the Division of Germany and the Origins of the Cold War* (Oxford: Clarendon Press, 1993).

38   M. M. Narinsky, 'The Soviet Union and the Marshall Plan' in this book. See also Mastny, *The Cold War*, pp. 27–9, 57–8; Zubok and Pleshakov, *Inside the Kremlin's Cold War* op. cit., pp. 104–8.

39   See Chapter 25 by A. Di Biagio, 'The Cominform as a Soviet Response to the Marshall Plan'. For a wider discussion see F. Gori and S. Pons, *Dagli archivi di Mosca. L'URSS, il Cominform e il PCI 1943–1951* (Rome: Carocci, 1998) as well as Aga Rossi and Zaslavsky, *Togliatti e Stalin*, op. cit.

40   See E. Di Nolfo's chaper in this volume, 'The United States, Europe and the Marshall Plan'.

41   The issue of western Europe's 'Americanization' has been tackled by numerous scholars. See for example in the Italian case P. P. D'Attorre, *Nemici per la pelle. Sogno americano e mito sovietico nell'Italia contemporanea* (Milan: Angeli, 1991), for the French case see R. Kuisel, *Seducing the French The Dilemma of Americanization* (Berkely/Los Angeles/London: University of California Press, 1993). For a broad view see D. W. Ellwood, *Rebuilding Europe Western Europe, America and the Post-war Reconstruction* (London/New York: Longman, 1992).

42   O. Rathkolb, 'First Budapest, then Prague and Berlin, why not Vienna? Austria and the Origins of the Cold War 1947/48'. On this topic see also A. K. Cronin, *Great Power Politics and the Struggle over Austria, 1945–1955* (Ithaca/London: Cornell University Press, 1986).

43   R. Girault's chapter, 'The Partition of Europe' in this volume.

44   We would like to remember his essays in R. Girault, *Etre historien des relations internationales* (Paris: Publications de la Sorbonne, 1998).

Part I

Plans for Postwar Europe, 1943–45

2
The United States and Europe from Roosevelt to Truman

Klaus Schwabe

What drew the United States into the Second World War was the Japanese attack on Pearl Harbor, and yet, in the years that followed, America fought primarily against Hitler and his 'New Order' in Europe. President Franklin D. Roosevelt, above all, insisted that Europe become America's principal military and political concern during the Second World War. Even before the United States had been involved in the war, he had seen to it that American contingency planning prepared for a Europe-first strategy, and he never deviated from that policy once America had joined the grand coalition to defeat Hitler. Thus, if Europe was Roosevelt's military priority, it should be all the more interesting, *first of all*, to know what his political plans were for Europe after Hitler's defeat, and whether these plans in any way anticipated the development of Europe from 1945 on up to the launching of the Marshall Plan. A thorough understanding of Roosevelt's ideas on the future of Europe is all the more necessary, as only on this basis it is possible, *secondly*, to find out whether his successor Harry S. Truman became the faithful executor of his last plans for the future of Europe or whether the new President adopted an approach that significantly differed from his predecessor's vision of Europe's future. In its conclusions this chapter will try to answer these two questions.

When Franklin D. Roosevelt informed the American Congress about the 'day of infamy', that was Japan's attack on Pearl Harbor, it was the second time within a generation that an American President asked Congress to recognize a state of war in connection with a conflict which had its roots in Europe. It was, therefore, only natural for Roosevelt to define America's aim in that second world conflict as a peace settlement that would last longer than the one concluded at Versailles and that would assure peace for Europe and the world for a foreseeable future. He considered the continued alliance with the Soviet Union an indispensable prerequisite to attaining that goal.

Basically, this was to him a global concern which had to be answered by a *universalist* concept. In view of the primarily European origins of two world wars, however, maintaining peace in Europe was a *regional* problem as well and, as we shall see, along with his universalist approach Roosevelt developed a *regional* blueprint for peace.

Roosevelt owed the basic ideas for a *universalist* and *multilateral* peace system to President Woodrow Wilson.[1] Together with the British Prime Minister, Winston Churchill, he reaffirmed the main tenets of this programme in the Atlantic Charter of 12 August 1941. These were self-determination for all peoples; the renunciation of territorial changes unless they accorded with the freely expressed will of the peoples concerned; the free access for 'all states, great or small, victor or vanquished' [. . .] 'on equal terms' 'to the trade and the raw materials of the world'; abandonment of the use of force; disarmament 'pending the establishment of a wider and permanent system of general security'.[2] The Soviet Union acceded to this declaration in 1942.[3] The gist of it was repeated during the war at various instances, most prominently at the end of Roosevelt's lifetime in the 'Declaration on Liberated Europe', which the Big Three agreed on at the Yalta conference in February 1945.[4] These principles, the President emphasized in his last speech at a joint meeting of Congress on 1 March 1945, spelt the end 'of the system of unilateral alliances, the spheres of influence, the balances of power, and all the other expedients that have been tried for centuries – and have always failed. We propose to substitute for all these, a universal organization in which all peace-loving nations will finally have a chance to join.'[5]

This universalist, quasi-Wilsonian approach was the *external* side of Roosevelt's blueprint for peace in the world. It supplied the basis of America's war propaganda. It inspired the war effort of the American people. However, it did not present the whole picture. The external side of Roosevelt's programme was coupled with an *inner* one, which was not made known to the American public. Kept strictly confidential, even within the administration, it sharply differed from what the President said in public, and had a distinctly *regional* as well as *unilateral* flavour. In part, it was developed by Roosevelt at a time when the United States was still neutral. It was based on the notion of four 'world policemen', which alone would be responsible for peacekeeping all over the world. These 'world cops' were the United States, the Soviet Union, Great Britain, and China. Each policing power – superpower, we would say today – was to look after peace and security in its own region: the United States for example in the Western hemisphere, China in the Far East and so on. It was a regionalist system of peace, which clearly recalled the good old system of zones of influence and a balance of power this time to be established between the four world policemen, who would contain each other by co-operation.[6]

This 'brave new world' would be a world without fully independent smaller nations. All of these smaller nations, foes or friends, including France, were to be totally disarmed. Military control of one global region thus would be exercised unilaterally by the respective 'policeman' – seen by the unarmed members as a 'system of permanent intervention', as de Gaulle disapprovingly called it, peeved as he was, because France had not been included in the club of world policemen.[7] Beyond that, it could lead to a European power vacuum, a Europe that would largely be dominated by the Soviet Union. As Charles E. Bohlen, a Soviet expert in the State Department, summed up what to him seemed to be the result of the conference at Teheran: Germany was to be broken up and kept broken up: 'The states of eastern, south-eastern and central Europe', he continued,

> will not be permitted to group themselves into federations or associ-
> ation. France is to be stripped of her colonies and strategic bases
> beyond her borders and will not be permitted any appreciable mili-
> tary establishment. Poland and Italy will retain approximately their
> present territorial size, but it is doubtful if either will be permitted to
> maintain any appreciable armed force. The result would be that the
> Soviet Union would be the only important military and political
> force on the continent of Europe [. . .].[8]

Perceived from the perspective of the superpowers and viewed on a global scale, it amounted to a system of a pluralist, co-operative imperialism. To Roosevelt such a system had become indispensable in view of what the world and he personally had experienced during the two world wars – the fact that small nations, their aspirations and their quarrels, had provided the breeding ground for global military confrontation. Roosevelt located such dangerously ambitious nations in Eastern Europe in particular.[9]

Obviously, this regionalist conception had a particular meaning in Europe. It raised many questions. First of all, which authority provided control over the controllers, that is the 'world policemen'? The more the war progressed, the more often Roosevelt referred to the projected United Nations as such a means of control, or more specifically to the

Security Council, in which the permanent members would obtain a privileged position. In this context, he hoped that the concept of an international police force guaranteeing global security would be acceptable to the American public. But what about the respective 'zones of responsibility' Roosevelt had envisaged? Where, above all, were they located – in Europe? Who would be in charge of them? What would be the role of the Soviet Union? How were the geographical and political limits of Soviet 'responsibility' to be defined? And, most important, how was what in reality amounted to military control to be made compatible with the right to self-determination of sovereign nations, large and small? How could the contradiction be overcome that existed between the ideal of a universal world organization to which all nations would be admitted on equal terms, and the military responsibility – one should rather say hegemony – assigned to the few privileged superpowers each being in charge of one sector of the globe?

How Roosevelt intended to implement his contradictory programme can be derived from his efforts to adjust it to the specific conditions prevailing in Europe in the last phase of the war when, on the one hand, the breakdown of Hitler's empire had become predictable, and when, on the other hand, the Red Army had crossed the prewar borders between Russia and Poland (1 January 1944). Inexorably, the Allied powers were confronted with the need to decide where geographically in Europe the responsibility of the Soviet Union would end and what the area of its responsibility would look like politically, or, more specifically, in terms of Poland's future, where that nation's future borders would be located and by what sort of regime it would be governed. Along with the further advance of the victorious Red Army this question became urgent with regard to all Eastern European nations, and to a certain extent even with regard to Greece, where the Communist underground was attempting to gain the upper hand militarily and politically.

There were two ways to cope with this question – first by the good old zones of interest to be set up in Europe – zones in each of which one superpower would be the police force. This was what Stalin and Churchill preferred and was confirmed by their famous percentage deal agreed on in early October 1944. This arrangement assigned Romania and Bulgaria 90 per cent to Soviet and 10 per cent to Western influence, Greece inversely was by 90 per cent subject to British and by 10 per cent subject to Soviet control. For Yugoslavia and for Poland – the latter with strong Soviet reservations – were to be influenced 50 per cent by Great Britain and 50 per cent by the Soviet Union.[10] But this was a deal concluded between the Soviet Union and Great Britain alone. How did

Roosevelt react to it once Churchill had informed him about it in general terms?[11] Following the inner logic of his regionalist approach and the concept of the 'four policemen' one would expect him to have agreed with it, and this was indeed the case as he hinted even after the conference at Yalta.[12] But how could that deal be applied to the awkward Polish problem? In August 1944, when German troops crushed the uprising of the Polish non-Communist underground virtually within sight of the Red Army, it seemed in Washington as if Stalin had actually welcomed the liquidation of Poland's non-Communist elites as an expedient to prepare a Communist take-over in that country.[13] With Poland subdued to the status of a satellite, the universalist principle of equality of smaller nations, of course, was gravely violated. However, seen purely from the perspective of the regionalist system of four policemen and the regional predominance of one of the superpowers, Roosevelt could very well have been expected to acquiesce in Poland's position of a Soviet satellite.

Actually, this was *not* the case, and this he demonstrated at the Yalta Conference in early February 1945. In compliance with an American proposal, the three participating powers adopted a 'Declaration on Liberated Europe', which demanded free elections and a Western system of government for all liberated European countries, Poland included, which, in addition, was the subject of a specific declaration.[14] It is true that the State Department had wanted more – an Emergency High Commission for Europe which was to provide the platform from which the three victorious powers would agree on a common policy for implementing the Declaration on Liberated Europe. Roosevelt rejected this proposal as bureaucratic and inflexible and, apparently, as a device that might endanger inter-allied harmony and co-operation.[15] At the same time, however, he underlined how seriously he took this inter-allied declaration by reminding Stalin that Poland would become the test case of its validity.[16]

At this point the ineluctable question arose: whether the United States was prepared to accept that the USSR would use its military presence in Eastern Europe to impose its political system on the (not so) liberated countries without bothering about the Yalta Declaration on Liberated Europe, or whether America would take this Declaration seriously and demand that the Red Army tolerate and protect free systems of government in that part of Europe. To a considerable extent, the future of Europe – the alternatives of an intact and of a divided Europe – depended on how the US government would answer that question. The records show that Roosevelt actually veered toward the more universalist aspect of his global concept for peace; he also modified the unilateral approach for security, which had originally gonealong with his regionalist concept of the four policemen. A significant indication of this change was his attitude towards France. As has been shown, he purposely had excluded it from the club of the exclusively armed superpowers. This restrictive attitude had something to do with personal reservations Roosevelt maintained *vis-à-vis* the Free French leader Charles de Gaulle, whom he considered a usurper. When, after the invasion, de Gaulle had succeeded in winning control over all of France, Roosevelt recognized the Gaullist regime.[17] At Yalta he yielded to Churchill's pleadings that France be accepted as one of the occupying powers for Germany. He even spoke of France as a future 'bulwark' against Germany – did he think of the Soviet Union in that role as well?[18] Roosevelt never divulged the motives for his change of heart regarding the future position of France. Possibly, it was his awareness that the US Congress might force an early American withdrawal from Europe that prompted him to accept an enhanced role for France in safeguarding peace and security in Europe.[19] In any event, he had watered down his original idea of the *unilateral* control of one policeman for one zone of responsibility.

To be sure, even in Yalta it was impossible for him to ignore the regional aspect altogether – an aspect that the Soviet Union forced him to take into consideration. When the Yalta Conference was held, Soviet troops had reached the Oder River. Roosevelt could not overlook that, once the Red Army had overrun all of Eastern Europe, Stalin would have the ultimate say in that area.[20] But did this necessarily mean that Russia would be permitted to impose the Communist system on these peoples? Roosevelt's answer was: no, because if the Soviet Union succeeded in this attempt, Europe would be split into British controlled and Soviet controlled halves, Anglo-Soviet tension, rivalry and conflicts were foreseeable, tensions likely to lead to another European conflict into which the United States would be drawn again. It was precisely such a course of events that Roosevelt wanted to prevent by all means, not because he was a pacifist, but because he heeded the advice conveyed to him in a memorandum of the Joint Chiefs of Staff. This memo warned that the United States could not win a war against the Soviet Union because it was militarily inferior to the eastern superpower; America should, therefore, avoid becoming entangled in a war the British might fight in the defence of their zone of influence in Europe. Thus it was America's national interest to keep zones of influence from being set up in Europe and to disassociate itself from British or Soviet attempts to do so and this is what Roosevelt did at Yalta. In other words he did not divide the 'old world', unlike what conventional wisdom would have him do.[21]

In the case of Poland, avoiding zones of exclusive influence meant, as far as Roosevelt was concerned, to prevent the transformation of that country into a Communist dictatorship and, instead, to make sure that it became a Western-style parliamentary democracy. This is why Roosevelt permitted Stalin to involve him in endless debates on Poland at the Yalta conference.[22]

Returning to a more universalist orientation in his European policy, not only did Roosevelt react to the situation in Europe, he reacted even more to what he considered to be the imperatives of domestic politics in his own country. What Roosevelt was aiming at during the last phase of the war was to win over the American public, the American people for the new universalist world order he kept advocating in the media. He was right in pointing out at Yalta that the American people, inspired by the ideals the Atlantic Charter had enunciated, would find it difficult, to say the least, to understand that in this new era Europe would again be carved up into zones of interest and that Poland would be forced to belong to the Soviet bloc. The same was true for example in the case of Yugoslavia. In that country it had become more and more evident that Tito aimed at a Communist controlled dictatorship and thus, so it seemed, at its inclusion into the emerging Communist bloc. As with Poland the United States objected and demanded that Tito's one man rule be supplanted by a new government in which all Yugoslav parties were represented.[23]

To Roosevelt more was at stake than simply public relations. The alternative, whether the American people would accept the future world order and the United States' active role in it, depended to a significant degree on the kind of agreements negotiated for the future governments of Poland, Yugoslavia and the other East European nations.[24] There was the deterring experience Woodrow Wilson had gone through: Roosevelt remembered very well how that American president had lost much of his credibility with the American people by abandoning American interests and ideals, as it seemed, when he signed the Versailles Treaty. This treaty was then rejected by the American Senate, which was supported by an uncomprehending public, and Wilson's world system of peace was in shambles. Roosevelt understandably wanted to avoid a repetition of such a chain of events. He wanted to prevent the Yalta Conference from being berated by the American public, disparaged as a thinly veiled process of old-style horse-trading.[25] Americans (not to speak of the millions of Polish Americans) he knew, were likely to consider the treatment of Poland as a touchstone for a peace that pretended to be based on the ideals of the Atlantic Charter and the Yalta declarations. This is why Roosevelt insisted at Yalta and afterwards on a regime for Poland, that was at least in part pro-Western in orientation and legitimized by truly free elections.[26]

But what could Roosevelt do to add pressure to his exhortations to the Soviet dictator to try to dissuade him from turning Eastern Europe into the backyard of a new Soviet Empire? Military pressure was out of the question. This was to Roosevelt not only a matter of conviction and the inevitable corollary to his resolution to continue the Soviet–American alliance into the postwar era; it was also in line with America's perceived military inferiority in Europe after victory.[27] Under these conditions a middle ground had to be found that, on the one hand, accepted the unavoidable *regionalism* of the new world order exemplified by Soviet military control of Eastern Europe, but that, on the other hand, retained some of the universalist features of Roosevelt's vision for a commonly shared future of Europe.

The compromise that Roosevelt accepted in Yalta – a mixed provisional Polish government coupled with a commitment to early free elections – showed what Roosevelt at that point understood by a 'zone of responsibility' assigned to one of the superpowers: Eastern Europe having become a Soviet 'zone' as the result of the war. Roosevelt, apparently, defined such a zone of responsibility primarily in a military sense: the superpower in charge of one of the zones of responsibility would have the right to look after its security interests in that zone, but *the exercise of this right was to be in harmony with the right of self-determination.* In the case of Poland, Roosevelt would not object to it being incorporated into a system of security controlled and run by the Soviet Union. At the same time, however, he wanted Poland to enjoy the freedoms of a parliamentary democracy Western-style. It was what later became the Finnish model which Roosevelt wanted to see adopted all over Eastern Europe – an 'open' zone of interest, as it has been called, which was under Soviet military dominance, but reserved domestic autonomy to its members, that is the free choice between a Western style democracy or Communist rule. The United States' role in Latin America served as an example for such an arrangement.[28]

If this was a blueprint for Eastern Europe, albeit a complicated one, the question arose as to how the United States would be able to carry it through against Soviet resistance, given the impossibility of building up military pressure. Roosevelt, evidently, counted on the time factor, which would increase the economic and financial leverage of the United States both *vis-à-vis* the Soviet Union and *vis-à-vis* Eastern Europe. Another trump card Roosevelt may have believed America could play was to grant access to the Soviets to nuclear know-how in exchange for Soviet concessions in Eastern Europe.[29] At any rate, the Declaration on Liberated Europe, though not enforceable, endowed the Western Powers with a *title* enabling them to mobilize world public opinion and to exercise moral and economic pressure on a recalcitrant Soviet Union.[30]

How did Germany fit into this half universalist, half regional programme? What would be, according to Roosevelt, defeated Germany's position in this system of security with open zones of interest? To whose zone was it going to belong – the Soviet or the Western? There was not the slightest doubt among the Allied powers that defeated Germany, Nazi-infested as it was, had to submit to an inferior international position (a sort of quarantine) which excluded any appeal on its part for protection under the Atlantic Charter and made it ineligible for UN membership. And yet, in spite of his personal hatred of Germany and the Germans of his own generation, Roosevelt felt that this pariah status for Germany would not last forever. Ultimately, so he hoped, the Germans would be re-educated and democratized.[31]

But even then the ever recurring German dilemma would come up, as had been the case after the First World War, assuming added relevance in the light of Nazi Germany's abuse of military power – the dilemma of how the victors could make it impossible for Germany to regain a military status that would be equivalent to its demographic and economic potential. One way of attaining this objective was to partition the country. For some time Roosevelt favoured this during discussions with his allies, at Teheran more enthusiastically than at Yalta.[32] But then the question arose as to where the dividing lines were to be drawn in Germany. Should they coincide which the borders of the future zones of occupation that had been agreed on in London on 12 September 1944? Did this partition not contradict the overall US goal of keeping all of Europe politically open and undivided?[33]

Another way to render Germany harmless was to deprive it of the sources of its economic wealth. It was Roosevelt's Secretary of the Treasury, Henry Morgenthau, who in the summer of 1944 developed a particularly drastic diet for the German people – in launching a plan for a far-reaching deindustrialization of the defeated country, and for its dismemberment as well. An inveterate disciple of Jefferson's teachings on the agrarian roots of democratic virtues, Morgenthau hoped that, even once Germany had been transformed into a primarily agrarian country, a tolerable standard of living could be maintained. His opponents within the Roosevelt administration like the Secretary of War, Henry Stimson, did not buy this argument. As Roosevelt at first took sides with Morgenthau the options of an agrarianization and/or of a partition of Germany began to dominate the intergovernmental discussion on the future of post-surrender Germany in Washington.[34]

Among the Allies the idea of Germany's dismemberment was not really pursued any further after Yalta. The same applied to its deindustrialization. What had happened? As far as deindustrialization was concerned, a fierce discussion continued within the US government, which lasted through the whole winter of 1944/45. Morgenthau's adversaries in the War and State departments were able to point to three obstacles which made deindustrialization seem counterproductive. For one thing, the Allies had envisaged that Germany make reparations in kind. These included reparations from current production. Morgenthau strictly rejected this kind of reparations because he justly saw they would deprive Germany of the means to restart its industrial production. But the Soviets were insistent. Morgenthau's scheme thus meant the rejection of a claim the Soviet ally had put forward with unquestionable justification. Did it make sense to decline this demand for the sake of the Morgenthau plan?[35] The other obstacle in the way of the Morgenthau plan was the European interest in using Germany's industrial potential for postwar reconstruction. A deindustrialized Germany would have been excluded from the process of an integrated European reconstruction with economically and politically damaging repercussions for the whole continent. This was a view held in particular by the State Department, which for a long time had been committed to a free trade policy and had at least discussed plans for an integrated European economy.[36]

But there was yet a third obstacle that made the Morgenthau Plan seem questionable – the United States' own fiscal interests. The more German territory US troops conquered, the more appalled US observers were at the degree of destruction they saw in German cities. It was obvious that the Germans would need a considerable amount of time, before they would be able to produce enough to assure a minimal standard of living for themselves by paying for the necessary imports of food and raw materials. As the victorious powers became responsible for Germany according to the agreements they had concluded, they would have to take charge of provisioning the German populations to keep them from starving. It was equally obvious that the power, which was best in a position to do so was the United States, that is, in the last analysis, the American taxpayer. Even Morgenthau acknowledged that after the dismantling of the Ruhr industries steps had to be taken to safeguard the subsistence of the local population, until it could find new work in areas that could not be abused for military purposes and leave the region.[37] The more German industries were dismantled or destroyed, the more dependent the Germans would become on imports of food from abroad, the more the American taxpayer would be impelled to finance their barest needs. The implementation of the Morgenthau Plan thus would ultimately be financially damaging to the United States. Roosevelt appears to have recognized this particular drawback of Morgenthau's plan and warned the Soviets at Yalta that the victors could not expect the Germans to be able to provide full compensation for the damage the war had caused, as the Germans had to retain some resources to pay for their own livelihood.[38]

As to Roosevelt's views on a partition of Germany, they were bound to be most revealing of his long-term plans, as the alternative to universalism and regionalism associated with the German question boiled down to an alternative between inter-allied condominium or simple partition of the defeated country. On some occasions – the last time at Yalta – Roosevelt made it clear that the definite partition of Germany was likely to result from its division into occupation zones and thus referred back to his regional ideas. In this he differed from his advisers from the State Department who considered any division forced on Germany utopian and untenable. Instead, they advocated a settlement that would leave Germany intact and provided for a unified Allied administration and concerted Allied measures to re-educate the German people. This was a universalist formula applied to postwar Germany. In spite of Roosevelt's preferences for partition the American representative at the Interallied Advisory Council initialled the London protocol of 12 September 1944, which divided Germany into three zones of occupation, but reserved a special status for Berlin as the common inter-allied seat of the military administration for Germany *as a whole*.[39]

The American acceptance of the London agreement was an indication that Roosevelt was not fixed on a partition of Germany. Actually, the nearer the end of the war, the more he turned to a 'universalist' treatment of Germany and gave up the idea of immediate partition. In the autumn of 1944 he had come around to the State Department's idea that Allied co-operation in dealing with Germany would become the testing ground for the solidity of the Grand Alliance and its interaction on the larger scale of the United Nations.[40] There was one minor voice of dissent: George Kennan, a young expert on the Soviet Union in the diplomatic service: he considered inter-allied co-operation a hopeless endeavour and advocated a clear-cut division of Germany and Europe between the Allies. The western half of Germany, he suggested, should become part of a Western European Federation.

Roosevelt did not follow this piece of 'regionalist' advice (if it ever reached him). Had he done so, Germany and Europe would have been purposely divided along the subsequent iron curtain line. Instead, Roosevelt had opted for inter-allied co-operation in defeated Germany. To be sure, Germany was going to be divided into occupation zones, each run by but one of the occupying powers. But the same Germany, as a whole, was to be treated as an 'open zone of responsibility', not unlike Eastern Europe. The whole German people was to be offered Western-style democracy, even though this was to be a democracy with a left-wing bias, as many planners for the US Military Government in Germany hoped, because they felt that any more conservative orientation had been discredited before and during Hitler's rule. By endorsing the non-Communist left in Germany, American planners also felt that they might meet the Soviets and their plans for a future Germany half way.[41] At any event, this was a 'Finnish solution' for Germany, which in the long run would be neutralized on the basis of a Four Power security treaty providing for Germany's indefinite disarmament, an arrangement that had been suggested to Roosevelt as early as on the eve of Yalta.[42]

On 12 April 1945 Roosevelt died of a brain haemorrhage. His successor Harry S. Truman at once declared that he would pursue the foreign policies of his great predecessor.[43] This was easier said than done. To do so he needed to know these policies. During Roosevelt's presidency he had been kept largely ignorant of the President's long range 'inner' views on postwar Europe. Undoubtedly, he had never heard of the latter's concept of four global policemen[44] and knew only the vague outlines of what had been discussed at the great inter-allied summit conferences. So he had to rely on advisers like Harry Hopkins, Roosevelt's personal aide, or the heads of the various departments, most prominently the State Department. Having listened to Roosevelt's war addresses he was familiar with the universalist outlook of Roosevelt's foreign policy conception. Various members of the State Department, who in general had always favoured universalist concepts and who now briefed him, confirmed this orientation. This meant that Truman wanted to continue collaborating with the Soviet Union within the framework of the United Nations, founded a few weeks later, and that he insisted that the United States should strictly adhere to the letter and the spirit of the agreements that had been concluded with the Allies; at the same time, he expected the Allies to do likewise.[45]

Like his predecessor he banked on the expected Soviet Union's economic dependence on the United States, a relationship that, if necessary, could be used to put pressure on the Soviet Ally to behave loyally.[46]

Voices from the State Department and from American career diplomats predicting a rivalry between the US and the USSR barely impressed him, at least in the first period after his accession to the presidency. Into the Potsdam Conference he remained convinced that Stalin shared basic interests with America, that he was a realist and that a deal with him was possible.[47] To an extent, he was aware that such a deal had to be based on mutual concessions, especially with regard to Poland. Indeed, on this thorny question Truman had accepted a compromise that Hopkins at his behest had negotiated with Stalin personally in late May. It provided for a limited participation of pro-Western Poles in the formation of the Warsaw government: this compromise certainly was not a breakthrough, it failed to commit the Polish Communists to early elections, although Stalin in his talks with Hopkins had confirmed that this had been agreed on at Yalta, but it did provide a formula that prevented Poland from being totally subjected to a Communist regime – at least this is the way Truman and his advisers saw it.[48]

Yet, more than Roosevelt, Truman kept his distance to both Stalin and Churchill. Probably, this had something to do with his taking Roosevelt's universalist policy, and the inter-allied agreements based on it, in a literal way and without the reservations Roosevelt had always made. Both Stalin and Churchill became the victims of this literalness, when Truman abruptly suspended American lend-lease aid to the two countries, as soon as the war in Europe had come to a conclusion. Soon afterwards, Churchill for his part, discovered the effects of this trend. Growing more and more distrustful *vis-à-vis* the Soviet war ally he desperately tried to persuade Truman to keep the armies of the two Western powers at their positions in those areas of central and north Germany that had been assigned to Soviet occupation by international agreement, but had been conquered by US and British troops during the last weeks of the war. In Churchill's view these areas should be used as a bargaining chip during the forthcoming negotiations with the Soviets over eastern and central Europe. Truman, however, wanted to have none of this. To the Prime Minister's dismay he insisted on the literal fulfilment of the London/Yalta agreement on Allied occupation zones in Germany and ordered the American troops to withdraw to the American zone of occupation without delay. Churchill had no alternative but to follow suit. In exchange for this evacuation, troops of the Western powers entered their respective sectors in the heap of rubble of what had been the capital of the Third Reich and which, in accordance with the London Protocol of 12 September 1944, was to become again the administrative centre of Germany, now under occupation.[49]

The withdrawal of the Western troops into their respective zones of occupation and the inter-Allied occupation of Berlin were only preliminaries to a more definite treatment of the German problem. This was put off until the tripartite Conference held at Potsdam from 16 July to 2 August 1945. Its result was merely a provisional settlement for Germany, although it was to provide the framework for Germany's development for the coming forty-five years and, as far as Germany's eastern border was affected, beyond. Our question is again to what extent did either *regionalist* or *universalist* notions pervade American policy at that crucial event. Truman, as we have already seen, felt committed to universalist solutions in dealing with the future of Europe. As far as Germany was concerned he went to Potsdam expecting an agreed inter-Allied settlement which would provide the basis for a long-term co-operative condominium of the four major victorious powers in Germany. At the conference Truman emphasized his universalist orientation by insisting that all four zones of occupation in Germany should be treated equally. In the European context he confirmed this by demanding that the Danube be placed under an international regime that would assure the unhampered international use of that river.[50] On opening the conference, he reminded Stalin and Churchill of the Declaration on Liberated Europe and urged its speedy implementation by the holding of free and internationally supervized elections in Greece, Romania and Bulgaria.[51] Curiously, he refused to refer to the Declaration on Liberated Europe in the case of Yugoslavia, where Tito was about to suppress his non-Communist adversaries, as he considered this problem as not yet ready for a decision and, very much to Churchill's disappointment, proposed to refer the case to the United Nations.[52] Whatever his hesitations may have been in that case, he had made it clear that he considered the future of Eastern Europe the common – in other words a 'universal' – concern of all of the Allies and never even alluded to regional responsibilities.

This was also his basic approach to the German problem. In this context, his primary concern was to arrive at an agreement for the immediate future of the conquered country. He wanted to avoid a failure by all means. He owed this to his great predecessor and could not afford to appear to lag behind on what Roosevelt had achieved by way of East–West co-operation. Public opinion in his country, in so far as it was loyal to Roosevelt, would have accused him of betraying his predecessor's legacy.[53]

Agreement with the Soviet Union thus was imperative. On it depended the solution of those problems that the Yalta Conference had left unsettled – above all the drawing of Germany's new eastern border with Poland and the fixing of a reparation sum for Germany. Among the minor problems that had been kept pending there was the question of whether or not to admit Italy to the United Nations. Truman's Secretary of State James Byrnes made a package of all three questions and thus paved the way for a compromise: Italy was promised admittance to the world organization as soon as a peace treaty was signed with it. For the time being and pending the conclusion of a formal peace treaty with Germany, the United States, misgivings notwithstanding, accepted the Oder-Neisse-border, which Stalin claimed for Poland. Truman felt obliged to enter this legal reservation out of regard of the American Senate's constitutional authority to pass judgement on treaties concluded by the executive. Otherwise, it seems, he did not fundamentally object to this new border. Apparently, he hoped that this Western concession would strengthen the non-Communist members of the Warsaw government. This was in line with his own and Roosevelt's determination to assure a partially Western orientation to Polish politics and thus underlined his adherence to a 'universalist' settlement for Europe.[54]

The provisional solution finally negotiated for Germany's reparations followed a different pattern: principally, it was agreed, that each occupying power was to rely on its own zone for the delivery of reparations, in other words, the Soviet Union had to accept to seek reparations largely from its own zone of occupation. Only 10 per cent of the eventual reparation output of the combined Western zones was set aside for Soviet Russia. In addition, the Soviet Union could receive a further 15 per cent of West German reparations in exchange for the delivery of an equivalent amount of food.[55] This solution boiled down to a partition of Germany as a source of reparations. It foreshadowed Germany's later division into a western and an eastern half, a danger that was already perceived by some members of the American Military Government in Germany, but dismissed by others. At any rate, it was a *regional* solution for the reparation question and anticipated the ultimate regional settlement of the German problem a few years later.[56]

Why did Truman accept this important qualification to his basic preference for a universalist peace settlement for Europe that would preserve, as far as possible, Western-style governments in Eastern Europe and keep Germany administratively and politically intact? Significantly, he followed in Roosevelt's footsteps in this matter as in others. As we have seen, the predominant opinion in the Roosevelt administration had rejected Morgenthau's option for a limitation of German reparations as a way to prevent Germany's reindustrialization. Instead, there was agreement that large-scale reparations would have to be extracted from Germany. At Yalta, Roosevelt personally had consented to a sum of $20 billion, of which the Soviet Union would receive 50 per cent. The real difficulty was that along with delivering reparations the German population had to produce enough to assure its own subsistence. If it did not, the United States, and ultimately the American taxpayer, as has been mentioned already, was bound to be expected to fill the gap, which meant to subsidize not only its own zone, but also the other ones to the degree that reparations were taken from them. In other words and as seen from the American perspective, a repetition of the post-first World War dilemma was to be feared in the sense that the United States would make indirect reparation payments to the other victorious powers. Again in line with Roosevelt, Truman flatly rejected such an apparent imposition. His experts insisted that the principle of the 'first charge' should be incorporated into the Potsdam agreement, that is that the occupying powers should agree that German imports assuring a minimal subsistence for the population would be the first charge on foreign currency earned by German exports, reparations coming only second. The USSR objected. Turning reparations into a matter for which each occupying power in its own zone was primarily responsible was the way out of the deadlock the discussion on reparations had reached at Potsdam.[57] The financial and economic interests of the Soviet Union, on the one hand, and of the United States, on the other hand, clashed openly at this point. Truman, with an eye on US Congress, espoused the financial interest of his own country. In doing so he tacitly accepted that the Potsdam settlement was contradictory: it maintained America's universalist claims for the future of eastern and central Europe; it upheld the principle of a common political treatment of Germany as a whole, but it made the crucial reservation that the reparation question was to be dealt with separately in the individual zones of occupation. As it turned out, different reparation policies in the four zones of occupation produced different economic policies, the result being that the economic unity of Germany, which had been set as a goal at Potsdam, was never attained.

It is noteworthy that during the period immediately after this and in spite of the reparation agreement for Germany, the Truman administration was far from abandoning the general universalist orientation of its European policies. It continued to demand free elections in all of Eastern Europe. Together with Great Britain it pressed for a commonly agreed-on policy of all four occupying powers in Germany. It succeeded only with regard to the Four Power-occupied former German capital: in

October 1946 a free election was held in all four sectors of Berlin and a Western-oriented city administration was set up headed by the social democratic party, which had won the election.[58]

As far as Germany as a whole was concerned, the United States proposed a 'universalist' international solution based on the preservation of the unity of Germany at the Paris Four Power Conference, held in the spring of 1946: returning to a project first discussed on the eve of Yalta it proposed to neutralize and demilitarize Germany for an indefinite period of time. The four occupying powers, it added, would enter into a treaty in which they committed themselves to coming to each other's assistance immediately, should Germany violate its obligation to remain disarmed. The Soviet Foreign Minister, Molotov, refused to entertain this proposition.[59] Simultaneously, while the Soviet zone of occupation developed as a separate political entity, the Western zones followed suit, the British and American zones combining at the beginning of 1947. Two Four Power conferences vainly attempted to bridge the gap that had opened up between the Soviet zone and western Germany. A 'universalist' solution of the German problem became less and less attainable.

During 1946 and 1947 the West and the Soviet Union clashed in other areas, beginning with Iran in early 1946. Any hope of seeing democratic regimes voted into office was dashed in most countries of Eastern Europe. In early 1948, a Communist coup in Czechoslovakia sowed further distrust among the former allies. In the Near East, the United States took over the role of regional policeman from Great Britain. The Truman Doctrine of March 1947 confirmed this commitment. At that time, the Truman administration had concluded that the estrangement between the West and the Soviet Union no longer left any room for a 'universalist', co-operative solution of the outstanding political problems of Europe, especially on the German question. There would be no longer any bargaining with Stalin. Containment of an inherently evil power by balancing it became the order of the day. It was the end of the hope that Roosevelt had clung to until his death, a hope that he had bequeathed to Truman, though the latter had loyally tried to espouse it. The Marshall Plan, an essentially regional approach to the problem of European reconstruction, marked the definite end of these illusions – although their shadow reappeared when Washington announced that Eastern Europe was included in the offer of American assistance. A Soviet veto on east European participation in the Marshall Plan dispelled this last vestige of American universalism.[60]

This was George Kennan's hour of opportunity. As we have seen, he had advocated a regional solution for Europe as early as 1944 – a clear-cut division that would avoid the overlapping claims of the victorious powers. In February 1946, in his famous 'long telegram' he called for a consistent policy for containing and discouraging Soviet expansion. Until 1946 a junior member of the US Embassy in Moscow, he had risen to the influential position of Director of the Policy Planning Staff in the State Department created by George Marshall.[61] During the crucial years of the implementation of the Marshall Plan (1947–49), he was not only the apostle of containment, but also, in conjunction with strong public pressure, one of the major initiators of an entirely novel approach in US European policy: if under the circumstances only a regional solution for non-Communist Europe was possible, he demanded that in this region the national state should still not be the ultimate political instance to be dealt with by America. Instead, he resurrected an idea that during the war had been advocated by himself and other officials of the State Department, but had been discarded by Roosevelt. It was the idea that seemed to offer a promising substitute for America's vanished universalist illusions – the idea of a regionally integrated Western Europe. This, it was hoped, would become a force that in the not too distant future would be able to become economically and, maybe, militarily self-sufficient and, as a third force, could contribute to the defence of the West against Soviet pressures. It would replace the *unilateral* responsibility of the United States as the police force for Western Europe by a *multilateral* responsibility.[62] Events of the following years – the Cold War, the nuclear arms race, the slow and incomplete pace of European integration – demonstrated that the Marshall planners' vision was premature. And so it seems, even today.

Our analysis has shown that Franklin Roosevelt's concept for the future of Europe presented a unique mixture between what we called universalist and regionalist elements. His regionalist idea of the control of the world by four superpowers amounted for Europe to its complete abdication as an independent military entity. As we have seen, Roosevelt gradually, although never completely, dissociated himself from this concept for Europe by espousing the universalist idea of 'open zones of responsibility' and by accepting the idea that at least France would become co-responsible for maintaining peace in Europe. At the same time he gave up the idea of partitioning Germany.

Did the final stage of his thinking and planning for the future of Europe anticipate later developments? This was the *first question raised* at the beginning of this chapter. From the global point of view, Roosevelt's idea of a primary responsibility of the major powers for world peace was reflected by the UN Charter and the institution of a Security Council with only a few permanent members. From the European perspective, developments after Hitler's defeat assumed a more regional character – Europe at large and Germany gradually being split up. This is what Roosevelt had wanted *to avoid* by espousing a more universalist approach for his European policy at the end of the war. In a way, of course, Roosevelt did contribute if not to the division of Europe, at least to the later estrangement between the Western powers and the Soviets. He anticipated the rift between East and West by claiming that Eastern Europe should become an open zone of responsibility and not a closed area of Soviet military, economic and political control as Stalin was aiming at.

It was this claim that Truman inherited from him and defended against the Soviet demand for exclusive and total predominance in Eastern Europe and Soviet occupied Germany. With regard to the enemy country, Truman at first fundamentally adhered to Roosevelt's universalist–co-operative approach by trying to assure a common treatment by the four victorious powers of an undivided Germany. For very basic economic reasons and once more as the faithful executor of Roosevelt's own policy he failed to uphold this universalist–co-operative formula in dealing with the reparation issue. In a way, Truman became a victim of the contradictions inherent in Roosevelt's own European policy. It is doubtful but cannot be proved whether a less contradictory and more forthcoming attitude toward the Soviet Union over the German question would lead to a more co-operative Soviet policy. But, basically, there can be no doubt that the division of Europe occurred not because, but in spite of, the universalist intentions that both Roosevelt and Truman had stood for.

What had been true of Roosevelt thus was true of his successor – both envisaged a Europe that would remain politically undivided, a Europe open to choose Western-style democratic governments. Neither of the two Presidents foresaw a development that would split the continent and result in a long term American military commitment in the Old World. Both had overestimated America's power in 1945 to steer events into a direction that would lead to political independence and economic prosperity for the whole of the European continent as was attained only more than forty years afterwards.

Notes

1 R. Dallek, *Franklin D. Roosevelt and American Foreign Policy 1932–1945* (New York: Oxford University Press, 1979) p. 441.
2 T. A. Wilson, *The First Summit. Roosevelt and Churchill at Placentia Bay 1941* (Boston: Houghton Mifflin, 1969) p. 206.

3 V. Mastny, *Russia's Road to the Cold War* (New York: Columbia University Press, 1979) quoted from the German translation: *Moskaus Weg zum Kalten Krieg* (München: Oldenburg, 1980) p. 54: Stalin made the reservation, however, that circumstances, requirements and peculiarities of the various member nations should be taken into account in applying the Atlantic Charter.

4 G. Lundestad, *American Empire* (Oxford: Oxford University Press, 1990) p. 144, and Dallek, *Roosevelt*, op. cit. p. 520.

5 Dallek, *Roosevelt*, p. 520.

6 W. Kimball, *The Juggler. Franklin Roosevelt as Wartime Statesman* (Princeton: Princeton University Press, 1991) pp. 85 ff., 103 ff., 191f.; Dallek, *Roosevelt*, op. cit., pp. 284, 342 ff.; H. Kissinger, *Diplomacy* (New York: 1994) p. 397, perceives a structural similarity between Roosevelt's idea of four world policemen and Metternich's Holy Alliance, although he does not introduce the idea of a balance of power into this particular analysis. See, however, J. L. Gaddis, *Strategies of Containment. A Critical Appraisal of Postwar American National Security Policy* (Oxford: Oxford University Press, 1982) pp. 9 ff., who refers aptly to a 'containment by integration' of the USSR.

7 C. de Gaulle, *Mémoires de guerre* (Paris: Plon, 1956) vol. 2, p. 291; R. Divine, *Roosevelt and World War Two* (Baltimore: Johns Hopkins Press, 1969) p. 59 ff.

8 C. E. Bohlen, *Witness to History 1929–1969* (New York: Norton, 1973) p. 153.

9 Kimball, *The Juggler* op. cit. pp. 98, 104.

10 A. Reiss, 'The Churchill-Stalin Secret "percentages" agreement on the Balkans', *American Historical Review*, vol. 83 (1978) pp. 372 ff.

11 Churchill to Roosevelt, 18 January 1944, in: W. F. Kimball ed., *Churchill and Roosevelt. The Complete Correspondence*, vol. 3 (Princeton: Princeton University Press, 1984) p. 359; Kimball, *Juggler* op. cit., p. 163.

12 Roosevelt took a much less rigid position on this issue than the State Department, which resented any arrangement that smacked of spheres of influence. To the US ambassador in Moscow, Averell Harriman, he pointed out that his major interest was to do everything possible to prevent the Balkans from entangling the US into another war (quoted by Kimball, *Juggler*, p. 162, see also pp. 164, 167, 170, and Roosevelt to Churchill, 22 October 1944, in: Kimball, *Churchill–Roosevelt Correspondence*, vol. 3, p. 365 ff.; Churchill to Roosevelt, 8 March 1945, ibid., p. 547; Roosevelt to Churchill, 11 March 1945, ibid., p. 562; Dallek, *Roosevelt* op. cit., p. 479.

13 G. Lundestad, *The American Non-Policy in Eastern Europe 1943–1947. Universalism in an Area Not of Essential Interest to the United States* (Oslo: Universitetsforlaget, 1978) p. 190.

14 *Foreign Relations of the United States (FRUS). Conferences of Malta and Yalta* (Washington: US Government Printing Office, 1955) p. 980.

15 L. C. Gardner, *Spheres of Influence. The Great Powers partition Europe from Munich to Yalta* (Chicago: I.R. Dee, 1993) p. 225 ff.

16 *FRUS, Malta and Yalta*, pp. 97 ff., 566 ff., 853; D. C. Watt, 'Britain and the Historiography of the Yalta Conference and the Cold War', *Diplomatic History* 13/1 (Winter 1989) p. 93; J. Gaddis, *The United States and the Origins of the Cold War* (New York: Columbia University Press, 1972) p. 158 ff.; Dallek, *Roosevelt* op. cit., pp. 163, 516; Kissinger, *Diplomacy* op. cit., p. 415.

17 Dallek, *Roosevelt*, pp. 408 ff., 458 ff.

18 J. L. Harper, *American Visions of Europe* (Cambridge: Cambridge University Press, 1994) p. 115; Dallek, *Roosevelt* op. cit., p. 509; also Robert Murphy, Memorandum of Conversation with President Roosevelt, 9 September 1944, Hoover Institution, Murphy Papers.

19 Dallek, *Roosevelt* op. cit., p. 510.

20 *FRUS, Malta and Yalta* op. cit., p. 589.

21 Leahy to Hull, 16 April 1944, quoted in *FRUS, Malta and Yalta*, p. 108; resubmitted after the invasion and VE day for American guidance at the Potsdam conference, cf. *FRUS, The Conference of Berlin (Potsdam)* (Washington: US Government Printing Office, 1960), vol. 1, p. 256 ff.; R. B. Woods *et al.*, *Dawning of the Cold War. The United States's Quest for Order* (Athens: GA: University of Georgia Press, 1991) p. 19; D. C. Watt, *Succeeding John Bull* (Cambridge: Cambridge University Press, 1984) pp. 100, 103; Kimball, *Juggler* op. cit., p. 100.

22 Dallek, *Roosevelt* op. cit., p. 515; Kimball, *The Juggler* op. cit., p. 96.

23 *FRUS, Malta and Yalta*, pp. 262 ff., 900; L. E. Davis, *The Cold War Begins. Soviet–American Conflict over Eastern Europe* (Princeton: Princeton University Press, 1974) p. 343 ff.

24 Kimball, *Juggler* op. cit., p. 171.

25 Kimball, *Juggler* op. cit., p. 191.

26 Gaddis, *Origins* op. cit., pp. 159, 163 ff.; Dallek, *Roosevelt* op. cit., p. 513; Kimball, *Juggler* op. cit., p. 172 ff.: Woods *et al.*, *Dawning* op. cit., p. 32.

27 Gaddis, *Origins* op. cit., p. 144; Kimball, *Juggler* op. cit., p. 182.

28 E. Mark, 'American Policy toward Eastern Europe and the Origins of the Cold War, 1941–1946: An Alternative Interpretation', *Journal of American History* 68/2 (September 1981), p. 313 ff., idem, 'Charles Bohlen and the Acceptable Limits of Soviet Hegemony in Eastern Europe: A Memorandum', *Diplomatic History* 3/2 (Spring 1979) p. 204 ff.; Kimball, *Juggler* op. cit., pp. 169, 182 ff. 1977. It was indicative that the United States was prepared to recognize Finland sooner than most of the other Eastern European states (Lundestad, *Empire* op. cit., p. 168; Davis, *The Cold War Begins* op. cit., p. 282 ff.).

29 Dallek, *Roosevelt* op. cit., p. 507 ff.; Gaddis, *Origins* op. cit., p. 191; Woods *et al.*, *Dawning* op. cit., p. 27 ff.; Mark, 'Charles Bohlen and the acceptable limits', p. 207 ff.; Kimball, *Juggler* op. cit., p. 100, footnote 71.

30 Lundestad, *Empire* op. cit., p. 159 ff.; Watt, 'Britain and the Historiography' op. cit., p. 93, who makes a revealing reference to Roosevelt's tactics *vis-à-vis* Hitler in 1938, which were quite similar; see also Kimball, *Juggler* op. cit., pp. 159, 195, 198.

31 Roosevelt stated as much, for example in a conversation with the Polish leader Sikorski on 2 December 1942, quoted in M.-L. Goldbach ed., *Dokumente zur Deutschlandpolitik*, first series, vol. 2: *Amerikanische Deutschlandpolitik, 11.8.1941 bis 31.12.1942* (Frankfurt: 1986) p. 714.

32 Kimball, *Swords or Plowshares. The Morgenthau Plan for the Defeated Germany* (Philadelphia: Lipincott, 1976) p. 110; R. D. Buhite, *Decisions at Yalta. An Appraisal of Summit Diplomacy* (Wilmington, DE: Scholarly Resources, 1986) p. 30 ff.

33 *FRUS, Malta and Yalta* op. cit., p. 612; Kimball, *Swords* op. cit., p. 53.

34 This discussion has many times been documented and analyzed. For one of the earliest and still best accounts see: P. Y. Hammond, 'Directives for the Occupation of Germany: The Washington Controversy', in H. Stein ed.,

American Civil–Military Decisions. A Book of Case Studies (Birmingham, Al.: Univessity of Alabama Press, 1963) p. 353 ff. See also: W. Kimball, *Swords* op. cit., pp. 25 ff., 106. Most recent German treatment: B. Greiner, *Die Morgenthau-Legende. Zur Geschichte eines umstrittenen Plans* (Hamburg: 1995).

35   O. Nübel, *Die amerikanische Reparationspolitik gegenüber Deutschland, 1941– 1945* (Frankfurt: 1980) pp. 80, 94, 121 ff.; Kimball, *Swords* op. cit., p. 110; J. Fisch, *Reparationen nach dem Zweiten Weltkrieg* (München: 1992) p. 48 ff.

36   Kimball, *Swords* op. cit., p. 89; for the opposite view held by Morgenthau see ibid., p. 107; P. Winand, *Eisenhower, Kennedy, and the United States of Europe* (Basingstoke: Macmillan – now Palgrave, 1993) p. 5 ff.

37   Greiner, *Die Morgenthau-Legende* op. cit., p. 177.

38   Big Three meeting, 5 February 1945, in *FRUS, Malta and Yalta* op. cit., p. 36 f. The same argument had already appeared at Teheran, cf. *FRUS. The Conferences of Cairo and Tehran 1943* (Washington: US Government Printing Office, 1961) pp. 243, 879. See also J. H. Backer, *Die Entscheidung zur Teilung Deutschlands. Amerikas Deutschlandpolitik 1943–1948* (München: Beck, 1978) p. 173.

39   The State Department had advocated the preservation of a single German state since America's entrance into the war: Goldbach, *Amerikanische Deutschlandpolitik* op. cit., p. 571. See also T. Sharp, *The Wartime Alliance and the Zonal Division of Germany* (Oxford: Clarendon Press, 1975) pp. 41, 46, 57; H. Notter, *Postwar Policy Preparation 1939–1945* (Washington: Department of State Publications, 1949) p. 554 ff.; Hammond, 'Directives' op. cit., pp. 397, 399, 409.

40   R. Murphy, *Diplomat among Warriors. Memoirs* (New York: Doubleday, 1965) p. 255; Hammond, 'Directives' op. cit., pp. 380, 404; H. Graml, 'Zwischen Jalta und Postdam', *Vierteljahrshefte für Zeitgeschichte* 24 (1976) p. 323.

41   W. Donovan to President Truman, 5 May 1945, Truman Library, Indep., Mo., Misc. Material filed by the Administration Asst. – with reference to the US aim of 'a democratic-socialist Germany balanced between the Eastern and Western blocs but aligned with neither'. Also: Hammond, 'Directives' op. cit., p. 420 ff.

42   A. Frohn, *Neutralität als Alternative zur Westintegration. Die Deutschlandpolitik der Vereinigten Staaten von Amerika 1945–1949* (Frankfurt: Metzner, 1985) p. 40 ff.; Gardner, *Spheres of Influence* op. cit., p. 225; *FRUS, The Conference of Berlin*, vol. 1, pp. 163, 450 ff.

43   M. Leffler, *A Preponderance of Power. National Security, the Truman Administration, and the Cold War* (Stanford: Stanford University Press, 1992) p. 25.

44   Kissinger, *Diplomacy*, p. 426 ff., takes it for granted that Truman 'pursued' Roosevelt's concept of four policemen without being able to prove that Truman actually was informed about it when he became president.

45   H. Truman, *1945. Year of Decision. Memoirs*, vol. 1 (New York: Doubleday, 1955) pp. 288, 290, 340.

46   Gaddis, *The United States and the Origins* op. cit., p. 191; F. J. Harbutt, *The Iron Curtain. Churchill, America, and the Origins of the Cold War* (Oxford: Oxford University Press, 1986) p. 104; Woods *et al.*, *Dawning* op. cit., p. 46; Leffler, *Preponderance* op. cit., pp. 31 ff.

47   E. May, *'Lessons' of the Past* (New York: 1976) p. 30 ff.; R. H. Ferrell ed., *Off the Record. The Private Papers of Harry S. Truman* (New York: Harper & Row, 1980) pp. 44, 57 ff. After Roosevelt's death regular summaries on current diplomatic

affairs were sent to Truman by the Secretary of State. They reflect the rather gloomy view the State Department was taking as to the state of Soviet–US relations (Special information for the President; Memoranda, 13 April 1945 and afterwards, President's Secretary's File, Harry S. Truman Library, Independence, Mo.).

48 *FRUS, The Conference of Berlin,* vol. 1, pp. 38, 41. Lundestad, *Empire* op. cit., p. 156 ff.; L. E. Davis, *The Cold War Begins* op. cit., p. 233 ff.

49 Harbutt, *The Iron Curtain* op. cit., p. 105 ff.; T. Andersen, *The United States, Great Britain, and the Cold War* (Columbia: University of Missouri Press, 1981) pp. 665, 772 ff.; Woods *et al.; Dawn* op. cit., p. 47 ff.

50 Truman, *Memoirs* op. cit., vol. 1, p. 34; H. Feis, *Between War and Peace. The Potsdam Conference* (Princeton: Princeton University Press 1960) pp. 241 ff., 297 ff.

51 *FRUS, The Conference of Berlin,* vol. 2, pp. 522, 643 ff. Stalin declined an international supervision and only promised freedom for the international press to report on the elections (ibid., p. 1493).

52 *FRUS, The Conference of Berlin,* vol. 2, pp. 127 ff., 1212 ff.; Woods *et al., Dawning* op. cit., p. 69.

53 Harbutt, *The Iron Curtain* op. cit., p. 104.

54 Feis, *Between War and Peace,* pp. 230, 259 ff.

55 Feis, ibid; W. Benz, *Potsdam 1945* (München: Deutscher Taschenbuch Verlag, 1986) p. 107 ff.; H. Graml, *Die Alliierten und die Teilung Deutschlands.Konflikte und Entscheidungen 1941–1948* (Frankfurt: Fischer, 1985) p. 100 ff.

56 Clayton, Collado to Thorp, 16 August 1945, in *FRUS, The Conference of Berlin,* vol. 2, pp. 938 ff.

57 Briefing Book, 12 January 1945, *FRUS. Malta and Yalta,* p. 191; Briefing Book, undated, *FRUS, The Conference of Berlin,* vol. 1, pp. 507 ff., also p. 519; Nübel, *Die amerikanische Reparationspolitik,* p. 186 ff.

58 H. Herzfeld, *Berlin in der Weltpolitik 1945–1970* (Berlin: de Gruyter, 1973) p. 92 ff.

59 A. Frohn, *Neutralität* op. cit., pp. 39 ff.

60 M. Hogan, *The Marshall Plan. America, Britain and the Reconstruction of Western Europe 1947–1952* (Cambridge: Cambridge University Press, 1987) pp. 44, 51 ff.

61 Kissinger, *Diplomacy* op. cit., p. 452 ff.

62 W. D. Miscamble, *George Kennan and the Making of American foreign Policy 1947–1950* (Princeton: Princeton University Press, 1992) p. 43 ff.; K. Schwabe, 'The United States and European Integration', in C. Wurm ed., *Western Europe and Germany, 1945–1960* (Oxford: Berg Publishers, 1995) p. 115 ff.

3
British Postwar Planning for Europe 1942–45

John Kent

Postwar planning for Europe under the Churchill and Attlee governments was never considered in isolation from the perceived need to secure Britain's future imperial role as a great world power. Europe was a key area because of the self-evident need to prevent a revived Germany launching a major war. It was also accepted that Britain's interests would not be served if a single power was to dominate the continent. Yet in some respects it is easy to overemphasize the significance of many areas of Europe for British postwar planners. In the first place while the war brought the British Isles into great danger, ultimately Britain survived relatively unscathed despite German control of the continent. This was to influence military planning both during and after the war when, with the Soviet Union as the new enemy, there was a perceived need to recreate the conditions which had enabled the British to emerge on the winning side. And this, in line with much interwar military thinking, did not involve a commitment to the land defence of western Europe. British military tradition and the role of the Empire/Commonwealth in embodying world power status led to the Middle East assuming much greater importance.

When planning first began in 1942, the general requirements of the new international organization assumed importance. In 1943 Churchill was very much in favour of a world order based on regionalism and, therefore, it was a question of defining the roles of the respective great powers in the European region. Roosevelt had suggested that the great powers acting as four policemen should play the key role in the preservation of peace and security, but the issue in Europe was whether or not this would involve blocs or spheres of influence. In November 1943 at Teheran, Stalin did not like the idea of applying Roosevelt's four policemen to Europe.[1] Instead the Soviet leader proposed something that resembled a regional committee for Europe comprising Britain, the US, the Soviet Union and possibly one other state.[2] But after Teheran there was more chance of a Europe emerging under Soviet and British auspices as the regional representatives of the new security organization with formal spheres of influence. For Britain this raised the question of how much of Europe would be under Soviet influence or domination.

In 1942 when the British ambassador in Moscow, Sir Archibald Clark Kerr, first assessed Soviet aims, he believed they would require eastern Poland, Bessarabia and the Baltic states to secure their frontiers.[3] Britain's main considerations were its vital imperial interests and its status in the postwar world relative to its two main partners. The more that the US and the Soviet Union surpassed Britain in terms of military and economic strength, the more concerned the British became about their great power status. Ultimately, postwar British policy towards both eastern and western Europe was to be significantly influenced by such concerns.

In 1944, the Foreign Office believed that an Anglo-Soviet alliance to contain Germany should be the basis of postwar planning for Europe. The paper the FO submitted to the Cabinet on this also suggested that the Soviet Union would not want to antagonize the West by undue interference in European countries.[4] It reflected a desire to create a stable Europe through Anglo-Soviet co-operation based on the rise of Soviet power; it did not reflect a naive assumption about the nature of this power or any illusions about what Soviet control would amount to in areas of Europe subject to that power. In April 1944 when the Soviet attack on Romania began, the British concern was not about Soviet domination of large areas of central and eastern Europe, but about this domination extending westwards and southwards.[5] The military study of the impact of Soviet policy on British strategic interests was undertaken by the Post Hostilities Planning staff. The PHP defined Britain's strategic interests as the security of the Commonwealth and Empire, their vital communications and the protection of Middle Eastern oil. The PHP in effect dismissed any idea of Britain having vital interests in large areas of eastern Europe as it assumed that Soviet influence would be dominant in Poland, powerful in Czechoslovakia and predominant in Hungary. In addition the Russians were expected to occupy Romania, to have a close interest in Bulgaria and great influence in Yugoslavia.[6]

The acceptance of Soviet domination in eastern Europe was not done without consideration of what Soviet dominance would entail. Sir Orme Sargent believed the Soviets would not permit the establishment of popular front governments. His view was that Stalin would want firm dictatorial regimes administering a system of state socialism. This, Sargent regarded as preferable to popular front governments comprising 'flabby democratic socialists' on the lines of the Blum model. If that kind of government were to be established by the Soviets then, claimed Sargent, 'heaven help us – it will mean corruption, inefficiency and Civil War'.[7]

This scenario of Soviet domination of most of the area east of Germany was dependent on the exclusion of Soviet influence from the territories in the Balkans closest to the Mediterranean. Officials in the Southern Department, traditionally hostile to Soviet influence in the eastern Mediterranean, were less concerned about the need to contain German power. The area of their responsibility covered Albania, Bulgaria, Greece, Italy, Romania, Turkey and Yugoslavia, all of which, apart from Romania, had a direct bearing on British influence in the Mediterranean. Indeed in 1943 and 1944 the main concerns of British planners were not with the countries of central and eastern Europe but with the Mediterranean countries of Greece, Turkey and Italy. There seemed to be no problems in securing Soviet co-operation over postwar planning for Germany or Poland. In October 1943 a European Advisory Commission had been agreed for Germany. The Polish question had been discussed at Teheran and it had been agreed to extend Poland's frontiers to the Oder.

The British were more concerned about the position in the Balkans. By October 1944, given the acceptance of the inevitable Soviet domination of significant areas of Eastern Europe, Churchill's aims were to get Stalin's agreement on the limits of that domination and preserve a special British position in Greece. On 9 October that formed the basis of the infamous percentages agreement.[8] The question since has been whether these arrangements were essentially a Churchillian whim or whether they assumed significance for FO planners. There were those in the FO who were not happy with the arrangement, notably Sir Orme Sargent, who was to be influential in securing the final rejection of spheres of influence arrangements. In addition Eden told Sargent that the agreements were symbolic.[9] On the other hand, there are a number of indications that the percentages agreement came to be seen, at least until the Yalta conference, as a key element of British foreign policy designed to protect British interests in Greece and to form the basis of Anglo-Soviet co-operation in Europe. Looking back, one official noted that the acceptance of percentages agreements involving Soviet predominance in Hungary and Romania in return for recognition of preponderant British interests in Greece was seen 'on reflection' as unsatisfactory. 'Nevertheless the British government set out to interpret them with the greatest possible strictness.'[10]

At the end of 1944 policy makers were still sanguine about Soviet control over parts of Eastern Europe. The JIC estimated that the Russians would have a postwar protective screen of Finland, Poland, Czechoslovakia, Hungary, Romania and to a lesser extent Yugoslavia and Bulgaria. Romania, the Joint Intelligence Committee (JIC) believed, would be only nominally independent. These assessments were confirmed by Gladwyn Jebb who believed the Russians would be 'paramount' in Poland, Czechoslovakia, Romania, Hungary, Bulgaria and possibly in Yugoslavia and Austria.[11] As the debate about whether to change policy developed in 1945, one official noted that 'we were before Yalta prepared to allow Russian predominance in the ex-satellite Balkan countries to which we agreed last October in Moscow, but it proved impossible to convince the Russians that the Yalta Declaration on Liberated Territories altered this and obliged us to interest ourselves in what the Russians were doing.'[12] The great catalyst for change was the Yalta conference which seemed to offer an alternative to a European settlement based largely on spheres of influence.

The British went to Yalta with some trepidation because of the high price that might have to be paid to preserve British influence in Greece and the Mediterranean. Yet despite his position of strength, Stalin appeared remarkably conciliatory. What astonished and pleased the British was Stalin's apparent acceptance of the Declaration on Liberated Europe which gave the British the right to influence the establishment of governments in Poland and other areas of vital interest to the Soviets. With hindsight it is easy to see that Stalin never took these seriously. Yet the Yalta agreements defined a European order governed by different principles to those of the percentages agreement. On returning from Yalta, Churchill told the Cabinet on 6 March that 'it would be for consideration whether the Yalta Declaration on Liberated Territories could be construed as superseding arrangements such as that in respect of Romania and Greece.'[13] It thus became necessary for the British to consider whether the abandonment of spheres would be beneficial to their position in the postwar international order or not.

The advantages of a spheres of influence arrangement for FO policy makers had clearly been reduced by the advance of the Red Army. Yet to abandon any idea of spheres of influence or blocs raised the question of how the British position in Greece could be maintained. Could spheres be abandoned in all European territories apart from Greece and Romania, which would allow greater British involvement in Poland and Bulgaria than provided for by the Moscow agreement? Or could there be some new deal involving a compromise between spheres of influence and a regime of international co-operation with a commitment to self-determination? In March, the ambassador in Moscow expressed his views on such matters. Clark Kerr argued that for Russians the word 'co-operation' meant something like the division of the world into spheres with no partner hampering or criticizing the other in their sphere. The Kremlin had a unique opportunity to control internal developments in Romania, Bulgaria and Poland but this did not indicate an abandonment of co-operation with the West. Moreover, Clark Kerr regarded these Soviet aims as limited objectives which did not endanger any of Britain's vital interests. The ambassador acknowledged that Poland could become a test case of Soviet behaviour but urged the FO to avoid fruitless arguments over Romania and Bulgaria. He believed Britain should be concerned with protecting its vital interests in Greece, Persia and Turkey.[14]

This in effect was a move to retain spheres of influence based very firmly on vital interests. As Britain had no vital interests in eastern and central Europe, co-operation with the Soviets could be maintained without too much concern over developments in such areas. However Sir Orme Sargent questioned whether the control of areas of vital interest by Britain and the Soviet Union would serve as an adequate basis for postwar co-operation. Sargent saw a danger in the Soviets consolidating what he referred to as their '*cordon sanitaire*' out of fear that Britain and the US would rehabilitate Germany, as they had done in Italy, to make it safe from communism. A Soviet sphere appeared to be taking shape in Poland, Romania and Bulgaria. Sargent feared this could be extended to Yugoslavia, Hungary, Austria, Czechoslovakia and possibly Turkey, but he accepted this could be prevented by a sphere of influence arrangement. Britain, he believed, could save Czechoslovakia, Yugoslavia, Turkey and Austria at the expense of Poland, Romania and Bulgaria by this method. It was an extraordinary estimation of Britain's capacity to influence events in postwar Europe but Sargent did not favour such a policy. He believed it would be a cynical abandonment of small nations and 'represent the abdication of our right as a great power to be concerned with the affairs of the whole of Europe and not just areas in which we have a special interest.'[15]

This was an attack on spheres of influence, not just because of their impact on small nations, but because whatever British vital interests might be secured, spheres of influence in Europe would not maintain Britain's status as a great world power. There was however a snag with planning for a Europe without spheres of influence. It was easy to reject them in eastern Europe where Britain had no vital strategic or geopolitical interests, but it would be difficult to reject them in those areas where

Britain did have vital interests and where the Soviets might want to be involved in the same way as Sargent wanted Britain to be involved with eastern and central Europe.

In early 1945 the Suez Canal Committee was considering future arrangements for the defence of the Canal Zone. It was divided over whether international arrangements should be made.[16] Eden submitted a paper to the Cabinet arguing that as the 'defence of the region was a matter of life and death for the British Empire', Britain could not afford to resign its special position in the area. Eden went on to argue that the future world organization should give each of the great powers special defence responsibilities in its particular area or areas and that the US and the USSR had areas of responsibility which were as vital to their interests as the Middle East was to Britain's. Thus 'the position of the United States in relation to the Panama Canal, is identical with our own in relation to the Suez Canal, as is the position of Russia with regard to certain areas of eastern Europe.'[17]

In the meantime the discussion of spheres of influence continued within the Foreign Office. F. K. Roberts argued that Britain would have to confront the reality of a Soviet sphere of influence in parts of eastern Europe. In his view Britain should expect to be excluded from Poland, Czechoslovakia, Bulgaria, Romania and even Yugoslavia. It would, therefore, be sensible simply to 'take a leaf out of the Russian book' and if Europe was going to be divided, concentrate British efforts on the western half.[18] Sargent's views were strengthened by growing concerns that Britain would be treated as a junior partner by the Soviets and the Americans. The concern about Britain's two allies orchestrating the postwar settlement in Europe culminated in July when Sargent wrote his famous 'Stocktaking on VE Day' memorandum which asserted that neither the US nor the Soviet Union would be 'likely to consider British interests overmuch if they interfere with their own and unless we assert ourselves.'[19]

However, in the summer of 1945 a more pressing concern developed. In June 1945 the Soviets informed the Turkish government that they would like to have bases in the Straits.[20] Clark Kerr regarded this as a disquieting feature as it suggested a threat to Britain's position in the Middle East. In response he called for a clear cut policy aimed at those areas for which Britain had long been responsible – the colonial Empire and the Middle East – and those new areas of responsibility in Germany.[21] In a sense this reflected a traditional British view of Europe. Britain was primarily a great imperial power whose real interests lay outside the continent. However, repeated German aggression required co-operation with the US and the USSR to control Germany. This could be assured and Britain's vital interests protected by a firm policy based on non-involvement in the other's areas of vital interest. While this co-operation over Germany prevailed it mattered little what military or other arrangements were made for the lesser states in eastern or western Europe.

The alternative view retained the idea of Britain as a great imperial power, but was concerned about Britain's relative decline in economic and military strength. Therefore, Britain would need to lead a constellation of states in the Commonwealth and western Europe in order to regain a position of equality with the US and the USSR. This view required firm opposition to any attempts to minimize Britain's European or imperial role. It also emphasized the importance of planning for postwar Europe in ways which were linked to Britain's imperial role particularly in the eastern Mediterranean and Middle East.

This was the view of Sir Orme Sargent who asserted in July 1945 that

it must be an essential feature of our European policy to maintain close and friendly links with Italy, Greece and Turkey, so as to secure our strategic position in the eastern Mediterranean, especially now that Russia, stretching down from the north is once again exerting pressure on this all important link between Great Britain on the one hand, and India, Malaya, Australia, New Zealand and our Persian and Iraq oil supplies on the other.

The only countries that Sargent believed might have to be accepted as under Russian domination were Romania and Hungary. These were the countries in which Britain had the least interest with regard to their eastern Mediterranean position. For Sargent, any threat to Britain's vital interests in the Mediterranean had to be avoided. Yet to abandon Eastern Europe would not be compatible with the great power status that Sargent saw as requiring the enrolment of France and the lesser western European powers, along with the Dominions, in a tripartite system that would make Britain equal to the US and the Soviet Union.[22]

In the Foreign Office it was pointed out that maintaining a British base in the Suez Canal Zone while denying the Soviets a base in the Straits was clearly illogical. Jebb considered the possibility of a spheres of influence deal which gave the British an exclusive zone in the eastern Mediterranean and Middle East in return for an exclusive Soviet sphere in most of eastern Europe. Yet, having considered this Jebb rejected such an option as 'to yield to *any* Russian demand would clearly mean we are not prepared to play the part of a great power which has been allocated to us in the present World Organization.'[23] Jebb's views reflected strong support for the views of Sir Orme Sargent and the policy which Bevin began to implement in the summer of 1945 was clearly based on these views rather than on the views of the Embassy in Moscow.

In eastern Europe it thus became important to deny the Soviets a sphere of influence while retaining a British one in the eastern Mediterranean and the Middle East. The policy was questioned by Attlee who was concerned about the financial costs and about the consequences of confronting the Soviets with the 'needs of the defence of the British Empire'.[24] However, it was warmly endorsed by Bevin and justified on the grounds that because the Soviet Union had acquired additional territory in eastern Europe it had no need of a sphere of influence. Whereas the British, who were seeking no territorial gains, should be allowed an exclusive Mediterranean and Middle Eastern sphere in order to ensure the security of the Empire/Commonwealth.[25]

Yet in seeking to realize this aim, British planners were determined to protect not only Britain's vital interests but her general position as a great world power. For this a Western European organization was necessary, as was denying the Soviets the right to a sphere of influence in most of eastern Europe. The British had initially hoped to secure a Europe without spheres but had adopted them in order to protect their interests in the Mediterranean, notably in Greece. Then, encouraged by Stalin's apparent rejection of exclusive zones of European influence, the British, worried about their standing as a great world power, abandoned spheres of European influence as the basis for co-operation. By the end of 1945 it was planned to unite western Europe, under British leadership, with the overseas dependencies in some kind of association that would provide Britain with the economic strength to match the Soviets and the Americans. Planning for Europe was geared to preserving and rebuilding Britain's position as a great world power.

Notes and references

1 *FRUS*, 1943, *The Conferences at Cairo and Teheran*, (Washington: US Government Printing Office) record of Roosevelt–Stalin meeting 29 November 1943, p. 530.
2 *Ibid.*
3 G. Ross ed., *The Foreign Office and the Kremlin: documents on Anglo-Soviet relations 1941–45* (Cambridge: Cambridge University Press, 1984), Doc 6, Clark Kerr to Eden 25 November 1942, p. 115.
4 PRO: CAB 66/53, WP(44)436, 9 August 1944.
5 One problem in dealing with British plans for, and attitudes to, Europe is the vague use of geographical terms by historians and by policy makers during the

war. There appears to be no clear geographical boundaries between central and eastern Europe for example let alone between eastern and south eastern Europe. Even the use of the term 'the Balkans' is rather imprecise and unless particular countries are mentioned by name there will always be some ambiguity as to which precise territories are being referred to. And even then, the inclusion of one country in a group defined by a particular criterion can often be followed by its subsequent exclusion from a similar group.

6   PRO: CAB 81/45, PHP(43)1, 1 May 1944.

7   PRO: FO 371/43335, minute by Sir O. Sargent, 11 June 1944.

8   There is a vast literature on the percentages agreement, which were initially Romania: Russia 90 per cent, the others 10 per cent. Greece: Great Britain (in accord with the US) 90 per cent, Russia 10 per cent. Yugoslavia 50–50 per cent. Hungary 50–50 per cent. Bulgaria: Russia 75 per cent, the others 25 per cent. It includes articles by J. M. Siracusa 'The Meaning of Tolstoy: Churchill, Stalin and the Balkans: Moscow 1944', *Diplomatic History* 3, 4 (1979) which reprints some of the official record; P. G. Holdich 'A Policy of Percentages? British Policy and the Balkans after the Moscow Conference of October 1944, *International History Review* 9, 1 (1987); A. Resis, 'The Churchill–Stalin Secret "Percentages Agreement"', *American Historical Review* 83 (1978); G. Ross 'The Moscow Conference of October 1944 (Tolstoy)' in W. Deakin, E. Barker and G. Chadwick eds, *British Political and Military Strategy in Central, Eastern and Southern Europe, 1944* (London: Macmillan, 1988); Warren F. Kimball 'Naked Reverse Right: Roosevelt, Churchill and Eastern Europe from Tolstoy to Yalta and a Little Beyond', *Diplomatic History* 9, 1 (1985). Details can also be found in B. Kuniholm, *The Origins of the Cold War in the Near East* (Princeton, NJ: Princeton University Press, 1980) and M. Gilbert, *Road to Victory: Winston Churchill 1941–45* (London: Heinemann, 1986) which includes details omitted from the official record.

9   PRO: FO 371/43647, Eden to Sargent, 12 October 1944.

10 *Document on British Policy Overseas*, series I, vol. II, doc 281, brief for the UK delegation at Moscow, 12 December 1945.

11 PRO: FO 371/40741B, minute by G. Jebb, 18 December 1944. 12 PRO: FO 371/47883, minute by D. L. Stewart, 12 July 1945.

13 Fraser J. Harbutt, *The Iron Curtain, Churchill, America and the Origins of the Cold War* (Oxford: Clarendon Press, 1986) p. 94.

14 PRO: FO 371/47941, Sir A. Clark Kerr to Eden 27 March 1945.

15 PRO: FO 371/47888, memorandum by Sir O. Sargent, 2 April 1945.

16 PRO: CAB 66/63, WP(45)197, 20 March 1945.

17 PRO: CAB 66/65, WP(45)256, 13 April 1945.

18 PRO: FO 371/47882, F. K. Roberts to C. F. A. Warner, 25 April 1945.

19 PRO: FO 371/50912, memorandum by Sir O. Sargent, 11 July 1945.

20 PRO: FO 371/48774, FO to Moscow, 5 July 1945.

21 PRO: FO 371/47883, Sir A. Clark Kerr to Eden, 10 July 1945.

22 PRO: FO 371/50912, memorandum by Sir O. Sargent, 11 July 1945.

23 *DBPO*, Series I, vol. I, doc 459, memorandum by G. Jebb, 29 July 1945 (emphasis in the original).

24 Ibid., doc 179, Attlee to Eden, 18 July 1945.

25 PRO: FO 371/50795, Heaton Nicholls to FO, 6 October 1945; Secretary of State to Heaton Nicholls, 11 October 1945; Secretary of State to Lord Halifax, 17 October 1945.

4

De Gaulle's Plans for Postwar Europe

Georges-Henri Soutou

When devising his plans for postwar Europe, de Gaulle's first concern was of course the German problem. But quite soon, and to a greater degree than has been often realized, he became conscious of the Soviet one and he foresaw quickly the onset of what was to become the Cold War. The dialectic between the German and the Soviet problems was probably at the core of his European policy.[1] One should keep in mind that most Frenchmen, not only de Gaulle, still considered France, leading its Empire, as able to regain soon its status as a major power. The preoccupation with 'le rang' was not by any means confined to de Gaulle. This can explain the undoubtedly over-ambitious plans devised at the time.

De Gaulle's postwar plans underwent considerable changes from 1943 to 1945. He began by relying on the Soviet Union; he mistrusted it deeply at the end. At the beginning he did not believe that the Americans would stay in Europe after the war, at the end he was trying to bring them to commit themselves to European security, not only against Germany but also against the Soviet Union. At the beginning he was contemplating an alliance with Great Britain, in 1945 he was refusing it at least for the time being. As for Germany, his plans were not definite before October 1945.

At the same time one can see four permanent factors in his policy. First, the conviction that traditional methods for controlling Germany – reminiscent of the period between 1914 and 1923 of French policy or even earlier ones – were still useful, appropriate and necessary. Second, the conviction that Europe was a new important dimension, and that France had to modernize its methods according to the evolutionary process and in order to form a western European bloc under its leadership. Third, that a major factor after the war would be the Soviet Union, either as an ally to control Germany, or as a menace. Fourth that eastern Europe had to remain politically, socially and ideologically independent from Russia, even if it was acceptable that it should be diplomatically and strategically aligned, so long as Moscow was striving for security and not for domination.

The Free French did not begin to reflect on the postwar problems before the constitution of the 'Comité Français de la Libération Nationale (CFLN)' in 1943, in Algiers. Basically the members of the CFLN were divided: they were either in favour of a coercive kind of peace in a national framework, or of a constructive one in a European framework. Of course in both cases they intended to achieve maximum security against Germany and a leading role for France in Europe, but those two basic orientations were to mark the immediate postwar period, until, in 1950, Paris finally chose the European construction policy. De Gaulle gave comprehensive instructions about French policies in the postwar period for the first time on 30 October 1943.[2] First of all, he believed characteristically, that Germany would not be the only problem. The 'Big Three' had developed imperialistic tendencies. After the war there would be two predominant and antagonistic powers, the US and the USSR. Through their rivalry a new war could happen, 'either because of Germany or about it', thus France should not align itself exclusively with any of the major powers.

International security organizations, although necessary, would not be enough for France. It would require close relations and a treaty of alliance with the Soviet Union against Germany, albeit with some precautions, in order not to be drawn into an eventual war in Asia, and to prevent Moscow from meddling in France's domestic policies. It would also need a treaty with Great Britain, opening the way for a trilateral security arrangement with London and Moscow. With the US there would be no formal treaty, but the traditional friendship between both countries. For its security against Germany, France would rely first on territorial measures: clear-cut separation of the Rhineland and the Ruhr from the Reich (their actual *régime* being postponed indefinitely). But de Gaulle also gave instructions to the effect that one should contemplate a political and economic 'federation' (the word is to be taken here in a loose sense) between France, Belgium, the Netherlands and Luxembourg, and to include the Rhineland and the Ruhr separated from Germany. Thus, De Gaulle was apparently attentive to the ideas of some members of the CFLN, who believed as Jean Monnet, did, that France would not be able to achieve its aims in a purely national framework, and would have to take into account the needs of the European economy. Indeed, as he explained, in de Gaulle's view this 'federation' was in fact intended to encompass Germany; as we shall see, it was also meant to enable France to assert itself alongside the major powers.

With regard to eastern Europe, France would limit its involvement to cultural and economic relations and renounce its prewar alliances. It was understood in Algiers that politically and militarily those countries would have to develop closer links with the Soviet Union. France no longer had the means to support them, and did not wish to antagonize the perceived Soviet security interest in that part of Europe.[3] From now on de Gaulle's plans for postwar Europe would thus include three major directions: alliances with the USSR and Great Britain; the separation of the Rhineland and the Ruhr from the Reich; and an organization for western Europe.

From the autumn of 1943 until the spring of 1944 the west European grouping – the 'federation' identified by de Gaulle – was to occupy an important place in Algiers thinking. De Gaulle contemplated a 'Bloc occidental', that is a 'strategic and economic federation' between France, Belgium, the Netherlands, Luxembourg, the Rhineland and the Ruhr, and eventually Great Britain.[4] On 18 March de Gaulle gave an important speech at the Provisional Assembly, in which he suggested for Europe 'a sort of western grouping'. These were not empty words: since the preceding autumn, different departments of the CFLN had been studying the possibility of such a western grouping. Its first aim would be, of course, to provide a framework in which to control Germany under French leadership, but there was also clearly a further motive: it was understood and stated that such a western grouping would also provide a means by which to balance Soviet power and influence after the war. In any case, and certainly correct, that was the Soviet's interpretation of the 18 March speech, against which the Russian representative protested forcefully as soon as 20 March, which led de Gaulle to abstain from referring to the 'western grouping' until 1945.

In January 1945 the preparations in Paris about Germany were stepped up. There was general agreement that the Rhineland and the Ruhr should be permanently occupied, that the Rhineland should be under French control and the Ruhr under international control, but there were for the remaining areas conflicting tendencies on some very important topics. Some were stressing French military security, and insisting on strategic control of the Rhine and absolute separation of the Rhineland and the Ruhr from Germany. Others believed that the main problem was an economic one and that a viable zone should be devised, to include the Ruhr, under strict international economic control, designed to benefit the economy of the neighbouring countries and of Europe as a whole, without necessarily separating that zone from the former Reich and with less insistence on complete French control of the Rhineland proper, which was seen as too narrow from an economic point of view and not viable.

Some insisted on French control of the western part of Germany and the adoption of an attitude of benign neglect to the rest of the country, or even with an express wish to see the break-up of Germany. It was stressed that France could not detach itself from development in Germany at large, if only for economic and reparations reasons, and because after all the Potsdam conference had postulated the unity of the former Reich. Although an issue which was not resolved at the time of the London Conference in September 1945, the question of German unity remained. Everyone agreed that Prussian centralism should be ended once and for all. But what should be done? There was in some quarters, apart from the separation of the Rhineland and the Ruhr, a wish to separate Prussia from the rest of Germany and to encourage Bavarian separatism. But there was also the fear, expressed as early as 19 July 1945 in the first directive of the 'Secrétariat général pour les affaires allemandes et autrichiennes', that a complete break-up of Germany could lead 'other powers' (by which one meant of course the USSR) to take control of eastern Germany, which would 'lead to an imbalance that might be fatal for Europe'. In that case the best solution might be to loosen the German confederation. Some diplomats, contrary to de Gaulle's opinion, were even in favour of setting up German central administrations, as decided at Potsdam.

Most Free French were expecting an early and strong alliance with Great Britain, as a cornerstone of France's postwar policy and the best way to control Germany. But this was not to happen before the Dunkirk treaty of 1947. In that respect de Gaulle's views were different, expressed in the 30 October 1943 guidelines, and personally explained to Stalin in Moscow on 8 December 1944. In de Gaulle's opinion, the alliance with Moscow took precedence over the alliance with London, because French and Soviet interests about Germany were similar, which was not the case with Great Britain, which was not a continental country and which would want, as after 1919, to quickly rehabilitate Germany for economic reasons. Therefore, France and the Soviet Union should establish their mutual security on three levels: the first and strongest level, would be the Franco-Soviet alliance; the second, less certain, level would be built around the Anglo-Soviet alliance of 1942 and the future Anglo-French alliance; the third and weakest level, would rely on collective security, in order to try to bring in the US, but without many illusions.

At the beginning of 1945 relations between London and Paris were not good and at that stage de Gaulle refused to contemplate an alliance with London as long as Great Britain refused to support French claims towards German territory (the separation of the Rhineland and the Ruhr) and towards Syria and Lebanon, the former French mandates in the Middle East.[5] They worsened in May, with the serious crisis in Syria. Thus the three-level security concept was doomed.

Nevertheless in December 1944, de Gaulle's priority was clear: the conclusion of an alliance with the Soviet Union. He did, in fact, sign the far-reaching Franco-Soviet alliance in Moscow, on 10 December. The Franco-Soviet pact amounted to a preventive alliance allowing each partner to take preventive measures against any menace coming from Germany, and obliging the partner to follow suit. This was a dangerous commitment for the weaker partner, but it now appears that it was the French who wanted it that way. The Soviets had originally envisaged a much less ambitious alliance, on the lines of the Anglo-Soviet treaty of 1942. But the French wanted an alliance as strong as the Franco-Russian alliance of 1892–94: their main objective was to eradicate the German menace forever. The Soviets had no difficulty in accepting that view and the treaty was drafted accordingly.

De Gaulle had certainly achieved his main goal in Moscow. However, Stalin had not agreed to the establishment of France's military border on the Rhine, nor had he impressed Stalin with his plea for Polish independence. Furthermore, he had had to accept the exchange of unofficial representatives with the puppet Lublin government, which in itself could be justified by the need to take care of French prisoners in Poland, but also he was obliged to exchange public announcements with the Lublin government to that effect, which amounted to a *de facto* recognition of this government, at a time when the British and the Americans were still recognizing only the exiled Polish government in London. Because of the historical links between France and Poland, it was a highly symbolic event, most useful to the Soviets who made it an absolute condition to the signing of the pact. De Gaulle was perfectly aware of the importance of the matter.[6] It is quite clear that, despite the achievement of the Franco-Soviet pact, which for him had been a clear priority, de Gaulle was bitter when he left Moscow. He had not achieved Soviet support for his aims in Germany; he had not been able to save Polish independence. He realized that perfectly.[7]

In the following weeks and months France's disenchantment with Moscow grew steadily. Stalin did nothing to invite de Gaulle to Yalta or Potsdam; he was against a French zone of occupation in Germany; and against French participation in the steering committee of the Reparations Commission. As early as May 1945 the Quai d'Orsay had reached the conclusion that Moscow was not taking seriously the Franco-Soviet pact and did not take any account of French interests or wishes in bilateral matters, for instance in the very sensitive question of French prisoners-of-war now in Soviet hands. But apparently nothing did more to convince de Gaulle that the Soviets were following a policy bent not on security but on expansion than the events in eastern Europe and in the Middle East. French diplomats and the Secret Service reported on the total and brutal political control Moscow was exerting in eastern Europe (events de Gaulle himself followed attentively as Poland and Yugoslavia were two countries in which he was interested) and on the changes introduced to the boundaries of those countries with the aim of building up what the Quai d'Orsay in a 13 August 1945 note called 'a powerful Slavic bloc' (de Gaulle himself would adopt this expression) with two prongs – towards the Danish Straits and the Balkans. In November the Quai d'Orsay was convinced that Moscow was encouraging the Poles to develop their links with the French in order to prevent the emergence of an Entente between France and the Anglo-Americans.

The French were also convinced that the Soviets were pursuing an ambitious policy in the Middle East, contrary to perceived French interests. In particular they noted the Soviets wish to participate in any settlement in that region, to establish a naval base in the eastern Mediterranean and also their support of the Kurds.[8] In addition the Soviets refused to support French aims towards Germany at the London Conference in September 1945, or on the occasion of Franco-Soviet discussions about Germany in December. And as early as July the French Communist Party began to try to exert pressure on de Gaulle, which ultimately would lead to his departure in January 1946. De Gaulle reacted to those disappointing and disquieting tendencies of Soviet policy in three directions: in August he initiated a rapprochement with Washington, he revived the 'Bloc occidental' in September and he finally established French aims towards Germany in October 1945 with an eye of course on the German problem, but also on the growing Soviet menace.

In August 1945 de Gaulle paid an official visit to the United States. The visit was a success; de Gaulle did not fail to notice that President Truman had a different approach, in his view more 'realistic', of world affairs than that of his predecessor. De Gaulle and Bidault stated the

French aims towards Germany: separation of the Rhineland and the Ruhr and suppression of German unity. The reason given was the usual one: the ever-present German menace. But they gave also a new one: a reunified Germany would fall under Soviet control and push Soviet influence to the Rhine. The perception of a German menace through Soviet control of Germany and a Soviet–German conjunction was an essential dialectical step in the process which led the French from the perception of the German menace to that of the Soviet one. This process would last until 1948–50; it had began already in 1945, sooner than frequently assumed, at least in the best-informed circles. The Americans did not concur with French reasoning and explained that they were still hoping to retain a good relationship with Moscow. But this did not deter de Gaulle from apparently going even further in the next weeks. He was informed in August that the Soviets were not demobilizing their forces, contrary to the American actions. In September 1945 he apparently contemplated military negotiations with the Americans in preparation for a secret alliance with them. De Gaulle's departure in January 1946 laid those plans to rest for the time being, but they were the early origins of the preparation of the Atlantic alliance, three years later.[9]

That de Gaulle was taking more and more seriously the Soviet threat to Europe is highlighted, apart from his evolving attitude towards America, by the revival of the Western bloc idea, which had been officially discarded in 1944, due to Soviet protests. Publicly he took up that idea again in an interview with the *Sunday Times* on 10 September 1945. He expressed forcefully the objective of a western European grouping, including the western part of Germany, during a visit to the Rhineland at the beginning of October.

The Soviets for one completely understood de Gaulle's new orientation. The Polish and Czech press were attacking forcefully the idea of a Western bloc. On 13 October 1945, Bogomolov, the Soviet ambassador in Paris, told Catroux, the French ambassador in Moscow, that the recent declarations of de Gaulle (implying of course the *Sunday Times* interview and the speeches in Germany some days earlier calling the Rhinelander to participate in the Western European grouping as 'Western European') proved that France had 'altered its orientation'. He was right, and that conversation marked the end of the policy of close links de Gaulle had tried to pursue with Moscow since 1941.[10]

The failure of the London Conference about Germany in September 1945 led de Gaulle, in instructions to his aides on 8 October, upon returning from his visit to the Rhine some days earlier, to formulate in a final and precise way French policy towards Germany. He aimed to solve the uncertainties and contradictions, which had marked his policy until then. He was now sure that the Allies would not accept the French aims, but it did not matter, because they would not be able to agree among themselves and to fulfil the Potsdam agreements. Therefore, France could pursue its own policy. The more so because with the end of Prussia – amputated by the Soviets and the Poles and occupied by the Soviet Union – came the end of German unity.

France would annex the Saar. France would occupy permanently, impose strict control on, and integrate economically, the Rhineland which would be separated from Germany and which would become an integral part of the Western bloc. The Ruhr, also separated from Germany, would be controlled by the Allies and its neighbours. The rest of the French occupation zone, that is part of Baden and part of Württemberg, should be reorganized and eventually France would exchange with the Americans their part of Württemberg against the rest of Baden. Baden and Württemberg would not be as closely integrated to France as the Rhineland; they would be allowed to form, with the rest of German States – Bavaria, Hannover and so on – a loose confederation. It was evident from de Gaulle's explanations to his aides at the time, and from the evolution of his policy towards Moscow in that period, that he hoped France would influence that confederation through Baden, and that this confederation would prevent a power vacuum west of the Soviet occupation zone, which would of course benefit the Soviet Union.

In other words de Gaulle tried at one stroke to solve three problems and reconcile all the various views expressed since 1943. The first problem, French security towards Germany, would be solved in the most rigid way, with an outright annexation of the Saar and control of the Rhineland that amounted to annexation, and the end of the German centralized State. The economic problems would be solved with the international statute of the Ruhr, which was a concession to the Monnet school of thought and to the people in the economic ministries, who were thinking more in terms of economic priorities in a European framework. And finally the Soviet problem would be solved with the integration of the Rhineland in the Western bloc and a loose confederation of the rest of Germany influenced by the southern states under French influence, in order to block the progress of Soviet influence as far as the Rhine.[11]

As we have seen, de Gaulle's postwar plans underwent considerable changes between 1943 and 1945. It would appear that despite changes in policy the constant aspiration from 1943 to 1945 and the fulcrum of his postwar plans for Europe, was to control Germany with the help of the Soviet Union (either with its direct help in the spirit of the Franco-Soviet pact, or with its indirect help through the fact of Soviet–Polish annexations of 'Prussian' provinces and through the Soviet occupation zone) and then to balance the Soviet influence in Europe with the Western bloc concept. By bringing Germany down Moscow would help, even unwittingly, France to achieve geopolitical control of the western part of that country and thus to form and lead the Western bloc. This would enable France to play a role far beyond its actual means after the war.

But this far-reaching concept was probably doomed to failure from the start, for two reasons. First, France did not possess the means by which to achieve those ambitious goals, particularly with the multiple factors de Gaulle had in mind – control of Germany by both the Soviet Union and France, and the formation of the Western bloc. All the more so when de Gaulle decided not to conclude an alliance with London immediately, thus isolating France and depriving it of the support of Great Britain. The second reason was expressed by the American diplomat Charles Bohlen, when de Gaulle went to Washington in August 1945. He told a French colleague: 'The Soviets do not wish to see a second major power standing up on the European continent.' Stalin had no intention of obliging de Gaulle, or to help him, even indirectly, to achieve his plans.

Notes

1 P. Gerbet, *Le Relèvement*, (Paris: Imprimerie Nationale, 1991). See G.-H. Soutou, 'Le général de Gaulle et l'URSS, 1943–1945: idéologie ou équilibre européen', *Revue d'Histoire diplomatique*, (1994) n. 4; G.-H. Soutou, 'Frankreich und die Deutschlandfrage 1943 bis 1945', in H.-E.Volkmann ed., *Ende des Dritten Reiches – Ende des Zweiten Weltkrieges*, (Munich: Piper, 1995).
2 R. Massigli, *Une comédie des erreurs*, (Paris: Plon, 1978) p. 37 ff.
3 G.-H. Soutou, 'Le général de Gaulle et l'URSS, 1943–1945: idéologie ou équilibre européen', and A. Marès, 'La France Libre et l'Europe centrale et orientale (1940–1944)', *Revue des Etudes Slaves*, LIV/3 (1982).
4 C. de Gaulle, *Mémoires de Guerre, L'unité* (Paris: Plon, 1956) p. 473.
5 Jean Chauvel, general secretary of the Quai d'Orsay, to René Massigli, ambassador in London, 4 January 1945; Massigli to Chauvel, 16 January 1945; Chauvel to Massigli, 23 January 1945; Paris, Ministère des Affaires étrangères (MAE), Papiers Massigli, vol. 94.
6 One notices that some parts of the protocols of his talks with Stalin concerning Poland were modified in his *Le Salut*, published in 1959. Compare with the

original text in *Documents Diplomatiques Français*, 1944–II, (Paris: Imprimerie Nationale, 1996).

7   Soutou, 'Le général de Gaulle et l'URSS, 1943–1945: op. cit.

8   For all this, ibid.

9   Ibid.

10   Ibid.

11   For all this see Soutou, 'Frankreich und die Deutschlandfrage 1943 bis 1945' op. cit.

5
Soviet Plans for Postwar Europe

Vojtech Mastny

To a greater extent than the Western planning for postwar Europe, the Soviet planning has been subject to retrospective misinterpretation. Indeed, as long as the Cold War lasted, the question of what Moscow had really been aiming to accomplish was the seminal point of dispute about its origins. In taking sides, both Stalin's admirers and his detractors at least tended to agree that he had systematically and purposefully worked toward the establishment of Communist regimes in those countries of the continent where such regimes were in fact established by 1949. Disagreements between pro-Soviet and anti-Soviet writers concerned the merit rather than the substance of this accomplishment. How justified is the image of Stalin's design for the postwar order?

Western revisionist historians have been more open than those of the traditional variety to the sensible proposition that Stalin, rather than implementing a rigidly set design, often responded to both challenges and opportunities. Yet they have usually underestimated the extent to which his choices had also been predetermined by his Marxist–Leninist preconceptions. Their abiding influence in providing the frame of reference within which Soviet policy was made, if not necessarily its goals, has been one of the more important revelations coming out of the Moscow archives since they opened their doors following the collapse of Communism in 1989. What were the effects of ideology on postwar planning?

At a time when the war was still in progress and neither its course nor its exact outcome could be reliably predicted, the resulting uncertainty inevitably shaped the planning for peace as well. Often decisions had to be made under the pressure of events whose long-term significance may not have been immediately clear. How effective was Stalin's control of policy in the increasingly complex and rapidly evolving international situation? In preparing for the postwar world, did he live up to his reputation of a self-confident and shrewdly calculating realist who knew what he wanted and how to go about achieving it?

Stalin was ill-equipped to preside over his country's successful entry into a peaceful postwar order. Having risen to supreme power by besting rivals in the deadly intrigue that was part and parcel of Soviet domestic politics, he tended to project its workings onto the international scene. A latecomer to foreign policy, he lacked first-hand knowledge of other countries. A despot with almost boundless levels of suspicion, he felt uncomfortable using power in an environment he could not control. His early forays into foreign policy had been clumsy and often disappointing, an experience which added a measure of caution, if not necessarily wisdom, to his management of Soviet foreign affairs, which by the end of the 1930s he had all but monopolized.

Stalin carried the burden of his August 1939 pact with Hitler. In trying to look after Soviet security as he understood it, however, he regarded the pact not so much a burden as an accomplishment. Its secret provisions about the division of eastern Europe into spheres of influence epitomized the concept of security by imperial expansion, which was Stalin's authentic and enduring contribution to the political thought and practice of the once revolutionary Soviet state. Not merely an expedient to buy time, the pact shaped in fundamental ways Stalin's European policy and left an indispensable legacy to his successors as well.

As implemented by mid-1940, Stalin's concept of security provided not only for the outright annexation of territories that used to belong to tsarist Russia, such as the Baltic states, eastern parts of Poland and of Finland, and Bessarabia, but also for a belt of states claimed by Moscow as a zone of its predominant influence. In competing with Hitler for such influence, Stalin sought to expand the zone by including in it areas that had never been in the Russian sphere before. During secret Berlin conversations in November 1940, his Foreign Commissar Vyacheslav M. Molotov claimed for his government a special role in Sweden, the Danish and Black Sea Straits, Hungary, Yugoslavia and even Greece.[1]

Such far-fetched demands, which Moscow at the time was in no position to enforce on its own, were a self-defeating way of soliciting Hitler's support and thus reassurance about his intentions; instead they helped to clinch his decision to crush the Soviet Union by force. His surprise attack, which almost succeeded, exposed another of Stalin's periodic miscalculations about Germany, the most serious so far but not the last. It showed that the quest for security by empire, far from providing real security, rather bred a false feeling of it, thus making the blow that came even worse than it need have been.

Yet Stalin proved notably unwilling to revise, much less discard, a concept to which he had so deeply committed himself. In 1941 he began his planning for the postwar order by merely trying to adapt his thinking to the new circumstances, which required Soviet participation in the alliance with the Western powers necessitated by the German invasion. In outlining his vision of the future to visiting British Foreign Secretary Anthony Eden in December 1941, he again envisaged a Europe divided into spheres of influence, only this time with Great Britain as the partner.[2] With the same 'incurable taste for future precision to offset [...] present confusion'[3] that characterized his tsarist predecessors during the First World War, he went into great detail in spelling out which countries were to be the Soviet, and which the British, responsibility.

Contrary to hindsight appearances, there was no straight line from Stalin's vision to the eventual partition of Europe as it took shape during the Cold War. Having failed in 1942 to obtain from the British an advance commitment to the division of the continent because of American opposition, Stalin never tried again. As long as the price of victory remained uncertain, it was better for him not to tie his hands lest he ask for too much, or else too little. His minimum aims, without which the war would have presumably not been worth winning, included the preservation of the territorial gains he had made as a result of his collusion with Hitler, the prevention of any regional combinations in eastern Europe capable of resisting Soviet wishes (particularly the planned Polish–Czechoslovak confederation), and the establishment throughout the continent of Communist centres of power to help implement whatever policies Stalin would eventually decide to pursue in different countries. Any further aims were flexible rather than fixed.

Shortly after the Stalin–Eden meeting, Deputy Soviet Foreign Commissar Solomon Lozovsky composed for Molotov and Stalin a memorandum dwelling on the need to study the problems of the postwar settlement. Afterward the Politburo decided to form several commissions, composed of Foreign Commissariat's experts, to address these problems. Yet while fighting was raging at the eastern front during 1942 without a clear outcome for either side, their activity apparently remained limited to the gathering of material. Rather than from their work, the Soviet thinking about the postwar order may be gleaned from Moscow's management of foreign Communist parties through the Comintern.

In trying to mobilize foreign Communists to assist Soviet policy as best as they could, the secret directives sent from Moscow did not conceptually differentiate between eastern and western Europe. They envisaged everywhere the formation of 'national fronts', distinguished from the 'popular' fronts of the 1930s by positing collaboration with not only left-wing but also other enemies of Fascism without any time limit.[4] This did not rule out, but neither did it postulate, eventual seizure of power by the Communists; as Stalin explained to the French party chief Maurice Thorez, their most urgent task was to expand their base of support by winning allies.[5] Other things being equal, they should best be able to control in the future the balance of power in their respective countries, which could then be manipulated from Moscow.

Not only were things not equal, however, but the wartime conditions often made it difficult to ascertain at a distance just how unequal they were. Contrary to the impression informed by later developments, the Soviet knowledge of the true situation in occupied Europe was inadequate. Compared with later periods, the size of the Soviet intelligence establishment was, according to the recollection of one of its veterans, 'simply laughable'.[6] Clandestine communication with underground Communist parties was sporadic and unreliable. In some countries, such as Czechoslovakia and Poland, the police managed to extensively infiltrate the Communist organizations.[7] Being left largely on their own did not necessarily make their members disloyal to Moscow; the Yugoslav Communists, in particular, were eager to oblige whenever they were able to find out what Stalin's wishes were.[8] Yet their inability to do so made them suspect in his eyes, thus limiting their utility for him.

When Soviet postwar planning began in earnest after the Red Army's decisive victory at Stalingrad in February 1943, Moscow's relations with foreign Communists were first on the agenda. The dissolution three months later of the Comintern, which controlled their utilization for purposes of Soviet foreign policy, came as a surprise and a shock to them; outsiders either wanted to believe that Stalin had finally given up Communism, or suspected a ruse. Yet the official announcement, which suggested that the wartime developments had accentuated differences in various countries, thus necessitating more flexible Communist policies, offered a fair indication of what really was on Stalin's mind.[9]

As Stalin explained to the Comintern's top officials, its disappearance was to make room for the launch of special committees to organize and indoctrinate prisoners-of-war from enemy countries, particularly Germany, Italy, Hungary, and Romania.[10] Once established, the committees proceeded to signal to the potential opposition back home that the Soviet Union might be amenable to terminating the war by a negotiated peace short of total victory.[11] While keeping this option open pending clarification of the course of the war and its exact outcome, the creation, for the first time, of an international department in the Soviet party Central Committee allowed for more flexible long-term management of foreign Communists. Under the expert supervision of the Bulgarian former General Secretary of the Comintern Georgi Dimitrov – a person thoroughly subservient to Stalin – the new organization could better assist different Soviet goals in particular countries regardless of whether the country qualified as Hitler's victim or his accomplice.

In anticipation of the great Allied conferences scheduled to meet in late 1943 to clarify the respective war aims, two commissions on postwar planning were established in Moscow in the autumn of that year. The first, headed by former Foreign Commissar Maksim M. Litvinov, was to generate ideas about the postwar order and the peace treaties that would underwrite it. The second commission, led by Politburo member Marshal Klimenti Ye. Voroshilov, was concerned with military matters, including the conditions of the armistice. Later on, a third commission was created under the chairmanship of former Soviet ambassador to London Ivan M. Maisky, which was to elaborate proposals for the treatment of Germany and its allies, particularly for the extraction of reparations.[12]

The papers of these commissions, now available from the archives of the Russian Foreign Ministry, provide the most important glimpse of the official Soviet thinking about the desirable postwar order. Although the commissions were staffed by relatively low-ranking officials these were close enough to the centre of power to be familiar with the preferences of the key actors, namely, Stalin and his thoroughly dedicated foreign policy manager, Molotov. Precisely because the planners were too junior to be involved in top-level decision making, they had to make special efforts to ensure that the ideas they outlined conformed to those which, to the best of their knowledge, were held by their superiors. Even if Stalin did not read the papers produced, and there is no reliable evidence that he did, their line of thinking could, therefore, never be too far from his own provided, to be sure, that he had made up his mind on any particular issue.

By the time the commissions started their work in early 1944, the Western representatives at the Allied conferences in Moscow, and especially Teheran, had given Stalin the impression that they were more supportive of his political aspirations than he had expected but less ready to assist Soviet military advance by opening the promised 'second front' in Europe.[13] While its launching six months after Teheran removed this particular uncertainty from his mind – reducing the prisoner-of-war committees from potential instruments of a negotiated peace into mere propaganda tools – enough other uncertainties remained to make his quest for a future European order a good deal more tentative than most outsiders have been inclined to believe.

In having to preventively protect themselves against any accusations of softness, Stalin's underlings had the incentive to err in the opposite direction. This applied also to the reputedly moderate and pro-Western Maisky and Litvinov, who appear from the papers of the planning commissions to be devotees of power politics hardly less ardent than Stalin himself. They saw nothing wrong about twisting the arms of weaker nations, looking forward to a postwar world in which the Soviet Union, as Maisky put it, would have 'become so powerful that [...] no state or a combination of states in Europe or in Asia could even think' of attacking it. Maisky calculated that after the ten years needed for reconstruction, in another 'thirty minimum, fifty maximum' years Europe would 'become socialist, thereby excluding the very possibility of a war on that part of the globe.'[14] Like Stalin, however, he did not see the encouragement of revolution to be in Soviet interest, nor did he anticipate revolution to occur as a result of the war.

Left to their own devices, subordinates sometimes produced more far-fetched proposals than Stalin subsequently allowed to be pursued. In northern Europe, for example, mid-level military and Foreign Commissariat officials favoured going farther than he considered prudent. In early 1944 they envisaged not only eastern Europe and most of Germany but also half of Norway as the Red Army's future area of occupation. Stalin ruled this out after the Western Allies had promised him more of German territory as a Soviet occupation zone than he had previously had reason to expect.[15] Subordinate officials also authored plans for forcing Norway to yield control of the Svalbard (Spitsbergen) archipelago and Bear Island,[16] and for establishing bases on the Danish Bornholm Island that would control access to the Baltic Sea[17] – ideas which echoed Molotov's proposals to Hitler during their conversations in November 1940. Although these projects never materialized they added to the picture of an open-ended and increasingly complex wartime situation in which Soviet policy was being shaped not solely by Stalin's vision but also by an interplay of often contradictory impulses from different officials and agencies, evolving haphazardly rather than by design.

Nowhere was the resulting incoherence more evident than in the Soviet plans for Germany. Having been burned before, Stalin seemed peculiarly reluctant to commit himself to any definite course in dealing with so unpredictable a nation lest it again misfire. Trying to find out from his Western partners what they proposed to do, he was anxious to ensure that they play their part in sharing the responsibility for anything that was to be done about Germany. He at first favoured but then became wary of its partition or dismemberment, which he feared might result in a lasting desire for revenge by the German nation.[18] While he preferred a weakened Germany, brought about by truncating its territory and restoring an independent Austria, he kept delaying a decision. While Stalin provided no authoritative guidance, Maisky went out of his way to propose a punitive treatment of the defeated enemy. Besides advocating dismemberment of Germany, he favoured taking out of it 'whatever can be taken out beyond the "starvation minimum"' and ensuring that for its people 'work would be tantamount to forced labour'.[19] More sensibly, A. A. Smirnov and Vladimir Semenov, of the Foreign Commissariat's German division, emphasized the importance of collaboration with the other occupation powers for securing Soviet access to the country's resources.[20] Concerning its political future, the German Communist exiles in Moscow looked forward to introducing a 'militant democracy', by which they meant a one-party state that they would run; before the war ended, however, their project had been discarded without an alternative in place.[21] Incredible as it may seem, the Soviets began their occupation of Germany with only hazy notions about its long-term future, made worse by an all too firm set of short-term, though often contradictory priorities, for its economic exploitation.[22]

Poland, rather than Germany, was for Stalin the key to Soviet security. He sought a postwar settlement that would depend less on the solution of the elusive German question, which required Western co-operation, than on the seemingly more straightforward Polish one, which he could hope to be better able to achieve on his own. He wanted a subservient, though not necessarily Communist Poland, or, as a 1943 Moscow directive to its underground party leadership called it, 'democratic' rather than 'socialist',[23] but had difficulty finding 'any Poles one could talk to'.[24] To ensure their subservience, he insisted on the cession of the territories he had acquired during his collusion with Hitler, demands he knew no Polish government could accept without being regarded by its people as a Soviet puppet. A willingness to accept this opprobrium was for Stalin the acid test of an acceptable Polish leadership.

Stalin would have preferred a deal with the Polish government-in-exile, or at least some of the London Poles, if he could have it on his terms, instead of having to rely on the Communists, whose base of popular support he knew to be thin. But rather than trying to win non-Communist politicians by conciliatory action he tried to show them by his intransigence that they had no choice but to submit, and serve as his puppets. Having failed in this tactic, he found himself with no choice but to install Communists and their fellow travellers in power on his army's bayonets; he still continued to hope that more respectable individuals would jump on the bandwagon to boost the regime's credibility. Although few did, he remained confident that 'the alliance will not break up over Poland.'[25] There hardly seemed to be a limit to Stalin's wishful thinking.

Elsewhere in Europe, Moscow's stakes were not so high nor were they necessarily fixed in advance; to a large extent they depended on the vicissitudes of the war. In the Balkans, for the Soviet Union – unlike for tsarist Russia not an area of primary strategic importance[26] – the Communists' ascendancy in the Yugoslav and Greek resistance movements embarrassed Stalin because of their revolutionary proclivities. After British Prime Minister Winston Churchill, in October 1944, casually suggested to him that he could divide influence in the peninsula by percentages, thus signalling a willingness to allocate to the Soviet Union more of the Balkans than he had so far been aiming at, Stalin concurred.[27] Although the exact meaning of the presumed deal was never clarified, the Soviet leader showed by his behaviour that he regarded Greece, though not Yugoslavia, as a British bailiwick. As long as London appeared to be accommodating, he encouraged the Yugoslav party chief Josip Broz Tito to proceed with his pet idea of a Communist-led confederation of Balkan states. But when the British, in early 1945, raised objections, Stalin ordered the project to be shelved.[28] Opportunistic rather than reckless, he was not impervious to pressure – a key difference between him and Hitler.

Even before the Red Army's advance into eastern Europe was an accomplished fact, its other feats had predisposed the West to accept a future Soviet sphere of influence there at least informally if not formally. No agreement was ever reached about the limits of the sphere or the nature of the influence, thus allowing each side to interpret them according to its preferences. Moscow did not consider the spheres as co-equal but presumed that in the eastern part of the continent its influence would be paramount while the western part would be open to political competition.

In August 1943, Maisky explained to Eden that 'there were two possible ways of trying to organize Europe after the war.' Either the Soviet
Union and the Western powers would 'agree each to have a sphere of
interest', which 'he did not himself think [. . .] was a good plan', or they
would 'admit the right of the other to an interest in all parts of Europe',
which he thought preferable.[29] In a secret memorandum written for
Molotov half a year later, Maisky argued that 'it is to our best advantage
that in postwar Europe there should be only one great land power, the
USSR, and only one sea power, England'.[30] He ruminated that France
ought to be restored 'as a more or less major European state' but not to
'its former military might', and while Italy was strategically insignificant, 'the Soviet Union is interested in the liquidation of the Franco
regime and restoration of the Spanish republic', preferably with its
former Prime Minister Negrín in charge of the government.[31]

More than Maisky and his superiors, Litvinov was rightly concerned
about the potential for conflict inherent in too vague a delimitation of
the spheres of interest. In a remarkably candid conversation with the
American left-wing journalist Edgar Snow on 6 October 1944, three days
before Stalin and Churchill concluded their 'percentages' deal about the
Balkans, the former Foreign Commissar lamented that 'we won't be able
to agree on a common programme on Germany'. While castigating what
he regarded as the 'revival of British traditional diplomacy in Europe',
particularly London's efforts to foster a bloc of western European countries under its auspices, Litvinov admitted that 'we are drifting more and
more in the same direction'. He remarked that 'diplomacy might have
been able to do something to avoid it if we had made our purposes clear to
the British and if we had made clear the limits of our needs, but now it is
too late, suspicions are rife on both sides'.[32] He still tried to influence his
government to seek 'an amicable separation of security spheres in Europe
according to the principle of geographic proximity', but there is no
evidence that either Molotov or Stalin ever read, much less acted upon,
the memorandum to that effect written by Litvinov in January 1945.[33]

Rather than a divided Europe, Stalin could confidently contemplate it
undivided but so weak and fragmented that none of its states would be
capable of resisting his will. He left no doubt that he considered France's
demise as a great power to be irreversible and sought to thwart the
tentative British efforts at supranational integration of its smaller neighbours.[34] The political collapse of Europe brought about by Germany's
aggression opened up for the Soviet Union the enticing prospect of
being able to act after the war as the arbiter of the continent. As summed
up by the Litvinov commission as early as March 1944, 'We must cherish

our position as the sole great land power in Europe, and we must not willingly share this position with anyone else'.[35]

In April 1945 Stalin is reported to have made his subsequently much quoted comment to Yugoslav Communist leader Milovan Djilas in which he suggested that 'this war is not as in the past; whoever occupies a territory also imposes on it his own social system. Everyone imposes his own system as far as his army can reach. It cannot be otherwise.'[36] The statement, if made as Djilas remembered it, was not so much incorrect as misleading: it provided a description of what was happening rather than a design for making it happen. In Stalin's scheme of things, military seizure of territory for political gain was not an overriding priority until the very end of the war. In their readiness to sanction in advance conquests that Stalin had not yet made, the Western powers mistook his ability to use force for a determination to use it. This may not have made a difference to the fate of Poland but could have done so to that of the less strategically exposed Hungary, where the Red Army moved in only when the British and Americans, for their own military reasons, chose to stay out, ignoring Stalin's proddings to land in the upper Adriatic and advance toward Hungary from the south.[37] Like them, he too preferred using his armies to bring the war closer to an end in ways he considered the most effective rather than delaying it for political motives. In 1944, Finland possibly escaped occupation by Soviet troops because they were needed to press on toward Berlin.[38]

Stalin made the attainment of his preferred postwar order dependent less on the vagaries of war than on the emergence after its conclusion of a congenial international environment. He tried to accomplish what he wanted with, rather than against, his powerful Western allies, whose support, or at least acquiescence he deemed indispensable for achieving the kind of security he craved. 'It was to our advantage to preserve the alliance', Molotov later reminisced,[39] and his underlings drafted their policy papers accordingly. His protégé Andrei A. Gromyko, at that time ambassador to Washington, predicted that since the United States 'would be interested in economic and political co-operation with the Soviet Union', their aims would be largely compatible. 'In spite of possible difficulties which from time to time may emerge in our relations with the United States', Gromyko wrote, 'the necessary conditions are clearly present for a continuation of co-operation between our two countries in the postwar period'.[40] The Cold War that later came was both unwanted and unexpected; it was nevertheless predetermined by Stalin's notion of security which required a weak and fragmented Europe in the shadow of Soviet power.

Nowhere beyond what the Soviet Union considered to be its borders did its policies initially envisage the installation of Communist regimes. In the part of Hungary occupied by the Red Army in early 1945, the Soviet authorities introduced four political parties of their choice; they included the Communist party as their instrument but directed its leaders to respect the multiparty set-up without any time limits.[41] Even in Bulgaria, the first eastern European country to be effectively controlled by the Communists as early as 1944, Stalin mused that he would not have minded Fascists as an opposition in the parliament, presumably because they were particularly corruptible.[42] Though not opposed in principle to Tito's Balkan unification scheme, at the same time he did not discourage resistance by Bulgarian Communists to the variant that would have amounted to their country's absorption into a greater Yugoslavia.[43] All things considered, the Soviet ruler preferred eastern Europe divided and pliable rather than Communist.

Of all countries in the region, Czechoslovakia suited best Stalin's purposes by offering itself as the main 'outpost of our influence in central and south-eastern Europe'.[44] Historically Russophile, even before the war it had a substantial Communist electorate, and now in London, a government-in-exile not only capable of getting along with the Communists but also intent on a special relationship with Moscow, which entailed voluntary subordination to Soviet foreign policy. In 1943 the Czechoslovak President, Edvard Beneš, took it upon himself to conclude with the Soviet Union the first of the 'friendship' treaties that would eventually tie to its fold all the eastern European member states of its empire.[45] Welcoming the initiative, Moscow dropped hints that the model might be suitable for France and Italy as well.[46] Even before coming to Moscow, Beneš had indicated to Soviet representatives that he did not care much about the future of the Carpathian Ukraine, a backward land allotted to his country by the peacemakers in 1919, although he expected it to remain part of Czechoslovakia. Since it had never belonged to Russia he assumed that the Soviet Union had no designs on it. This was a correct assumption until the Red Army approached the area in the summer of 1944, by which time Stalin changed his mind, most likely because he wanted direct access to Hungary. Invoking the Ukrainians' alleged desire to unite within the Soviet state, he could cite the Czech leader's own previously expressed indifference to the future of the territory.[47] Much of the Soviet planning for the postwar order was proceeded by such improvisation; taking advantage of opportunities rather than implementing a design.

In shaping the future of Europe in accordance with Soviet preferences, the Yalta conference of February 1945 was not as crucial as its later notoriety suggested. No deal about the division of Europe into spheres of influence was struck there; the Soviet drive for the establishment of 'friendly' but preferably non-Communist governments in eastern Europe did not substantially differ before or after the conference. What did happen at Yalta was that Stalin misjudged the extent of Western tolerance for his aspirations while the Allies misjudged the extent of his willingness to exercise restraint. The Western representatives could not believe that Stalin would find it in his interest to impose unrepresentative governments in Poland and elsewhere in eastern Europe, whereas he could not imagine how they could possibly expect him to do anything else. Directing Molotov to sign the American-drafted 'Declaration of Liberated Europe', which affirmed its peoples' right to self-determination, he did not 'mind signing it. We can fulfil it in our own way. What matters is the correlation of forces.'[48]

Despite their growing apprehension about Soviet intentions, the Western Allies did little to discourage Stalin from thinking that he could take their acquiescence for granted. The outcome of the August 1945 Potsdam conference was seen in Moscow as amounting to their acknowledgement of having 'lost eastern Europe and the Balkans'.[49] By the end of the year they accepted, however unhappily, the Soviet *faits accomplis* in the region after changes had been made in the local governments that attached, in George F. Kennan's memorable phrase, 'some fig leaves of democratic procedure to hide the nakedness of Stalinist dictatorship.'[50] Stalin's quest for security by empire could hardly have been more successful, or so at least it appeared to his contemporaries. Potsdam confirmed the principle of joint responsibility for the administration of occupied Germany, for Moscow the necessary prerequisite for a satisfactory solution of the German question. A peace conference that would render the defeated enemy permanently harmless was generally expected to follow soon. The Soviet Union particularly cherished the establishment of the Council of Foreign Ministers, inaugurated in London in September 1945, as a great-power directorate which would enable it to share in all important international decisions, thus helping to secure its 'foreign policy gains made during the War'.[51]

The victory in the Second World War promised the Soviet Union more security than it had ever had, yet it was not enough for Stalin. His insatiable craving for security was the root cause of the growing East–West tension, regardless of his and his Western partners' desires for manageable, if not necessarily cordial, relations. None other than Litvinov, one of the chief Soviet planners of the postwar order, expressed through his indiscretions to visiting Westerners the opinion that his government's drive for security without clearly defined limits was the primary cause of trouble, while the West's failure to resist it early and firmly enough was an important secondary cause.[52] But Molotov, Stalin's chief diplomat, saw nothing wrong. He retrospectively explained the origins and nature of the quarrel as follows:

> All this simply happened because we were advancing. They [the Western powers], of course, hardened against us, and we had to firm up what we had conquered [. . .]. Everywhere it was necessary to make order, suppress the capitalist ways. That's what the 'Cold War' was about.

Molotov agreed with Litvinov in his judgement that the conflict had arisen from Soviet actions, but insisted that Stalin 'knew the limits'.[53]

This may have been true in the sense of Stalin knowing that there were limits somewhere but not exactly where. In 1945 Soviet marshal Semen Budenny is said to have egged him on to let the Red Army keep marching on into western Europe, to which the dictator reportedly raised the rhetorical question of who would then feed all its people.[54] Nor, in 1945, did Stalin tolerate his Yugoslav disciples' attempts to grab parts of Italy and Austria, for which he would have been held accountable by the West. For the same reason, he discouraged their Greek comrades from resuming the civil war against the pro-British Athens government.[55] Yet in other places the post-victory euphoria made Stalin less resistant to the imperialistic temptations which he had earlier not allowed his subordinates to translate into action. Perhaps goaded by his sycophantic security chief and fellow Georgian Lavrenty P. Beria, he attempted to intimidate Turkey to cede to the Soviet Union territory in the Caucasus and military bases in the Black Sea straits.[56] Delaying the evacuation of Soviet troops from Iran, he sought to establish a client regime in its part of Azerbaijan to gain dominant influence in this other historic area of Russian expansionism.[57] And he cast his eyes beyond that area by having Molotov at the London foreign ministers conference claim a share in the administration of Italy's former African colonies – an idea originally hatched by Litvinov.[58]

The failure of the other ministers to entertain Molotov's expanding desiderata should have been taken in Moscow as a warning; instead it was received there with surprise and indignation as evidence of unwarranted Western hostility. Neither side yet realized that the slide into the Cold War had already become irreversible. Although Stalin considered Europe the area of primary strategic importance for his country the wartime Soviet planning for the future was notable for its vagueness. The plans elaborated by the special commissions set up in Moscow during the war never achieved even the limited influence that was exerted by their Western counterparts. Even more than Churchill and Roosevelt, the Soviet leader believed in deciding the future of the continent, if not the world, by wheeling and dealing with his peers within the Alliance. He had clear enough notions about what he wanted to accomplish, namely, acquire as much power for himself and the Soviet state as he could safely claim, but proved reluctant to committing himself in advance to any particular ways of proceeding, lest these prove to be counterproductive.

Stalin's disposition to leave so much open to be decided later was the result not only of his own insecurity but also of his Marxist–Leninist belief that history was on his side, and could, therefore, be counted upon to eventually arrange the future to Soviet advantage. Hence, much though he desired the relations with his capitalist allies to remain manageable, in gearing his policy to conform with the presumably irresistible advance of Communism at their expense, he was bound to strain those relations beyond tolerable limits. It is, therefore, hardly surprising that instead of the greater security Stalin craved to find in a congenial European order under Soviet supremacy he eventually brought upon himself a confrontation in a divided continent, which gave him and his country far less security that he had hoped for.

Notes

1 'Poezdka Molotova v Berlin v noiabre 1940 g.' (Molotov's Trip to Berlin in November 1940), *Novaia i noveishaia istoriia*, (1993), no. 5: pp. 64–99.
2 Soviet minutes in O. A. Rzheshevskii, 'Vizit A. Idena v Moskvu v dekabre 1941 g.: Peregovory s I. V. Stalinym i V. M. Molotovym' (Eden's Visit to Moscow in December 1941: Conversations with Stalin and Molotov), *Novaia i noveishaia istoriia*, (1994), no. 2: pp. 85–102.
3 A. J. P. Taylor, 'The War Aims of the Allies in the First World War', in Richard Pares and A. J. P. Taylor eds, *Essays Presented to Sir Lewis Namier*, (New York: St. Martin's Press, 1956), p. 480.
4 J. Barth Urban, *Moscow and the Italian Communist Party: From Togliatti to Berlinguer* (Ithaca, N.Y.: Cornell University Press, 1986), pp. 154–61.
5 Record of Stalin–Thorez conversation, 19 November 1944, 'Zaniatsia Podgotovkoi Budushchego Mira' (Preparations for a Future World), *Vestnik Arkhiva Prezidenta Rossiiskoi Federatsii* 4 (1955): pp. 114–58: 152–8.
6 In the Moscow headquarters there were, reportedly, no more than 150–200 officials at the beginning of the war. Vadim A. Kirpichenko, 'Razvedka vykhodit iz zony molchaniia' (The Intelligence Services End Their Silence), *Voennoistoricheskii zhurnal*, 1995, no. 2: pp. 80–7:84.

7   Josef Klecka, 'O zradě' [On Treason], *Odboj a revoluce* [Prague] 5, no. 4 (1966): pp. 47–52, and Vilém Kahan, 'O některých nedostatcích v konspirativní činnosti' ('Some Shortcomings in the Conspiratorial Activities'), *ibid.* 5, no. 4 (1967): pp. 97–98; Władysław Gomułka, Pamiętniki (Memoirs), vol. 2 (Warsaw: BGW, 1994), pp. 160–257, 349–59.

8   M. M. Drachkovitch, 'The Comintern and the Insurrectional Activity of the Communist Party of Yugoslavia in 1941–1942', in M. M. Drachkovitch and B. Lazitch eds, *The Comintern: Historical Highlights* (New York: Praeger, 1966), pp. 184–213.

9   'Statement of the Praesidium of the E.C.C.I. on the Dissolution of the Communist International', 21 May 1943, in Jane Degras ed., *The Communist International, 1919–1943*, vol. 3 (London: Oxford University Press, 1965), pp. 477–9.

10 G. M. Adibekov, *Kominform i poslevoennaia Evropa, 1947–1956 gg.* (The Cominform and Post-war Europe), (Moscow: Rossiia Molodaia, 1994), pp. 7–10.

11 V. Mastny, 'Stalin and the Prospects of a Separate Peace in World War II', *American Historical Review* 77 (1972): pp. 1365–88.

12 A. M. Filitov, 'Problems of Post-War Construction in Soviet Foreign Policy Conceptions during World War II', in F. Gori and S. Pons eds, *The Soviet Union and Europe in the Cold War, 1943–53*, (London: Macmillan – now Palgrave, 1996), pp. 3–22: 4.

13 V. Mastny, 'Soviet War Aims at the Moscow and Teheran Conferences of 1943', *Journal of Modern History* 47 (1975): pp. 481–504.

14 Maisky to Molotov, 11 January 1944, 'Zaniatsia Podgotovkoi,' pp. 124–44, at pp. 124–5.

15 J. Laufer, 'Die UdSSR und die Zonenteilung Deutschlands (1943/44)', *Zeitschrift für Geschichtswissenschaft* 45 (1995): pp. 309–31, at pp. 328–9.

16 S. G. Holtsmark, *A Soviet Grab for the High North? USSR, Svalbard, and Northern Norway 1920–1953* (Oslo: Institutt for Forvarsstudier, 1993), pp. 57–64.

17 S. G. Holtsmark, 'The Limits to Soviet Influence: Soviet Diplomats and the Pursuit of Strategic Interests in Norway and Denmark, 1944–7', in Gori and Pons, *The Soviet Union and Europe in the Cold War*, pp. 106–24.

18 G. P. Kynin, 'Germanskii vopros vo vzaimootnosheniiakh SSSR, SShA i Velikobritanii 1941–1943 gg.: Obzor dokumentov' (The German Question in the Relations between the U.S.S.R., U.S., and Great Britain in 1941–43: A Survey of Documents), *Novaia i noveishaia istoriia*, 1995, no. 1: pp. 91–113:93.

19 Maisky to Molotov, 3 March 1944 and 10 November 1943, quoted in A. M. Filitov, 'Problemy poslevoennogo ustroistva v sovetskikh vneshepoliticheskikh kontseptsiiakh perioda vtoroi mirovoi voiny' (Problems of the Postwar Order in Soviet Foreign Policy Conceptions during World War II), in F. Gori and S. Pons eds, *The Soviet Union and Europe in the Cold War.* op. cit.

20 Filitov, 'Problems of Post-war Construction', op. cit., pp. 19–20.

21 H. Laschitza, *Kämpferische Demokratie gegen Faschismus* (Berlin: Deutscher Militärverlag, 1969), pp. 136–8. Cf. P. Erler, H. Caude and M. Wilke eds, *'Nach Hitler kommen wir': Dokumente zur Programmatik der Moskauer KPD–Führung 1944/45 für Nachkriegsdeutschland* (Berlin: Akademie, 1994).

22 N. M. Naimark, *The Russians in Germany: A History of the Soviet Zone of Occupation, 1945–1949* (Cambridge, Mass.: Harvard University Press, 1995), pp. 9–68.

23   Dimitrov to Finder, 2 April 1943, 'Perepiska Generalnogo Sekretaria IK KI G. M. Dimitrova s rukovodstvom Polskoi Rabochei Partii (1942–43)' (Correspondence between Secretary General of the Executive Committee of the Communist International G. M. Dimitrov and the leadership of the Polish Workers' Party), *Novaia i noveishaia istoriia*, 1964, no. 5, p. 122.

24   As related by Czechoslovak President Edvard Beneš in V. Mastny, 'The Beneš–Stalin–Molotov Conversations in 1943: New Documents', *Jahrbücher für Geschichte Osteuropas* 20 (1972): pp. 367–402:379.

25   Minutes of Stalin's meeting with the Polish Committee of National Liberation, 9 October 1944, in A. Polonsky and B. Drukier eds, *The Beginnings of Communist Rule in Poland: December 1943–June 1945*, (London: Routledge & Kegan Paul, 1980), p. 298.

26   Presuming Soviet recognition of the Yugoslav communist party as *primus inter pares* in Europe as early as 1941 means projecting the postwar situation backwards: G. Swain, 'Stalin's Wartime Vision of the Post-war World', *Diplomacy and Statecraft* 7, no. 1 (1996): pp. 73–96:79.

27   Albert Resis, 'The Churchill-Stalin Secret "Percentages" Agreement on the Balkans, Moscow, October 1944', *American Historical Review* 83 (1977–78), pp. 368–87.

28   B. Petranović, *Balkanska Federacija, 1943–1948* (The Balkan Federation), (Belgrade: Edicija Svedolanstva, 1991), pp. 128–35.

29   Eden to Clark Kerr on conversation with Maisky, 31 August 1943, quoted in V. Mastny, *Russia's Road to the Cold War: Diplomacy, Warfare, and the Politics of Communism, 1939–1945* (New York: Columbia University Press, 1979), p. 107.

30   Quoted in A. M. Filitov, 'V komissiiakh Narkomindela . . . ' (In the Commissions of the Commissariat for Foreign Affairs), in *Vtoraia mirovaia voina: Aktualnye Problemy* (The Second World War: Topical Issues) (Moscow: Nauka, 1995), pp. 54–71:57.

31   Maisky to Molotov, 11 January 1944, 'Zaniatsia Podgotovkoi,' pp. 127–8.

32   Record of interview with Litvinov, by Edgar Snow, 6 October 1944, Russia 1945, President's Secretary's file, Franklin D. Roosevelt Library, Hyde Park. Cf. V. Mastny, 'The Cassandra in the Foreign Commissariat: Maxim Litvinov and the Cold War', *Foreign Affairs* 54 (1975–76): pp. 366–76.

33   'On the Question of Blocs and Spheres of Influence', 11 January, 1945, quoted in Vladimir O. Pechatnov, 'The Big Three after World War II: New Documents on Soviet Thinking about Post War Relations with the United States and Great Britain', Working Paper no. 13, *Cold War International History Project* (Washington, DC: Woodrow Wilson International Center for Scholars, 1995), p. 12.

34   Mastny, *Russia's Road to the Cold War* op. cit., pp. 128, 229–30; K. Larres, 'A Search for Order: Britain and the Origins of a Western European Union, 1944–55', in B. Brivati and H. Jones eds, *From Reconstruction to Integration: Britain and Europe since 1945*, (Leicester: Leicester University Press, 1993), pp. 71–7.

35   Quoted in A. O. Chubarian, 'Sovetskoe rukovodstvo i nekotorye voprosy evropeiskoi integratsii v nachale 50–kh godov' (The Soviet Leadership and Problems of European Integration in the Early 1950s), in A. S. Namazova and B. Emerson eds, *Istoriia evropeiskoi integratsii (1945–1994)* (A History of European Integration), (Moscow: Institut vseobshchei istorii RAN, 1995), pp. 108–17:114.

36 M. Djilas, *Conversations with Stalin* (New York: Harcourt, 1962), p. 114.
37 Mastny, *Russia's Road to the Cold War* op. cit., p. 211.
38 J. Nevakivi, 'A Decisive Armistice 1944–1947: Why Was Finland Not Soviet-ized?' *Scandinavian Journal of History* 19 (1994): pp. 91–115:114.
39 Entry for 17 August 1975, in F. Chuev, *Sto sorok besed s Molotovym* (Hundred and Forty Conversations with Molotov) (Moscow: Terra, 1991), p. 76.
40 'On the Question of Soviet-American Relations', 14 July 1944, quoted in Pechatnov, *The Big Three after World War II* op. cit., pp. 6–8.
41 C. Gati, *Hungary and the Soviet Bloc* (Durham, N.C.: Duke University Press, 1986), pp. 33–7.
42 V. Dedijer, *Novi prilozi za biografiju Josipa Broza Tita* [New Supplements to the Biography of Josip Broz Tito], vol. 3 (Belgrade: Rad, 1984), p. 325.
43 E. Kardelj, *Boj za priznanje in neodvisnost nove Jugoslavije: Spomini* (The Struggle for the Recognition and Independence of New Yugoslavia: Memoirs) (Ljub-ljana: Drěavna zaloěba Slovenije, 1980), pp. 103–4.
44 Maisky to Molotov, 11 January 1944, 'Zaniatska podgotovki', p. 138.
45 Mastny, 'The Beneš–Stalin–Molotov Conversations' op. cit., pp. 367–402.
46 Speech by Molotov, 1 February 1944, *Izvestiia*, 2 February 1944; M. Toscano, 'Resumption of Diplomatic Relations between Italy and the Soviet Union in World War II', in his *Designs in Diplomacy* (Baltimore, Md.: Johns Hopkins Press, 1970), pp. 294–5.
47 Mastny, *Russia's Road to the Cold War*, op. cit., pp. 226–9.
48 Entry for 15 August 1975, in Chuev, *Sto sorok besed*, p. 76.
49 Molotov's estimate reported by Yugoslav ambassador Vladimir Popović, cited in L. Ia. Gibianskii, 'Doneseniia iugoslavskogo posla v Moskve ob otsenkakh rukovodstvom SSSR potsdamskoi konferentsii i polozheniia v vostochnoi Evrope (avgust-noiabr 1945 g.)', (Reports by the Yugoslav Ambassador about the Assessments by the Soviet Leadership of the Potsdam Conference and the Situation in Eastern Europe), *Slavianovedenie*, 1994, no. 1: pp. 3–13:6.
50 G. F. Kennan, *Memoirs, 1925–1950* (Boston: Little Brown, 1967), p. 284.
51 Molotov's evaluation of the London conference cited in V. V. Shustov, 'A View on the Origins of the Cold War and Some Lessons Thereof', in G. Lundestad and O. A. Westad eds, *Beyond the Cold War: New Dimensions in International Relations*, (Oslo: Scandinavian University Press, 1993), pp. 23–37:30–1.
52 E. Snow, *Journey to the Beginning* (London: Gollancz, 1959), p. 357; Harriman to Secretary of State, *Foreign Relations of the United States*, 1945, vol. 5, p. 921.
53 Entry for 28 November 1974, in Chuev, *Sto sorok besed*, p. 86.
54 *Izvestiia*, 11 February 1992, p. 6.
55 J. O. Iatrides, 'Civil War, 1945–1949: National and International Aspects', in J. O. Iatrides ed., *Greece in the 1940s: A Nation in Crisis*, (Hanover, N.H.: University Press of New England, 1981), p. 203.
56 *Khrushchev Remembers: The Last Testament* (Boston: Little, Brown, 1974), pp. 295–6.
57 L. L'Estrange Fawcett, *Iran and the Cold War: The Azerbaijan Crisis of 1946* (Cambridge: Cambridge University Press, 1992), pp. 83–107; N. I. Egorova, '"Iranskii krizis" 1945–1946 gg. po rassekrechennym arkhivnym dokumen-tam' (The 'Iranian Crisis' of 1945–1946 from Declassified Archival Docu-ments), *Novaia i noveishaia istoriia*, 1994, no. 3: pp. 24–42.
58 Pechatnov, *The Big Three after World War II* op. cit., p. 20.

6
The Balkan Union: an Instance in the Postwar Plans of Small Countries

Stevan K. Pavlowitch

The postwar plans made during the Second World War by eastern European governments in exile usually went no further than to restoring their own states. At times they envisaged improving on the earlier peace settlements and occasionally considered frameworks for better regional co-operation. They all failed to have any impact on the course of events, and thus, if for no other reason, form a small part of 'the failure of the peace in Europe'. They might just about be worth looking at for some of the ideas that they contain.

Interwar regional security pacts such as the Little and Balkan ententes had been made between smaller beneficiaries of the Great War, but only for their common interests against smaller losers attempting to disrupt the peace. They contained no commitments against the greater losers who soon returned to the front of the stage, nor did the greater winners stand by them after they had provided initial encouragement. After the Reich had conquered most of the European continent, some of the exiled political leaders of the states that had been wiped off the map began to think again of regional unions. As early as November 1940, the Czechoslovak President Beneš and the Polish Prime Minister Sikorski had begun negotiations on some kind of union. The outcome was a formal protocol in 1942 setting out the principles of the projected 'confederation' between Poland and Czechoslovakia, and leaving the door open for the accession of other states. The move was encouraged by the British Foreign Office, but the real progress achieved fell short of its ostensible goals, as the fundamental problems diving the two partners were not tackled seriously.

Another scheme that the British had very much favoured was the Balkan Union Agreement of 1942, signed between the exiled Yugoslav and Greek governments.[1] No sooner had Yugoslavia collapsed under the Axis onslaught, and its government had found exile in the Near East, than its Foreign Minister Nincić was thinking of postwar relations with its neighbours. On arriving in London in June 1941, he explained his views to Eden: his government hoped to form a bloc with Greece and with those elements in Bulgaria that were not connected with its present pro-German rulers. Both he and his Prime Minister Simović, agreed on the importance of joint action with Greece. It could stabilize the Balkans under the influence of those countries that had been on the side of the Western democracies in both world wars, it could hope to come to an arrangement with a new regime in Bulgaria, and it could prevent the interference of foreign powers intent on exploiting differences between the states of the region.

The exiled Greeks were ready enough to accept the idea. The Tsouderos government, like the Simović government, had been sworn in on the eve of the collapse, thus marking an end to the previous authoritarian regime. There was no difficulty in agreeing with 'our Yugoslav friends' on the need to pick up again the threads of a policy of Balkan co-operation. The Yugoslavs, however, also knew that the Greeks were more than apprehensive about extending contacts with neutral Turkey or with expatriate representatives of the Bulgarian opposition. When the Greek government had also arrived in London, public references were being made to a postwar community of the Balkan peoples, and formal negotiations on a treaty to establish the foundations of a union were initiated, but it was not before late November that drafts were ready.

The delay had been caused by difficulties on both sides. There were differences of attitude towards Bulgaria even within the Yugoslav government. The Serbian Agrarians had maintained links with their Bulgarian counterparts, and had continued to keep in friendly contact with those of them who had come out to the Near East. The Bulgarian Agrarian Union had always advocated an alliance with Yugoslavia, and a regional federation or confederation as a context within which to adjust territorial questions. In exile, both sides talked of the extension of Yugoslavia to include Bulgaria. Nincić envisaged a Balkan community as eventually including a chastened, though independent, Bulgaria. He even considered the possibility of union as the outcome of a stage-by-stage evolution, but he did not see it as an aim to be proclaimed from London with Bulgarian exiles.

The Greek government had got wind of the Agrarian Serbo-Bulgarian talks, and did not like them. Right from the start of their exile, the

Greeks had held that Bulgaria would have to be punished, and they had their own differences with Nincić's proposals. The Yugoslav Foreign Minister was of the opinion that it was better not to tamper with existing frontiers in the Balkans, particularly in the case of Albania, whom the Yugoslavs wanted eventually to bring into the union as an independent partner. He felt that Greek claims would cripple Albania, frighten it away and trigger off Yugoslav claims, but he tried not to show that he actually opposed the Greek government on this point. The Greeks too had something which they did not want to tell the Yugoslavs, and that was that they wanted to readjust the Macedonian border with Yugoslavia for reasons of territorial security. Once the Greek government had examined the Yugoslav draft, it had given its formal agreement to negotiations, but with reservations, as it found it too 'confederal'. It wanted a statement of principles, but not implementation clauses in the case of other possible Balkan partners who were enemies or, at best, in the case of Turkey, neutral. It wanted to stop the Yugoslavs from planning ahead to form links with other countries. Counterproposals were put forward and Eden eventually brought Tsouderos to accept something closer to the original Yugoslav proposals.

On 15 January 1942, Greek and Yugoslav plenipotentiaries signed an agreement, which established the bases for a Balkan Union: co-ordination of foreign policies and cultural co-operation; co-ordination of trade policies with a view to establishing a customs union and monetary union; co-ordination of defence policies. It listed the common organs to be set up and it looked forward to welcoming to the union other Balkans states '*régis par des gouvernements librement et légalement constitués*', but did not spell out the details of future membership procedure. The two kings spoke of the Balkan Union as the first step towards the realization of a political and economic *communauté* of southeast Europe, while the Yugoslav monarch also expressed the hope that it would link up with a parallel central european union, and contribute to the creation of a new international order in Europe. A few days after the signature of the Balkan Union Agreement, the Beneš–Sikorski agreement was also formalized in a protocol setting out the principle of a Polish–Czechoslovak confederation, similarly meant to be the nucleus of a central european union.

Just as in the early 1930s Yugoslavia had sought to find some greater measure of security by connecting the Little Entente and the Balkan Entente, so in 1942 the exiled government saw itself as a potential link between future Central European and Balkan regional associations. When, four days after the signature of the Greek–Yugoslav treaty, President Beneš gave a luncheon for King Peter, the two exiled heads of state spoke of the future of their part of the world, based on the two regional agreements. *The Times* described their meeting as 'the first step towards linking the Czechoslovak–Polish and the Greco-Yugoslav alliance'. The Greek government took exception to this line. Tsouderos feared Soviet reactions, and did not want his country's postwar diplomacy to be hampered by ties which he did not consider to be of immediate interest. He drew Nincić's attention to the danger of giving the Russians the impression that the east Europeans were trying to re-establish a *cordon sanitaire*. He saw the Greek–Yugoslav nucleus as aiming simply at the preservation of peace in the Balkans, in close friendship with both Britain and the Soviet Union.

Neither did Nincić wish to get on the wrong side of the Russians; Sikorski's explicit anti-Soviet aim made him adopt a more reserved position. The two governments had informed Russia, Turkey and the United States of their intention to sign a treaty, and explained to them its general aims. While the Turks and the Americans had welcomed the project, the Soviet minister to the exiled governments had taken the information without comment. Along with Eden, the US and Soviet representatives had been invited to the signing ceremony at the Foreign Office. The Russian had replied that his attendance depended on his government's decision. This, he claimed, had not been received by the appointed date, and his American colleague was then asked not to come, so as not to stress the Soviet absence. It was only subsequently that the Soviet envoy openly expressed his government's displeasure. Nincić wanted good relations with the USSR. He dreaded a peace settlement which would leave his country out in the cold. Like most of his Yugoslav and Greek colleagues, he was terrified of the possibility of a Communist take-over during the period of chaos which could follow the collapse of the Axis and he was not sure that British support would be forthcoming. He did not want to be tied exclusively to London and believed that to strike a balance with the Soviets would improve the chances of survival for the countries of eastern Europe.

Tsouderos, however, was worried by any action which, in raising its suspicions, could incite the USSR to interfere in the Balkans. This is why any extension of the regional plans beyond the Greek–Yugoslav nucleus was most unwelcome to him. So indeed was any gesture which could appear to disregard the Greeks' susceptibilities concerning Albania and its Italian protector. Precisely such a gesture was the meeting between Nincić and Sforza during King Peter's visit to the US in July 1942. It had been the result of the one-time Italian Foreign Minister's repeated attempts to communicate with Yugoslav exponents. Nincić had seen him for a private exchange of views. What he told the Italian exile can be surmised from Sforza's papers and from a statement made by Nincić to his cabinet colleagues: it would be in Italy's interest to let Albania join a Balkan union; it was in the interests of Italy and Yugoslavia to establish a joint bulwark against German predominance; although he fully endorsed Croatian and Slovenian claims against Italy, such questions would not be so important after the war, and he would prefer not to make any public statements for the time being. Croatian and Slovenian members of the Yugoslav government, however, were alarmed by the 'Sforza connection'. They told the Greeks so and the Greeks probed State Department and Foreign Office.

The Greek Prime Minister had also heard something of a Yugoslav–Soviet treaty. The more he feared Russian designs, the more Nincić wanted good relations with the USSR. Yugoslavia was already somehow linked to the Soviet Union by the treaty signed the day of the German attack, and never ratified. He thought of reactivating it, and of arranging for King Peter to be invited to the Soviet Union after he had been to the US. The renovated treaty would have been signed, and the aims of the Balkan Union would have been explained, along with the Yugoslav government's views of the future of Europe. Nothing would come of that plan, but once again the Greeks had not been consulted, had come to hear of it, and objected.

They were frank when they met on 10 August, Tsouderos with his reproaches, Nincić with his explanations, and they made it possible for a formal Greek–Yugoslav 'summit' to discuss all the issues arising out of the Balkan Union Agreement, less than seven months after its auspicious signature in Whitehall. Southeast Europe was a sensitive spot, where Britain and Soviet Russia suspected each other's long-term aims. Eden kept his Balkan allies ignorant of his suspicions concerning Soviet intentions and of his talks with Soviet representatives. Soviet attempts to neutralize the British-encouraged regional plans began to produce results, and by September 1942 there were signs of Foreign Office reluctance to continue with them, for fear that the Soviet Union would oppose British plans in western Europe as well.

So it was that, in September 1942, Greeks and Yugoslavs agreed to do no more about extension plans until after the war. Nincić had had to defend his Balkan policy on home ground as well. Although the Greek treaty did earn general support in the Yugoslav government, the Foreign Minister was criticized there both for trying and for failing to please the Russians, both for being too lenient and for being too harsh towards

Albania, Bulgaria and Italy. Tsouderos was worried by Soviet hostility to the Balkan agreement, and by the British attitude as well, for he conducted his foreign policy on the assumption of a preponderant British influence in his country after the war. He may also have become less keen on such close ties with a partner whose future, by the middle of 1943, was beginning to look dubious. By that time, exiled Greeks and Yugoslavs had both taken fright at the way in which the Turkish government displayed signs of wanting to give the Balkan combination an anti-Soviet look, and Eden had virtually abandoned the east European regional schemes.

On 15 February 1942 the *Sunday Times* had carried an interview with Ninčić, under the characteristic title adapted from Litvinov's famous phrase, 'The Peace of Europe is Indivisible'. In it he aired his views on Europe. The Balkan Union was not merely a security pact, but a contribution to the rebuilding of Europe. Regional associations would not in themselves be sufficient to guarantee peace. They would have to be tied together and merged into a higher and common European organization. Ninčić knew how to antagonize colleagues and King Peter got the impression that to sacrifice him would help propitiate the British. Ninčić resigned in January 1943, eventually to be replaced by Grol who had often deputized for him and who continued on the same lines, though more cautiously, until the shaky coalition of Yugoslavia's prewar parliamentary parties put together on 27 March 1941 eventually fell apart in August 1943.

Ninčić had wanted to ward off a potential Soviet threat, but, although fearful of Communism, he cannot be described as anti-Soviet. The exiled Yugoslavs were anxious that regional associations should help them both keep Soviet Russia at bay and bridge the gap with it. After Churchill's approach to Turkey in 1943 on the subject of confederation in southeast Europe, they wanted to know more about Allied attitudes to regional schemes. Thereafter they tended to stick to the letter of the Balkan Union Agreement and avoided any further mention of extending the links. Born of the common experience of April 1941, based on a tradition of good neighbourliness and on not dissimilar views of the Soviet Union and encouraged by the British, the treaty signed by the exiled governments of Greece and Yugoslavia had little effect on the situation in their occupied homelands. Furthermore, it characterized a certain difference of approach. The Greeks, who had not entirely exercised their bitterness at Yugoslavia's behaviour in the early stages of the war, wanted to pin down their northern neighbours seeking the support of a Balkan partner in progressing territorial claims at the peace conference. They wanted to remain under the wing of Great Britain and not to antagonize the Soviet Union. The Yugoslavs, who realized their mistake, on the eve and in the early stages of the war, of trying to placate the Axis powers unilaterally, also sought the support of a Balkan neighbour in forming a wider regional community. They wanted the benefits of friendly relations with both the UK and the USSR.

'Federation' is the term most widely used in the Foreign Office documents that refer to the arrangements of the Greek and Yugoslav governments, as though to show that the word, when applied to regional associations in Europe, was misunderstood in British political parlance in the 1940s no less than in the 1990s. The word used by both contracting parties at the time of the settlement was 'community', in their diplomatic French and in their own languages. We have shown elsewhere that, at least for the Yugoslav politicians in charge of foreign policy, the idea was one of association, where states would gradually shed some of their sovereignty. Nincić and Grol shared such a broad approach. They had their differences, their limitations and their prejudices, but both looked for a new type of political organization to take the place of the nation which, to them, seemed to have become dangerous and outmoded as such, if not as a historical and cultural entity. They groped for a community where rationality would replace bloodshed and suffering, where ethnic groups realized that they were condemned to living with one another, that they must combine in order to survive, that they must also deserve rather than impose their rights. This applied to Yugoslavia, to the Balkans, and to the rest of Europe.[2]

Greeks and Yugoslavs were hardly free agents in London. Their diplomacy did have an air of unreality in the middle of a world war, caught as they were between the reality of their homelands and that of the Anglo-Soviet alliance. Britain initially encouraged their scheme and then virtually abandoned it in the face of Soviet opposition. Greeks and Yugoslavs in London planned a Balkan Union for which no other partners were immediately available. In considering other possible links, they took so much notice of what Britain and the Soviet Union would think, that it created difficulties among themselves. Yet it still led the diplomats of the two powers to complain of the Greeks' and the Yugoslavs' unwillingness to think primarily in terms of the objectives of their great power patrons.

Nevertheless, it was a diplomacy that, for all its limitations, took account of precedents and, even more so, of past mistakes in order to look forward to a new sort of Europe – one that can almost be said to have looked forward to the formation of the European Community. And yet its proponents hailed from the Balkans, which has come to mean disunity and strife in current European jargon, but which simply means 'wooded mountains' in Turkish.[3]

Notes

1 See S. Pavlowitch, 'The Balkan Union Agreement of 1942', *Storia delle relazioni internazionali*, III, (1987).
2 S. Pavlowitch, *Unconventional Perceptions of Yugoslavia, 1940–1945*, (New York: Columbia University Press, 1985) chapter II.
3 See also the following published diaries and memoirs: B. Ubrilovi, *Zapisi iz tudjine*, (Sarajevo: State Printing Office, 1946); M. Grol, *Londonski dnevnik, 1941–1945*, (Belgrade: Filip Višnji, 1990); S. Jovanovi, *Slobodan Jovanovic u emigraciji: razgovori i zapisi*, (Belgrade: Dosije, 1993); I. Juki, *The Fall of Yugoslavia*, (New York and London: Harcourt Brace Jovanovich, 1974); A. Mazarakis-Ainian, *Mémoires*, (Salonika: Institute for Balkan Studies, 1979); E. Tsouderos, *Diplomatika paraskinia, 1941–1944*, (Athens: Aetos, 1950).

7
Setting the Limits of the Soviet Hegemony in Europe

Elena Calandri

The failure by the victorious powers to agree on a peace settlement for Europe was a turning point on the path leading from the wartime alliance to the Cold War. Understanding wartime intentions for the postwar order from the point of view of the major global powers and lesser European countries, can highlight some of the perspectives and shortcomings of the unsuccessful search for a peaceful Europe.

It is probably as a result of the 'end of the ideologies', if all chapters looked at in this part of the book – except to some extent Stevan Pavlowitch's – make little room for 'grand designs'. If international politics can follow either normative or realistic guidelines, usually falling somewhere between the two, the essays by Klaus Schwabe, John Kent, Georges-Henri Soutou, Vojtech Mastny and Stevan K. Pavlowitch, leave no doubts that the 1943–45 elaboration of war aims in the would-be winners felt very close to the 'realistic' end of the line. No wartime leader revived Wilson's clamour for 'peace without victory', and none was driven by the moral compulsion and the intellectual drive to build a 'just' order. Nor did self-determination, democracy, or nationality inspire the definition of the political map of postwar Europe. The big powers were determined to impose peace on Europe and to make it a stable, peaceful element in a larger global sharing of power. All the people and the governments involved in the Second World War shared worries about Germany, and had vivid memories of the common failure to contain Hitler and to establish stable foundations for a lasting continental order. Besides leaving shameful memories and a conscience of the weakness and limits of European power, the 1930s had taught a lesson of realism to the decision makers that had had a role in the Paris settlement and in interwar policy.

The answer was given in geopolitical terms. The Soviet Union, as the major European continental power, was the logical end of any such discourse. As the war turned in favour of the 'Democracies', nobody in London, Washington, the French leadership or in the exiled eastern European governments, doubted the Soviet right to sit among the governors of the international system. Nobody ignored the shift eastward of the continental balance of power, nor denied the well-founded impending influence of the Soviet Union on eastern Europe. Around this role moved five years of ambivalent and wavering attitudes and practises. The question to address remains: why between 1943 and 1947 the attempt to accommodate not so incompatible war aims failed in such a fateful and traumatic way.

Klaus Schwabe's analysis of American attitude starts from two 'classic' questions: the 'double' nature of Roosevelt's policy and the impact of the Roosevelt–Truman succession. F. D. Roosevelt proclaimed universalism encompassed, which is well known, a regional arrangement for Europe under the predominance of Britain and the Soviet Union. Once again, the myth of FDR's idealism short of ingenuity did not stand the test. Behind the screen of a 'just war' and peace and democracy, Roosevelt's plans for postwar Europe were shaped in meeting with domestic constraints and US national interest. In Klaus Schwabe's reading, the 'four policemen' concept appears an outspoken oligarchy with no proclivity whatsoever to representativeness. Instead this concept aimed at short-cutting in a permanent way minor powers' sovereignty and reserving for the four, the monopoly of the use of force in international relations. At the Yalta conference, Roosevelt took his position against personal spheres of influence, to prevent the United States from becoming embroiled in an Anglo-Soviet clash for continental primacy. Accordingly, the President defended self-determination for the peoples in both eastern and western Europe in the name of freedom and democracy because he feared that American public opinion would refuse US involvement in a world order not in line with accepted official American ideals and interests. Domestic considerations were the dominant reason for the 'idealistic' shell of the American position: postwar Europe had to be consistent with domestic constraints lest the permanent temptation of the American public opinion toward disengagement and isolation prevailed. Not a member of the FDR inner circle, and lacking Roosevelt's utopian intellectual coldness, Harry Truman knew only the public, universalist façade of the President's plans for postwar order. Once in power, he keenly stuck to this façade, and he was labelled as the first 'cold warrior' on the merit of the FDR entourage and his own deference to his predecessor. Indeed, he resolved to move on to the 'Truman doctrine' and that quintessential 'regional' initiative that was the Marshall Plan, only after becoming convinced that the Soviet Union was pursuing unilateralism and expansionist policies.

FDR's designs for the future of Europe were consistent with British intentions. For no matter how many disagreements Washington and London had concerning extra-European affairs, they shared the idea of the European continent as a political headache, an area to be settled in order to leave resources free for commitment in other areas and plans. John Kent's study on British imperial policy appear to be an enlightening starting point to understand the limits of British continental commitment. If great power status was the aim, and empire was the mean, then it becomes all the more understandable that in 1943–44 Churchill and most of the Foreign Office endorsed a Soviet sphere of influence in Eastern Europe. The limits of British military and economic resources suggested the necessity of an Anglo-Soviet 'partnership' in Europe, and London was ready to accept a broad definition of Soviet security requirements – including a free hand in imposing communist *regimes* in eastern European countries – provided that Soviet expansion had clear boundaries and did not jeopardise British vital national and imperial interests. So the much debated percentages agreement was indeed a partition of influence in the Balkans aimed, on Churchill's side to preserve British control, and on Greece's side to set the limits of the Soviet sphere of influence in the Balkans. In this coherent attitude, the Yalta conference and the Declaration on Liberated Europe allowed Britain a say in the eastern European countries' future, and changed the terms of the problems as shown in the quotation from Sargent in Kent's study: 'the preservation of great power status now required Britain to use her right, no more just to preserve her influence in south-eastern Europe and the Middle East.' Therefore, the Yalta conference recovered a major role in the diplomacy for postwar Europe, imposing a revision of planning based on spheres of influence and regionalism.

Unilateralism was not the choice of the Soviet leadership. Given that the opening of Soviet archives is far from complete, these remarks raise many doubts and questions on Stalin's policy. Stalin's own thoughts remain undocumented, because he did not commit to paper his purposes or plans, nor register conversations with Molotov – the only person with whom he talked openly and, indeed, who shared his foreign policy outlook. Notwithstanding the assumption that no real debate could have developed in the atmosphere of Stalin's dictatorship, Vojtech Mastny accepts that the Foreign Ministry officials in charge of planning merely wrote down – with sometimes interesting nuances – what they assumed to be Stalin's views. Relying on recently opened official records he elaborates on insecurity as being the deepest feeling underlying Stalin's policy, unveils the psychological as well as rational roots of Stalin's dream of security by empire, and illustrates his improvization, incoherence and opportunism in shaping a postwar Europe in which the Soviet Union would be the only continental power. The other states would be ruled by 'friendly' governments, that were not necessarily Communist, but ready to adopt Moscow's wishes and interests. Such an attitude was not intrinsically incompatible with American and British views and expectations. A poorly defined, or plainly unlimited, concept of Soviet security requirements and a misperception of the limits of Anglo-American acceptance of Soviet claims, led Stalin and Molotov to reduce their own genuine willingness to establish such European order in agreement with the Western allies. As London began to meet Moscow's greediness by signalling limits, Stalin's fears and suspicions rapidly escalated into self-assertiveness, mistrust and autarchy.

The 'Big Three' was a closed system, and the postwar European order, or its failure, was indeed the result of their interaction. Other states, whether they were major like France, or small like Poland and Czechoslovakia, had a common attitude to postwar planning: to find the best possible position in an Anglo-Soviet 'partnership'; to prevent themselves being strangled in exclusive relations with one of the dominating powers; and to find a balanced position between the two, securing a margin of independence and freedom of action.

Charles de Gaulle, just like Churchill and the British Foreign Office, was determined to work with the Soviet Union. Indeed, the entente with Moscow had become a cornerstone of French foreign policy and almost a symbol of the Third Republic's mistakes of the 1930s. 'Maybe the wartime leader whose plans for postwar Europe underwent most radical changes.' De Gaulle's European policy, as Georges Soutou put it, resulted from the 'dialectic between France's German and Soviet problems'. On the other hand, de Gaulle perceived the hegemony of the Big Three, as well as the impending global bipolarism, and was determined to lighten their suffocating hold on France. With his peculiar combination of backwardness and modernity, he relied both on post First World War strategies and on new concepts. Plans to separate the Rhineland and the Ruhr from Germany went hand-in-hand with plans to create an organization for western Europe and to enter into an alliance with the USSR and Britain. Choices that afterwards appeared to be mutually exclusive were conceived as a whole, complementing each other in order to render France *rang* and independence. Between 1943 and 1945, de Gaulle came to realize that alliances with Britain and the Soviet Union would not deliver what he sought. In Moscow he achieved a Franco-Soviet alliance against Germany, but he had to renounce the defence of Polish independence and failed to secure Stalin's support for wider French aims in Germany and western Europe. Indeed, a total reversal of the positive French stance towards the Soviet Union came as early as May 1945. However, the partial dismemberment of Germany, through Soviet occupation and the newly imposed eastern borders, implemented a part of de Gaulle's German policy. In spite of France's longstanding presence in eastern Europe, an early consensus soon emerged in the Algiers government that France should renounce her prominent prewar position, as she did not have the political, military and economic capabilities to play a meaningful role. Unlike the British case, however, Soutou detects a critical French attitude towards the incoming Soviet hegemony: diplomatic and geopolitical alignment with the USSR was not expected to mean the general imposition of the Soviet model of political society on the eastern countries. Therefore, the brutal and forceful Sovietization of eastern Europe precipitated a crisis of confidence in Paris and the end of any illusion of entente with the Kremlin.

The east European minor powers shared the French assumption of British–Soviet bipolarity domination of postwar Europe. In the final study of this section, Stevan K. Pavlowitch recollects exiled east European governments' plans for regional co-operation in central Europe and in the Balkans, that further stresses the contrast with the first *après-guerre* and the then small powers' ability to foster their national aims over the débris of the Habsburg empire. Fully aware of the failure of the Versailles system, as well as of the new geopolitical reality of Soviet power, important Polish, Czechoslovakian, Yugoslavian and Greek politicians elaborated on their plans, formulated while in exile in London, aimed at moderating the dominant Soviet role and involving Britain in the political balance of eastern Europe. The renunciation, to some degree, of national sovereignty and the entering into some sort of federal arrangement, was the answer Yugoslavian politicians considered to be the only possible way out from perpetual local conflicts and/or subordination to the Soviet Union. Well before west European leaders such as Schuman or De Gasperi started on the path towards the 'European construction', in the East some people had already elaborated a supranational answer to the security problems of 21st-century Europe. But as Pavlowitch comments, how serious were such plans and how much those who advanced them believed in their implementation, remains to be seen. However they were prevented from demonstrating their seriousness by the British who were seeking an agreement with Moscow. This incorrect assumption, and Britain's leading role in continental Europe remains today a lasting, though highly problematic, topic in the search for a stable European arrangement.

Part II
East–West European Relations in the Aftermath of the Second World War: the View from the West

8
Great Britain, the Balkans and the Division of Europe, 1943–45

Bruno Arcidiacono

In literature devoted to inter-allied diplomacy during the Second World War, Great Britain's attitude to Russia and the establishment of a Soviet sphere of influence in eastern Europe has long been treated as a relatively marginal issue: in any case as a subsidiary issue compared with the American policy (or 'non-policy') in the face of the 'Bolshevikization' of the countries occupied by the Red Army. Hence, this historiographical production, completely dominated by the Cold War perspective and obsessed by the search for responsibilities,[1] ordinarily proposes two antithetical views of the British position, both aimed at better highlighting, by way of contrast, the moral and political flaws or virtues of the United States' position.

The first view attributes to Great Britain a kind of natural propensity for appeasement, to the benefit of the USSR this time, and a deep lack of interest in the fate of east European nations: two elements which, when combined, translate into the readiness to acknowledge a Soviet sphere of influence where the Muscovite proconsuls would have the right to act entirely as they pleased. The second view, on the other hand, credits the authorities in London with a clear and early awareness, nurtured by years of experience, of the threat of Russian expansion, and alleges their firm resolution to counter this threat everywhere and as vigorously as their means (unfortunately scarce) allowed.

In both cases the British inclinations are presented as exactly opposed to those of the Americans. Thus the cynicism that some reproach the English for serves to emphasize the United States' righteous aversion for anything that resembled, from near or far, the carving up of the continent into separate spheres of influence; the lucidity and spirit of resistance that advocates of the second view claim His Majesty's government to have demonstrated in relations with the Soviet Union allow them, on the contrary, to better underscore the naive optimism of the Washington administration, and in particular Roosevelt's illusions in this field.

Even more recent studies specifically devoted to London's Russian policy, and based on material from the Foreign Office's archives, rarely depart from these two stylized pictures.[2] The second view is taken up and broadened by the authors who, reacting to the usual under-assessment of the British side in the triangular relationship, make Great Britain the real pioneer of the Cold War: it is Great Britain who, in pursuing its own objectives, is said to have deliberately led or pushed the Americans into the path of confrontation with the USSR. Other historians, dealing with internal discussion and formulation of the British attitude to Russia, describe this process at times in terms of *contradiction* between the two extreme options, appeasement and resistance, at times in terms of *oscillation* from one to the other. An insurmountable and paralyzing contradiction, in one case, a perpetual pendular motion without the least strategic continuity, in the other: which produced either an 'English non-policy', or a neurotic *volte-face* sequence, devoid of any intellectual coherence.

The question that must be asked at the outset, when studying the British approach to the problems raised by the Balkans in general – and by the enemy countries of the region in particular – during the years between 1943 and 1945,[3] is whether this strictly binary conceptual basis, dictated in fact by later developments in international relations, is adequate to represent the object of the analysis. The reply is immediately apparent: it is not adequate at all. As the documents make it clear, in London the choice during this period was not between two mutually exclusive policy lines, one 'Russophile', in favour of the division of the continent and indifferent to the fate of States and peoples subjected to Soviet occupation, the other 'anti-Russian', hostile to the division and attached to the independence of these States and to the liberty of these peoples. The first objective of this chapter is to argue for a somewhat more subtle definition of the possible options. The suggested method combines three criteria:

a)   the attitude with regard to postwar co-operation with the USSR and the general configuration of the new international order;

b)   the attitude to the division into exclusive spheres (the type of division which would entail for each party complete freedom of action in its zone, including the freedom of imposing regimes of its own choice);[4]

c) the attitude to the distribution of roles between the three Allies in the political administration of occupied Europe, and in particular the appreciation of the *degree* and *type* of intervention permitted to or required of Anglo-Saxon powers in eastern Europe during Soviet occupation.

By adopting these variables we escape the straitjacket of the above mentioned dichotomy and get, in the last analysis, four different political formulae. One of these (here is the central thesis defended in the following pages) corresponds to the Foreign Office's 'official' strategy *vis-à-vis* Russia and the Balkan countries it had conquered, and allows a faithful, intelligible and perfectly coherent representation of this strategy – whatever the opinion anyone may form of its intrinsic value. Indeed, London's Balkan policy associated:

a) the idea that it was in Great Britain's interest to preserve tripartite co-operation and to build on this basis the postwar international system, a revised version of the old Concert of Europe;
b) the rejection of any hypothesis implying the fracturing of the continent into two sectors, abandoning the eastern sector to the Russians and accepting its reduction to vassalage;
c) the conviction that, in order to reconcile (a) and (b), it was necessary first and foremost to reassure the Russian government of Western intentions in its regard: it was, therefore, not only right but expedient to take into account its legitimate security interests by restraining within strict limits and by calibrating very carefully Anglo-American political activities in eastern Europe.

In other words, as far as the Foreign Office was concerned, rejection of all excessive Western interference in enemy countries controlled by the Red Army coexisted, in an intellectually coherent context, with opposition to the integration of these countries into a permanent Soviet sphere: opposition to the logic of spheres, because the geographic division of Europe would have led sooner or later to the political and military dislocation of the coalition;[5] recognition of Russia's pre-eminent political role in the East at the end of hostilities, not because the Foreign Office intended (or recognized as inevitable) to give the Kremlin free rein, but because it hoped in this manner to *avoid* the Sovietization of the occupied countries. If this point is not grasped, one is necessarily reduced to depict a British policy, which fluctuates unceasingly between accommodation and resistance, depending on the circumstances and mood of the moment.

As to the three other possible combinations, they correspond to solutions advocated or practised, respectively, by an influential portion of the British press and opinion, which felt that postwar collaboration with the USSR and the permanent abasement of Germany were conceivable only on the basis of a clear and lasting division of Europe into *Arbeitszonen*;[6] by the American administration after Yalta and still more after Potsdam, when it decided that it was possible and necessary to impose upon the Russians the principle of joint responsibility in the occupied east European countries, and to consider Moscow's reaction to this requirement as the test of its real will to co-operate; and by the few critics, English and American, of the very idea of tripartite co-operation, according to whom it was neither possible nor necessary to perpetuate the inter-allied concert and it was thus advisable to build a postwar Europe not based on restraint of Germany but on containment of Russia. It should be added that each of these options was to find its supporters within the London diplomatic community at one time or another, without undermining however, at least between 1943 and 1945, the Foreign Office's faith in the 'orthodox' doctrine.

The three points to be now examined (and which will only be touched upon) are, first, the unspoken (or half-stated) assumptions underlying this doctrine; second, its positive manifestations during the period under consideration here; and finally, the trials and challenges these assumptions had to face, especially after the Crimea conference.

1) The Foreign Office's prevailing view of Russia during the war was one of a power whose policies were not (or no longer) spurred on by messianic ideology, who wished like its Allies the survival of the coalition into the postwar era, and who did not *premeditate* Bolshevikization of the half of Europe over which its troops would have acquired military control before the end of hostilities; on one condition however: provided it did not perceive any new threat against its strategic security.[7] It was, therefore, essential for the Western powers, on the one hand, not to give the Kremlin this impression and, on the other hand, to see to it that the factors *internal* to the region, and to each country in the region, did not push the Russians along this path. In particular, the local 'bourgeois' parties and their leaders had to do everything possible to persuade the occupiers that Russia was not condemned in the Balkans to counting on the Communists alone in order to get

'friendly governments' and guarantee its security. Hence the Foreign Office's attempt to reach an agreement with the USSR which, while giving a certain role to London in the occupied countries (that of junior partner, in varying shades according to local situations), assured the Russians that Great Britain was not planning to pursue an independent policy, prejudicial to their interests: on the contrary, it intended to help them protect these interests, working hand-in-hand with them and encouraging native moderate forces to do the same.

Would Great Britain have been worried about regimes that were going to be formed in the countries conquered by the Red Army, as some assert? The aim of the British policy was *precisely* that of preventing the Bolshevikization of the Balkans, and its immediate problem lay in getting through the crucial stage of the Russian military occupation (that is to say, the period between the armistices and peace treaties) without irreparable damages. During this transition phase, the Kremlin was not to adopt, or be forced to adopt, irreversible measures in this part of Europe, transforming it into its preserve, normalized internally and closed off to all exchanges with the outside world. For if this were to happen, not only would the direct strategic interests of Great Britain be affected (for instance in Bulgaria), but the tripartite alliance would not have survived long. In brief, it was a matter of safeguarding the future – both the future of inter-allied relations and that of the countries concerned.

2) In the first half of 1943, when the Foreign Office thought of resolving the Balkan question 'by securing Russian agreement to Anglo-Russo–American collaboration there',[8] its idea, in fact, was that of a general entente with Moscow establishing the principle of joint responsibility and certain forms of tripartite supervision of political affairs in all of the territories destined to be invaded by the coalition armies, whoever the occupier: 'some uniform system applying to the whole of Europe', *western* Europe first, then eastern Europe.[9] But the system designed by the Foreign Office proved to be unfeasible in Italy, and more generally in all the enemy countries which, like Italy, would remain theatres or bases of military operations after the armistices.

After this failure, the instruments of British policy adapted to the circumstances but its strategic co-ordinates remained unchanged. Contrary to what some affirm,[10] the Foreign Office continued to reject the idea of a division of the continent into exclusive and permanent spheres. In 1944 the negotiation on the 'Greece for Rumania exchange', initiated in May by Eden with the Soviet ambassador Gusev, and the 'division' of the Balkans which resulted five months later in Moscow (the so-called percentages agreement), constitute different means to attain the same end. Indeed, the first move did not involve an exchange at all and the second, in the Foreign Office's mind, was not a division in the usual sense of the term. Neither the one nor the other sought to save Greece by 'sacrificing' Rumania, Bulgaria or Hungary: both were supposed to ensure *at the same time* that the USSR would not act against British interests in Greece and that it would not destroy the independence of the other countries for fear of hostile manoeuvres from the Western powers.[11] The Foreign Office did not intend to authorize the Russians to intervene freely in the internal affairs of their sphere of occupation; it wanted to reassure them that Great Britain would not intervene there against them, for according to its theory that would *restrain* Moscow from all excessive interference. 'While it is true', Sargent wrote in June 1944, 'that it is part of our policy to endeavour to work hand in hand with the Russians in the Balkans, this in no way means that we are intending to divide the area up into spheres or influence. We have no such intention and we have entered into no commitments on this subject with the Soviet government or anyone else.'[12] In fact, the Moscow agreement contained more than a mutual self-denying ordinance. It was not only a matter of each party renouncing pursuit of an independent policy in a specific area: it was also a matter of supporting the other party's policy in that area. Thus the concept of exchange is worse than unsuitable, it is misleading.

This policy was reflected in the political directives given by London to its missions in the three Russian-occupied enemy countries. British envoys who travelled to Rumania, Bulgaria and Hungary between the end of 1944 and the beginning of 1945 went there to co-operate with the occupiers and to encourage co-operation on the part of local political forces over whom Great Britain had (or believed it had) influence. At the same time, however, the missions had the task of monitoring the general situation and, if necessary, countering any slide towards 'Communization' which could occur in one of these countries, from whatever source.[13]

It is true that in 1945 the development of the general situation in the half of Europe occupied by the Red Army led the Foreign Office to have serious doubts regarding one or two axioms of

British policy and to produce a series of documents which ex-plored alternative solutions: whether it be a 'real' division, or a harder line towards Russia. But in the end there was no policy reversal.[14] Moscow had the right to friendly governments at its borders. The question raised after the establishment of the Groza cabinet in Bucharest was whether this right could imply the installation of a government where Communists would play a majority role. After much hesitation, the Foreign Office's reply was in the affirmative, at least in countries where there were no other forces on the political market acceptable to the Russians and ready to co-operate with them (which was the case in Rumania).

In London's view, the regimes set in place or kept in power by the USSR in the three occupied countries were certainly unsatis-factory, distasteful, even repulsive in some respects, but to con-sider them as the worst of evils was to reveal a singular lack of imagination; and they probably were not an irreversible evil. Hence, the Foreign Office *disapproved* of the 'tough line', the policy of exerting pressure on the Russians initiated by the Ameri-cans after Yalta and pursued more strongly after Potsdam; and in order to emerge from the impasse created by this policy, it recom-mended immediate recognition of the governments in power and rapid conclusion of peace treaties, for it was the only way not to worsen further tripartite relations and to keep open the perspec-tive of an improvement of the political situation in the Balkans.[15] At the end of the year, in the brief prepared for Bevin before the Moscow conference – a document considered by some as the last in a long series of *volte-face*[16] – the Foreign Office summarized arguments and reaffirmed recommendations perfectly in line with all of its previous Balkan policy. The Groza and Georgiev regimes, which the Russians viewed evidently as a guarantee of security, had to be accepted (with some cosmetic changes) not out of indifference or resignation to the inevitable fate of the coun-tries in question but, on the contrary, to avoid their complete Sovietization and because Great Britain still hoped there to be able to 'gradually re-establish [its] influence'.[17]

3) As to the challenges, they emanated from four different sources. First of all the Russians, whose occupation policies often (but not always or everywhere) proved to be not in keeping with the postu-lates on which the British theory was based. Second, the local moderate parties who, as has been seen, had a central role in the scenario envisaged by the Foreign Office; but, instead of fulfilling

this role, they generally preferred the suicidal policy of playing the Anglo-Saxons against the Soviets, thereby pushing the latter to identify their interests with those of the Balkan Communists alone. Then the Americans, and the interest they began to display for south-east Europe in 1945 and which translated quickly into a policy line profoundly different to that of the Foreign Office; a line which ultimately led the State Department to encourage against all reason the anti-Russian schemes of the local 'bourgeois' forces. Last but not least, the British representatives themselves in Rumania, Bulgaria and Hungary, not having taken much time to detect a contradiction between the two tasks assigned to them (co-operating with the Soviet occupiers and protecting the independence of the occupied countries), they increasingly tended to give priority to the second task and became progressively the most acerbic critics of the strategy they should have been applying. In fact, together with their American colleagues and with their local information sources, they developed an interpretation of Russian policy and of its objectives which was just the opposite of the prevailing view in London: an expansionist and predatory policy, ideologically motivated, religiously devoted to the spreading of Communism.

Despite everything, the Foreign Office refused to simply jettison its own doctrine. Indeed, the story of the year 1945, retraceable from the British documents on the 'Balkan question', is not at all one of a confused and inconsistent oscillation between resistance and resignation. It is the story, typical of situations where a conceptual paradigm enters into a crisis, of the intellectual exercises by which London diplomacy, faced with this quadruple challenge, attempted to preserve the essence of its system of hypotheses and assumptions about Russia, before abandoning it in 1946 and adopting another: the paradigm which in the meantime its own envoys in Bucharest, Budapest and Sofia had contributed to forging.

Notes

1   M. A. Stoler, 'World War II Diplomacy in Historical Writing: Prelude to Cold War', in G. K. Haines and J. S. Walker eds, *American Foreign Relations. A Historiographical Review* (Westport: Greenwood Press, 1981) pp. 187–206, and 'A Half Century of Conflict: Interpretations of US World War II Diplomacy', *Diplomatic History*, XVIII (1994) 3, pp. 375–403.
2   Apropos British policy towards Russia in the years 1943–45 see for example K. Hamilton and A. Lane, 'Power, Status and the Pursuit of Liberty: The Foreign

Office and Eastern Europe, 1945–46', in M. Dockrill ed., *Europe within the Global System, 1938–60* (Bochum: Brockmeyer, 1995) pp. 31–54; J. Kent, *British Imperial Strategy and the Origins of the Cold War, 1944–49* (Leicester: Leicester University Press, 1993) and 'British Policy and the Origins of the Cold War', in M. P. Leffler and D. S. Painter eds, *Origins of the Cold War. An International History* (London/New York: Routledge, 1994) pp. 139–53; J. Zametica, 'Three Letters to Bevin: Frank Roberts at the Moscow Embassy, 1945–46', in J. Zametica ed., *British Officials and British Foreign Policy, 1945–50* (Leicester: Leicester University Press, 1990) pp. 156–88; S. Greenwood, 'Frank Roberts and the "Other" Long Telegram: The View from the British Embassy in Moscow, March 1946', *Journal of Contemporary History*, XXV (1990) 1, pp. 103–22; M. Kitchen, *British Policy towards the Soviet Union during the Second World War* (London: Macmillan – now Palgrave, 1986) and 'Winston Churchill and the Soviet Union during the Second World War', *Historical Journal*, XXX (1987) 2, pp. 415–36; G. Ross, 'Foreign Office Attitudes to the Soviet Union 1941–45', in W. Laqueur ed., *The Second World War: Essays in Military and Political History* (London/Beverly Hills: Sage Publications, 1982) pp. 255–74; D. Reynolds, 'Churchill the Appeaser? Between Hitler, Roosevelt and Stalin in World War II', in M. Dockrill and B. McKercher eds, *Diplomacy and World Power. Studies in British Foreign Policy, 1890–1950* (Cambridge: Cambridge University Press, 1996) pp. 197–220; G. Warner, 'From Ally to Enemy: Britain's Relations with the Soviet Union, 1941–48', *ibid*, pp. 221–43; D. C. Watt, 'Britain, the United States and the Opening of the Cold War', in R. Ovendale ed., *The Foreign Policy of the British Labour Governments, 1945–51* (Leicester: Leicester University Press, 1984) pp. 43–60, and 'British Military Perceptions of the Soviet Union as a Strategic Threat, 1945–50', in J. Becker and F. Knipping eds, *Power in Europe? Great Britain, France, Italy and Germany in a Postwar World, 1945–50* (Berlin: De Gruyter, 1986) pp. 325–38; P. Boyle, 'The British Foreign Office View of Soviet-American Relations, 1945–46', *Diplomatic History*, III (1979) 3, pp. 307–20; R. Merrick, 'The Russia Committee of the British Foreign Office and the Cold War, 1946–47', *Journal of Contemporary History*, XX (1985) 3, pp. 453–68; R. Smith and J. Zametica, 'The Cold Warrior: Clement Attlee Reconsidered, 1945–47', *International Affairs*, LXI (1985) 2, pp. 237–52; V. Rothwell, *Britain and the Cold War 1941–47* (London: Jonathan Cape, 1982); P. J. Taylor, *Britain and the Cold War. 1945 as Geopolitical Transition* (London: Pinter, 1990); H. Thomas, *Armed Truce. The Beginnings of the Cold War, 1945–46* (London: Hamish Hamilton, 1986).

3   Concerning British attitude towards the 'Balkan question' see for example E. Barker, *British Policy in South-East Europe in the Second World War* (London: Macmillan, 1976); the essays collected in W. Deakin, E. Barker and J. Chadwick eds, *British Political and Military Strategy in Central, Eastern and Southern Europe in 1944* (London: Macmillan, 1988); R. Garson, 'Churchill's Spheres of Influence: Rumania and Bulgaria', *Survey*, XXIV (1979) 3, pp. 143–58; P. G. H. Holdich, 'A Policy of Percentages? British Policy and the Balkans after the Moscow Conference of October 1944', *International History Review*, IX (1987) 1, pp. 28–47; A. Resis, 'The Churchill-Stalin Secret "Percentages" Agreement on the Balkans, Moscow, October 1944', *American Historical Review*, LXXXIII (1978) 2, 368–87; J. Siracusa, 'The Meaning of Tolstoy: Churchill, Stalin, and the Balkans, Moscow, October 1944', *Diplomatic History*, III (1979) 4,

pp. 443–63; and B. Arcidiacono, *Alle origini della divisione europea. Armistizi e Commissioni di controllo alleate in Europa orientale, 1944–46* (Firenze: Ponte alle Grazie, 1993).

4   The distinction between an 'exclusive' and an 'open' sphere is made in E. Mark, 'American Policy towards Eastern Europe and the Origins of the Cold War, 1941–46: An Alternative Interpretation', *Journal of American History*, LXVIII (1981) 2, pp. 313–36.

5   'By abdicating our responsibilities [...] we may encourage the growth of zones of influence leading to the division of Europe into rival camps [...] which, in the long run, is bound to be detrimental to Anglo-Soviet relations': see 'British Interests in South-Eastern Europe', 14 April 1944, Public Record Office, FO 371, U 3322/491/70 (40733).

6   A. Foster, 'The Times and Appeasement: the Second Phase', in W. Laqueur ed., *The Second World War, op. cit.*, pp. 275–99, and 'The British Press and the Coming of the Cold War', in A. Deighton ed., *Britain and the First Cold War* (New York: St. Martin's Press, 1990) pp. 11–31. See also E. H. Carr, *Conditions of Peace* (London: Macmillan, 1942) p. 205; G. D. H. Cole, *Europe, Russia, and the Future* (London: Victor Gollancz, 1941) pp. 15, 153; L. B. Namier, *Facing East* (London: Hamish Hamilton, 1947) pp. 96–7; A. J. P. Taylor, *A Personal History* (London: Hamish Hamilton, 1983) p. 181.

7   B. Arcidiacono, 'Between War and Peace: The Western Perception of Soviet East European Policy', in A. Varsori ed., *Europe 1945–1990s. The End of an Era?* (London/New York: Macmillan/St. Martin's Press, – now Palgrave 1995) pp. 47–61.

8   C. F. A. Warner, 2 January 1943, in G. Ross ed., *The Foreign Office and the Kremlin. British Documents on Anglo-Soviet Relations, 1941–45* (Cambridge: Cambridge University Press, 1984) p. 119.

9   'Secret record of meeting held in Jebb's room', 3 March 1943, in B. Arcidiacono, 'The "Dress Rehearsal": The Foreign Office and the Control of Italy, 1943–44', *The Historical Journal*, XXVIII (1985) 2, p. 420.

10   See for example A. Resis, 'The Churchill–Stalin', op. cit., p. 387.

11   B. Arcidiacono, 'Dei rapporti tra diplomazia e aritmetica: lo "strano accordo" Churchill–Stalin sui Balcani (Mosca, ottobre 1944)', *Storia delle relazioni internazionali*, V (1989) 2, pp. 245–77.

12   PRO : Sir O. Sargent to Sir H. Knatchbull-Hugessen, 2 June 1944, R 8130/349/67 (43646).

13   PRO: see the 'Political Directives' for the British sections of the Allied Control Commissions in Romania, September 1944, R 15283/294/37 (44009), in Bulgaria, October 1944, R 17949/13941/7 (43616) and in Hungary, October 1944, C 13947/5439/21 (39280).

14   PRO: see Sargent's memoranda of 13 March 1945, R 5063/5063/67 (48129), and 2 April 1945, N 4281/165/38 (47881); the 'orthodox line' is reaffirmed in 'Questions at Issue with the Soviet Government', 17 May 1945, R 9256/81/67 (48192).

15   'We are inclined to reconcile ourselves to the fact that a Communist majority in the Government[s] is inevitable for the time being' (W. G. Hayter to the political representative in Bucarest, J. H. Le Rougetel, 27 October 1945); 'We must accept the lesser evil [...] in order to [...] create conditions in which there is at least some hope of the emergence of democratic government'

(Foreign Office to Le Rougetel no 687, 15 June 1945): see respectively PRO: R 17268/28/37 (48560) and R 10240/28/37 (48554).

16 For example J. Zametica, 'Three Letters to Bevan...', op. cit., 65.

17 Sargent to the political representative in Sofia, W. E. Houstoun-Boswall, 26 November 1945, PRO:R 19541/81/67 (48194).

9

Franco-Czechoslovak Relations from 1944 to 1948 or the Munich Syndrome

Antoine Marès

When France was liberated in the summer of 1944, the continuity of its foreign policy was assured by the Free French government. It was, therefore, on the foundations laid in London and Algiers that General de Gaulle's central European policy was built, and not on the heritage left by Vichy, which was not at all clear for that zone anyhow.[1]

The relations with Czechoslovakia were complex at the time, due to a difficult heritage and to actors who were deeply marked by their diplomatic and ideological experiences. A difficult heritage, because the Munich agreements stood in the background, be they considered to be with regret (Maurice Dejean), an experience never to be repeated (René Massigli), a stain to be removed at all costs (Edvard Beneš) or a bad memory to be erased because it reflected the powerlessness of France (General de Gaulle). Yet, mutual sympathy had subsisted between the Franco-Czechoslovak couple, separated but not divorced, since September 1938. On the French side, the sympathy towards Prague was reinforced by the feeling of having gone through a shared and parallel experience of German occupation and exile in London. On the Czechoslovak side a Francophile sentiment persisted, though moderated by past experience and overshadowed by the failure of 1938 and by a new Russophile sentiment.

The actors of this foreign policy had themselves a different heritage. General de Gaulle, marked by his experience in the Soviet–Polish war – which ought not, in principle, to have encouraged feelings of sympathy towards Prague – was indisputably anti-Munich. Since Munich had signified the debasing of France, his ties with the Czechs were tightened in London. Georges Bidault, former editor of *L'Aube* and a fierce opponent of the Munich treaty, also had privileged ties with Prague, as did the president of the Republic, Vincent Auriol, who had long-standing friendly relations with Edvard Beneš. Among the diplomats, the positions were more contrasting, although one cannot speak of outspoken antipathy, more of a critical distance.

Among the Czechs, the Munich trauma had been even stronger. For Beneš, it was a real obsession, which determined his policy and his reactions. At the Ministry of Foreign Affairs, Jan Masaryk was doubly restricted by the narrowness of his freedom to operate and by the presence of a Communist Vice-minister, Vlado Clementis. Jindrich Nosek, the Czechoslovak ambassador in France – he returned his *lettres de créance* on 18 November 1944 – was more clearly Francophile.

Finally and above all, Franco-Czechoslovak relations were to be marked, during these four years, by the evolution of the Soviet–American relations.

1)   The heritage and the premisses: from 1944 to March 1946

As soon as instructions were sent in August 1942 from Beiruth by General de Gaulle to his Foreign Affairs Commissioner, Maurice Dejean, to prepare the negotiations for the repudiation of the Munich agreements,[2] sanctioned by the adoption of an exchange of letters made public on 29 September 1942, one observes great caution. In June 1943, Beneš recognized the *Comité Français de Libération Nationale*, but from then on his geopolitical analysis led him more clearly towards the east. Although he still considered that France had to play a role after the war, he was more inclined to consider that the predominant role in central Europe would be taken by the USSR, which explains the December 1943 Soviet–Czechoslovak treaty, so strongly disapproved of by the Anglo-Saxon powers. For the French diplomats, it was clear that the *cordon sanitaire* policy had definitely changed to the advantage of the USSR in the spring of 1944.

What united the French and the Czechs was their common experience of occupation, their suspicion towards the Anglo-Saxons, their marginalization on the international scene and their pursuit of the struggle against Germany. What divided them was the importance of their reciprocal agreements: when on 10 June 1944 Beneš proposed to the French an univocal alliance that would liquidate the shadows from the past, he was confronted by a certain degree of suspicion. Although Maurice Dejean clearly stated his support for that idea because the Czechs were a constant support for the *Gouvernement provisoire*, those in Algiers[3] were much more reluctant. There resulted a text elaborated on 17 August and signed on 22 August by de Gaulle, Dejean, Šrámek and Masaryk, a text of resounding vagueness. The caution, that stand as a permanent feature in the bilateral relations, on the one hand was linked to the difficulty of appraising the balance of power in central Europe and, on the other hand, to a desire not to enter into ill-considered agreements.[4]

A note of January 1945, addressed to the minister Georges Bidault, stated: 'It would be premature to precisely define the French policy in Central Europe.' Nevertheless, Paris 'must defend certain essential interests on the Danube implied by the Bohemian and Austrian issues', stay firm as regards the small powers and position itself above their quarrels.[5] Bidault did not follow these suggestions, being too absorbed by the German question. Another unknown quantity lingered: in December 1944, at the Foreign Office, there were serious doubts as to the future of President Beneš and of his ministers. It was said about the Russians that their support would last 'as long as they considered the President likely to serve their purpose'.[6] Thereby, the fears expressed would soon reveal themselves to be well founded, both on the return of the Czechoslovak authorities from London to their national territory and concerning the destiny of sub-Carpathian Ukraine which was annexed by force to the USSR.[7] The Czechs placed themselves in an ambiguous position when Hubert Ripka greeted the first anniversary of the Soviet–Czechoslovak treaty and praised the alliance with the USSR, which was from now on considered 'natural'. Of course, in these words one must weigh the constraints deriving from the massive presence of Communist ministers within the government, from the treaty of December 1943 and from the fact that the Czechoslovak territory was on the verge of being liberated by the Red Army.

Besides, in February 1945, Beneš said to Massigli that 'the future would be bleak without a close collaboration between France and England. It is essential for my country' and Massigli concluded by stating 'M. Beneš could not highlight more clearly his fears of seeing the pressure from Moscow weigh on Prague without any counterweight'.[8] During his visit to Moscow in March, Beneš was not enthusiastic about the result of his negotiations with Gottwald.[9] The British did not share the same hesitations as the French. A member of the Cabinet in London indicated to René Massigli that the Polish, Hungarian, Austrian and Trieste questions were all part of the same problem, 'that of the Russian expansion in Europe'. Besides, Paris had rapidly reached a conclusion as to the consequences of the Polish situation.[10]

In spite of these reservations, in the spring of 1945, the Franco-Czechoslovak relations were marked by a seal of friendship as seen in the discussions on cultural issues[11] and, on 1 June 1945, in the warm telegram from General de Gaulle to President Beneš.[12] Nevertheless, locally, the opinions regarding the role France could still play were mixed.[13] From a military point of view, the disengagement was obvious, even if Czechoslovakia had to remain a *plaque tournante* for French information on central Europe.[14] From a political point of view, the new Chargé d'Affaires Louis Keller – who arrived on 3 June with his British counterpart Nichols – had not lost hope of 'making Prague a bridge between us and Moscow'.[15] A bridge? It was true that the Czechs 'wonder[ed] why the Allies, although having victorious armies at their disposal, did not want to go against the wishes of the Soviet command and expect[ed] the Czechoslovak people to become the champion, in central Europe, of Western conceptions.'[16]

On 4 July 1945 Beneš presented his position to Keller during a very long discussion that was also a *plaidoyer* for his country: 'only Czechoslovakia can serve as a model for the other countries of western and eastern Europe', he claimed with a characteristic assurance that profoundly irritated ambassador René Massigli in London.[17] And he insisted on privileged cultural relations for France. For the economy, the orientation towards the USSR was obvious. Beneš underlined, on the same occasion, the understanding by the Soviets of the German problem in Czechoslovakia. It was, and will be, his fundamental criteria for judging real allies and friends.[18] Basically, in the light of his experience of 1938, Beneš suspected France from now on.[19] This long period of exploration ended with the visit to Prague of General Leclerc's mission, decided by General de Gaulle, who wanted to express his ties with Czechoslovakia at the highest level and solemnly mark the 14 July. General Leclerc had orders to resume the cultural exchanges and to thaw the relationship with Prague. He left his short visit with the feeling that not all was lost. As early as 15 July,[20] Keller plunged head first into the opening left by his recommendations. In an unsigned note of 29 October 1945 addressed to the minister, the relations with Prague were described as virtually ideal.[21]

As regards the USSR, the interpretations oscillated between several poles: were Moscow's motivations purely ideological? Did they derive from the Russian traditional approach in establishing protective areas and in moving towards the warmer seas? Bogomolov, the most prominent diplomat to whom the French spoke, alternatively blew hot and cold. In October, he explained to General Catroux that the Soviet Union did not plan to make eastern Europe its exclusive hunting ground. It only wanted to give itself guarantees.[22] Several days earlier, Henri Roux had expressed the position of the General's cabinet, probably in view of the approaching visit to Paris of Vlado Clementis, Vice-minister of Foreign Affairs:[23] 'The new Czechoslovak regime basically seeks to combine a profound social revolution with the upholding of democratic forms. It represents a sort of compromise between Eastern governments and those of the West. From an exterior point of view as well, Czechoslovakia, although strongly influenced by the East, does not omit to look westwards. Its rulers would like it be a link between the two.'[24]

A new phase in Franco-Czechoslovak diplomatic relations started with the posting of Maurice Dejean to Prague. A former Free France Foreign affairs commissioner, he was trusted by President Beneš. Dejean immediately evaluated the situation 'The attitude of the Czechoslovak press regarding us largely follows the Prague idea of our relations with the USSR.'[25] 'Obviously, nobody doubts that at the moment, the Soviet influence is all-powerful in the new Czechoslovak republic.'[26] But Dejean was convinced that this weight was temporary and that if the Communists postponed the legislative elections, it was because they feared a decline of their influence. During a discussion between Clementis and Dejean on 12 January 1946, several points of friction appeared: the passage of Otto of Habsburg into the Austrian occupied zone; the French reservations regarding Tito's Yugoslavia; the claims of the French companies which had been nationalized. On the other hand, the Deputy Minister expressed his understanding of the French policy in the Rhine region.[27] In effect Germany did remain a common preoccupation. Beneš declared on the same day to Dejean during a two-hour lunch 'The existence of a strong Germany is incompatible with an independent Czechoslovakia.'[28] But Beneš also advised that France should bide its time and not get involved in Europe's fate.

As regards the territorial disputes with Poland and Hungary, Paris was more in favour of Prague, due to the commitments contracted in the agreement of 29 September 1942.[29] The enactment of this principle revealed itself to be a delicate matter. Budapest continuously postponed negotiations about population exchanges with Prague. And France, which had acknowledged the Hungarian government, was considered jointly responsible for this elusiveness, after having made declarations that had been interpreted as univocal promises of support. The question of the eviction of Germans was dealt with in theory during the war; on the other hand, the question of Hungarians remained at the heart of Czechoslovak diplomatic efforts until the signature of the peace treaties in March 1947.

2) The year of transition, April 1946 to July 1947

Until the spring of 1946, Franco-Czechoslovak relations consisted in patching up older agreements. The situation suddenly evolved at end of April following the Czechoslovak alarm at rumours of a Franco-Polish agreement. Ambassador Nosek expressed his fears to the Quai d'Orsay. Coulets denied, claiming it to be no more than discussions concerning a joint declaration.[30] Nosek expressed his government's wish to proceed to a relatively urgent clarification of Franco-Czechoslovak relations, a 'real alliance treaty' to be discussed when Masaryk came to the Paris Peace Conference due to take place in June.[31] The Czechs would like the conclusion of a treaty that would replace those of January 1924 and October 1925 and 'that would be elaborated according to the model of the Franco-Soviet Pact of December 1944 and the Alliance Treaty between the USSR and Czechoslovakia.'[32] The date? The day following the elections in both countries.

This initiative by Prague can be explained: the Czechs were afraid of being left behind by the Poles and feared that support from Paris could reinforce Warsaw in the frontier dispute. On the other hand, with the Paris Peace Conference approaching, Prague was looking for allies to resolve the question of the Hungarian minority. Nosek made a long presentation to Couglets on the 27 April regarding the Czechoslovak desiderata on the Hungarian transfer, the suburbs of Bratislava and the frontier rectification with Germany. Nosek told his government that Bidault supported the re-establishment of pre-Munich frontiers and the modification of the Slovak capital's suburbs, but remained cautious on the question of the Hungarian transfer. As for the claims on Germany, Bidault would agree to everything but for the Glatz area.[33] In spite of this reluctance confirmed by Couve de Murville to Nosek,[34] the public scene was apparently idyllic, as the Czechoslovak Council of Ministers of 9 July 1946 approved the idea of negotiating an alliance treaty based on the declaration of 17 August 1944,[35] so long as Moscow did not disapprove. Molotov and Vychinski seemed not to have expressed any hostility towards the initiative.[36] The celebrations of 14 July, in the presence of the Assistant State Secretary to Information, Bichet, went so well that it was claimed 'Munich is erased.' At this point the chronology is important: between the April initiative and the July decision the legislative elections had taken place, to the surprise of Beneš and Dejean.[37] The French observers were indeed quite intrigued by Soviet troop movements in and around Czechoslovakia (transit of 200 000 men) from the 20 to the 29 May.[38]

In fact, Bidault maintained his position on the Hungarian question, which was at the centre of Czechoslovak worries,[39] even if a few days later he agreed to pass on the Czechoslovak requests while recommending caution. Britain's Foreign Secretary Bevin remained very reluctant too. As for the US, Byrnes was hostile to the idea.[40] Hence, Molotov, whom Masaryk and Clementis had met on 30 June, was also cautious.[41] Finally, Bidault sent a telegraph to Dejean on 16 July that said 'The openings offered to him by the Prague government must be accepted with great caution.'[42]

At the end of July, Beneš declared in a grand speech in Kromeriz:

> In my view, our foreign policy should never have been, even during the first republic, exclusively Western or exclusively Eastern, but should have been, depending on the situation on the international scene, Western and Eastern or Eastern and Western. Situated in the centre of Europe, we cannot sever ourselves from the West. To all who come to see me at the Castle, I repeat that we are in Czechoslovakia, not in between the West and the East and that, geographically, we are between the Soviet Union and reactionary Germany. In case of conflict our attitude would be predetermined. We would walk alongside our ally. Our geographical situation is unchangeable and so is our policy line.[43]

Hence the defence of a democratic Slav policy questioned by the Christian-Democrats.[44] The systematic support by Prague of Moscow's position on Germany, on one hand, and Molotov's obvious intention of encouraging the estrangement between the French and Anglo-American powers, on the other, therefore explain the respective positions of France and Czechoslovakia.

Henri Roux wrote in a secret note to the Eastern Europe desk that if 'the USSR is in fact the master of Czechoslovak destiny, our alliance with it is *sufficient* [. . .].' There was therefore no political commitment on the French side. This did not prevent a Commercial Agreement from being concluded on 29 July[45] and the first draft of a treaty to be handed in on 7 August to Maurice Dejean.[46] The initiative thus lay in the hands of the Czechs. Everything leads us to think that the Quai d'Orsay had adopted a voluntarily cavalier attitude. On the British side, information confirmed that Czechoslovak docility had been clearly evaluated, but there was still some hope that Czechoslovakia would keep a margin of autonomy, even 'if the Soviet influence will remain stronger than in Austria.' [47] Actually, the Foreign Office's position comforted that of the Quai.[48] In Prague, Maurice Dejean had another view of the situation. He noted that France had returned to its initial position of December 1945 and he began to plead in support of the treaty.[49]

When *Le Figaro* published a denial regarding the negotiation of a Franco-Czechoslovak treaty, Clementis reacted by demanding explanations from Dejean. The latter explained that the Quai thereby sought to diminish Anglo-American dissatisfaction. Dejean then saw Bidault who, according to him, did not agree with the Quai and would have liked to resume discussions in approximately ten days. In this game of hide-and-seek, Clementis suggested to his compatriots that they should remain aloof in order to cast the French in a bidding role.[50] Apparently, on the Czechoslovak side, positions started to diverge. Upon his return from Paris, Dejean saw President Beneš who asked him if, in France, 'Czechoslovakia [was] considered as already attached to one of the existing blocs.' This question confirmed his worries and doubts. Dejean cautiously answered that France understood there were 'certain imperatives'. As for the Franco-Czechoslovak talks, 'I answered that in the course of the conversation I had had with him on 14 August, just before my departure from Paris, the President of the Provisional Government had charged me to inform Masaryk and Clementis that we were ready to begin discussions from now on.'[51]

One comes across such ambiguities again concerning the Hungarian question: while speaking to Pál Auer, the Hungarian minister in Paris, Courcel confirmed that Bidault was not in favour of the Hungarian transfer. But if a reasonable basis for agreement was not found, 'France would tend to be in favour of the Czechoslovak request, as long as it is subordinated to specific guarantees concerning the conditions of transfer of the population.' Finally, the Conference sub-commission was to support the rectification in favour of the *avant-pays* of Bratislava and a transfer limited by guarantees. In October, the USSR had apparently abandoned its univocal support of Prague in view of the transfer.[52]

It is useful to note that on the Czechoslovak political scene, the famous October 1946 speech by Churchill in Zurich caused unanimous commotion. Hubert Ripka, the Minister of Trade, a National-Socialist close to Beneš, and the organ of the (Catholic) Popular Party voiced the same protests against the exclusion of the USSR. It was not a case of sovietophile sentiment but rather the conviction that the autonomy of Prague was based on the maintenance of an East–West dialogue. At the general assembly of the Paris Conference, on 12 October 1946, Clementis reaffirmed the Slav policy, repeating that it did not imply a satellization around the USSR, but that it was the result of the reaching of history.[53] October was also the month when the Americans suspended their credits in favour of Prague because of its representatives' attitude at the Paris Conference. Ambassador Steinhardt explained that this measure was meant to reinforce democracy and fortify the moderates. The Czech unanimity was once again disturbed: the National-Socialists and especially the People's Party disagreed. Beneš felt it to be regrettable for the Czechs to have criticized Washington. But, he added, it was 'illogical to blame Czechoslovakia for staying in the wake of the USSR when it was the Anglo-Saxons themselves who, during the Teheran Conference, had handed Czechoslovakia over to the Soviet Union. It was they who put us in the Russian zone. Now we are there. Russia is at our door and we need it against Germany.'[54]

Despite all this, the year of 1947 began with signs of a revival: the president of the Foreign Affairs Commission at the Czechoslovak National Assembly regretted that France had not paid more attention and had not responded in a more positive manner to the proposals coming from Prague regarding a project 'that took into consideration, right from the start, reality as crudely as it came, that is the situation of Germany coming in between Strasbourg and Prague.' If that were so, the Czechoslovak's operational leeway had been considerably reduced. The instructions given to the Czech delegation in January 1947 for the London Conference reflected that. 'For the Saar, the delegation can support the requests from France on condition that the French delegation support the specific requests of the Czechs and that in conjunction with the Soviet delegation, the delegation makes sure that the French requests do not go against the USSR's interests.'[55] On 30 January, Bidault reproached Prague for not having supported Germany's federalization preferred by Paris, even if the press highlighted the Czechoslovak support on the Saar issue.[56] The following day, Beneš met Dejean for two hours: Czechoslovakia '[was] achieving the integration of communism into democracy', which was 'the great task of our time', he said. As to the German issue, Beneš reaffirmed his conviction that federalization was not a further peace token; he feared the inclusion of Austria in a German confederation. He insisted on the identity of Franco-Czechoslovak relations, holding that Germany '[had] not ceased to be a danger'. Against all expectations, Beneš did not raise the issue of a common treaty, probably so as not to fall into the previous *ornements*. However, Václav Kopecký, Minister for Information, insisted with Louis Joxe during his visit, on tightening the bounds between the two countries.[57]

Talks were finally started by Masaryk and Clementis in Paris. Within Ramadier's government, Georges Bidault took Leon Blum's place at the Ministry of Foreign Affairs on the 22 January. From now on, France was to work at the obviously more important Franco-British and Franco-Czechoslovak treaties. From the Quai, François Coulet cabled to the Moscow and Washington embassies that 'the moment has come to begin the planned discussions with the Czechoslovak government, even if the signature is not to happen before that of the Franco-British pact.'[58]

It was on 14 February, a few weeks after the signature of the Paris treaties, that the beginning of discussions was officially announced at the Palais Cernin.[59] It was greeted with favour unanimously in Prague and the Czechoslovaks even began to wonder if it would be possible to close the talks before the Moscow conference, as Bidault was going to Moscow via Prague, but the *Quai* refused.[60] Dejean then suggested stopping in Prague on his way back from Moscow, around the middle or at the end of April.[61] As soon as the Franco-British treaty was signed on 4 March 1947, a great difficulty was removed. Masaryk announced to the National Assembly that Charles Tillon, Minister of the Air, has assured him that the signature would occur 'in the shortest possible time, as befits the importance of such a pact', a fact meanwhile which was not well received by Moscow.[62] This was when French hesitations surfaces again. Meeting with Ambassador Nosek, President Vincent Auriol declared that: 'We do not wish for the creation of two hostile blocs and hope to be the link between the so-called great and small powers.'[63] From London, on the other hand, Ambassador Massigli confidentially made known the reaction of the permanent under-secretary of state at the Foreign Office, Sir Orme Sargent: 'Let us not make the same mistakes as before the war'. The British believed in possible results only in economic and cultural matters.[64] René Massigli's views most certainly counted at the Quai d'Orsay. As to the treaty, President Vincent Auriol declared to Jindrich Nosek on 28 March that the new organization of France's political relationships was to be all the more crucial as France was once again going to play an important role among the great powers.[65]

The criss-cross of information between London, Paris and Prague gives a clear but complex image of the situation. Faced with the permanent reluctance of the French, a certain number of Czechoslovak political forces – in particular the Christian Democrats, the 'People's Party' – urged a treaty with Britain. Ivo Duchacek, President of the Foreign Affairs Committee, evoked this possibility before Parliament.[66] London made the most of this situation by developing cultural and economic ties with Czechoslovakia, poaching the French cultural 'monopoly'.[67] On the whole Massigli saw therein a manoeuvre by Czech government to put pressure on the French, for the purpose of accelerating the discussions, which in return puzzled Dejean.[68] In a telegram to his minister on 6 May,[69] he asked the question in the clearest terms: 'One wishes to know if France aims at claiming a stake in Central Europe, or is resigned to evacuating the area in political terms, just as requested by Germany after Munich.' The Americans[70] were also greatly annoyed by this pactomania in central Europe. But the Quai's 'defence' consisted in saying that these pivotal pacts should facilitate East–West negotiations and prevent a split in Europe.[71] The two governments exchanged their respective treaty projects. Prague's foresaw mutual support, not only in the case of German aggression (as did the Quai's version), but also in the case of another state directly or indirectly joining forces with Germany. While the Czechoslovak press announced that France did not intend to bring the treaty to a conclusion,[72] Georges Bidault – ever more disappointed by the Soviet position at the Moscow Conference – and the Quai's General Secretary had then met Nosek to deny this and the French text for Prague[73] was indeed handed to him on 31 May. He arrived in Prague with this text, although Dejean had not been previously informed. The differences became apparent immediately.[74] The atmosphere seemed to have hardened in Prague.[75] Paris maintained its position, except for a few minor changes, and suggested that Bidault travel to Prague at the end of the month for the signature.[76]

Meanwhile, the Marshall Plan was presented. On the 19 June, Masaryk wrote to the Czech embassy in Moscow that the decision would depend on whether the plan was to contain only economic terms in its implementation, as well as on the Allied position.[77] Simultaneously, Beneš suggested a visit to France, as well as an immediate signature, despite the fact that the Council President, Gottwald, had not given him a definitive answer. Still on 20 June, Gottwald and Masaryk asked for Moscow's position on the Franco-Czechoslovak treaty: the telegram was phrased ambiguously, exposing Prague's worries, and thus bolstered Molotov's argument in favour of a negative reply.[78] The only element in favour of its conclusion was the prevention of the separation of Europe into two halves!

Concerning the Marshall Plan, which remained at the forefront of current issues, the Czechoslovak instructions insisted on the notion of the state's independence and the rebuttal of any influence being exerted on previous economic choices made by the participants.[79] After the Soviet rejection on 2 July the government decided, two days later, to send a delegation to Moscow, while certain Communist ministers were said to have spoken in favour of waiting for the French Communist ministers to achieve power before signing the treaty.[80] On 6 July, Masaryk met the *Chargé d'Affaires* on Soviet issues in Prague, who handed him a memorandum in which Moscow rejected the Marshall Plan as an instrument of interference 'in aid of the dollar' within the European economies.[81] This did not stop the Council of Ministers from deciding in favour of Czechoslovakia's participation at the future conference which was to begin on 12 July in Paris. It was on 9 July that the 'appearance' before Stalin took place.[82] On the 10th, Nosek noted what interest the wait for Prague's definitive answer was arousing in Paris since Poland, Romania, Bulgaria and Yugoslavia had already refused.[83]

One hour after receiving this telegram, the government turned its back on its *engagement*. It must be noted that the members of the delegation in Moscow had insisted on receiving Prague's answer. The pressure from Gottwald and, apparently, Masaryk was obviously very strong. At 21:30, Clementis met the British ambassador, P. H. Nichols, and the French ambassador, Dejean, to inform them of his government's retreat.[84]

3) The illusions' end: summer 1947 to February 1948

The Franco-Czechoslovak treaty was by then in jeopardy. Hala, minister of postal services and leader of the People Party, in a letter to Bidault on 26 July regretted that it had not been finalized in February.[85] On the 13, Bidault and Ramadier had expressed their desire to achieve this goal, but by drafting a counter-proposal, extended the treaty to include Germany's potential allies. The unlucky Masaryk wrote to Nosek on 28 July pleading with Bidault to be patient and insisting on the fact that he 'wanted' the treaty.[86] Bidault and Couve de Murville remained sceptical on the issue of any extension to the satellite states, but did not shut the door entirely.[87] Clementis questioned Warsaw about this new draft at the end of September; a new delaying tactic. The issue now lay at the heart of the battle for power in Prague while the Communist press ascribed the blame for the interruption of the discussions with France as being 'due to a shift to the right'. Dejean concluded a long brief on 21 October 1947 in the following manner:

> Despite the attempts to patch things up, the ideological breach which appears to divide Europe and the world in two seems to have split the national front.

Already, there was talk of dissolving the non-Marxist parties and of Beneš resigning.[88] In a letter to Beneš on 22 November, Clementis refuted the parallel drawn by the President between past opposition to the Soviet–Czechoslovak treaty and present opposition to the Franco-Czechoslovak treaty.[89]

The tension in Europe was such during that autumn that certain American analysts [90] believed that in France and Italy the Communists might grab power. From Moscow, however, General Catroux did not believe that the Soviets were ready to enter into war: they were making preparations while fearing it and their real aspiration was peace.[91] Petr Zenkl, Vice-president of the Council and head of the National-Socialist Party, came to Paris at the end of November to try to relaunch the discussions. During a lunch with André Marie, the radical Minister of Justice, he drew a relatively optimistic portrait of the situation in his country, describing the Communists' and their allies' recent failures within social democracy, as well as the need to reinforce the non-Communist elements within the government by linking Prague to the West. However, France delayed her decision until the next London conference. What was to befall Germany at its outcome? And if it were cut in two, what would be the eventual guarantees?[92] In London, there was rejoicing at the abandonment of this treaty which threatened to immobilize France.

Within Czechoslovakia, the situation deteriorated. For Gottwald, there was no question, from now on, of his country continuing to play an intermediary role between the USSR and the Western nations. Well-informed minds considered that by and large, France's position in Czechoslovakia henceforth depended on the relationship between Paris and Moscow, as Dejean noted in January 1948. Numerous incidents and social clashes in November and December 1947 in France precipitated the Franco-Czech relationship. On 1 January, Dejean declared that the Franco-Czech pact could not be signed

> as the division of the world into two blocs was already a definite fact. [...] It becomes obvious that a treaty which is mostly an act of faith in the future of a unified Europe can only bear fruit in an international context which does not at present exist.

Franco-Czech negotiations failed anyhow in January 1948. The warming of the Franco-British relationship was a heavy blow to partisans of an East–West modus vivendi.[93] It was to be a tough year for Masaryk.

> I hope we can hold fast thanks to the prestige of President Beneš. But if the international crisis were to persist in developing in this manner,

I have serious doubts on the possibility of maintaining a system consistent with our national traditions and the true aspirations of our people.[94]

And Dejean predicted on 29 January 1948:

All is happening as if the Communists had received instructions to take absolute control of the government and to have the country set on the same course as the other Eastern democracies by election time (April–May).[95]

These worries proved to be justified. In February, Beneš was convinced that the separation of Europe into two blocs would inevitably lead to renewed conflict. He ascribed the blame to both Czechoslovak Communists and the Anglo-Saxons, regretting that France was not able to play its mediating role. Masaryk shared these same worries a few weeks before his death.[96] It was under these circumstances that the Prague coup took place; a 'pre-fabricated revolution', 'bloodless coup', which, in American eyes, 'only crystallized and confirmed Czech politics'. However, they were concerned about possible repercussions in western Europe. General Catroux drew strategic conclusions from the crisis, which the Soviets had begun, because the rewards were great and the losses few.[97]

On 26 February, France – a meagre compensation – took the initiative with a common Western protest. The grabbing of power by the Communists became a counter-model 'masterpiece of Soviet strategy', with many lessons of all sorts to be learnt.[98] Prague was no longer a potential ally, but rather a privileged observation post for Maurice Dejean. The post became more and more difficult, materially and psychologically, and Dejean asked to leave in November 1948. General Papousek, of the Ministry of Defence, was to say a few months later to Colonel Helliot: 'For us, France is finished.'[99]

Notes

1 Cf. A. Marès, 'Free France and Central and Oriental Europe (1940–1944)', *Revue des études slaves*, LIV/3, (1982), 305–36.
2 Ibid., pp. 313–14.
3 Ibid., pp. 330–1.
4 Example, Nosek's 2 July 1945 brief n. 6811 (Archives of the Czechoslovak Ministry of Foreign Affairs, henceforth AMZV, 'in' briefs n. 2357/Paris 112a, secret).
5 Robert Luc's 6 January 1945 brief, A/1836, 9 pages, private archives.
6 AMAE, Europe series 1944–1949, Czechoslovakia n. 36 (henceforth AMAE, TS), T. secret 18 December 1944/AL/CL 132 of J. E. Paris, London to Paris.

7   Ibid., Czechoslovakia n. 56, T de Garreau n.182–7, 28 January 1945 from Moscow, and information of the 5th desk of the EMA, 29 May 1945 and this despite the guarantees given by Beneš to Massigli (*Ibid*, Czechoslovakia. 48, V. confidential brief n. 553 26 February 1945, from London for Bidault).

8   Ibid.,

9   Rep. by General Catroux, France's ambassador to Moscow. *Idem*, Czechoslovakia. n.36, tel. n. 1107–111, 28 March 1945.

10 AMAE, Poland n. 54. Sent there by General de Gaulle, Christian Fouchet concludes on 3 March 1945 'France must be satisfied with maintaining her spiritual and cultural influence in Poland [...]. Not to abandon the London government out of fidelity to a body that died of a violent death would be to abandon the Poles.'

11 AMZV/general secretary sources/ Zourek 1945–54, n.3, brief from London, 10 May 1945, n. 11477/45, confidential to Nejedlý, Minister of Culture.

12 AMZV, 'in' briefs, ZU 1945 box n. 84, D. n.187 from Paris, 1 June 1945. (Ibid., *Nouvelles politiques de Paris*, PZ Paris 1945, message 29 May, from London 12 June).

13 AMAE, ibid., Czechoslovakia. n. 48, 20 May 1945 report, top secret and n. 68, brief Europe Dep., 12 June 1945.

14 SHAT, EMGDN/ 2nd desk, brief by Lt.-Col. Escarra n. 978.

15 Idem. n. 58, briefs 9 and 11 June 1945. In brief n. 9 he specified 'It is useless denying the considerable reduction of our situation on the political level in Prague. Though our retreat is not so much due to our military defeat or our material poverty as to the presence of the fearsome ally with which Czechoslovakia will henceforth have a common border.' Then he mirrored Prague's claims by writing to the Quai: 'I would like to have a far-left professor and a Communist party member. That would show our friends that we, too, look at these formulas which scare them so awfully, and our enemies that we are not replacing fascism [...]. At least, as long as the Russians are here, we cannot accept that Prague become a battlefield where we have already lost.' A relatively optimistic point of view shared by the military attaché, General Flippo. (Archives of the Army's History Department (SHAT), EMDGN, 5 p. 65, reports of 15 June and 7 August 1945), victim of certain gullible discussion partners in good faith. In fact, General Svoboda was constantly two-faced with his French discussion partners. The introduction of his 'cultural officers' was to be a definitive step towards taking control of the army. Their first national conference took place in September 1947.

16 14 June 1945: brief by Robert Luc, A 2932, AMAE, Czechoslovakia n. 48 (visa by Henri Roux).

17 'I consider it slightly excessive that the Czechoslovak president should present as a model of acceptable democracy for Western Europe a system in which it is only with the agreement of a foreign government that the inner reform programme is drafted and in which Moscow's approval is sought before that of the number of political parties whose existence is allowed.' (Ibid., n. 1845 EU, 31 July 1945 to Georges Bidault.)

18 Ibid., brief n. 51, 5 July 1945.

19 Which he put in these terms a few months later 'The French must understand that they will succeed in this country only by treating it fraternally, on even ground, and always consider their mission in the light of reciprocity.' Cf. *Une*

Histoire de l'Institut Français de Prague. Les cahiers de la Stepanska, (Prague, 1993) p. 35.

20 Ibid., General Leclerc's report of July 1945, *vis-à-vis* Bidault, Dejean and Roux and a secret note by Keller brought back by Leclerc and approved by Bidault. (Europe binder n. 68.) On 18 August, after dinner with General de Gaulle, René Capitant, Maurice Dejean and some civil servants from the Foreign Office, Nosek wrote to Prague that he could measure the impact of Leclerc's favourable report on the French position. (AMZV, PZ Paris, July 1945, Nosek to London, and note on the economic ties between Czechoslovakia and France, 5 March 1951, General Secretary, box 150, n. 3552.) Financial and commercial discussions were begun simultaneously that month, after Hervé Alphand's initiative, before resulting in a six-month agreement, signed in Paris by Ripka and Bidault on 24 October, based on an old agreement of 2 July 1928.

21 AMAE, Czechoslovakia. n. 58. 'Not a single important question divides both Republics, who have similar visions of democracy and who are both aiming at the reform of similar structures. France has engaged to help Czechoslovakia gain its independence again and its territorial integrity.[...] We should beware of disappointing our Czechoslovakian friends.' The author added that France would soon profit from the U-turn which could take place concerning the Soviets. The content of this brief was taken up again on 7 December (cf. Czechoslovakia. n. 36, signed J. G., under-desk Oriental Europe, for General de Gaulle).

22 AMAE, USSR n. 33 and 54.

23 The visit was delayed because of the dissolution of the French government (AMZV, in telegrams ZU 1945, volume n. 4).

24 AMAE, Czechoslovakia. n. 36.

25 AMAE, TS n.58, T. n. 358–61, 28 December 1945.

26 Ibid., TS n. 56, D. Europe n. 55, 9 January 1946.

27 AMZV, General Secretary, box 65, 14 January 1946 brief, n. 7478/A/46.

28 AMAE, TS n. 48 (T. top secret 14 January 1946, n. 76).

29 Confidential telegram n. 45–6, 18 January 1946 AMAE.

30 This was in fact an alliance and assistance treaty project submitted by the Poles to the French on 15 October 1945 instead of the text of 19 February 1921: the French handed it back on 19 April 1946 after having altered it considerably concerning the engagements towards Germany.

31 T. n. 368–9 of 24 April 1946 from the Ministry to Prague, reserved and top secret from Paris n. 1232/B/46, Nosek (AMZV, 'in' briefs, Paris archive).

32 Confidential T. n. 614–17, 27 April 1946.

33 AMZV, 'in' briefs, Paris reserves, n. 1235/B/46.

34 Ibid., n. 1315 and 1316/B/1946, 5 May 1946.

35 AMAE, TS n. 58, T. confi., 10 July 1946, n. 931–3.

36 Ibid., confid. T. n. 949–50, 15 July 1946.

37 Beneš did not understand 'his' National-Socialist party's defeat. Dejean explained this result by the fact that the Communist Party stood as a government party with an agile agricultural policy, and because they occupied the Home Office and Ministry of Information cabinet posts. AMAE, TS n. 37, T. 775–7, 28 May 1946.

38 AMZV, General Secretary, box 65, brief on talk between Clementis and Dejean, 24 June 1946.

39   The 29 July Czechoslovakian indications before the Paris Conference specify that 'our delegation should most of all make sure of solving the Hungarian problem by forcing Hungary to accept all the Hungarians remaining on our soil after the exchanges and the re-Slovakization' (AMZV, General Secretary 1945–1954, box 87).

40   AMZV, General Secretary, 1945–1954, vol. 89, T. from Heidrich to Moscow n. 118, 27 June 1946. Ibid., France vol. 148, a note of 28 June on talks between Bidault, Clementis and Masaryk in Paris the day before.

41   AMZV, ibid., and AMAE, T.S. n. 53, 5 July tel. by Dejean n. 910–12.

42   AMAE, TS n. 58, secret tel. n. 665–6.

43   SHAT, TS, report n. 434 of 30 July 1946, archive. Military Attaché in Prague.

44   Pavel Tigrid denounced this direction in *Lidova Demokracie* and the fact that Prague would benefit 'neither from the West's nor the East's confidence'. He underlined the contradiction between the intellectual and economic links his country had with the West and its diplomatic and military ties with the East, whose artificial nature he implied.

45   For one year, which was to be prorogued by six months in July 1947 (cf. AMAE, TS n. 64).

46   AMAE, TS n. 58 and Dejean Papers, tel. n. 1017, 3 August 1946.

47   Ibid., TS n. 49, brief n. 2864 to Louis Roche, Chargé d'Affaires in London, to Bidault, 27 July 1946.

48   Dejean Papers (AMAE), note from the summer of 1946 (in the dossier 'Franco-Czechoslovak project', not signed) recapitulated the arguments in favour and against it and came to the conclusion of 'not rushing into things'.

49   He attributed this change of style to a favourable evolution in French home politics – confirmed by the visits by the Communist Jacques Duclos and the Socialist Gaston Defferre – which can be explained by the insufficient Soviet aid in the Hungarian episode, the compatibility of the Alliances between Paris and Moscow, by the re-emergence of France on the international scene and by the worries arising from traditional dangers: German, Polish and Hungarian.

50   AMZV, 'in' briefs, Paris archive, n. 2178/B/1946, Clementis to Gottwald, 19 August 1946, n. 220.

51   AMAE, TS n. 58, 26 August tel., visa by H R (Roux).

52   AMAE, TS n. 53, volume on the Hungarian question.

53   AMZV, General Secretary, 1945–1954, box 87, handwritten and corrected text.

54   Ibid., TS n. 49, T. n.1320, very confidential, by J. P. Garnier, to Prague, 6 November 1946, visa by HR and FC (Roux and Coulet).

55   AMZV, archive. General Secretary 1945–1954, box 87.

56   AMZV, political briefs in Paris 1947, n. 63, confidential, Nosek, 31 January 1947, 'in' briefs n. 332/B 47, same day, n. 58.

57   For the Mixed Commission reunion foreseen by article 2 of 29 July 1946 ruling, in Prague from 27 January to 3 February 1947.

58   AMAE, TS n. 58.

59   'Within the context of the current international discussions', so as to 'alter the existing treaties in time to make Franco-Czechoslovak collaboration tighter concerning general security and the reconstruction of Europe and the World.' AMZV, General Secretary, arch. Zourek n. 4.

60   AMAE, TS n. 58, 19 February from Dejean and brief on Nosek's visit to Chauvel, General Secretary of French Foreign Ministry.

61 Ibid., tel. 27 February n.115–17, and AMZV, General Secretary, box 65, brief on talk between Dejean and Clementis 26 February 1947.

62 *L'année politique*, Editions du grand siècle, 1947, p. 89 and AMAE, ibid., and n. 56. Dejean also announced the imminent signature of a Polish–Czechoslovak treaty which he attributed to the 'tenacity with which the Kremlin rulers are pursuing their politics of solidarity among Slavs. The fact that the communists exert great influence over the Prague and Warsaw governments is not irrelevant either.' Brief n. 309/EU 5 March, AMAE, TS n. 52. The pact was effectively settled for 20 years on 10 March. Soviet pressure explained this conclusion in many ways. If Dejean was able to see positive aspects, the Quai's notes on the document proved the astonishment of those who read his brief. In fact, the French ambassador was, in a prewar historical perspective, unaware of their dependence on Moscow and the creation of blocs.

63 Cf. his '*Journal du septennat*', tome I 1947, (Paris: Armand Colin, 1970), July and even August, Auriol continued to believe in France's capacity as a mediator.

64 The Ambassador added: 'I can see the moral advantage we will gain by a document which would erase the memory of Munich in Czechoslovakia, but [...] I'd rather we were careful and not put ourselves in a position where, if one day a conflict of interests concerning Germany were to occur between Prague and Moscow, we'd find it difficult to honour our engagements.' Brief, 31 March 1947, n. 909.

65 AMZV, political briefs, Paris 1947, confidential brief n. 197, 1 April 1947, secret.

66 Cf. Dejean papers, T. n. 669, 18 June by Dejean (AMAE, TS n. 49).

67 Cf. brief n. 570, 14 May and n. 669, 18 June by Dejean (AMAE, TS n. 49).

68 A real dispute then ensued between both diplomats: cf. Dejean Papers, correspondence with Massigli, who concludes on 28 June with a personal letter to Chauvel: 'the future will say if I was right or wrong.'

69 Ibid., TS n. 58.

70 AMAE, TS n. 48, ambassadorial counsellor Bombright to Courcel, 22 May 1947 brief, about 'the regrettable effect of bilateral pacts'. It does in fact concern the Polish–Czechoslovak pact, rapidly ratified on 14 May by the Czechoslovak parliament.

71 Cf. AMAE, TS n. 58, brief by Epinat 26 May 1947.

72 One can see in these echoes the double intoxification of those who wished to hurry the signature and those who wished to arouse defiance towards France. One should remark on the huge presence of senior Soviet officials in Czechoslovakia during the month of May – Marshall Konev, General Antonov, Vychinsky and so on. Cf. AMAE, TS n. 58.

73 AMZV, 'in' brief, n. 1303/B/4, Nosek, 10 May.

74 While Prague wanted the subject of the treaties with Yugoslavia and Poland to be brought up, Paris only mentioned the USSR and Great Britain. There was no question of extending the guarantees to 'potential allies of Germany' either, even if Gottwald insisted on this, said Clementis, as a guarantee against Hungary. Ibid., n. 1395/B/47, 13 June 1947, talk between Nosek and Couve de Murville; General Secretary, box n. 65, secret report of the talk between Clementis and Dejean, 6 June, and T. by Dejean, 6 June n. 428–34, visa by F. Coulet (AMAE, TS n. 59).

75   Ever since 14 June, he had stated that differences had appeared between Masaryk and Clementis, the first wanting to precipitate the signature, the second to defer it. On 16 June, Clementis requested of Dejean that the USSR, Yugoslavia and Poland be consulted. The dilatory manoeuvre was obvious and Dejean replied by saying he did not see the use of such contacts. AMAE, ibid., T. by Dejean. Finally, he suggested coming between 28 June and 13 July (AMAE, TS n. 59).

76   AMZV, 'in' briefs Paris, n. 1621/B/1947, Nosek n. 338, 14 June.

77   Ibid., General Secretary 1945–1954, box 87, t. 132 104/GS/47.

78   Ibid., box 150, n. 132 102/GS/47, 20 June 1947.

79   In this case the 1947–48 current biennial plan. Ibid., box 87, June–July 1947.

80   AMAE, TS n. 59, T. n. 540–6 from Prague, 3 July.

81   Ibid., brief to Viliam Siroký, president of the Slovak Communist Party, 6 July.

82   Cf. ibid., Dejean's report after speaking to Masaryk, Drtina and Heydrich, brief of 15 July, v. secret n. 623.

83   Ibid., Nosek n. 388, 10 July 1947.

84   It would be superfluous to describe this episode, amply described by Czechoslovak witnesses. The precise date of the Soviet rejection however remains unknown. Were the previous delays on 2 July mere tactics?

85   AMAE, TS n. 59.

86   AMZV, General Secretary, box 150, brief n. 160 388/A/47. Finally, an initial delay of two weeks was mentioned during a meeting between Dejean and Masaryk on 1 August (ibid., archive. Zourek, box 5).

87   AMZV, 'in' briefs, Paris, n. 2054/B/47, Nosek 421, 31 July 1947.

88   AMAE, TS n. 39, brief n. 1030/EU.

89   AMZV, General Secretary, France 1945–1954, n. 150. Letter in Slovak.

90   Namely Joseph and Stewart Alsop, close to Bohlen, on the Saturday Evening of 20 November 1947.

91   AMAE, URSS, n. 36, b. n. 1124, 19 November 1947.

92   AMAE, TS n. 59. Brief, 4 December 1947.

93   Ibid., T. secret n. 3, 2 January 1948.

94   Ibid., TS n. 49, T. n. 1028, 12 December by Dejean.

95   Ibid., TS n. 50, T. secret by Dejean, 29 January n. 88–91 (vis-à-vis Europe).

96   Ibid., TS n.50.

97   Ibid., TS n. 40, T. by Catroux, 27 February, n. 403–8, from Moscow. 'It appears that to escape these [Soviet] plans, it is now up to Europe to establish a counterweight system able to oppose power with power as soon as possible and thereby force Moscow to act.'

98   'While President Beneš loyally tried to establish a transition zone in the heart of Europe where both rival political attitudes would meet, while he attempted to create a synthesis between Communist Russia and an Eastern democracy, Gottwald's friends were quietly grabbing the reins of power.' 'A decisive factor in the passage from governmental activity to revolutionary activity has been the decay of the international situation during the past summer [. . .] October's events seemed to announce February's [. . .] it is likely that the Kominform had put its plan to advance Czechoslovakia in line with the Eastern bloc.' Ibid., TS n.41, 18–page brief by Dejean, 5 March 1948, n. 143/EU.

99   Ibid., TS n. 34, Helliot n. 54, 8 March 1949.

10
Italy and Eastern Europe, 1943–48

Giorgio Petracchi

Reading the volume *Il Ministero degli Affari Esteri al servizio del popolo italiano, 1943–1948*,[1] one discovers the typical *trompe l'oeil* which historians, and readers of E. H. Carr, have learnt to regard as 'neither unusual, nor astonishing'. The book, published in 1949, aims to give the general public an idea of the achievements of Italian foreign policy, with a detailed report of Italy's policy towards the West, and its remarkably successful achievements in this area. On the other hand, relations with east central Europe and the Soviet Union, where there had been hardly any tangible results, receive hardly any mention at all. Central Europe, the Danube States and the Balkans are left in the wings for the entire period, except when they make a brief appearance between September 1943 and September 1944; the Soviet Union is given a timid walk-on part.

The true state of affairs is rather different. In the first instance, Italian foreign policy did not follow blindly in the footsteps of Western policy. From 1944 to 1946 and later, Italian diplomacy tried to compensate for the overwhelming presence of the Anglo-American forces in the peninsula by maintaining constant and active diplomatic relations with Moscow.[2] Italian politicians followed suit in trying to establish stable relations of friendship and collaboration with the Soviet Union and with those European countries that were entering its sphere of military, political and economic influence.

This may have been an illusion: yet Italian diplomacy believed it could use geography (some have called it Italy's 'geographical Machiavellism') to establish, between 1944 and 1947, a policy of equidistance from both Britain and Russia. To be equidistant, or to act as a link or bridge between Britain and Russia, was an illusion held by several politicians: certainly by Communist Palmiro Togliatti, possibly because of his political affinities; but by the Socialists too, like the elderly Ivanoe Bonomi and the leader, Pietro Nenni; or by instinct as in the case of the Christian Democrat leader, Alcide De Gasperi; or even the Republican Ferruccio Parri and Carlo Sforza, the heirs to the Risorgimento. Obsessed by the idea of a division of Europe into two opposing blocs and eager to discover the exact centre for a position of equidistance, both politicians and diplomats turned to Moscow with expressions 'that can today be held, quite rightly, as either visionary or unusefully servile'.[3]

The foreign policy of the Kingdom of the South towards eastern Europe was conceived during the winter 1943–44 and launched on 14 March 1944 by re-establishing diplomatic relations with the Soviet Union.

With rare exceptions, Italian historians have underestimated the international significance of this debut, considering it to be merely a preliminary of the 'Salerno turning-point' (the entry of the Communist Party into the Badoglio government) – that it was an expression of domestic policy. This omission is deliberate, rather than casual. Communist historians wished to affirm the continuity of the PCI's Italian tradition, whereas the Action Party historians wished to underscore the current controversy over the form of the State. Liberal historians saw this move towards Moscow as merely contingent on the need to escape the straitjacket of the armistice. Here was yet another reductive interpretation that, during the Cold War, tended to diminish the international significance of renewed relations with the USSR.

There is another reason why the international significance of the 'Salerno turning-point' in relations with the USSR and east-central Europe and the Balkans has been virtually ignored. First, the overtures made to Moscow were a deliberate move by Italian professional diplomats. At a moment in which the machinery of State and politics had almost ground to a halt, the few remaining career diplomats were able to wield real influence over Italian foreign policy. To renew relations with the USSR was undoubtedly a traditional move, based on pre-Fascist (as well as Fascist) doctrine.[4] We have seen how this emerged between 1900 and 1914, during the golden era of the Kingdom of Italy's foreign policy. When it was reformulated in 1943–44, it corresponded not so much (or not only) to the ideological motive of granting the Communist Party a constructive role, but to nationalist motives, that is the defence of the State by safeguarding its national territory, its economic interests and political influence. Italian diplomats had noted that the balance in Europe had shifted eastwards. As in the past they had always sought the protection of the strongest power, here, too, they tried to lean on the state that was to play a hegemonic role in the area. The shift towards

Moscow, as a strategy, was meant to exploit traditional Russian sympathy for Italy to the full.

The man chosen to represent this policy in Moscow was Pietro Quaroni, one of Italy's a most brilliant career diplomats, who possessed a thorough knowledge of Russia and Communism. He was a nationalist (and not even very moderate), who applied the parameters of the political realism he had learnt from Gaetano Mosca and Vilfredo Pareto. To complete the picture, one must add that he nurtured a strong anti-British sentiment. In the British Foreign Office, people remembered that when Quaroni was minister in Afghanistan, he had been pretty keen on anti-British activities. Quaroni himself, once in Moscow, boasted how, in association with Chandra Bose, he had arranged anti-British plans 'to outwit my British friends'.[5] Briefly, Quaroni was believed capable of any intrigue and seen as a *thoroughly 'faux bonhomme'*[6]. Suspicions increased because of his wife, a Russian *byvshaja* (*ci-devant*), considered to be 'a violent communist'[7] and 'a most dangerous woman'.[8] Quaroni, in other words, was considered to be a rather undesirable person from the British point of view. The British, therefore, had been rather surprised to hear of Quaroni arriving in Moscow in May 1944. During the first months of his mission, both Sir A. Clark Kerr, British ambassador, and Averell Harriman, his American colleague in Moscow, suspected Quaroni and his wife of playing 'the Russians off against the Western Powers'.[9] Quaroni arrived in Moscow on 27 May 1944. The government had already given him the task of making Russia Italy's advocate vis-à-vis the Allies. Quaroni saw at once that this task could never have been achieved. Thus, he changed his line. He conducted a policy aimed at the future, trying to edge the government towards granting Italy a position within Russia's European policy. In setting the sights of Soviet behaviour, he played the role of prompter for the 'policy of equidistance' between the Russians and the Anglo-Americans. In accordance with Quaroni's analysis, Italy's (still called the Kingdom of the South) east European policy was conceived to gain Russian confidence. Nevertheless, by September 1945, Quaroni was already becoming more and more disillusioned with the Russians.

As far as Italy's interests were concerned, the effects of the war and of the '8th September' on eastern Europe could be divided into three scenarios, distinct in both the situations and problems they had left behind. The first scenario centred on the Gulf of Trieste; the second comprised central Europe; the third included the States of the Danube and the Balkans, Hungary, Romania, Bulgaria – the former satellites of Germany.

The question of Trieste and of the eastern frontier was becoming, once again, like the problem of the Adriatic in 1919–20, the crucial issue in Italian politics. The question is so well-known and has caused so much ink to flow, that we shall not deal with it here, except with regard to Italy's Eastern policy.

Beginning with the renewed relations with Poland and Czechoslovakia, the case of Poland proves the lengths to which Italian diplomacy was prepared to go in order to gain Moscow's friendship. The Polish issue was the first and the most acute test for the Big Three. Obviously, this involved recognizing the legitimate Polish government: but which government should be recognized as legitimate, the one in exile in London since 1940, or the Polish National Committee of Liberation, set up by the Soviets at Lublin during the summer of 1944? The problem arose in the summer of 1944 and came to light in the winter of 1945.

In September 1943, the Polish Embassy in London approached the British Foreign Office asking for the protection of Polish interests in Italy. The matter was postponed until the capture of Rome, but the presence of the Polish 2nd Corps in Italy gave the request of the 'London Poles' particular weight.

When Rome had been liberated (June 1944), the Polish government appointed as its representative with the Allied authorities in Italy and requested the Allies consent, Mr Sydom Maciej Loret, who was a kind of esteemed *Kunsthistoriker* and former Polish Chargé d'Affaires in Rome during 1920–21. After the Fascist government had closed the Polish embassy in Rome, in June 1940, the former Polish ambassador in Italy, Wieniawa-Dlugoszowski, had asked Loret to stay in Rome in an unofficial capacity as the representative of Polish interests in Italy. Contacts with him had been established via the Polish embassy at the Holy See. The Poles also nominated a consul for Southern Italy and other agents to deal with displaced persons.

On 14 June, the Polish ambassador in London, Władisław Kulsky, demanded the presence of a Polish representative with the Allies in Italy, not an independent representative to the Italian government like the Soviets had, but a sort of representative besides a consul.[10]

The proposal was, for reasons of prestige, connected with the part played by the Polish troops in the Italian campaign and in view of the entry of the Red Army into Poland and of the extent of the Soviet presence in Italy.

The Polish government wanted to go far and fast with the Italians. The 'London Poles' feared that if they did not take the initiative and did not send a diplomatic representative to Rome, the Italian government would have proceeded to something like recognition of the Lublin Committee.[11]

The unofficial mission of Maciej Loret led in fact to the virtual re-establishment of direct relations between Poland and Italy with the exchange of letters on 8 and 10 November 1944.[12] On January 1945, the Polish government in London appointed Stanisław Janikowski to Rome as its Chargé d'Affaires ad interim to the Italian government.[13] Italy did not do likewise.

As early as September 1944, Quaroni had convinced the Italian government that it should regard the Lublin Committee as Poland's only true government.[14] Yet, the Italian Premier and Foreign Minister, Ivanoe Bonomi, influenced by the Vatican's diplomatic channels, was prepared to recognize the Polish government in London.[15]

The international situation had changed – as Quaroni pointed out again on 21 December.[16] It had changed to the disadvantage of the Polish government in London and in favour of the Lublin National Committee (it was transformed into the Polish Provisional Government on 31 December 1944, when it took office in Warsaw; in Italy it was called the Lublin or Warsaw government). The Italians asked for more time.[17] They realized how important it was not to offend the Soviet authorities, hoping to co-operate with them to provide some relief to Italian refugees in Poland, numbering no less than 50 000. Therefore, they laid no emphasis on the re-establishment of diplomatic relations with the 'London Poles', and recommended that any official appointed to represent the Italian government with the Polish government while in London should also be accredited to Norway and Czechoslovakia.[18]

In the meantime, Quaroni and Zygmunt Modzelewski, the ambassador to Moscow of the Polish Provisional Government in Warsaw, negotiated an agreement to assist and repatriate Italian prisoners-of-war in Poland. Quaroni wished to endow the agreement and the exchange of delegates not only with humanitarian, but with political, value too. Alcide De Gasperi, the new Foreign Minister, would have certainly preferred to restrict it to its humanitarian aspects only.[19] He knew the hostile joint position of the British Foreign Office and the US State Department on the Italian recognition of the Lublin Committee: they were making joint representations to Prunas, the Secretary-General of the Italian Ministry for Foreign Affairs, pointing out that they 'could not view with any favour any move by the Italian government to send a diplomatic representative to Lublin'.[20] Therefore, De Gasperi was careful to send no one to Lublin other than an official with Red Cross duties.

Quaroni's arguments, in the light of the results of the Yalta conference, were inspired by political realism. Quaroni felt the Italian government should recognize the Provisional government in Warsaw so long as
Italy wanted Polish coal, Polish co-operation for the welfare and repatri-
ation of the Italian prisoners, Poland's support on the question of Trieste
and, also, if Italy wanted to obtain Moscow's friendship. De Gasperi's
thinking was determined by other, equally realistic, circumstances: Italy
could not set itself up against Great Britain and the US, and against the
'London Poles', so long as the Polish contingent was fighting gallantly
on the Italian front.

In fact, the agreement signed in Moscow on 28 April 1945 by Quaroni
and Modzelewski lent itself to a broader interpretation in that it implied
de facto recognition.[21] Without doubt, problems with communications
between Rome and Moscow favoured these discrepancies in important
respects.[22] The account of the agreement communicated on 3 May by
Prunas to Noel Charles, the British representative in Rome, differed in
important respects from a statement broadcast from Moscow on the
same day. In the Prunas communication the agreement appeared to
contain six articles,[23] while in Moscow's broadcast of the text contained
ten articles. What was more important, Article 8 of the agreement
appeared to treat the Lublin Committee as the government of all Polish
nationals in Italy, and Article 9 stated that 'both Governments have
come to an understanding about the exchange of diplomatic representatives within the shortest time possible'.[24] In any case, Prunas played
on the discrepancies between the articles he had received and those that
had been published by the Polpress Agency and on their possible different interpretations.

In the words of Beckett of the Foreign Office, it was a 'very muddled
question from a legal point of view'.[25] To the Anglo-Americans, Prunas
protested that the conclusion of the agreement did not imply any Italian
recognition of the Warsaw government at all.[26] On the other hand, he
had reassured the Soviets that the agreement was 'a real contract *de facto*'
namely he called the Lublin Committee the Polish Government.[27]

A Northern Department official of the Foreign Office drew the more
realistic conclusion: 'From the Italian point of view the agreement with
the Lublin government appears highly satisfactory, at least on paper' –
noted Ross, who added: 'All this was, of course, inevitable once the
Italian government took the first step. Considering the probable
number of Italians in Poland I find it hard to blame them.'[28]

Nevertheless, Anglo-American official pressure on Prunas compelled
the Italian Foreign Minister to accept the agreement's more restrictive

interpretation, underscoring the humanitarian role of the delegates and to delay the departure of the Italian Red Cross delegate, Count Eugenio Jaccarino, who left for Poland on 2 September 1945.

On 6 July 1945, the Italian government at last recognized, together with Great Britain and the US, the Polish Provisional Government of National Unity. Then, it disclaimed the 'London Poles', closed its consular offices in Italy, and accepted the appointment of the Polish Provisional Government representative in Rome, Eugeniusz Markowski. At the same time, Eugenio Reale, a leading member of the Italian Communist Party, was appointed ambassador in Warsaw. The 'second phase' of the Polish question in Italy was just beginning. Italo-Czech relations serve as a 'case study' on the two countries' attempts to find an 'equidistance'. It shows how, from 1944 to 1946, both diplomats and politicians (De Gasperi and Nenni, no less than Jan Masaryk and Eduard Beneš) endeavoured to remove their respective countries from the logic of the spheres of influence, trying to build a somewhat autonomous bridge between Prague and Rome. In both countries it was the Socialists who supported this policy.

Following the days after the '8th September', Minister Paolo Cortese and all the Legation secretaries of the Italian mission to Slovakia remained loyal to the Italian Monarchy. On 28 September, when Slovakia's government acknowledged Mussolini's Republican Government, the male personnel were interned.[29] A year later, during the session of 26 September 1944, the Italian Council of Ministers repudiated the Munich Agreements of 29 September 1938, together with the so-called Vienna award of Ciano and Ribbentrop of 2 November 1938.[30] By repudiating its past, the Italian government showed it wanted to renew co-operation with the states that had re-emerged from the former territory of Czechoslovakia. This was achieved within a few months. By early April 1945, Gastone Guidotti became Chargé d'Affaires *ad interim* with the Czech government in exile in London, and the Czech consul general Vladimir Vanek became minister in Rome.[31]

Italian diplomats sought Czech support on the defence of Italy's eastern frontier and the possession of the city of Trieste, on the colonies and reparations, as well as the Alto Adige issue. Nor was the economic programme less intense: co-operation went ahead until an agreement was signed (10 February 1947) to send Italian workers to Czechoslovakia in exchange for coal.[32] In the end, almost nothing remained of these premisses and programmes. After Beneš had made the first overtures, the Czech government towed the Moscow line on all issues, which involved the question of Slav brotherhood. Italian analysts felt that

Beneš was forced to agree with Moscow in his attempt to conduct an independent domestic policy and maintain some ties with the Western Powers.

In Germany's three satellites – Hungary, Romania and Bulgaria – we can speak of a real '8th September' in diplomacy, which is best recounted chronologically.

Bucharest and Budapest had simultaneously two Italian delegations, one for the Republic of Salò, the other for the Kingdom of the South. The Hungarian and Romanian governments recognized both, giving rise to absurd diplomatic incidents.

Bulgaria was a case apart. Members of the Italian Legation remained faithful, on the whole, to the Kingdom in the South. Unfortunately for them, the country was still under the military and diplomatic control of Germany, so that the Badoglio diplomats were interned in the Varchtes camp. However, thanks to the complicity of the Bulgarian authorities, the head of the mission, Francesco Giorgio Mameli, via the Italian Legation in Ankara, carried on a precarious and sporadic correspondence with the government in the South of Italy. Then, on September 1944, the Soviet tanks entered Sofia; the Legation resumed its role of representing Italian interests, continuing to do so throughout Soviet occupation.[33] The same was true of the Legation in Bucharest. The Salò diplomats in both countries were arrested and delivered to the Russians, who conveyed them to Moscow and imprisoned them for years.

The Legation in Budapest had a harder time of it: on March 1944, when the Germans invaded Hungary, they interned all the members of the Badoglio Legation: a year later, when the Soviet troops liberated Budapest, they were first set free, only to be interned again and expelled on March 1945. A split within the personnel of the Italian Legation between two tendencies, the so-called 'Badogliani' and the so-called 'reds', contributed to their expulsion. There was to be no Italian representative in Hungary until the autumn of 1946.[34]

The fact that Italian diplomats remained in Bucharest and Sofia, meant that Italian interests continued to be represented, as best they could, even vis-à-vis the Soviet occupying authorities. In Hungary, where Italian political influence and interests were strongest, the Soviets cleared the area of any form of representation to prevent Italy from having a basis on which to build new relations.

The question of how to defend Italian interests in the Danube and Balkan area was, of course, paramount for the Italian government. Article 25/B of the Long Armistice Terms conferred upon the United

Nations the right to determine the extent of the Italian government's diplomatic relations with neutral and former enemy countries. In practice, Italian Legations abroad could only communicate with the Italian government through the Allied Control Commission in Italy.

Of course, after Soviet recognition (14 March 1944), the Italian government tried to move fast along the path towards resuming its relations with former enemy countries. The Italian government emphasized that diplomatic relations between Italy and Romania, as between Italy and Bulgaria, were never formally broken off, but merely suspended for a period due to *force majeure*. The Romanian government also was eager to resume relations with Italy. On 22 December 1944, Mr Teodoro Scorzescu, Counsellor of the Romanian Legation to the Holy See, was appointed Minister *ad interim* of the Romanian Legation to the Quirinal.[35] During the session of 18 January 1945, the Italian Council of Ministers repudiated the so-called 'Second Vienna Award' drawn up by Ciano and Ribbentrop on 30 August 1940 relating to the Hungary–Romania dispute over Transylvania.

In principle, the Russians and Anglo-Americans would not permit the re-establishment of direct diplomatic relations between Romania, Bulgaria and Italy so long as the three principal Allies had only informal representation in Bucharest. On February 1945, the Big Three reached a general agreement on the point, deciding to allow a few Italian diplomats to remain in Sofia and Bucharest to establish 'unofficial' contacts with those governments.[36] The Italian government relied on Quaroni's good offices with the Soviet authorities to ensure that Italy's diplomatic capabilities were extended to Sofia and Bucharest to safeguard Italian interests in these countries.

As early as September 1944, Quaroni had had the foresight to predict Britain's defeat in the Balkans. Naturally, what he meant was that the British would lose all political influence there.[37] Even in September 1944, Quaroni thought the USSR would opt for a system of collective security, rather than the creation of zones of influence. In his view it was quite natural for the Soviet Union to seek strategic frontiers, protected by a belt of 'friendly states'. He was quite adamant that Stalin did not intend to turn the occupied countries into Communist states.[38]

Within this framework, Quaroni urged Italy to detach itself from the British policy in the Balkans and, second, to modify its own anti-Slav policy, based on Hungary and partly on Romania.[39] Between the autumn of 1944 and that of 1945, Quaroni slowly changed his view of Soviet foreign policy. After 'mature reflection', he decided that Stalin had reverted to the doctrine of 'spheres of influence' in eastern

Europe.[40] The Italian ambassador in Bucharest, Bova Scoppa, had reached the same conclusion a year earlier.[41] Vojtech Mastny has pointed out that in Stalin's view a quest for security underlay the Ribbentrop–Molotov pact. In the second postwar period this quest was transformed into the search for a kind of 'total security' through the replication of the Soviet system in eastern Europe.[42]

In autumn 1945, Quaroni lost any illusion of 'making the Russians the advocates for Italy'. The disillusionment of the ambassador fell on the anti-Russian attitude of the Italian newspapers. In October 1945, the Italian Communist leader, Palmiro Togliatti, complained to Prunas about the deterioration in Italo-Russian relations, when he emphasized that 'the two countries were on better terms under Marshal Badoglio's government'.[43]

Soviet efforts to carry favour with the Italians had included: a promise to repatriate Italian prisoners of war and to export the raw materials necessary to enable Italian shipyards to build ships for the USSR; the Polish–Italian commercial agreement to send monthly 100 000 tons of coal; Molotov's 'most friendly' reception of De Gasperi on 24 September 1945 in London. All this left the Italian government apparently indifferent. Why? The Russians had realized that Italy was binding itself politically and economically to Great Britain and the United States. On the contrary, the Anglo-Americans were trying to prevent the Soviets from achieving the same goals in Romania and in Bulgaria. Nothing could be done. Least of all to try to play 'la grande politique' – wrote Quaroni – by exploiting friction between the Soviets and the Anglo-Americans:

> If we aspire, not so much to friendly relations, but merely to decent relations with the USSR one of the first essential conditions is to avoid the very semblance, in the Balkans and in Central Europe, of pursuing a policy that will cross Russia's path.[44]

And he began to prepare his government to accept the idea that all Italian property in Hungary, Bulgaria and Romania was to be expropriated as a form of reparations.

Quaroni's analysis became more specific in the light of the bilateral economic agreements, from 1945 to 1946, between the USSR and east-central Europe and the Balkan states. These agreements gradually included the economies of these countries within the Soviet five-year plans. In other words, the Soviets were trying to put into practice the Marxian concept of the uniqueness of the historical process; or rather they were translating foreign policy into the terms of domestic policy.

The adverse attitude Russia adopted towards Italy on many issues should be seen in the light of this 'extreme dialectic simplification'. According to Quaroni, it depended in many respects on Soviet disappointment that the Italian government had not introduced radical reforms, such as nationalization, agrarian reform and radical purges. This, then, was the structural stumbling block that Italian diplomacy first, and the Italian government later, found in the path of an Italian policy towards central Europe and the Balkans.

Yet, there was another objective limitation: the concrete impossibility of expanding economic relations with countries almost entirely without any surplus, which were then being integrated, more and more firmly, into the Soviet economic system. And last, there was the very real political limitation of the question of Trieste and of the Italo-Yugoslav frontier. Both of them were connected with the Polish problem in Italy, the 'second phase', which finally deserves a mention.

At the end of 1945 there were some 110 000 Polish troops in Italy – the great majority of which were formed by the Polish 2nd Corps, a united and strong fighting formation and a large proportion of the total number of troops under British command in Italy. These 'Anders' Polish' were known to be hostile to the Polish Provisional Government and linked to the underground opposition in Poland. From the military point of view the Polish troops played an important role in maintaining security and order in Italy: they were deployed along the whole line between Bologna–Ferrara–Padoa–Venice–Treviso–Udine to ensure the security of Venezia Giulia and maintain communications with Austria. This movement, apparently drawn up facing the Yugoslav frontier, was denounced by the Yugoslav Deputy Foreign Minister, Bebler, in an aide-mémoire on 14 February 1946. And Vyshinsky, Deputy Foreign Minister of the Soviet Union, brought the Yugoslav memorandum to the knowledge of the members of the UN Security Council.[45] The Communist international press aroused virulent attacks on General Anders and his followers for stirring up anti-Russian trouble in Poland and for anti-Communist activities in Italy.[46] Of course, the maintenance of the Polish 2nd Corps – violently hostile both to the Soviet government and to the Polish Provisional Government – was very prejudicial to Italy's relations with Russia, Poland and Yugoslavia and to whatever strategy the Soviets intended to apply on the Italian peninsula.

According to Litvinov's proposal to Stalin, Italy would be part of a zone of disengagement, a neutrality belt stretching from Norway to Italy. This situation, 'in combination with the dismemberment of Germany, if adopted, could have led to an ever greater power vacuum in

Europe that would arouse fears and competition between the East and the West'.[47] It is a fact that, as long as 'Anders' Poles' stayed in Italy, they filled not only any Italian political vacuum but also any Italian military weakness. They were withdrawn in the summer of 1946, after which the Italian Communist Party lost the elections in June 1946 for the Constituent Assembly, thus losing all hope of conquering the peninsula through political means.

Therefore, the Soviet accusation (as indeed that of the Italian Communist party) that the Italian government had not turned their sights firmly eastwards, hardly respected the truth. It served to camouflage an 'arrière-pensée'. In point of fact, in Italy there were two opposing concepts of what its policy should be towards Eastern Europe: the strategy espoused by the traditional political forces which pursued the national interest, and that of the Communist Party which pursued an internationalist policy hoping to slide Italy into the camp of 'progressive democracies'. Italian foreign policy stakes had to be placed on whatever model of society chosen, rather than where to stand on the international scene. If in the summer of 1920, the Red Army's advance on Warsaw had been on the point of determining Italy's change of camp, in 1945–47 this seemed to be about to happen again and more, when the 'iron curtain' ran from Lubeck via Eisenach, all the way to Trieste.

If the Communists were unable to conquer the peninsula politically, it must fall increasingly into a power vacuum, pointed out Quaroni at the end of 1946, 'dragging the Italian national spirit down towards desperation'.[48] It is a fact that, whereas in the eastern countries the Communists came to power by associating with nationalism, in Italy the Communist Party sacrificed Italian national prestige to Communist prestige elsewhere. In this growing military and political depression, action by Tito, as Quaroni pointed out, in co-ordination with internal movements in Italy and France would, in the opinion of the Communists, decide the outcome of the situation.

Notes

1 *Il Ministero degli Affairi Esteri al servizio del popolo italiano, 1943–1948* (Rome: Ministero degli Affari Esterli, 1949).
2 Legatus (R. Cantalupo), *Vita diplomatica di Salvatore Contarini* (Rome: Sestante, 1947) p. 142.
3 R. Gaja, *L'Italia nel mondo bipolare. Per una storia della politica estera italiana, 1943–1991* (Bologna: Il Mulino, 1995) p. 65.
4 G. Petracchi, *Da San Pietroburgo a Mosca. La diplomazia italiana in Russia, 1861–1941* (Roma: Bonacci, 1993); and by the same author, 'Le relazioni tra

l'Unione Sovietica e il Regno del Sud: una riconsiderazione della politica sovietica in Italia, 1943–1944', *Storia contemporanea*, XV (1984) pp. 11–83; B. Arcidiacono, 'La politique soviétique en Italie (1943–1945)', *Relations internationales*, n. 45 (1986) pp. 35–49.

5 Quaroni made these indiscrete references to former anti-British work at the reception given at the Polish Embassy on 23 April 1945 in connection with the signing of the Polish–Soviet Treaty. PRO: FO371/49961: ZM 2687/2687/22, letter of Frank Roberts from Moscow to Douglas F. Howard (Southern Dep.), 29 April 1945

6 PRO: FO371/49961: 4939/2687/19/G, letter from F. R. Hoyer Millar to Frank Roberts, 25 September 1945.

7 Ibid.

8 PRO: FO371/49961: ZM 2882/2687/22, letter from G. F. Squire, C. I. E. Kabul, to C. W. Baxter, 5 June 1945.

9 PRO: FO371/49961: 4939/2687/19/G, note of Hoyer Millar, 30 and 31 August 1945. As Roberts wrote to Hoyer Millar, 'Quaroni and his wife are notorious gossips, and we have to be careful as in a town like this any chance remark which could be construed in a anti-Russian way would certainly be passed on by them'. PRO: FO371/49961: ZM 5317/2687/22, 8 October 1945.

10 PRO: FO371/43965: R 9416/4173/22, letter from Kulsky to Laskey, 14 June 1944.

11 PRO: FO371/43965/: R 9416/4173/22, note of G. L. McDermott, 21 June 1944.

12 *Documenti Diplomatici Italiani DDI*, Series X, V.1, no. 496, pp. 578–9, 27 October 1944, and no. 524, pp. 600–1, 10 November 1944.

13 *DDI*, Series X, V.2, no. 47, p. 62, 30 January 1945.

14 *DDI*, Series X, V.1, no. 408, 16 September 1944.

15 *DDI*, Series X, V.1, no. 513, p. 590, 5 November 1944.

16 *DDI*, Series X, V.2, no. 11, p. 15, 20 December 1944 (received on 13 January 1945).

17 The Poles requested the appointment of an Italian representative several times. *DDI*, Series X, V. 2, no. 47, p. 61, 30 January 1945; and *Diario di Nicolò Carandini 1944–45* (Italian representative to London), introduction by Giustino Filippone Thaulero, part one, *Nuova Antologia*, 2144 (1982) pp. 353, 356–7, 359.

18 Count Carandini's proposal to the British Foreign Office; the Poles had not received any Italian representative without first obtaining British agreement. PRO: FO371/49882: ZM 313/208/22, note of A. D. M. Ross, 1 February 1945.

19 *DDI*, Series X, V. 2, no. 35, p. 47, 16 January 1945.

20 Note of A. D. M. Ross, 1 February, cit. Prunas' memorandum to De Gasperi, 1 February 1945, Archivio Storico Ministero Affari Esteri (ASMAE), Affari Politici (A.P.) 1931–1945, Polonia, b. 20, fasc. 1.

21 The original French text in ASMAE, A.P., Polonia, b. 20, fasc. 2

22 Because of the lack of secret communications between Rome and Moscow, the diplomatic correspondence was deliberately filled with allusions: *DDI*, Series X, V.2, no. 194.

23 PRO: FO371/49882: ZM5309/202/22, Sir Noel Charles to Foreign Office, no. 780, 11 May 1945. According to Prunas, the text received by telegram from

Moscow had undeciphered groups; Sir Noel Charles to Foreign Office, n. 799, 11 May 1945, ZM5292/202/22.

24   Polpress Agency on 2 May emphasized the 'mutual exchange of representatives of the two Governments'. PRO: FO371/49882:ZM2670/2O2/22.

25   PRO: FO371/49882:ZM2670/202/22, note of Mr Beckett, Northern Dept, 25 May 1945.

26   Prunas reassured Sir Noel Charles that 'it is superfluous to emphasize that agreement is for the purpose of assistance only and does not imply any recognition on our part of Warsaw Government'. Sir Noel Charles to Foreign Office, n. 799, 11 May 1945, quoted in note above.

27   *DDI*, Series X, V. 2, no. 118, p. 157, Prunas' memorandum res. to De Gasperi, 8 April 1945.

28   PRO: FO371/49882:ZM2670/2O2/22, note of A. D. M. Ross, 15 May 1945.

29   PRO: FO371/37344:R12686/8900/22, report of Guido Rocco, Italian ambassador to Ankara, on the 'Situation Réprésentation Royale en Slovaquie', 17 November 1943.

30   *DDI*, Series X, V. 1, no. 438, p. 526.

31   ASMAE, A.P., 1931–1945, 'Cecoslovacchia', 1944–45, b. 30, fasc. 9.

32   At first, it was mooted that at least 100 000 Italian workers could be sent to Czechoslovakia. The agreement of 10 February provided for the first transfer of 5 000 Italian workers. ASMAE, A.P., 1946–1950, 'Cecoslovacchia', b. 6, fasc. 7, file: 'Mano d'opera italiana in Cecoslovacchia'.

33   M. Viganò, *Il Ministero degli Affari Esteri e le relazioni internazionali nella Repubblica Sociale Italiana, 1943–1945*, (Milano: Jaca Book, 1991) pp. 207–71; comp. *DDI*, Series X, V. 1 (9 Settembre 1943–11 Dicembre 1944). Because all the communications between the Italian government in the South and its representatives in neutral and satellite countries passed through the hands of the Allied Control Commission, this diplomatic correspondence is also in PRO: FO371/37343–37344/8900/22.

34   See M. Petricioli, 'Quell'inverno a Budapest', in Ilona Fried ed., *Tra totalitarismo e democrazia, Italia e Ungheria, 1943–1953*, (Budapest, 1995) pp. 1–17; G. Reti, 'Il ristabilimento delle relazioni diplomatiche italo-ungheresi dopo la seconda guerra mondiale', *Rivista di Studi Politici Internazionali*, LXIII (1996), no. 251 pp. 390–8.

35   *DDI*, Series X, V. 2, no. 26, p. 35.

36   PRO: FO371/49834:ZM/29/22 (Resumption of Italo-Romanian and Italo-Bulgarian relations); DDI, Series X, V. 2, no. 70, p. 89.

37   *DDI*, Series X, V. 2, no. 407, p. 490. See B. Arcidiacono, *Alle origini della divisione europea. Armistizi e Commissioni di controllo alleate in Europa orientale, 1944–1946* (Florence: Ponte alle Grazie, 1993).

38   *DDI*, Series X, V. 2, no. 409, p. 500.

39   Ibid., p. 501.

40   *DDI*, Series X, V. 2, no. 145, p. 203.

41   R. Bova Scoppa, *Colloqui con due dittatori* (Rome: Ruffolo, 1949), Aide-Mémoire (21 October 1944) p. 188.

42   V. Mastny, 'Pax Sovietica', in R. Ahmann, A. M. Birke and M. Howard eds, *The Quest for Stability. Problems of West European Security* (London: Oxford University Press, 1993) p. 382.

43 PRO: FO371/49825:ZM5150/19/22, Sir Noel Charles to Foreign Office, n. 1563, 7 October 1945.

44 ASMAE, A.P. 1946–1950, Romania, b. 20, f. 5, 'Accordo economico romeno-russo', no. 848/376, 1 October 1945.

45 PRO: FO371/56464:N2230/86/55, Vyshinsky to Trygve Lie, 15 February 1946.

46 K. Syers, 'Polish Army in Italy is centre for intrigue', *News Chronicle*, 15 February 1946.

47 Vl. Zubok and K. Pleshakov, *Inside the Kremlin's Cold War from Stalin to Khrushchev* (Cambridge, Mass.: Harvard University Press, 1996) p. 38.

48 PRO: FO371/60653:ZM4334/316/22. On 18 December 1946, Mr Osborne, British representative appointed to the Holy See, transmitted to the Foreign Office the translation of a memorandum on Italy within the framework of Russian policy, purported to be written by Quaroni who had just been appointed to the Italian delegation at the Paris Peace Conference. The memorandum was discussed and believed to be genuine. On 18 January 1947, A. D. M. Ross noted: 'This intelligent Italian diplomat knows his Russians and has the knack of putting himself in their position.'

11
Socialist Parties between East and West
Wilfried Loth

During the Second World War many prominent European Socialists had sought to reach an agreement with the principal members of their fellow parties on the shape of postwar Europe, and in this way several pro-European associations had been formed, such as the Socialist Vanguard Group, the Laski Group in Great Britain with its journal the *International Socialist Forum*, and the International Group of Democratic Socialists in Stockholm.[1] At the end of the war it was all the more important to build on these contacts and arrangements since the Socialist parties had achieved government office in several liberated countries and were thus able to exert an active influence on foreign policy. Accordingly the French Socialists in particular, but also those of Germany, Austria, Holland and Italy pressed for the early establishment of a new Socialist International to co-ordinate the activities of the national parties.[2]

However, the chances of reviving the International were not good. There were bitter memories of the failure of the Socialist Workers' International, whose members had not even succeeded in reaching agreement on their attitude towards Hitler's expansionist policy.[3] In addition there were numerous structural and substantive differences among the parties: between Socialists of the Allied countries and those of enemy and neutral states; between the Labour Party in power in Britain and the continental parties which had only survived the war in exile; between those for and against forming a united front with the Communists; and between Western parties and those which found themselves in the Soviet sphere of influence from 1944–45 onwards. Thus, before the international community of Socialist parties could become an instrument of European union, it was first the scene of conflicting views according to the parties' special interests in their respective countries.

The leading role in these debates fell to the British Labour Party. During the war it had taken under its wing most of the continental Socialist leaders in exile, and after the landslide victory of July 1945 it was the sole party of government in Britain, the third great power alongside the USA and the USSR.[4] This gave it such a preponderance over the continental parties that a reorganization of international Socialism was for the time being unimaginable except under British leadership. The Labour Party, however, reacted with great reserve to proposals for a new International. Its leaders were interested in co-operation with their fellow Socialists abroad, but chiefly for the purpose of facilitating their own political tasks; they were chary of allowing an international association of parties to restrict their freedom of action. In the British view, if there was to be a new International it could only be created by degrees, and steps would have to be taken to make the parties more homogeneous than they had been during the time of the unsuccessful Socialist Workers' International.[5]

For this reason, when the National Executive Committee of the Labour Party agreed in September 1944 to the formation of an 'International Labour and Socialist Preparatory Committee', only Socialist representatives from Allied countries were permitted to attend.[6] The Preparatory Committee convened a first conference in London on 3–5 March 1945, the agenda of which did not even mention the reorganization of international Socialism: instead, its declared purpose was to reach agreement on the principles which should govern the peace settlement. Representatives of 12 Socialist parties attended the meeting: those of Britain, Czechoslovakia, France, Holland, Italy, Norway, Poland and Sweden, also the Palestinian (Jewish) Mapai and the *Bund* of Polish-Jewish Social Democrats. Other groups from allied countries were prevented by logistic difficulties.[7]

The delegates in London soon found common ground in evoking the traditional doctrine of collective security, but had difficulty in agreeing on specific measures to make the ideal a reality. In particular the question of how to treat conquered Germany led to controversy between those, like the French Socialists, who wished to see Germany integrated into the future community of states, and those who advocated strict control of the German people, as did the Dutch, Norwegian, Polish and British representatives. In the Declaration on the German Problem the French managed to exclude any reference to the 'division of Germany into several states', but had to agree to a provision approving 'necessary changes of frontiers' as well as 'a special regime for the Rhineland, the Ruhr and the Saar' and to an indefinite postponement of German reintegration. For the immediate future, the conference demanded 'a prolonged and total military occupation' of Germany 'by the United Nations' which should be carried out 'by an army composed of American, British, Soviet and French troops, and if they so desire Belgian, Dutch, Polish and Norwegian and Czechoslovak.' After the period of direct administration by the occupation army, the conference imagined 'a period during which Germany can and indeed should be administered by Germans', but 'under the supervision of the United Nations.'[8]

As regards the organization of world peace, delegates took the view that the draft of the UN Charter as it had emerged from the Dumbarton Oaks and Yalta conferences did not satisfy the principle of collective security. While accepting realistically that the great powers' right of veto was unavoidable in the present state of world affairs, the conference put forward several proposals, intended to strengthen the new organization. Prominent among them were 'the immediate setting up of machinery for the international control of the private and public production of armaments', 'the rapid constitution of the first nucleus of an international police force' and the building up of 'a true Democracy within the boundaries of every nation.' As regards Europe, the conference welcomed vaguely 'any regional arrangement or grouping, on condition that groups shall not be set up or act in opposition to each other and that all remain within the framework and under the supervision of the international organization.'[9] The British and French in a bilateral declaration called for the speedy conclusion of an alliance between their two countries: 'They consider that such a treaty of alliance is the indispensable corollary of the Anglo-Soviet and the Franco-Soviet pacts and the necessary foundation for unity between the East and West of Europe.'[10] Further resolutions were passed on the international economic system, the future of the Relief and Rehabilitation programme, relief for prisoners of war and displaced persons, and the Jewish problem.

At the end of the conference, on a French initiative, a further committee was set up to consider the re-establishment of the International. However, its work was blocked by the Labour Executive. At the next conference, held at Clacton-on-Sea from 17 to 20 May 1946, the main objective of the Labour leaders was that the Socialist parties should firmly dissociate themselves from the Communists; the representatives of France, Belgium, Austria and Switzerland argued in vain for the creation of an effective International. The Scandinavians were no less cautious than the British, and the east European party leaders advocated combining with the Communists to form a single International.[11] In these circumstances all that could be achieved was to set up a 'Socialist Information and Liaison Office' (SILO) in London headed by Denis Healey, who was also head of the International Department of the Labour Party.[12]

The advocates of a new International were scarcely more successful at the two following conferences, at Bournemouth from 8 to 10 November 1946 and at Zurich from 6 to 9 June 1947. The east European Socialists, who were increasingly under the thumb of Moscow, made it clear that they had no interest in the present circumstances in reviving the Socialist International; their attitude put an end to the arguments of those who hoped that such an International would be a means of averting an East–West split in Europe. At Zurich the representatives of Belgium, France, Austria and Switzerland urged that international Socialism should use its strength to counter the formation of the Eastern and Western blocs and unite Europe on a Socialist basis. An appeal in this sense was made in the opening speech by Hans Oprecht, chairman of the Swiss Social Democratic party, as host and president of the conference.[13] After a lively debate on the admission of the German SPD to the international Socialist organization,[14] Max Buset, chairman of the Belgian Socialist Party, and Guy Mollet, secretary-general of the French Socialist Party (SFIO), argued for the creation of a new International as a step towards European union. However, Morgan Phillips, Secretary of the British Labour Party, rejected the idea as 'premature', so that the conference reached no agreement. All the advocates of a new International could achieve was the establishment of another committee to consider the question of organization.

At the end of October 1947 this body agreed to strengthen the Information Office by creating a standing committee of party representatives to make preparations for international Socialist conferences and see that the decisions taken there were carried out. This 'Committee of International Socialist Conference' (Comisco) was officially set up at the Antwerp conference held from 28 November to 1 December 1947. In this way international socialism was given a somewhat more concrete organization than the British and Scandinavian leaders would have desired; but the system fell far short of satisfying those who believed in the need for concerted international action by the Socialist parties.[15]

The practice of confining attendance at international Socialist conferences to parties representing the Allied countries was soon given up. The Social Democratic Workers' Party of Sweden was already present at the London conference of March 1945, and at Clacton in May 1946 the Socialists of Austria, Hungary and Romania were invited, as well as those of neutral Switzerland and some non-European parties.[16] On the other hand, there was great difficulty over the admission of the German Social Democratic party (SPD). The German comrades, who were considered partly to blame for the collapse of the Weimar Republic, were deeply mistrusted, and only by degrees did the opinion prevail that encouraging the SPD might help towards the democratization of Germany. In addition many party leaders, especially those from eastern Europe, regarded the uncompromising anti-Communism of the SPD chairman, Kurt Schumacher, as an argument against the unconditional readmission of the German social democrats into the bosom of international socialism. Hence Schumacher was not given an opportunity to present his party until the Zurich conference in June 1947, and the necessary two-thirds majority for its admission was not forthcoming until the Antwerp conference in November 1947. The representatives of Israel, Hungary, Czechoslovakia and Poland still voted against admission. Those of the *Bund* of Polish–Jewish Social Democrats abstained, as did the Italian Socialist Party, which advocated a united front with the Communists.[17]

The expulsion of the east European parties was a much more rapid process than the decision to admit the SPD. The latter question brought about the first signs of tension in East–West relations within the Socialist community. During the second half of 1947 the Socialist parties in Soviet-dominated eastern Europe lost more and more of their autonomy, and a profound rift between them and the West was created by the divergence over the Marshall Plan and the Cominform declaration of war on Western social democracy. At the end of 1947 the International Socialist Conference of Socialist parties once again attempted to formulate an agreed viewpoint on the European peace settlement which could be accepted by the Socialist parties of eastern Europe.[18] After hours of debate the conference passed a resolution which deprecated the formation of blocs and the division of Europe but offered no remedy beyond a vague reference to closer co-operation among Socialist forces. American economic aid to Europe was welcomed in principle, but at the same time it was emphasized 'that no aid can be accepted which may threaten national independence and the possibility of Socialist reforms of any Nation.' The conference formally rejected Cominform attacks on the Socialist parties,[19] but did not directly criticize Soviet actions in eastern Europe. The resolution[20] was adopted by 14 votes with four abstentions. Italy, Poland and Hungary abstained following the rejection of a Polish–Italian counterdraft calling for a united working-class front against the capitalist offensive; the Dutch PvdA, on the other hand, abstained on the ground that the resolution was not firm enough in disavowing Soviet behaviour and supporting the Marshall Plan.

At the first Comisco meeting on 10–11 January 1948 the Eastern parties refused to agree to a general discussion of the Marshall Plan, whereupon the Norwegian and British representatives successfully moved that the plan should be discussed at a separate conference of those parties whose countries were recipients of Marshall aid.[21] Then, the Communist take-over in Prague on 25 February 1948 put an end to the attempts of western Socialists to find a basis for agreement with the Socialist parties of the Soviet bloc. Henceforward most Socialists shared the general fear of Soviet expansion, with the result that advocates of a clear separation of democratic socialism from Soviet communism were able to achieve their aim. When Comisco held its second meeting in London on 19–20 March 1948, the Socialist parties of Romania, Bulgaria and Hungary were declared to have, as a consequence of their absorption into the Communist movement 'by an arbitrary decision of their leaders', excluded themselves from the Committee of International Socialist Conferences. The Czechoslovak Socialists were expelled because of their leaders' collaboration in the Prague coup; and the Polish Socialists, who had not been granted visas to attend the meeting, as well as the Italian Socialists, were urged to resist absorption by the Communists: they should 'prove by their deeds', it was said, 'that, faced by the choice between subjection to the Cominform and free Socialist cooperation in European reconstruction, they have chosen the Socialist way.' Pietro Nenni, the chairman of the Italian Socialist Party, who had argued at Antwerp for a common line with the fellow parties of eastern Europe, withdrew in protest from the London meeting.[22]

The Polish party thereupon withdrew from Comisco of its own accord. The Italian Socialist Party (PSI), which held out for a united front with the Communists, did not take part in the subsequent conference on the Marshall Plan, condemned by Nenni as a device for splitting the Socialist movement. As far as specific policies were concerned, the consensus of the International Socialist conferences extended initially to calling for a strengthening of supranational elements in the United Nations Organization; a greater degree of unanimity among the victorious powers, especially in European affairs; and strict supervision of the democratization of Germany. Regional arrangements under the UN were welcomed provided they did not lead to the formation of hostile blocs, and importance was attached to the internationalization of the Ruhr district as a means of controlling Germany.[23] The idea of a European 'third force' capable of overcoming US–Soviet tension and averting the division of Europe found much sympathy among the Socialist parties,[24] but was not accepted by the leaders to the extent of becoming an explicit guideline for international Socialism. As East–West tension increased during 1947 the basis for inter-party agreement shrank steadily. Some leaders, especially those of the Labour Party, pressed for a clear dissociation from Soviet policies, which were increasingly espoused by the east European parties.

After the exclusion of the east European parties, the reconstruction of western Europe under the Marshall Plan became the basic agreed theme of International Socialist conferences.[25] Efforts to play an independent role between East and West gave way to a generally pro-Western alignment; however, the parties of neutral countries such as Sweden and Switzerland held to their tradition of avoiding political and military commitments, and the other parties in varying degrees worked for the relative independence of western Europe within the Western alliance. How far this entailed a closer degree of union among west European countries was a matter of dispute. The French and Dutch Socialists especially, but also the Belgians and the Socialist Party of Italian Workers, called for decisive steps towards a European federation. The British Labour Party, on the other hand, while admitting the need for closer co-operation, pointed to the numerous difficulties that stood in the way of a supranational Europe; and the Scandinavians took advantage of British scepticism to avoid being involved in binding obligations.[26]

The International Socialist Conference thus aligned itself formally with the advocates of west European integration; but the form was deficient in substance. The federalists were unable to pin down the hesitant British in favour of a supranational Europe, and Scandinavian agreement was out of the question. Instead, the British hindered the continental Socialist leaders from coming to terms with the European Movement in its first phase in 1948, and then prevented them for nearly two years longer from venturing into a European union without British participation.[27] However, when in May 1950 the French Foreign Minister Robert Schuman took the initiative for a supranational coal and steel community, the pro-European parties could no longer be prevailed on to frustrate the creation of a 'Europe of the Six', without Britain. Attempts were once again made to persuade the British to change their minds; but from that point on the Socialist parties in practice went their different ways as far as European union was concerned.[28]

Thus the conference of Socialist parties did not develop into an instrument for transforming international relations, such as had seemed necessary to committed internationalists. Its true function was rather to make possible a rapprochement between the different viewpoints of Socialist parties, which mostly reflected national conditions and, when that was not achieved, to preserve a remnant of solidarity that could be of benefit at a later date. The solidarity was not strong enough to resist the splitting of Europe into East and West. However, the deliberations among Socialist parties helped to promote the process of European integration, which was not actively supported by all member parties but which at least they all tolerated. And they also contributed to the equilibrium within the European community, especially between France and West Germany. In the latter sphere, efforts to strike a balance between security and self-determination led repeatedly to recommendations for a 'European' solution, for example in the question of the Ruhr, vital to European security, and that concerning the future of the Saar.[29] In these cases too, national interests and considerations were not eliminated to such an extent that international Socialism could of itself effect a solution; but the statements on the basis of which it was possible to reach agreement embodied ideas that proved fruitful in the course of time.

At its meeting in London on 2–4 March 1951 Comisco resolved, on Belgian initiative, that the International Socialist Conference should henceforth be known as the Socialist International. This did not signify a belated triumph of the internationalists, but was only intended to improve the public image of the Conference's work: its method of proceeding did not change after 1947–48.[30] The International held its inaugural congress at Frankfurt from 30 June to 3 July 1951; it passed a basic resolution on the need for European union, but adopted no position in the current debate on the ECSC and the EDC.[31] The Socialist International continued to exert no more than a modest influence on the progress of European integration. A special role for the Socialists between East and West was no longer at stake.

Notes

1 W. Lipgens, 'Views of Socialist and Trade Union Associations on the Postwar Order in Europe', in W. Lipgens ed., *Documents on the History of European Integration, vol. 2: Plans for European Union in Great Britain and in Exile 1939–1945*, (Berlin/New York: 1986), pp. 653–98. The chapter is based on existing literature and on research in the Archives of the Socialist International, preserved in the International Institute for Social History in Amsterdam. My hearty thanks are due to Mr Bernt Carlsson, former secretary-general of the Socialist International, for granting permission to consult these archives,

and to Mrs Daisy E. Devreese of the Amsterdam Institute for her active help in procuring this material.

2   R. Steininger, *Deutschland und die Sozialistische Internationale nach dem Zweiten Weltkrieg*, (Bonn: Neue Gessellschaft, 1979), pp. 22, 27 ff., 31–5; on the French Socialists W. Loth, *Sozialismus und Internationalismus. Die französischen Sozialisten und die Nachkriegsordnung Europas 1940–1950*, (Stuttgart: Deutsche Verlags-Anstalt, 1977), pp. 65 ff.

3   Consequently it had proved incapable of taking practical action after the Munich agreement of October 1938. Cf. J. Braunthal, *Geschichte der Internationale*, vol. 2, (Hanover: Dietz, 1963); 3rd edn (Bonn: 1978), pp. 512–14; Steininger, *Deutschland*, pp. 13–17; W. Röder, *Die deutschen sozialistischen Exilgruppen in Grossbritannien 1940–1945*, 2nd edn (Bonn: Neue Gelleschaft, 1973), p. 164 ff.

4   K. O. Morgan, *Labour in Power 1945–1951*, (Oxford: Clarendon Press, 1984).

5   Cf. a memorandum compiled by John Price in February 1945 for the Party Executive's Advisory Committee on International Questions: German text in Steininger, *Deutschland*, p. 39; for the further views of Labour Party leaders see ibid., pp. 29 ff., 32 ff., 36 ff.

6   Representatives of the Stockholm Group and the Laski Group protested strongly against this decision. For this protest and the following passage cf. O. Dankelmann, 'Zwischen SAI und Sozialistischer Internationale. Zur Genesis des International Labour and Socialist Preparatory Committee in London 1940–1945', in *Zeitschrift für Geschichtswissenschaft* 24 (1976), pp. 1394–1413, esp. p. 1409 ff.; K. Misgeld, *Die 'Internationale Gruppe demokratischer Sozialisten' in Stockholm 1942–45*, (Uppsala: 1976), pp. 120–3; Steininger, *Deutschland*, pp. 36 ff. and 40.

7   Loth, *Sozialismus* op. cit., pp. 66–71; Steininger, *Deutschland* op. cit., pp. 40–3.

8   Published by the Press Department of the Labour Party, and reprinted in W. Lipgens and W. Loth eds, *Documents on the History of European Integration, vol. IV: Transnational Organizations of Political Parties and Pressure Groups in the Struggle for European Union, 1945–1950*, (Berlin/New York: de Gruyter, 1991), pp. 446–9.

9   Ibid. pp. 443–6.

10 *Report of the 44th Annual Conference of the Labour Party 1945*, (London: 1945), p. 170.

11 On the attempts for a reunification of the 'worker parties' see D. Staritz and H. Weber eds, *Einheitsfront – Einheitspartei. Kommunisten und Sozialdemokraten in Ost- und Westeuropa 1944–1948*, (Köln: Wissensdraft und Politik, 1989); on the crucial German case see the more recent A. Malycha, *Auf dem Weg zur SED. Die Sozialdemokratien und die Bildung einer Einheitspartei in den Ländern der SBZ*, (Bonn: 1995).

12 J. Braunthal, *Geschichte der Internationale*, vol. 3, op. cit., pp. 169–72; Loth, *Sozialismus*, pp. 70 and 113 ff.; Steininger, *Deutschland*, pp. 44–8; K. Misgeld, *Sozialdemokratie und Aussenpolitik in Schweden. Sozialistische Internationale, Europapolitik und die Deutschlandfrage 1945–1955*, (Frankfurt und New York: 1984), pp. 59–62.

13 Cf. Braunthal, *Geschichte* op. cit., vol. 3, p. 174 ff.; Loth, *Sozialismus* op. cit., p. 114 ff.; Steininger, *Deutschland* op. cit., pp. 52–7; Misgeld, *Sozialdemokratie* op. cit., pp. 83–5; excerpts from Oprecht's speech in Lipgens *Documents* vol. IV, p. 450 ff.

14 See below.
15 Cf. Braunthal, *Geschichte* op. cit., vol. 3, pp. 172–7; Loth, *Sozialismus* op. cit., pp. 114–16; Steininger, *Deutschland* op. cit., pp. 51–9; on the work of the committee set up at Zurich see Misgeld, *Sozialdemokratie* op. cit., pp. 100–10.
16 Besides the UK, the following countries were represented at Clacton: Argentina, Austria, Belgium, Canada, Czechoslovakia, Denmark, France, Holland, Hungary, Italy, New Zealand, Norway, Palestine, Poland, Romania, Sweden and Switzerland. Minutes and documents in the Labour Party Archives, London, cited by Steininger, *Deutschland* op. cit., p. 46.
17 For a full account see Steininger, *Deutschland* op. cit., pp. 60–89; extracts from the Bournemouth and Zurich minutes, ibid., pp. 217–66; further information in Loth, *Sozialismus* op. cit., p. 116 ff., and Misgeld, *Sozialdemokratie* op. cit., pp. 62 ff., 73 ff., 83–5.
18 Summary of Proceedings, draft resolutions and correspondence in Socialist International Archives, International Institute for Social History; extracts of the Summary in Steininger, *Deutschland* op. cit., pp. 282–98. Further details of the conference ibid., pp. 58 ff. and 87 ff., and in O. Dankelmann, *Die Genesis sozialreformerischer Integrationspolitik 1914–1951* (thesis), (Halle: 1975), pp. 301–8; also Loth, *Sozialismus* op. cit., pp. 115–17, and Misgeld, *Sozialdemokratie* op. cit., pp. 110–15.
19 The final communiqué of the inaugural conference of the Cominform on 2 October 1947 attacked 'Right-wing Socialists, especially in Britain and France' as allies of American imperialism: cf. *The Cominform. Minutes of the Three Conferences 1947/1948/1949*, (Milano, Annali Fondazione Giangiacomo Feltrinelli: 1994).
20 Reprinted in Lipgens *Documents* op. cit., vol. IV, pp. 451–3.
21 Cf. Loth, *Sozialismus* op. cit., p. 202 ff.; Steininger, *Deutschland* op. cit., p. 92 ff.; Misgeld, *Sozialdemokratie* op. cit., p. 121 ff.
22 Braunthal, *Geschichte* op. cit., vol. 3, p. 229 ff.; Loth, *Sozialismus* op. cit., p. 180 ff.; Steininger, *Deutschland* op. cit., p. 93; Misgeld, *Sozialdemokratie* op. cit., p. 132 ff.; Resolution quoted later in Lipgens, *Documents* op. cit., vol. IV, pp. 454 ff.
23 Cf. declarations of the London conference of March 1945 at note 10.
24 For France cf. Loth, *Sozialismus* op. cit., pp. 79–83, 137–75; for Great Britain J. Schneer, 'Hopes Deferred or Shattered: The British Labour Left and the Third Force Movement, 1945–49', *Journal of Modern History* 56 (1984), pp. 197–226.
25 See Lipgens, *Documents* op. cit., vol. IV, p. 454 ff.
26 Details of the French position in Loth, *Sozialismus* op. cit., pp. 156–66, 187 ff., 223–5; for the British attitude W. Lipgens, *A History of European Integration*, vol. 1, (Oxford: 1982), pp. 155–201 and 489–95, and G. Warner, 'Die britische Labour-Regierung und die Einheit Westeuropas 1949–1951', *Vierteljahrshefte für Zeitgeschichte* 28 (1980), pp. 310–30.
27 Loth, *Sozialismus* op. cit., pp. 204–14, 225–9, 244–50 and 257–60; on relations with the European Movement, also A. Hick, 'The European Movement', in Lipgens, *Documents* op. cit., vol. IV, pp. 318–435.
28 Cf. Lipgens, *Documents* op. cit., vol. IV, pp. 471–4.
29 At the International Socialist Conference in Copenhagen on 3 June 1950 French and German Socialists agreed in principle that the Saar problem could

only be solved on a European basis. Cf. Loth, *Sozialismus* op. cit., p. 261 ff., and Steiniger, *Deutschland* op. cit., pp. 128–30; text of resolution in Lipgens, *Documents* op. cit., vol. IV, pp. 469–71.

30 Braunthal, *Geschichte* op. cit., vol. 3, pp. 235–9; Steininger, *Deutschland* op. cit., pp. 169–72; Misgeld, *Sozialdemokratie* op. cit., pp. 264–9.

31 Text of resolution in *Report of the First Congress of the Socialist International*, Frankfurt, 30 June–3 July 1951 (Circular 100/51), in Socialist International Archives, International Institute for Social History.

12
Minor and Major Powers and the Failure of the Anti-Fascist Wartime Alliance

Antonio Varsori

It is not easy to summarize the main aspects of the chapters dealt with in this section. I would stress that one of the main assumptions on which the volume was based was as follows. During the last stages of the Second World War and the early stages of the postwar period the partition of Europe into two opposing camps was not regarded by most decisionmakers as an obvious consequence of the conflict, on the contrary numerous political leaders, in particular the European ones, both in the West and in the East, shared the goal of creating a continent which could be regarded as a single entity, as well as the ambition to overcome the divisions which had characterized the interwar period. A further aim of the volume was to pinpoint what room for manoeuvre was left to European decision-makers, both in the West and in the East, in spite of the emerging Cold War.

The chapters presented in this section, seem to suggest that we must draw a line between, on the one hand, the intentions and policies pursued by the major victorious powers and on the other hand, the goals and solutions worked out by minor actors. As far as the major victorious powers are concerned, it seems that, at least in the immediate postwar period, neither Britain nor the United States thought that Europe was going to be divided and their plans aimed at maintaining a continent which, in spite of the obvious political, social and economic differences, as well as of the presence of the Soviet Union, could be regarded as a single entity characterized by peaceful relations among the different states. Such an attitude has been carefully and convincingly examined in Bruno Arcidiacono's chapter and such an hypothesis appears to receive support in other contributions to the volume. However, as far as Soviet intentions are concerned, other contributors have focused their attention on this aspect and they seem to imply that Stalin's policy was responsible for the partition of the European continent into two spheres between which any form of contact was to become impossible.[1]

As far as Western European actors are concerned, the rejection of the idea of dividing the continent appears to be a common feature stressed in each chapter, even though the differences between the views of a great power such as Britain and those of a minor power such as Italy are of particular relevance. As far as the United Kingdom was concerned, for most British decision-makers the European settlement could only be the outcome of an agreement among the great powers, in particular between London and Moscow. On the contrary the minor powers were regarded as mere pawns on a chessboard and Britain did not seem to be very much interested in developing autonomous relations with the local leaderships of the countries of central and eastern Europe. The events which took place in countries such as Romania or Bulgaria, or Hungary, were perceived in London as a mere backdrop and those countries' future could be changed as a consequence of some agreement or compromise worked out by the great powers.[2] Was there any exception to such a scheme? Poland for instance? Were some local leaders able to exert some influence on Britain's policy towards east and central Europe? As for France, which was struggling in order to recover its great power role, Antoine Marès' chapter convincingly points out that Paris excercised a keen interest in maintaining in central Europe some of the ties France had developed in the interwar period.

Italy's policies towards east-central Europe, which have been skilfully analyzed in Giorgio Petracchi's chapter, offer a completely different view. Italy came out of the war as a defeated enemy country, but unlike Germany, it could rely on some room for manoeuvre and it is of considerable significance that the Italian authorities almost immediately looked with great interest to east central European countries and it was Rome's intention to renew relations with traditional partners such as Poland and the countries of the Balkan–Danubian area. Furthermore Giorgio Petracchi has pointed out Italy's traditional interest towards the Adriatic Sea. In this connection the authorities in Rome appeared to disregard the ideological implications and it is of great interest how a diplomat of the 'old school', such as Pietro Quaroni, was ready to develop official contacts, on behalf of his government, with the Lublin Committee, which was largely dominated by Communist elements. Italy's attitude could perhaps be explained also on the basis of its domestic policies. The tendencies on the part of Italian moderate forces to avoid an open confrontation with the parties of the Left, in particular with the Communist Party, played a part in Rome's eagerness to develop close contacts with some central and east European nations in the immediate postwar period.[3] Moreover it is very likely that economic considerations were a significant factor in shaping Rome's foreign policy; in the interwar period Italy had developed fruitful economic ties with some nations in east central Europe. Last but not least, Petracchi's study seems to imply that the 'Salerno turning point' and the establishment of full diplomatic relations with the Soviet Union were aspects of a broader strategy, in part based on the assumptions of the conservative forces that, in the postwar period, it would have been impossible to neglect Moscow's increasing influence in the European continent.

In fact if, at least for a while, we focus our attention on some Western European political forces, an eagerness to maintain some form of fruitful co-operation with east central Europe appears a distinctive feature of their policies during the immediate postwar period. Most members of Catholic, democratic and Socialist parties in western Europe could not immediately forget the experience of their anti-Fascist co-operation with the Communist parties which had characterized the Second World War, in particular in the Resistance movement. Such an attitude is underscored in Wilfried Loth's chapter about the Socialist parties. It is therefore, likely that the lukewarm attitude shown by most Western Socialist parties towards the creation of a new Socialist International was as a consequence of the western European Socialists' desire to avoid serious conflict with the Communists, as well as with the Soviet Union which had disbanded the Third International in 1943. Furthermore such an attitude could be regarded as a way to ensure some room for manoeuvre for the Socialist comrades from east central Europe. However, some Western Socialists believed in a fruitful dialogue with the Communist movement, a hope shared by a few French and Italian Catholics. In this connection I would stress the position of the British Labour Party towards the Italian Socialist Party. Transport House favoured the condemnation by the Socialist International (Comisco) of the Nenni Socialists on the eve of the Italian elections of April 1948, in spite of the close alliance the Italian Socialists had developed with the Italian Communist Party and in 1947 the moderate Labour leadership rejected the proposal that the Italian Social Democrats, who in January 1947 had left the Italian Socialist Party led by Nenni, could join the Socialist international organisation.[4]

A further element which appears to confirm this intention to avoid open confrontation and a partition of Europe is the will showed by most European nations in the immediate postwar period to resolve, albeit in a dramatic way, one of the sources of deep friction which had character-ized the interwar years: the presence of strong ethnic minorities in some central and east European states. In this connection one should recall in particular the fate of the German minorities in Czechoslovakia and Poland and also that of the Italian minority in Yugoslavia. Moreover, it is of some significance that the victorious Western powers did not raise great objections to this sort of 'ethnic cleansing'. And if we think about the case of Venezia Giulia we can attach a certain validity to such an interpretation.[5] But we may wonder whether London and Washington's compliance with such policies was the outcome of a clear-cut position worked out during the wartime years or just the reaction to a phenom-enon that neither Britain nor the United States were able to deal with.

We may now consider whether the chapters have identified the reasons why, in spite of the goodwill which was shown by several actors, Europe was about to be split into two opposing camps. Drawing on some of the contributions, it appears that there were two issues on which the prospect of dialogue was curtailed very quickly. First I would stress what we might call the 'Soviet' factor, as opposed to a possible 'Russian' factor. In 1945, everybody in the Western camp seemed eager to comply with Moscow's need for security, as well as with the prospect of a sphere of influence in east central Europe where the Soviet Union would exert the leading role. This point is expanded in Bruno Arcidiacono's chapter where he deals with Britain's strategy in their relations with the Soviet Union; in Marès' chapter where he deals with France's attitude towards Czechoslovakia; in Petracchi's contribution on Italy; and in Wilfried Loth's study. But some Western powers opposed the ideological implica-tions of Moscow's policy in east central Europe; they perceived Soviet policy as one aimed at changing, in a dramatic way, the character of this part of the 'old world', as well as at blocking any possible form of Western influence, however minor.[6] This is clearly shown for instance in Antoine Marès' contribution.

Furthermore as the Western leaders became convinced that Stalin's policy was inspired by deep-rooted ideological convinctions, it became logical for them to fear that Moscow nurtured expansionist ambitions and that the Kremlin sought the creation of a continent-wide hegemony as an early step towards the imposition of world-wide Communist rule. This ideology appears to be confirmed by some considerations in Loth's chapter: Western Socialists – and we must not forget that in the immediate postwar years some of them were in government – were willing to maintain some form of dialogue with their Socialist 'brothers' of east central Europe until early 1948. The 'turning point' was the Prague 'coup' of February 1948, which was perceived both as evidence of growing repression in east central Europe by the Communists against the moderate Socialists and as the 'annexation' of the left wing of the Socialist parties by the Communist parties. 'Left understands Left' was no longer valid among western European Socialists.[7]

The second factor which favoured the partition of the European continent into two opposing camps was Germany. The evidence presented in this section does not deal directly with the German question. At any rate, if in the Western camp almost everybody was ready to find a compromise with the Soviet Union as far as east central European countries were concerned, was it true? Was Germany's fate the real reason for the failure of peace in Europe? In this connection we must stress that relations between the Western zones of occupation and the Soviet one between 1945 and 1947 became strained very early on.[8]

There is a third factor, which has not been considered in this section, but which is of relevance: the United States' position. In fact Washington radically changed its attitude towards Europe's future between 1945 and 1947. By early 1948 the prospect for peace in Europe was rapidly fading.[9]

Notes

1 On Stalin's foreign policy see V. Mastny's chapter in this book. Furthermore see V. Zubok and C. Pleshakov, *Inside the Kremlin's Cold War From Stalin to Khrushchev* (Cambridge, Mass.: Harvard University Press, 1996) and V. Mastny, *The Cold War and Soviet Insecurity The Stalin Years* (New York/Oxford: Oxford University Press, 1996).

2 On Britain's attitude see B. Arcidiacono, *Alle origini della guerra fredda. Armistizi e Commissioni di controllo alleate in Europa orientale 1944–1946* (Florence: Ponte alle Grazie, 1993). For a broader view of Britain's policy see V. Rothwell, *Britain and the Cold War 1941–1947* (London: Jonathan Cape, 1982).

3 On this aspect see the important contribution of E. Aga Rossi and V. Zaslavsky, *Togliatti e Stalin. Il PCI e la politica estera staliniana negli archivi di Mosca* (Bologna: Il Mulino, 1997).

4 See for example A. Varsori, 'Il Labour Party e la crisi del socialismo italiano (1947–1948)', *Socialismo Storia. Annali della Fondazione Giacomo Brodolini e della Fondazione di studi storici Filippo Turati*, 2 (Milan: Angeli, 1989).

5 G. Valdevit, *La questione di Trieste 1941–1954. Politica internazionale e contesto locale* (Milan: Angeli, 1986), and G. Valdevit (ed.), *Foibe. Il peso del passato. Venezia Giulia 1943–1945* (Venice: Marsilio, 1997).

6   See my paper A. Varsori, 'Do We Need Turning Points? Some Reflections on the Origins of the Cold War (1944–47)' in O. A. Westad ed., *Reviewing the Cold War: Approaches, Interpretations, Theory* (London: Frank Cass, 2000).

7   D. Healey, *The Time of my Life* (London: Michael Joseph, 1989).

8   On Germany see for example: N. Naimark, *The Russians in Germany: A History of the Soviet Zone of Occupation 1945–1949* (Cambridge, Mass.: Harvard University Press, 1995); A. Deighton, *The Impossible Peace: Britain, the Division of Germany and the Origins of the Cold War* (Oxford: Oxford University Press, 1990); E. Ninkovich, *Germany and the United States: The Transformation of the German Question since 1945* (Boston: Twayne, 1995); C. Buffet, *Mourir pour Berlin. La France et l'Allemagne 1945–1949* (Paris: Colin, 1991).

9   On US foreign policy see R. Pruessen's Chapter 20. For a broad view see M. Leffler, *A Preponderance of Power. National Security, the Truman Administration and the Cold War* (Stanford, Cal.: Stanford University Press, 1992) and J. L. Gaddis, *We Now Know Rethinking Cold War History* (Oxford: Clarendon Press, 1997).

Part III
East–West European Relations in the Aftermath of the Second World War: the View from the East

13
Bulgarian Cultural Elites' Perception of Europe, 1944–48

Svetla Moussaková

This chapter sets out to discuss the case of the Bulgarian cultural élite[1] and its perception of Europe during the period between two major events that mark the history of Bulgaria after the war: the political coup of 9 September 1944 which paved the way to 'popular democracy', and the Fifth Congress of the Bulgarian Labour Party (Communist), which put an end to the pluralist political system and established the single-party model, after the Stalinist example of the Soviet Union. It was a terrible period, and the replacement of the political, cultural and military élite took place through a bloody rift with the democratic tradition, ending up with the physical extermination of opposition leaders. The successive waves of purges against the opposition parties, through numerous political trials, were in keeping with the evolution of the policies implemented by the great powers: the Soviet Union, the United States and Britain who all put pressure on the Bulgarian government of the time. In this chapter, we will try to describe the evolution of a hesitating European vision derived from the specificity of political history in Bulgaria.

Europe, a contradictory and controversial symbol, was ever-present in the Bulgarian imagery of the time. Even though it was held to be hostile and threatening on the political stage, it generated immense hope among cultural circles. Let us recall that the first European point of reference between 1944 and 1948 was the Allied Control Commission, set up under Article 18 of the armistice. Chaired by General Tolbukhin, the Commission controlled all political, cultural and economic activities in Bulgaria.

On the other hand, Bulgaria remained a German satellite country in the European vision, resulting in the country's political isolation.[2] That negative image and its political and cultural consequences were energetically contested by the Patriotic Front, the coalition in power. That is the reason why the issue of how to improve the international image and prestige of Bulgaria, of 'Bulgarian propaganda abroad' was central to the political strategy of the successive governments of the Patriotic Front. First, it is worth noting that, in this mostly tense political situation, the national view concerning the various European countries took on features which were derived directly from that political context. Second, one of the characteristics of the government's pro-European policy – which remained steadfast in its desire to improve Bulgarian international prestige – was to depend more and more on the representatives of the cultural élite. Thus, a strategy was developed whereby, contact between intellectuals, artists, writers, scientists and academics played an active part in state policy. In this way, the cultural network linking the cultural élite represented a specific policy choice for the Patriotic Front government during this period of international and political isolation. Finally we will follow the evolution of that national view vis-à-vis the Soviet Union, Great Britain, the United States and France.

In Bulgarian contemporary history, the date of 9 September 1944 is a crucial one – it is that of the political and military coup against the 'bourgeois' government, which brought a coalition of the Patriotic Front political parties to power; a coalition comprised of the Bulgarian Labour Party, the left wing of the Agrarian Union, the Zveno political circle, the Social-Democrat Party and a group of independent intellectuals.[3] The main role was played by the Communist Party, which in the period considered, (1944 to 1948), was called the Bulgarian Labour Party (Communist). With the aid of the Red Army, the new government set up a political and social system, which implied the restoration of the Constitution and a breech with the Fascist past: the democratization of the country; the abolition of exploitation, social equality; and a new Bulgarian political prestige on the international stage. Yet, very quickly that new 'popular democracy'[4] political system became a national variant of the totalitarian political system by then in power in the Soviet Union.

What were the determinant factors of the transition? First, the political situation of the country. It is worth recalling that Bulgaria's historical fate at the end of the Second World War depended exclusively on the negotiations between the great powers who had won the war. In August 1944, the country's situation was very bad – Bulgaria was at war with Great Britain, the United States, Greece, Yugoslavia and some of their allies. None of the armistice talks with the Western democracies ended positively, and in that context, the Soviet Union declared war on

Bulgaria on 5 September 1944. The Red Army entered the country, to pave the way for Soviet hegemony and thus, offered the opportunity of a quick political victory to the pro-Soviet forces, centred on the Patriotic Front. After the Moscow and Yalta negotiations, the United States and Great Britain allowed the Soviet Union great freedom of action in Bulgaria and in the Balkans. If one adds that the armistice clauses permitted the Soviet army to remain on Bulgarian territory for three years (1944–1947), the Soviet influence appears to have been a decisive factor in strengthening the Patriotic Front's power base. Moreover, Stalin himself considered that the coalition did not come to power through popular insurrection, but thanks to Soviet support.[5] In that context, there was no alternative choice of a political model: the Soviet-inspired totalitarian system.

It is obvious that the impact of the Soviet Union as the first anti-Fascist force, that greatly contributed to the defeat of Nazism in Germany, was very important in Bulgaria. Coupled with centuries of close historical ties between the Bulgarian and Russian Slavonic peoples, with their strengthening cultural, religious and political links, that influence undoubtedly contributed to the popular support lent to the Soviet presence in Bulgaria. However, Europe, which had also defeated Fascism, remained a symbol of freedom and democracy. France, which had a long tradition of contact with Bulgaria, remained the first European point of reference both for its culture and for its glorious fight against Fascism. In the political context of that transition period, France enjoyed support from representatives of various political trends, whereas the Bulgarian perception of Great Britain and the United States was conditioned by political connotations which resulted from the domestic political context.

On 10 January 1945, the leaders of the four coalition parties signed a common statement concerning the national situation.

> The Patriotic Front is not a temporary political coalition. It is a stable coalition of the people's revolutionary forces whose main objective is to get rid of the heavy inheritance left by fascist regimes in order to build a new strong, free and democratic Bulgaria. [...] The Patriotic groups are aware of the importance of those goals, and declare they will concentrate all their forces in the implementation of this programme [...].[6]

It is also interesting to note the principles underlying the foreign policy political programmes of the four parties embraced by the Patriotic Front.

They were unanimous on the government's future international relations: an end to relations with Germany and its allies; establish contacts with the anti-Fascist coalition countries; and build the political prestige of the Patriotic Front.

Several times articles and comments were published in the press, which showed explicitly, or implicitly, that the Bulgarian government envisaged very early use of its international cultural contacts as a way to improve Bulgaria's international standing.[7] The arguments that support this interpretation are as follows:

- the disastrous economic situation and the political isolation of the country did not facilitate a quick economic revival;
- it is probable that officials in several European countries remained cautious concerning their interpretation of the situation in Bulgaria, and showed reluctance to revive normal diplomatic relations with the country;
- in the difficult Bulgarian political context, a cultural strategy had the advantage of favouring contacts between European artistic and cultural clubs and organizations, since the intellectual élite with its long-established tradition of cultural dialogue, was not homogeneous in terms of political and ideological commitment.[8]
- The intellectual exchange programme was often stimulated by personal contacts and often remained independent of the government's official political trends. However the Patriotic Front's political programme also hoped to enhance the international image of Bulgaria through cultural channels, a process which may later contribute to the normalization of the relations with West European countries.[9]

Without going into great detail, we can say that in 1945, the emergence of opposition within the Coalition in power reflected a long political evolution of the parties themselves. The political evolution in the Agrarian Union, the Zveno Circle, the Social-Democrat Party led to the constitution of several trends and groups which opposed the Patriotic Front's political programme. Their representatives did not accept the hegemonic role of the Communist Party in the coalition, nor did they approve of its interference in their parties' political lives. As to the Coalition in power, it did its best to silence dissenting groups. Thus, anti-Communist groups and tendencies left the Coalition to create an opposition outside the Patriotic Front.[10] From then on, public opinion considered the images of Great Britain and of the United States as first and foremost linked to the political ambitions of the opposition. The political representatives of the United States and Great Britain on the

Allied Control Commission gave their full backing to the pre-election activity of the opposition forces in 1945. They pointed out that the Yalta conference between Stalin, Churchill and Roosevelt required the populations of the Axis satellite countries, including Bulgaria, to solve their economic and political problems through democratic means.[11]

In August 1945, American and British pressure increased. Maynard Barnes,[12] the American political representative, sent a first note (13 August 1945) to Kimon Georgiev, the Bulgarian Prime Minister, outlining the American government's alarm concerning progress towards the country's parliamentary election.[13] In a second note (20 August 1945), Barnes declared that the American government wished to establish diplomatic relations 'with a government representing all the essential elements of democratic opinion', and which 'would take all the necessary measures for the organization of a free election, with no constraints, in conditions which would favour the free expression of political opinions as well as the free exercise of civic rights.'[14] On 21 August a note on the same subject was sent by the British government.[15]

Official opinion in Bulgaria considered that the election had been postponed because of American and British interference in Bulgarian political life. This was felt deeply in the national psyche and strengthened the negative image of both countries in Bulgaria. According to the most wide-spread thesis in some circles, the opposition forces used the difficult Bulgarian international situation to resolve the internal problems of their own political groups. According to information from the Ministry of Foreign Affairs, some British newspapers were the first to publish the opposition's claims with an openly favourable comment on their political programme. In that way, a majority considered Great Britain and the United States to be hostile countries, emphasizing their refusal to recognize the Patriotic Front government and, thereby undermining Bulgarian efforts to bolster their prestige with the west European sphere.

What was the Communist Party's opinion of the opposition? We cannot contend that the existence of the opposition was the result of a trend towards democracy on the part of the Communist government. It was born more of a situation imposed by the Western forces, as well as by the country's concern for its international image. Besides, the Bulgarian Labour Party representatives themselves asserted that the emergence of the opposition had been 'dictated from abroad'.[16] It is interesting to recall here Georgij Dimitrov's viewpoint that the 'presence of non-fascist opposition in the parliamentary election was an absolutely normal condition in democratic Bulgaria, currently governed by the Patriotic Front.'[17] Yet, this remark is distinct from Stalin's position, expressed during a meeting with the Bulgarian government's representatives in Moscow: 'It is always better to make the opposition legal, then you can control it and force it to be loyal and not to go underground. [...] For you, it is even better to have a 50–60 person-opposition, so that you can boast in front of Bevin that you actually have an opposition.'[18]

It is worth going into a bit more detail as far as the image of the Soviet Union is concerned. The traditional relations between the two Slavonic countries have already been mentioned. In national imagery, Russia's emblem was 'Father Yvan', who had twice freed their Bulgarian brothers from foreign invaders. Given the political influence at that time, and the fragmentation of the world into zones of influence among the three great powers, political, economic, and especially cultural relations between Bulgaria and the USSR, were closer than ever. The first exchanges of writers, artists, scientists and academics also had taken place with Russia. It is interesting to note that the intensive activity within the USSR field of culture was never contested by the opposition. Their representatives, for national historical and cultural reasons, were often connoisseurs of Soviet and more especially Russian literature. We should remember that Russian literature had been one of the most important vehicles for the conveyance of European culture in Bulgaria since the time of the National Awakening of the 1830s. Concurrently, the opposition preferred that the contacts between Bulgaria and the USSR be developed in the cultural field rather than in the political or economic ones. On principle, the opposition refused to show openly anti-Soviet attitudes.[19]

In that context of tension and political debate, on 18 November 1945, the parliamentary election took place. The election brought the parliamentary system back to Bulgaria, and legitimated the political changes which had taken place after the political coup of 9 September 1944. How to constitute the new government had not been thought out because the election did not bring about any changes: 88.14 per cent of the vote went to the Patriotic Front. On 31 March 1946, the Second Patriotic Front government was appointed. The opposition contested violently the Second Patriotic Front government. This provoked a second wave of repression, whose most extreme expression was a series of political trials, starting immediately after the second law for the defence of the popular power was passed.[20]

Great Britain and the United States continued their active support of the opposition forces. Official circles in Bulgaria continued to consider the British position as hostile and as mostly poisonous to Bulgaria's image abroad. After some diplomatic exchanges – General Stoytchev had been sent as the diplomatic representative to Washington in August 1945 and on 27 November 1945, the French ambassador Jacques Paris went to Sofia – Great Britain was the only country of the three powers 'to stick to its unchanging position' as far as the Bulgarian representation in London was concerned. The Bulgarian newspapers published comments showing how British public opinion was divided on this issue and the Labour Party left-wing's criticisms of their own government generated hope. The Bulgarian government considered that, given the fact that the United States had agreed to welcome a political mission to Washington and that the relations between Bulgaria and the USSR had been re-established, the British position was senseless. However, the non-recognition of the Bulgarian government remained part of British policy.

The hope that relations between the two countries could return to normal was generated by a first contact between government sponsored cultural institutions. In March 1946, Colonel Barbruk arrived in Sofia as the representative of the British Council. If we examine the proposals made, we can surmise that, above all, Britain was more interested in a collaboration in all cultural and artistic fields (music, science, publishing) than in opting for a policy of total normalization of the cultural relations.[21] Thus, cultural relations between Bulgaria and Great Britain became the epitome of the negative consequences of the political tensions between the two countries, especially given the absence of traditional cultural exchanges.

The negative position of Britain towards the Patriotic Front government worsened polarization within intellectual circles. The British–Bulgarian association created at the end of 1944 gathered representatives of various political trends who often disagreed on the evolution of these contacts. The differences of opinion increased significantly after autumn 1945, that is after the opposition was constituted. Besides, the cultural circles of the opposition did not wish official relations between Bulgaria and Britain to improve. They considered that the British negative position towards Bulgaria could be utilized as a determinant psychological factor in the fight against the Patriotic Front.

On April 1946, John Mac, the Labour MP, went to Sofia for a non-official visit. Several times he met Georgij Dimitrov, who made it clear in one of his speeches that Bulgaria was eager to establish friendly links with Britain, the country 'which gave the world the first co-operative movement, the first trade-unions, parliament, and the birthplace of a wonderful culture and literature.'[22] In the articles that he published later in London, John Mac mentioned the Bulgarian cultural élite's interest in British culture. He wrote that he thought that the élite was in favour of collaboration with Britain and was looking forward to the resumption of diplomatic relations between the two countries. Mac also considered that British public opinion had been misinformed on the Bulgarian political situation, and that the Patriotic Front government was a democratic one.[23] However, that visit, together with that of Colonel Barbruk's, were only episodes in the contacts between the two countries. Public opinion in Britain continued to see Bulgaria as a German satellite state.

The comparison with the specificity of the American image is interesting. The most famous character in Bulgaria at that time was Barnes, who arrived in Sofia at the end of 1944. He had a lot of contacts within the intellectual circles and actively engaged with the opposition. Even at the end of his term, in 1947, when the United States changed strategies in the Balkans, Barnes continued to rally public opinion in his country urging them to save the Bulgarian opposition leaders. On the eve of the October 1945 Bulgarian election, Mark Ethridg – a publisher in Louisiana who also worked for the *Washington Post* and who was there to represent James Byrnes, the American Secretary of State – arrived in Bulgaria. He had several meetings with representatives of Bulgarian cultural circles.[24] Ethridg's attitude, judged to be 'haughty and distant', demonstrated his reluctance to commit himself towards those circles and generated ambiguous interpretations of his visit to Bulgaria. Some cultural circles evoked his visit as one of the 'deplorable episodes' of the relations between Bulgaria and the United States. Comments in newspapers underlined the 'humiliation' Bulgaria had to undergo due to the country's difficult political situation as a result of the British and American refusal to recognize its government.[25]

That incident deeply marked Bulgaria's image of the United States. Nevertheless, the contacts between the two countries became more active thanks to Slavonic committees; traditional cultural clubs formed by expatriates created in the United States during the 1920s. There were about 125 000 Bulgarian immigrants in the United States (the figure varies according to sources and the inclusion of different waves of emigration into the United States, Canada, and Australia).[26] As that very interesting but seldom studied theme is beyond the scope of the present study, we will only mention the principle of such cultural action.

Very active and particularly well-organised in the Slavonic committees, the expatriates represented the main intermediaries in the process of improving the Bulgarian image and prestige in the United States. As an example, one can quote the campaign for support to Bulgaria which was organized by the American, Canadian and South American Slavonic committees, and which gathered thousands of supporters in Barbison Palace in New York, on 9 May 1946, just before the Peace Conference in Paris. The participants signed an appeal to American public opinion to support Bulgaria and its government. On that occasion, a 'Help Bulgaria' fund was created; action that generated once again the hope that contact between Bulgaria and the United States – whatever its nature – would normalize the situation.

Within the context of a 'hostile' Europe threatening Bulgarian international prestige, France was the only country to be the symbol of some hope. Three important reasons for this support are given here, briefly:

1. the French language traditionally has been spoken among Bulgarian cultural circles and it had been the language of culture and education during the two previous centuries;
2. France was considered to be the Western country where freedom and the ideals of democracy were express by linked to the fight against Fascism;
3. France was the only Western country where the cultural policy of the time remained independent of the political context.[27]

The priority was for cultural and intellectual dialogue in order to safeguard a long-established cultural tradition of links with France. The will to maintain bilateral relations in all fields of culture was expressed several times and represented a major divergence from British or American cultural strategies, which preferred to remain cautious and outside the cultural sphere so that they would not be forced to recognize the Patriotic Front regime. The historiography of the time, as well as current analyses, saw the French cultural policy as benevolent, friendly, tolerant and expressing the will to understand the national context. The French cultural associations and the great capacity to adapt French cultural action were at the roots of its positive image. In this way, France managed to increase its political influence in the Balkans and particularly in Bulgaria.

Spring 1946 marked the beginning of intensive bilateral co-operation, starting with scientific and academic collaboration. In autumn 1945, Jacques Paris was appointed French ambassador to Sofia. The first delegation of French intellectuals, chaired by Claude Morgan, the chief editor of *Les Lettres Françaises*, was sent to Bulgaria. At the same time, the Alliance Française and the French Institute resumed their activities. French culture was warmly welcomed in Bulgaria: 1946 was marked by a rich French cultural programme: concerts, exhibitions, conferences. The Franco-Bulgarian club, created in December 1946, had more than 3000 members. Among the numerous French diplomats involved in that cultural action, we can quote young Romain Gary, who arrived in the same year, as the Secretary of the French Legation. His novel *European Education*, which won the Review's prize, was immediately translated into Bulgarian. Later he wrote of his time in Bulgaria in his book *The Night Will Be Calm* (1974) retelling a few now famous, anecdotes.

It is interesting to note that all cultural circles were happy with the cultural co-operation. The newspapers supporting the Coalition in power, and cultural propaganda, emphasized the revolutionary tradition of French culture and the present impact of anti-Fascist intellectuals. The opposition newspapers also welcomed it, underscoring the universal humanist and democratic values of the French cultural tradition. We can also claim that public opinion unanimously defended the positive image of French culture. Of course, in 1946 and 1947, the most intensive contacts were those between the Bulgarian government and the French Communist Party. Eminent writers, translators, poets, journalists and academics visited Bulgaria. They were in demand across the country, and political and cultural exhibitions were organized. The example of Louis Aragon and Elsa Triolet's trip throughout Bulgaria remains of particular significance. It was the most important event in the cultural relations of the two countries during the summer of 1947 evidenced by Aragon's influence within the publishing sector, which operated according to the French poet's guidance during the three years following their visit, as far as the translation and publication of French literature was concerned. It is important to underline that Louis Aragon and Elsa Triolet were welcomed with unanimous and enthusiastic admiration in all the cultural circles.[28] Moreover, in the narrative of her journey,[29] Elsa Triolet wrote that 'nowhere else is France so respected as it is in Bulgaria'.

After this rapid survey, we can conclude that France, as the Western country most open to Bulgaria, remained its European hope. No wonder then that Bulgarian opinion considered that co-operation with France in western Europe would be the equivalent of that with the USSR in eastern Europe.[30] That interpretation, which was very popular at the time, stated clearly the place of France in the national perception.

On 22 November 1946, the Third Patriotic Front government was appointed. Opposition soon organized protest meetings against the government and its programme. As a reaction, the government banned the opposition newspapers and organized a third wave of arrests and retaliation. These events coincided with a change in American political and military strategy in Europe and in the Balkans. From then on, the American political line was no longer to intervene in eastern Europe. In return, the Soviet Union had to adopt the same policy in western Europe. That is how American military interests led to the total abandonment of the opposition forces in Bulgaria.[31] Thus, once again, Bulgaria's political life was totally dependent on the great powers' postwar interests. The American strategic U-turn allowed the long war against the Bulgarian non-Communist opposition to start – the climax in that third and last stage was the trial of Nikola Petkov, the Agrarian Party leader.

In current Bulgarian historiography, the topic of how the West suddenly abandoned the opposition remains ever present. The historians underscore the international events which coincide with Nikola Petkov's trial: on 5 June 1947, the American Senate ratified the peace treaty with Bulgaria, and Nikola Petkov was arrested on the very same day; on 15 September, the treaty was brought into force and on 18 September the Court of Appeal confirmed his death penalty; on 19 September Washington announced they would recognize the Bulgarian government, and three days later, Nikola Petkov was executed.[32] Once again, Bulgarian political life was dictated by the great powers' interests – according to the peace treaty with Bulgaria, the Soviet armies were to leave Bulgarian territory three months after it had come into force. That explains why the non-Communist opposition was suppressed so brutally and cruelly. Moscow approved of the Bulgarian Labour Party, which did not need its opposition any longer. The 'democratic transitional' period ended with the Fifth Congress, held on 5 December 1948, it marked the beginning of the move towards a Stalinist totalitarian society.[33] The Fifth Congress gave its name to the Bulgarian Communist Party and put an end to the pluralist political system, using the Stalinist political model for the organization of politics and society in Bulgaria.

From then on, the vision of Europe changed again. After the rise of the Zhdanovist ideology the cultural élite was increasingly supressed. Europe, which was the hope of Bulgarian intellectuals, remained more and more distant. Yet France was still endowed with some symbolic value. In Bulgaria, the French cultural impact did not need a political pretext to operate in the cultural field. Of course, the political context changed with the Cold War, and France was to face ideological opposition in the years that followed. In the field of aesthetics, priority was given to socialist realism and so-called democratic and humanist literature. Nevertheless, a parallel network of French-speaking intellectuals was set up, which perpetuated the desire for cultural dialogue.

Notes

1   We use the phrase 'cultural élite' in a broad sense, to include those who create and those who transmit culture. Without wishing to enter the debate about notion and definition, let us say that our interpretation is close to Gramsci's, mentioning the 'individuals who lend their own roles to various social groups'. In that way, it is obvious that the issue of cultural élite cannot be isolated and analyzed outside a social context whose political destiny determines their identities. A. Gramsci, *Quaderni dal carcere* III (Torino: Einaudi, 1975) pp. 1511–52.

2   The theme of the country's isolation inside Europe due to its past as a German satellite state, haunted public opinion just after the war. The ambiguity of the Bulgarian position towards Germany led to the fact that Bulgaria never fought the USSR, that it declared war on Germany in 1944 and then sent its first army to the Russian front under the command of Marshal Tolbukhin. However, the country had joined the Tripartite Pact in March 1941, but even after 22 March 1941, Sofia maintained its diplomatic relations with Moscow. The pro-Russian attitude of some politicians, as well as the active anti-Fascist resistance organized by the Communists, were the bases of opposition to Germany at that time.

3   The most powerful political party after the war was the Bulgarian Labour Party (Communist). There are various reasons for that: first, because it was the political force in office which sustained the structures of its underground organization during the resistance; it was the dominant party in the Patriotic Front coalition; and had a concrete political programme. The Bulgarian Labour Party was supported by Moscow, especially after Bulgaria entered the Soviet sphere of influence. The number of Party members increased four-fold in a 40 day-period – before 9 September, when the Party enrolled about 13 700 members, and towards the end of 1944, that figure had grown to more than 250 000. The first issue of the Party's journal *Rabotnitchesko delo* was published on 18 September 1944. Between 20 September and 12 November, the Party organized a regional and district election. The twelve members of the political committee were also elected in September. The political or first-Secretary, Traicho Kostov, (who later became one of the victims of the Stalinist trials) maintained permanent contact with Georgij Dimitrov, in the USSR.

The Agrarian Union (The Bulgarian Popular Agrarian Union), the second party in the coalition in office very quickly engineered its political reconstruction. On 14 and 15 October 1944, during the national Conference of the Union, the office and the head committee were elected (48 people). The elected General Secretary was Dr Georgij M. Dimitrov. Nikola Petkov was elected chief editor of *Zemedelsko zname*, the Party's journal published for the first time on 14 September. It is interesting to note that the number of Agrarian Union members reached more than 100 000 within a few months, and thus the Union became the most influential agrarian party in the country. Nevertheless, the Party's coherence was torn by various political trends. First and foremost, there was no social homogeneity, because the party attracted members from different levels of society. Furthermore, there was a lot of disagreement about the political position of the Agrarian Union towards Communist hegemony within the Coalition. All these political and social differences led to the creation of three trends inside the Union: a left-wing one, a moderate one and a right-wing one, which led to a crisis, towards the end of 1944.

The third party inside the Coalition was the Bulgarian Social-Democrat Labour Party. The first meeting of its central committee was held on 16 September 1944 to elect the leading committees, with a central committee of 25 people; the General Secretary was Kosta Lulchev, and the chief editor of *Narod*, the party's paper, Dimitar Bratanov, was appointed on 4 October 1944.

The Zveno political circle became a political party during its national conference held on 1 November 1944. Kimon Georgiev was elected President of the central committee, Vassil Youroukov became the chief editor of *Izgrev* and the first issue was published on 9 October 1944. The political programme was that of the Coalition in office, and it is interesting to note that at the beginning of 1945, the Party was made up of only 15 000 members. This indicates its weak social influence, yet the Party's impact remained unquestionable within the organs of government.

4   The analysis of the 'popular democracy' period still divides Bulgarian historians. In his writings Mito Issoussov defends the thesis that during this period real chances existed for the creation of a democratic socialist society due to the influential positions of the Bulgarian Communist leaders like Dimitrov and Kostov. A younger generation represented by Iskra Baeva and Dragomir Draganov support the thesis that the only way for the Bulgarian Communists and more so for the other Communists in Europe, was to pursue the Soviet model. This explains the hypothesis that popular democracy does not represent an autonomous model, but leads to an obligatory path towards the already existing model of Socialism.

5   This thesis is developed in the work of M. Issoussov, *Stalin and Bulgaria* (Sofia: 'St Klement of Ochrid' University Editions, 1991).

6   *Building and Strengthening the Popular Democratic Power* (September 1944–May 1945), collection of documents (Sofia: the Bulgarian Academy of Sciences Editions, 1969) p. 432.

7   *Otetchestven Front*, no. 8, September 1944; *Rabotnitchesko Delo*, no. 11, October 1944.

8   V. Tchitchovska, *International Cultural Activity in Bulgaria 1944–1948* (Sofia: the Bulgarian Academy of Sciences Editions, 1990) pp. 24–5.

9   Cf T. Dobryanov, 'Overcoming Bulgaria's Isolation on Foreign Policy' (1944–1947) in *Problems of the Transition from Capitalism to Socialism in Bulgaria* (Sofia: 1975).

10 On 7 September 1945, the opposition was legalized by decree. As a consequence, political groups formed were known as the legal opposition to the Patriotic Front: the Agrarian Party lead by Nikola Petkov, the (United) Social-Democrat Party whose Secretary was Kosta Loultchev, and the Democrat Party under the supervision of Nikola Mouchanov and Alexander Guirguinov. Those parties' journals, notably *Narodno zemedelsko zname*, *Svoboden narod* and *Zname*, became the new opposition press.

11 G. Gounev and I. Iltchev, *Winston Churchill and the Balkans* (Sofia: Patriotic Front Editions, 1989) pp. 230–40.

12 Maynard Barnes arrived in Bulgaria at the end of 1944 as the political representative of the American mission of the Allied Control Commission.

13   *Rabotnitchesko Delo*, no. 283, August 1945.
14   *State Central Public Record of the Republic of Bulgaria*, fund 1, record unit 1, sheets 89–94.
15   Ibid., sheets 3–4.
16   K. Dramaliev, *The Patriotic Front's Educational Policy* (Sofia: Otetchetven Front, 1947) p. 50.
17   *Savremenen Pokazatel*, no. 20–1, 25–30, May, 1990, p. 33.
18   Quoted from M. Issoussov, *Stalin and Bulgaria* op. cit., p. 33.
19   See the first chapter of V. Tchitchovska, *International Cultural Activity in Bulgaria*, op. cit..
20   M. Issoussov, *Stalin and Bulgaria* op. cit., pp. 177–8.
21   *Izgrev*, no. 496, 13 April 1946.
22   V. Tchitchovska, *International Cultural Activity in Bulgaria* op. cit., p. 140.
23   *Otetchestven Front*, no. 493, 10 April 1946 and no. 496, 13 April 1946.
24   About Ethridg's report to the Secretary dated 7 December 1945, *Otetchestven Front*, no. 493, 10 April 1946 and no. 496, 13 April 1946. see *Foreign Relations of United States (FRUS)*, 1945, vol. V, p. 633.
25   *Izgrev*, no. 331, 30 October 1945.
26   See N. Altankov, *The Bulgarian–Americans* (Palo Alto, Ca: 1979).
27   Italy was the second Western country to show it was willing to co-operate with Bulgaria in the cultural field. Like France, Italy implemented a cultural strategy after the war in order to reinforce its international political influence.
28   *Rabotnitchesko Delo*, no. 161, 16 July 1947; *Narod*, no. 842, 16 July 1947; *Otetchestven Front*, no. 842, 16 July 1947.
29   E. Triolet, 'The Sentimental Journey', *Le soir*, 19 October 1947, p. 1 and 20 October 1947, p. 1.
30   See V. Tchitchovska, op. cit., pp. 108–12.
31   L. Ognianov, *The State and Political System in Bulgaria 1944–1948* (Sofia: Academy of Sciences Editions, 1993) p. 157.
32   L. Ognianov, op. cit., pp. 179–80, G. Gounev, *The Edges of Freedom or Nikola Petkov and His Time* (Sofia: Informatzionno obsloujvane AD, 1992) pp. 132–3, 142–3.
33   L. Ognianov, op. cit., pp. 233–4.

14
Soviet Economic Imperialism and the Sovietization of Hungary

László Borhi

The point at which Sovietization of Hungary differed most from that of Romania, Poland or Bulgaria was that it was the country's economy that was conquered first, making Hungary a case of economic imperialism, as Hans J. Morgenthau described it in *Politics among Nations*:

> The common characteristic of the policies we call economic imperialism is their tendency, on the one hand, to overthrow the status quo by changing the power relations between the imperialist nation and the others and, on the other hand, to do so not through the conquest of territory but by way of economic control [...].[1]

There is a plethora of Cold War literature dealing with American economic imperialism, but Soviet economic expansionism has received little attention so far. Intentionally or unintentionally, historians thus tacitly adopted the Marxist argument that economic colonialism is a feature of capitalist nations but not of political systems organized along Marxist lines. Yet, research on Soviet–Hungarian relations, based on newly available evidence from Hungarian archival sources, suggests that the Soviet Union was involved in economic colonialism. Moscow-imposed commercial and economic agreements reoriented Hungarian commerce towards the Soviet Union and provided Moscow with significant financial benefit. The economic agreements gave the Soviets control over Hungarian mining and mineral wealth – coal, oil, bauxite and manganese – under colonial terms, as well as control over the strategically significant parts of Hungarian industry. Soviet companies in Hungary enjoyed extraterritorial rights; their existence was not bound by any time limit, their *modus operandi* violated Hungarian sovereignty.

The Soviet Union's economic objectives in Hungary in the aftermath of the war were determined by three major considerations: on the one hand, the requirements of reconstruction. Second, the acquisition of long term control over the Hungarian economy so that it could serve the needs of the Soviet economy, in other words, to integrate Hungary economically into the Soviet sphere. These objectives were not limited to Hungary alone: in the postwar years Moscow is calculated to have extracted US$ 14 billion from eastern Europe through economic exploitation[2] and extended its control over the Romanian, Bulgarian and other economies as well. Finally, not only did the Soviet economic exploitation of Hungary yield significant material benefits, but, at least as importantly, it prepared the ground for political conquest. Our account of Soviet economic penetration in Hungary aim to add a new dimension to the history of that country's Sovietization as discussed in earlier literature.[3]

The exploitation of Hungarian resources was begun by the Germans and continued by the Red Army. Requisitions and robbery were every day occurrences, the Soviet army was supplied with food by the Hungarian population. The Soviet units did not spare the banks either: while the Hungarian Arrow Cross looted 9 billion pengôs[4] worth of bank notes, the Soviets took 3 billion pengôs worth, plus 55 kg of gold bars and 1.75 billion pengôs worth of securities.[5] Hungary was forced to supply the Red Army, even though the armistice agreement, which had been concluded with Hungary on 20 January 1945, provided for the supply of the Allied Control Commission (ACC) only. This led, according to a memorandum by Hungary's Minister of Foreign Affairs, János Gyöngyösi, to 'the complete exhaustion of Hungarian food supplies. The value of foodstuffs given to the Soviet Army in the months of April, May and June [1945] alone amounted to 1.5 billion pengôs.'[6]

The Red Army's requisitions brought about an economically dangerous situation and even put the Hungarian Communist Party's prestige at risk. In a letter from József Révai to Communist Party leader Mátyás Rákosi in January 1945 we read that 'if the Red Army continues to waste livestock there will not only be famine, but we will be unable to do the spring works or make up, at least in part, for what was not done in the autumn [according to Nagy, 10 per cent of the sowing area], but we won't be able to conclude the land reform either and all this will fall back on us Communists. We asked for urgent measures.'[7] More or less ten per cent of the GNP was used up in supplying the Red Army. In addition, the Soviet units dismantled production units as war booty. The most significant, although by no means unique example of this was the dismantling of the part American owned, Egyesült Izzó (Tungsram) plant in March–April 1945. It took the Soviets eight weeks to dismantle and take away the 600–700 wagonfuls of equipment estimated at US$ 12 million.[8] The Hungarian government attempted to persuade the Soviet Union to deduct this amount from the reparations deliveries, but Moscow had no intention of doing so. Not even Prime Minister Ferenc Nagy's personal visit to ACC Chairman Klement Voroshilov could change the Soviets minds.[9]

The Soviet method of collecting reparations made it impossible to reconstruct the Hungarian economy on a market-oriented basis and facilitated the introduction of a Soviet dominated centrally-planned economy. Although the American government wanted reparation payments to be commensurate with the productive capacity of the defeated nations' economies, the Soviet leadership insisted on the payment of fixed amounts. In Hungary's case this was US$ 300 million, of which US$ 200 million was to go to the Soviet Union in six years (the balance to Yugoslavia and Czechoslovakia). Washington considered this was within Hungary's capacity to pay, but did not reckon with the drastic decline of the Hungarian economy's productive capacity. Even so, Washington's ambassador in Moscow, Averell Harriman, warned: 'Whoever controls reparations deliveries could practically control Hungarian economy and exercise an important influence in other directions.'[10]

Nevertheless, only the Soviet Union controlled the Hungarian reparations payments. The issue of reparations reflected elements of Soviet economic policy: the acquisition of resources needed for its own reconstruction and economic expansion. Reparations were regulated by a secret bilateral agreement signed on 15 June 1945, the text of which had only recently been declassified. The Soviet Union unilaterally insisted that 1938 world market prices be applied to goods to be shipped under the agreement, in spite of the fact that the Armistice Agreement contained no such provision. This in itself meant a heavy increase in the reparations burden, although Moscow did allow a 10–15 per cent premium. However, the products ordered contained individual specifications prescribed by the Soviet authorities. Obviously then these products could not have had a 1938 world price, a fact which added an element of arbitrariness to the price negotiations.

The goods to be shipped were grouped into three categories:

1) 'existing equipment', which meant that operational facilities had to be handed over, such as the Weiss Manfréd Works, the Lampart Factory, the Rimamurányi Salgótarjáni Iron Works or the Almásfüzitő Alumina Works, all of which were pillars of Hungarian industry;

2) new equipment made according to technical specifications prescribed by the Soviets – railway equipment, ships, metals;
3) agricultural products.

The Hungarians would have preferred the third category of goods to
prevail in the shipments, but Moscow insisted on the first two. For this
reason, 90 per cent of the heavy industry was tied down in reparations,
although this branch was crucial for reconstruction. According to a
memorandum prepared by the Hungarian government in 1947, shipments valued at US$ 145 million were in fact worth US$ 225 million due
to under-pricing. Disregarding actual 1938 prices, 550 radial drilling
machines were shipped at one-third of the real price, 525 locomotives
at half, 15 thousand electric engines for only 15 per cent, and so on.[11]
Furthermore, one reparation dollar cost the Hungarian economy 10.2
pengôs and not the official 5.15 pengôs.[12] The cost of packaging
and shipping added a further 15–20 per cent and penalty for late
delivery another 5 per cent to the original cost. In this way reparations
cost Hungary 2.5 billion pengôs instead of 1 billion as originally conceived.

This figure constituted an average 30 per cent of the GNP, but in late
1945 and early 1946 – the crucial months from the perspective of
economic recovery – this sum was even higher. All this had far-reaching
consequences, since the immense burden, which by far exceeded the
capacity of the Hungarian economy, led to hyperinflation and, with the
pretext of stabilization, the elements of a centrally-directed economy
were introduced in 1946. In 1946, as a result of American pressure
Moscow reduced the reparations burden but this did not mean much.
By then hyperinflation had set in and the concessions were offset by
new demands.

Another significant element of reparations which the Western powers
carelessly sanctioned and which reflected the expansionist tendencies of
the Soviet Union even more clearly was the execution of the Potsdam
Declaration. Accordingly, the Soviet Union was given the right to claim
German and Italian assets in Romania, Bulgaria, Hungary and the Soviet
zones of Austria and Germany. In reality this meant that Moscow could
acquire virtually any property it desired. The only thing that could have
tied its hands was the 1943 London Declaration, which Moscow signed,
according to which assets acquired forcefully by the German Reich as a
result of the occupation of a country could not be regarded as German-
owned. The Soviet Union chose to disregard this provision. The American minister in Budapest, Arthur Schoenfeld, held the view that the

Potsdam Declaration made a significant contribution to the implementation of Soviet aims in Hungary by giving Moscow an Anglo-American license for its attack on the independence of the Hungarian economy, which the Soviets did in fact take advantage of.[13]

On 14 April 1945 the ACC presented the Hungarian government with a provisional list of German assets to be handed over. It was compiled on the basis of a list prepared in 1942 which contained the names of those companies which had been allowed to transfer dividends to Germany. All Austrian assets – factories, firms, banks – which were acquired by Berlin after the *Anschluss* (1938) and all those of which the ownership was not clear, were deemed German. The list attested to Moscow's intention of seizing the strategically important sectors of the economy. An enumeration of some of these companies will suffice to illustrate this point. The acquisition of the Count Zichy Urkuti Mine Works Ltd (Hungary's largest manganese mine), Dunavölgyi Alumina Ltd, Transdanubia Bauxite Ltd, the Bakony Bauxite Ltd and the Aluminium Ore Industry Ltd obviously served military purposes. It is worth mentioning that at the time Hungary was one of the world's most important producers of bauxite. Furthermore the Soviets got hold of numerous coal mining companies in addition to the Dunai Aircraft Factory Ltd, Ganz and Partner Machine, Wagon and Ship Plant, the Hungarian Siemens Electric Ltd, the Orenstein and Koppel Industrial Railway General Machine Factory Ltd and notable units of the Hungarian textile industry. The Hungarians had documentary proof that almost none of these were German. Thus for example the Bakony Bauxite Ltd was Swiss-owned, the Salgótarján Coal Mine Company's German shares had been purchased by Hungary earlier, just like those of the Urikány Zsilvölgy Hungarian Coal Mine Co., and the Felsômagyarországi Coal and Foundry Co. Only 5 per cent of Ganz's shares were German, those of the Dunai Aircraft Factory Ltd and the Telephone Factory were solely Hungarian property.[14]

The Potsdam Declaration involved the bank sector as well. Perhaps the most disputed case was the one of Magyar Általános Hitelbank (Hungarian General Credit Bank) which controlled 40 per cent of Hungarian industry. The Office of Reparations handed over 205 290 shares, that is 23.3 per cent of its registered capital, to the Soviet Union. These shares were the property of the German Dresdner Bank, yet the Germans acquired them through coercion from a French group under Banque de l'Union Parisienne and Union Européenne in 1941. This was obviously a case to which the London Declaration applied, but Moscow thought otherwise and the French protests fell on deaf ears.[15]

The companies acquired by the Soviet Union under the Potsdam Declaration came to be known as Soviet companies in Hungary and operated extraterritorially, producing for the Soviet Union. In 1952 Budapest and Moscow signed a protocol according to which what remained of the companies – 77 altogether – were resold to Hungary.[16]

A bilateral agreement signed on 9 December 1947 settled the issue of German claims payable to the Soviet Union. According to the peace treaty signed with Hungary, Hungarian debts to Germany could be claimed by the Soviet Union while Hungary's claims against Germany – which were much higher – were waived. There had been a clearing agreement in effect between Hungary and Germany in which the former had a significant surplus. Nonetheless ACC Vice-Chairman Sviridov demanded a payment of US$ 200 million. This particular issue was settled after months of negotiations in Moscow between Hungarian Minister of Finance Nyárádi and the chairman of the Soviet government agency in charge of Moscow's property abroad, General Merkulov. As a result of the settlement, the sum was reduced to US$ 45 million. Out of this Moscow had to invest US$ 30 million in Hungary, and the remaining amount was payable in four years.[17] In addition, Hungarian companies were obliged to pay their outstanding debts to former German companies which had been seized by the Soviet Union under the Potsdam Declaration. Few of these firms were able to pay their debt in cash and instead were forced to settle the financial claims against them by handing over all, or part of, their shares. This in turn enabled the Soviets to acquire the claims of *those* companies. This 'snowball' effect gave the Soviets one more opportunity to extend their control over Hungarian industry.

On 27 August Minister of Commerce Ernö Gerö (the second man in the Communist Party) and Minister of Industry Antal Bán (Deputy Secretary-General of the Social Democratic Party) concluded a commercial and economic treaty of co-operation in Moscow without the authorization of the government. Gerô, who initialled the agreement, thought that 'the foundations of a lasting economic and commercial co-operation between Hungary and the Soviet Union had been laid.'[18] Not all agreed with his assessment. Thus for example the President of the Smallholders Party (and later Prime Minister) Ferenc Nagy opposed the treaty's ratification arguing that 'it could involve the monopolization of the whole Hungarian economy, which in turn could facilitate the growth of the Soviet Union's political influence.' Nonetheless, the commercial part of the agreement was widely accepted. This was echoed by the head of the Office of Reparations, János Erös, who thought that the

'Hungarian–Soviet trade of 30 million dollars will make it possible for Hungarian industry to make a giant leap in the field of reconstruction.' Beside raw material for the textile industry, the Soviets sold iron and other metals, tractors, fertilizers, lorries, even sugar and raw materials for the chemical industry as provided by the agreement.[19] In return for the 30 000 tons of Soviet cotton and 1800 tons of wool Hungary exported textiles and lumber. In 1946 the Soviet Union's share in Hungary's imports of iron ore was 36.6 per cent, 47.1 per cent of coke, 96.7 per cent of charcoal, 100 per cent of tin, the same of lead and 84 per cent of copper.[20]

The second part of the agreement provided the Soviet Union and Hungary with an equal, 50–50, share in important spheres of Hungarian mining, industry and transport in the form of joint venture companies and in such a way that guaranteed Soviet control over the key branches of Hungarian economy and their exploitation for Moscow's ends. The significance of the treaty was not lost on the American representative in Budapest: in Schoenfeld's view the ratification of the treaty 'remains a critical Hungarian political issue', but admitted that without outside assistance ratification would be unavoidable.[21] While the Soviet leadership threatened to dismantle the German assets in Hungary in case ratification was refused, the State Department decided not to support the Hungarian opposition to it, because it was well aware that neither the United States nor the other Western powers could make up for the Soviet raw materials or the economic losses that Hungary would suffer and would be unable to provide the goods, capital and technical assistance which Hungary would be receiving from Moscow under the agreement.[22] Eventually the treaty was approved by a special session of the Ministers' Council and was ratified not by parliament – the majority of which was opposed to sanctioning it – but by the precursor of the Soviet type Presidential Council, *Nemzeti Fôtanács* (National High Council).

Although the short term effects of the agreement were obviously beneficial, in the long run it was both economically and politically detrimental. Economically, because the Soviet Union became Hungary's chief trading partner, thereby rigging Hungarian production to the needs of a market with low expectations. Furthermore Hungary's economy became unilaterally dependent on the shipment of Soviet raw materials. Thus, by 1948, 60 per cent of the nation's iron ore, raw iron and coke and 100 per cent of its asbestos came from the powerful eastern neighbour.[23] In 1946–47 the Soviet Union was Hungary's number one partner for exports and third most important for imports. By 1949 Moscow became the most important Hungarian source of imports as well. It is interesting to mention that in 1948 the Soviet Union accounted for 24.9 per cent of Hungarian exports and 21.44 per cent of Hungary's imports, which is more or less equivalent as the position its expansionist precursor in the region, Nazi Germany, enjoyed vis-à-vis Hungary in 1937: in that year Berlin absorbed 24.1 per cent of its exports and supplied 26.2 per cent of its imports, but the magnitude of Hungarian–Soviet trade in 1949 remained below that of the 1939 Hungarian–German one. Three years later the Soviet share climbed to 30 per cent. Such a high figure for a country like Hungary, which achieves its GNP largely in foreign trade, almost 50 per cent, in itself suggests *political* dependency. By 1949, as a result of the Comecon's drive for economic autarchy and Western embargo, Hungary was unable to acquire machinery, know-how and capital that would have been essential for its development.

The Western powers repeated their policy of the 1930s when they refused to provide a market for the agricultural surplus of the east central European nations. Then it was Germany which exploited the opportunity for its own economic expansion. After the war, for example, the United States refused to sign a trade agreement with Hungary, making it easier for the Soviets to increase their own role. Yet, the most important means of Soviet economic penetration was the establishment of joint-venture companies, which intensified not only the Soviet Union's economic but also its political stranglehold on Hungary. Moscow's contribution to these companies was either capital or property acquired by virtue of their 'German' ownership. This system operated in other countries such as Romania, Bulgaria and even China as well.

A secret Soviet–Hungarian naval agreement was signed on 29 March 1946, which set up a joint Soviet–Hungarian navigation company (Magyar–Szovjet Hajózási Részvénytársaság – Hungarian–Soviet Navigation Co.). It was to control Hungarian navigation on the river Danube and its tributaries, on Lake Balaton and the high seas; the operation of ports, stations, buildings, workshops; the management of ship factories, ship repair facilities and companies dealing with the supply and distribution of fuel. A supplementary agreement signed in 1947 improved Hungary facilities for navigation at sea by providing that both nations could use each others' ports on a most favoured nation basis. This was a help for landlocked Hungary. A similar – again secret – accord came into being in the field of air transport: the Magyar–Szovjet Légiforgalmi Társaság (Hungarian–Soviet Airlines Co.) was established. The company was given a 30 per cent right to use all civilian airports and their facilities and to construct new airports. A protocol attached to the agreement gave the Soviet air fleet landing and transit rights. Planes other than Soviet or Hungarian ones could fly over or land in Hungary with *Soviet permission* only.[24]

On 8 April 1946 the two countries signed an undisclosed agreement on the bauxite industry. Three companies were set up. The Soviet Union received a 50 per cent share in the Aluminum Ore Mine and Industry Ltd and its subsidiaries which controlled 90 per cent of the country's bauxite resources. Moscow obtained half the shares of the second largest company in the bauxite as well. As their contribution the Soviets brought in the former German assets of Magyar Bauxite Bánya Rt (Hungarian Bauxite Ltd) seized under the Potsdam Declaration and the equipment they had acquired for reparations. Special provision was made for the increase of bauxite production for internal consumption and export, with the stipulation that *the Soviet Union's needs would enjoy priority*. The new companies were granted their predecessors' rights to explore new bauxite deposits for an indefinite time. The three Soviet–Hungarian bauxite companies were set up without a time limit. The agreement provided that Hungarian authorities were to place their foreign currency at those companies' disposal without limitation to help cover their expenses abroad. This provision put them in an exclusive position since other Hungarian and foreign companies were not allowed to keep their income and were not allocated foreign currency under the pretext of currency shortage. The Soviet joint companies were in an exceptional position also in the sense that they were exempted from all taxes and duties. The companies were controlled by the Soviet managing directors. Although they were theoretically required to operate within the Hungarian legal system, in reality they often acted arbitrarily.[25]

The same day as the bauxite agreement was signed, another one was concluded in the oil industry. It goes without saying that this was also kept secret. Two companies were established: Magyar–Szovjet Nyersolaj Rt (Hungarian–Soviet Crude Oil Ltd) and Magyar–Szovjet Olaj Társaság (Hungarian–Soviet Oil Co.). The former inherited an earlier German concession to explore, drill and exploit oil and gas on the left bank of the Danube, to process oil and gas and finally to sell crude oil and oil products. It acquired the Hungarian state's 15 per cent share of oil extracted in the country, which it was empowered to sell. The other company was created from the previously Hungarian-owned Hungarian Oil Works in such a way that the Soviet Union was given 50 per cent of its shares and the Hungarian government was compensated for them. Its activity was oil refining, and was allocated 15 per cent of all crude oil refined in Hungary, plus a share of the remaining 85 per cent.[26]

On 9 December 1947, a protocol was signed which provided that Hungary was to give an advance payment of circa US$ three million on profits and dividends to the Soviet Union in commodities. The figure was established *before* the annual financial balance was known. While the Hungarian Treasury had to advance profit and dividends to the Soviets, Hungarian and other foreign companies were not allowed to pay dividends to their shareholders or dispose of their profits. Thus the protocol violated the most favoured nation clause of the Hungarian peace treaty. The same protocol provided for the joint bauxite companies' right to prospect for bauxite. If an applicant sought a concession for a territory also requested by an Hungarian–Soviet company, the latter automatically enjoyed priority, but it was obliged to offer the conditions promised by its competitor.[27]

After 1948 the construction of a central-directed economy was completed in Hungary. Although the Soviet–Hungarian companies received special treatment, the centralized economic system was often disadvantageous even for them. In the course of Soviet–Hungarian negotiations in 1949 the fusion of the oil and bauxite companies and the fitting of these firms into the new Hungarian economic system was discussed. The serious conflicts which resulted from the operation of the joint companies as well as the absurd inner contradictions of the centralized economic system now surfaced. Moscow was represented in the talks by the deputy head of the Supreme Directorate of Soviet Property Abroad (Gusimz), which proved that Moscow attributed some importance to the talks. The Hungarian delegation protested that 'the institution of the managing director lends the companies a Soviet character and certain Soviet organs in Hungary instruct those companies as if they were Soviet ones. The managing directors should be part of the uniform system of control and the Hungarian side would like to secure full influence on the functioning of the companies [. . .] the institution of managing director means that the companies are looked upon as Soviet ones.'

The question of prices created an ambiguous situation. As co-owner, the Soviet Union had a legitimate claim to participate in formulating bauxite and oil prices, but in the new system only the Hungarian Office of Prices had such a right. Moscow could also refer to the fact that it was the number one customer of these commodities and wished to involve the Soviet state authorities in fixing the prices. The Hungarians complained that this demand infringed their country's sovereignty. The two parties did agree, however, on the absurd idea that the newly-fashioned oil company's profit should be set at a fixed sum several years in advance, including the annual growth of the profit. The only disputed thing was how big this amount should be and how it should be arrived at. Moscow also wanted to decrease the Hungarian government's royalty on oil from 15 to five per cent and to change the 1911 Mine Act in order to eliminate the mine concession, so that the right to drill and extract oil could be vested directly in the joint company.

Since foreign and domestic trade had become a state monopoly, the companies had to renounce their right to dispose of their own products. State agencies of foreign and domestic trade had to take their commodities, but the Hungarians insisted that these agencies be obliged to take only the amount prescribed by the State Planning Office. This violated the Soviets' right to influence the production of their own company. They sought to resolve the issue by a demand to harmonize the two countries' plans. This again raised the problem of Hungarian sovereignty.

Hungary wanted to settle the joint companies' financial issues, which had been handled by a bank located in Budapest, but owned by the Soviet Union. Moscow did not agree to include the joint companies into the Hungarian National Bank's single-account system, but did allow some of those companies' accounts to be transferred to the Hungarian National Bank.

As a result of the talks, the bauxite and oil companies were merged. The agreement signed on 21 December 1949 provided that the Hungarian authorities consult with the 'Soviet representative in the company' about prices. The Hungarian government was required to purchase the amount of products fixed by Hungary's economic plans, but no mention was made of the harmonization of the two nations' plans. Nothing was said about how the fixed profit would be calculated, which had to be paid only in case the annual production exceeded 50 000 tons.[28] The leadership of the joint companies – with the exception of the newly founded Pécs Coalmine Co. – remained in Soviet hands. The two parties exchanged shares: they handed one another the shares of those companies in which each had an interest below 50 per cent. This was a good occasion for Hungary to pay the Soviets: 143.4 million florins were transferred to the Soviet Union in four years as compensation for the loss it incurred in the transaction.[29]

The story of the joint companies continued in 1952 when the joint companies' scope of operation was extended. The Soviet–Hungarian Oil Company now received the concessions of the former Hungarian–American Oil Company which had been nationalized in 1948.[30] This concluded the process whereby the Soviet Union gained a direct influence over the Hungarian economy and was able to control and exploit key segments for economic and political ends. The brutal and very rapid Soviet penetration began well before Hungary's political Sovietization came into full swing. This points to the conclusion that the country's full Sovietization by 1949 was a result of a process that had begun as early as 1945. The Sovietization of Hungarian economy, which seriously curtailed the country's sovereignty, buttressed the Soviet economic reconstruction, and political and economic expansionism. It was given a legal cover by the Hungarian armistice agreement, but chiefly by the Potsdam Declaration, both of which bore the sanction of the Western Allies.

From the above it is clear that until the history of Soviet economic expansionism has been written, our understanding of postwar Soviet foreign policy will be less than complete.

Notes

1   H. J. Morgenthau, *Politics among Nations – The Struggle for Power and Peace*, (New York: Knopf, 1967) p. 56.
2   See C. Gati, *The Bloc that Failed – Soviet East European Relations in Transition*, (Bloomington: Indiana University Press, 1990) p. 123.
3   See for example C. Gati, *Hungary and the Soviet Bloc*, (Durham: Duke University Press, 1986); B. Kovrig, *Communism in Hungary from Kun to Kádár*, (Stanford: Hoover Institution Press, 1979); S. D. Kertész, *Between Russia and the West-Hungary and the Illusions of Peace Makin*, (Notre Dame: University of Notre Dame Press, 1984); S. M. Max, *The Anglo-American Reponse to the Sovietization of Hungary*, (Ann Arbor: University of Michigan Press, 1986).
4   The pengô was Hungary's legal currency prior to August 1946. In 1938 1 US$ was equal to 5,15 pengôs.
5   Magyar Országos Levéltár (Hungarian National Archives – HNA) Szu tük. XIX-J-1-j IV-482 23. doboz 441 sz.n. 1945. Record of discussion on valuables taken by the Red Army.
6   HNA vegyes admin. XIX-J-1-k 41fh 165. doboz ikt. sz. n. 1945.
7   Published in: *Moszkvának jelentjük – Titkos dokumentumok 1944–1948* (Reports to Moscow – Secret Documents 1944–1948) I. Lajos and K. Miklós, eds (Budapest: Századvég, 1994), p. 35. Révai's letter to Rákosi, January 1945.
8   HNA KÜM Szu tük. XIX-J-1-j IV-536 30. doboz ikt. sz. n. 1945.
9   HNA KÜM vegyes admin. XIX-J-1-k 41fh 165. doboz 174/F.B. 1945. The Foreign Minister's note.
10 National Archives Washington DC (–NAWDC) RG 59 740.00119. Harriman to the Secretary of State, 31 December 1944.
11 HNA KÜM Szu. tük. XIX-J-1-j IV-536.2 30 doboz 452/Pol./res-1947. The Foreign Minister's verbal note.
12 HNA KÜM Szu. tük. XIX-J-1-j IV-526.5 28. doboz ikt. sz. n. 1945. Note on Hungary's reparations obligations.

13 NAWDC RG 59 864.00–3146. Schoenfeld to the Secretary of State, 31 January 1946.
14 HNA KÜM Szu. tük. XIX-J-1-j IV-536.4 31. doboz 96–615/II–1945. The Prime Minister's (Zoltán Tildy) note to the Chairman of the ACC (Voroshilov).
15 HNA KÜM Szu. tük. XIX-J-1-j IV-510/c 26. doboz ikt, sz. n.
16 HNA KÜM Szu. tük. XIX-J-1-j IV-548/3 35. doboz 1717. sz. VIII. 9–1952.
17 HNA KÜM Szu. tük. IV-526.5 28. doboz ikt. sz. n. For an account of the negotiations see N. Nyaradi, *My Ringside Seat in Moscow.* (New York: Crowell, 1952).
18 Quoted in Sipos Péter-Vida István, 'Az 1945. augusztus 27-én megkötött szovjet-magyar gazdasági egyezmény és a nyugati diplomácia' (The Soviet-Hungarian Economic Agreement of 27 August 1945 and Western Diplomacy), *Külpolitika*, (1985/4), p. 102.
19 HNA KÜM Szu. tük. XIX-J-1-j IV-571/a37. doboz ad respol 1945.
20 For the figures see Pécsí. Kálmán, *A magyar–szovjet gazdasági kapcsolatok 30 éve*, (Thirty Years of Hungarian–Soviet Economic Relations) (Budapest: Közgazdasági és Jogi Kiadó, 1979).
21 *Foreign Relations of the United States* 1945, IV, Schoenfeld to the Secretary of State, 6 October 1945, p. 882.
22 NAWDC Department of State Research and Analysis Branch. Microfilm no. 3467.
23 Kálmán, op. cit.
24 NAWDC RG 59 864.50/5–747. Memorandum on Soviet Economic Penetration, 7 May 1947.
25 HNA KÜM Szu. tük. XIX-J-1-j IV-548 34. doboz 97 res/h 1946.
26 Ibid.
27 HNA KÜM Szu. tük. XIX-J-1-j IV-548 34. doboz 97 res/h 1946.
28 HNA KÜM Szu. tük. XIX-J-1-j IV-548.1 35. doboz ikt. sz. n. The 31 December Soviet–Hungarian agreement.
29 The protocol of the 31 December 1949 agreement.
30 HNA KÜM Szu. tük. XIX-J-1-j IV-548/3 35. doboz 1717 sz. and NAWDC RG 59 864.053/7-1052; 764. 00/0–2152.

15
Yugoslavia between the Two Emerging Blocs 1943–48: a Reassessment

Giampaolo Valdevit

It is conventional wisdom that, between 1944 and early 1948, the Yugoslav–Soviet relations became more and more strained, the area of disagreement wider and wider so that the final clash – the Cominform resolution of 28 June 1948 – was the last step of an escalation in mutual challenges. This interpretation was firmly established in the late 1940s and later confirmed by the Yugoslav leaders in their memoirs.[1] Further-more, according to the conventional wisdom, it was the Yugoslav dyna-mism in the field of foreign policy and the Yugoslav project to play a leading role in the Balkans, that produced the split between Tito and Stalin. There is also a corollary to this interpretation: on one side it holds that the Soviets perceived nothing but Yugoslav national interest in its foreign policy; on the other the Western view of Tito was equally unilat-eral: here was a Communist leader intent on expanding the frontiers of Communism. The outcome was to be an 'intelligence failure'.[2]

Actually Tito's policy was much less unilateral than it appeared. 'At times Tito tends to consider Yugoslavia as something apart, outside the general course of the proletarian revolution and the Socialism', Kardelj stated to the Soviet ambassador to Belgrade in early June 1945 after a compromise settlement put an end, at least temporarily, to the Trieste crisis.[3] Kardelj's statement clearly identifies the two pole stars guiding Tito's policy: the Communist revolution and Yugoslav national interest. Moreover, it identifies Tito's basic aim: to make both these aims coexist. Two years later at the first conference of the Cominform the statement was to be reinforced. 'Within the framework of the national liberation war [Kardelj and Djilas said] we carried out a democratic revolution.' Such a statement later would become a sort of Yugoslav self-portrait.[4]

For the Yugoslav partisan leadership only such a coexistence could reverse the course of Yugoslav history and recompose the prewar ethnic and political fractures. They knew all too well that Yugoslavia was a country deeply fractured along ethnic rather than political lines, characterized by sharp conflicts among the leading prewar groups, inviting the destabilizing intervention of foreign powers; and they considered the dismemberment of Yugoslavia after the Nazi invasion of April 1941 as the epilogue of this history.

From such a perspective the main challenge to the Yugoslav Communist leadership came essentially from the Yugoslav past. Therefore the Committees of National Liberation, that were set up in September 1941, were considered to be the embryo of the people's power, the postwar governing authorities. Accordingly the Titoists did not view the conflict in Yugoslavia as a clash between Fascism and anti-Fascism. On the contrary, what was at stake was not only liberation from Nazi occupation, but also the building of a postwar Communist society: this was the only alternative to the ethnic conflict (Croatian ustasas versus Serbian chetniks) hidden behind the confrontation between respectively Fascism and anti-Fascism. Moreover they saw in the relations within the Grand Alliance the seeds of a conflict between the interests of the 'proletarian revolution' and those of British 'reaction' and/or American 'imperialism'. Furthermore, the Yugoslav revolution (Communist and national) was expected to produce integration among the various Yugoslav ethnic components and consequently lead to national unity. The favourite catchword was *Bratstvo in Jedinstvo* (brotherhood and unity): in other words Communism and national unity, a supranational and a national perspective. They put *Bratstvo* first – and such a term defined the relationship between the CPs; they put the supranational dimension before the other one.[5]

Thus the Communist option – Communism being seen as an expansionist force – was the first identity, that lent meaning to the national interest; and conversely the defence of the national interest was what gave strength to international Communism as such. Moreover Tito's definition of the Yugoslav national interest fulfilled and integrated many previous expectations. In favour of the Slovenians he claimed Carynthia and Trieste, the outlet to the sea; for the Croatians the Istrian peninsula and the Dalmatian coast in order to strengthen the position of Yugoslavia as an Adriatic power. To the Macedonians he proposed a larger Macedonia including the Pirin territory and to the Serbs he offered the project of a Balkan federation. In this regard two possibilities had been considered during wartime: 6 + 1 (the six republics of

Yugoslavia and Bulgaria) or 1 + 1 (Yugoslavia and Bulgaria), the former being preferred by the Yugoslav leadership. It would have made Serbia the aggregating force in the Balkan peninsula and, therefore, the leading power in this region.[6]

In Tito's project the national interest could only take shape within a Yugoslav framework. Consequently he censured the territorial claims announced by the Croatian Committee of National Liberation (*Zavnoh*) in September 1943, immediately after the Italian unconditional surrender had been announced. He considered that such a claim could lie only within the authority of the Yugoslav Committee (*Avnoj*), who, at the end of November 1943, presented the whole territorial claims without making any reference to the former Croatian decision. Moreover, the Yugoslav leadership pursued the Communist option and the national interest with extreme rigour, which served also as a shield from the great powers' intervention.[7] By the end of the Second World War Tito's double polarity had created a mixture (power politics and Communist takeover) which exploded in May 1945 during the Trieste crisis.[8]

On the Soviet side Stalin needed Tito as an instrument to test in particular the British intentions in the Balkans, especially after the Greek crisis of late 1944, and British objections to a Yugoslav–Bulgarian federation. Moreover at the Yalta conference the British, fearing a new 'Greek experience' in Venezia Giulia (that means basically civil war), suggested a demarcation line be drawn across this region; on the American side it fell on deaf ears: what then were the American intentions?[9] Stalin very probably knew that Tito was planning a Communist takeover of Venezia Giulia and that the Yugoslav army was aiming at the control of all the claimed territories. He warned him 'not to create tensions with the neighbouring countries and not to be on the point of "waging war" on the whole world', but Stalin needed Tito. At any rate, by mid May when the Americans showed they were determined to resist the Yugoslav pressure in Venezia Giulia, for Stalin the test was over. He pushed Tito towards the negotiating table and virtually forced him to accept a compromise settlement: the Belgrade agreement of 9 June 1945, dividing Venezia Giulia into two zones to be administered by a military government (a British–American one in the western zone, including Trieste and a Yugoslav one in the eastern zone, the larger part of former Venezia Giulia).[10]

From this moment on the national and the supranational dimensions of Tito's project ceased to coexist peacefully. But the crisis of Trieste cannot be considered as the first episode in a difficult relationship between Yugoslavia and the USSR that was to explode in 1948. Probably

Tito drew a very different lesson: that in order to defend the national interest it had to be closely knit with the 'proletarian revolution', in other words with the Soviet interests in the field of foreign policy. Therefore, he carefully monitored the general course of Soviet foreign policy. From the Soviet pressure against Iran and Turkey, and later from the outbreak of civil war in Greece, he came to lend an extremist interpretation to Soviet foreign policy and adjusted his own foreign policy accordingly. So he exerted his own pressures: first of all against the Allied Military Government of Venezia Giulia intending to destabilize the internal situation in the Zone A, to make it difficult for the military authorities to hold the 'domino' Trieste (as it was defined in the second half of 1947). Later, pressure against Greece evolved into a sort of encirclement. The treaty with Bulgaria that was announced in August 1947 (which was delayed by the Soviets) and the tutorship of the Yugoslav CP over Albania were part of this plan.[11]

The motivating force undoubtedly was the Yugoslav national interest – a project for Yugoslav leadership to prevail in the Balkan area; in any case Tito's regime still considered the Yugoslav national interest to be 'inseparably connected' with the interest of the 'proletarian revolution', and the Yugoslav foreign policy with the Soviet foreign policy. But this was basically a Yugoslav misconception and, as such, the source of the crisis that was to erupt in June 1948.

After the failure of the Moscow meeting of the Conference of Foreign Ministers to reach any agreement on Germany and the announcement of the Marshall Plan, the USSR was on the defensive. The reaction to the Marshall Plan, and in particular the Polish and Czech intention to join it, showed that the Soviet bloc was still loosely knit; centrifugal tendencies appeared to be at work. In order to reverse this trend the Soviet leadership decided to force the rigid alignment of east European countries with the USSR: the 'democracies of the new type' had to be rapidly transformed into 'people's democracies' and 'a common point of view' on the international situation had to be elaborated. Therefore, if the ERP was perceived as American interference in the Soviet sphere intended to create the conditions of a 'colonial enslavement', the Soviet response aimed at consolidating the relationship within the eastern European context rather than intruding into western Europe.[12] Thus, the Soviet leadership decided at least temporarily to block the treaty of co-operation between Yugoslavia and Bulgaria because, Stalin said, it could be exploited by 'reactionary Anglo-American elements [as] a pretext to speed up their military intervention in Greek and Turkish affairs.'[13] The ritual language did not conceal the fear that the Soviet interest in the Balkan area could be misread and the treaty considered as a source of (Soviet) pressure against Greece and particularly the American intervention in Greece.

The preparatory papers for the meeting of the Cominform and the minutes of the conference at Szklarska Poreba in September 1947 tend to confirm this view. In Poland Zhdanov announced the 'two-camp theory', a bipolar approach to the international situation that seemed to reveal the Soviet intention to seal off eastern Europe. On the other hand there was sharp criticism of the PCF and the PCI, who in particular were blamed for not having 'a plan of attack'. An appeal was made 'to unmask the subjugation' to the United States, to fight for 'national independence' and to turn to extraparliamentary action against the ERP. All that can be interpreted as a Soviet tendency to act beyond the iron curtain, even though the eastern European CPs were left without any clear directives on how to conduct an offensive against the United States. Thus to a certain extent Zhdanov's message was still ambivalent.[14] Ambivalence dominated Soviet thinking on Yugoslavia as well. The preparatory papers mentioned Yugoslav 'national narrowness' and pointed to 'certain tendencies among the Party leaders [...] to try to make the Yugoslav CP a "leading" party in the Balkans.' On the other hand at Szklarska Poreba Yugoslavia was proclaimed 'a bastion of peace and democracy in the Balkans.'[15]

For their part, Kardelj and Djilas could see complete correspondence between the national and the supranational dimension of Yugoslav foreign policy. 'The alliance between Moscow and Belgrade was the fundamental support of our independence', they stated; and they depicted the internal 'reaction' ('the enemies of the people's powers') as a force directly controlled by the 'international reaction'.[16] In the Soviet decision to station the headquarters of the Cominform in Belgrade they perceived an intention to establish a special relationship between Yugoslavia and the USSR. Moreover they were already accustomed to the statements contained in Malenkov's report: 'sharp class struggle has now shifted, for the USSR, into the international arena'; a struggle between two tendencies: on one hand the American tendency to 'world domination' and 'enslavement of the weakened capitalist countries of Europe and of the colonial and dependent countries', and on the other the tendency 'aimed at undermining imperialism.'[17] Such a definition resembled the two-camp theory, but the militant tone of Malenkov's report did not suggest the division of Europe could be a synonym for the stabilization of Europe.

Such a perspective was already commonplace for the Yugoslavs during the war, and Kardelj's reference to Greece is revealing of his extremist interpretation of Soviet foreign policy. 'I am sure [Kardelj said] that a "Greek situation" in Italy and France, alongside the original one in Greece, would signify a very severe blow to imperialism, would mean the ruin of the current imperialist offensive against the progressive forces.'[18] Moreover, the Greek CP followed the Yugoslav pattern – 'the popular front from below' – and in September 1947 set up a provisional government; obviously the Titoists concurred. From all that the Yugoslavs drew the conclusion that 'a new phase of revolutionary advance' had started.[19] Such a statement implies that the Yugoslavs were considering Zhdanov's and in particular Malenkov's report much more as a guide for future action than as an instrument of ideological cohesion for the Eastern bloc (as the Soviet leadership preferred to see it).

Yet in the last months of 1947 the Yugoslav interpretation of Soviet foreign policy met with no opposition from Moscow, even though the Soviet ambassador to Belgrade often stressed 'Tito's limits'.[20] In November 1947 Yugoslavia signed the treaty of co-operation with Bulgaria that had been delayed for several months on Soviet initiative; in December similar treaties with Romania and Hungary followed it. On 17 January 1948, in a conversation with Djilas, Stalin recognized the dominant position of Yugoslavia in Albania, even to the point of unification.[21] Tito got the message that he could go farther and reacted by raising the level of the tension with Greece. Two days after the meeting between Djilas and Stalin, he proposed to the Albanian Communist leader Hoxha that Yugoslav troops be introduced into Southern Albania as a defence against the threat of invasion by 'Greek monarcho-fascists backed by the Anglo-Americans.' Moreover, on 17 January in a press statement, Dimitrov announced the creation of a federation of eastern European people's democracies. Greece was included in the project because, he said, the Greek CP was waging a civil war, whose aim was to establish a people's democracy.[22]

The manifest attempt to escalate the crisis in Greece produced a shift in the Soviet policy towards Yugoslavia. At this point letting Tito off the leash could send a message to the Western powers, especially the US, that Stalin himself considered the Balkans as the main theatre of Soviet foreign policy. It would have been a misleading message from Stalin's point of view considering that his priority was Germany, where the Western powers were putting the final touches to the country's division. As a response to this the Berlin blockade was planned in Moscow in March: it was to be the last chapter in the division of Europe.[23] In conclusion, what had been stated ambiguously at Szklarska Poreba needed to be clarified immediately.

Some days after Dimitrov's statement to journalists, an editorial statement appeared in *Pravda*, in which the project of an eastern European
federation was defined as premature.[24] On 10 February a meeting in
Moscow with Kardelj and Dimitrov started with their being harshly
rebuked. Particularly important was Stalin's statement on Greece: he
dismissed as irretrievably lost the cause of Communism in that country:
he referred to the 'naked illusion' of a Communist victory there.[25]
Greece, said Stalin, now lay within the borders of the Western bloc. To
a certain extent it was now clear what was still open to different interpretations at Szklarska Poreba: the division of Europe and the Soviet
Union's tight control over the Eastern bloc were the two keystones of
the Soviet foreign policy.

However Stalin did not push bilateral relations to breaking point.
During the meeting with Kardelj and Dimitrov he hinted at the idea of
three federations in central and eastern Europe and invited them to
carry on with the project of a Yugoslav–Bulgarian federation, which
could eventually include Albania. Thus Stalin unambiguously established the range of compatibility between the Soviet and Yugoslav
(and Bulgarian) foreign policies. Only now did Tito fully realize that
Soviet foreign policy was far from his expectations and could become a
straitjacket for himself: a few days later the Yugoslav Politburo promptly
dismissed the idea of a Balkan federation because within the framework
of Stalin's recommendations it could prove to be a 'Soviet Trojan
horse'.[26] From his point of view Stalin's definition not only looked like
an attempt to normalize Yugoslav foreign policy, but a threat to his
whole Yugoslav design. Since it was Communism as an expansionist
force that gave meaning to the national interest, he tried to save one
so as to save both. He had no other choice but to resist Stalin. In fact on
21 February during a meeting with Zachariades in Belgrade he continued to support the Greek CP and did not inform him of Stalin's
view on Greece.[27]

Probably at this point Tito still believed that an open clash could be
avoided, but again he misunderstood the Soviet priorities: he underestimated the Soviet determination to make clear the direction of Soviet
foreign policy. Therefore, Tito's behaviour forced Stalin to shift the
confrontation to another playground while he was under pressure
from the Western powers (on 20 March the French, British and American governments released a joint declaration favouring the restitution
of the whole Free Territory of Trieste to Italy).[28] According to the Soviet
tradition any clash of interests should be traced back to ideological
orthodoxy. So, Suslov's memorandum for the Foreign Policy Depart-

ment of the CC of the CPSU, with its typical opening ('Intoxicated by their achieving [. . .]'), and the 28 March letter from Stalin and Molotov to Tito, was a long list of 'deviations'. At this point the only choice between resistance and surrender was left to Tito; and Yugoslav resistance turned the dispute into an ideological conflict.[29]

In the end the Soviet–Yugoslav confrontation went well beyond the sphere of bilateral relations. It became the testing ground for the Soviet ability to build 'the Socialist common front against the imperialism', mentioned by Zhdanov at the second conference of the Cominform in June:[30] whoever tried to get out of it would be isolated. From then on any interplay between the national and the supranational dimension within the Communist bloc was over; the purges against the 'Titoist deviationists' in the eastern European countries were dramatic evidence of this. Later any encounter of the two dimensions would only produce explosions (Hungary, 1956 and Czechoslovakia, 1968).

In the early postwar period the Western relationship with Yugoslavia was strongly influenced by the problem of Trieste. Even though it did not turn immediately into a Cold War issue, from mid 1946 on the British and American military authorities in Trieste perceived the combination of an external threat (the Yugoslav Army) and an internal one (the Yugoslav-led CP); therefore the Allied military presence in Zone A was seen as a shield against subversive projects, considered to be sponsored directly by Yugoslavia and supported indirectly by the USSR. From this perspective the former was seen as subservient to the latter and this view was widely held in Washington. Inspired by Kennan's views, encroachment and its synonyms (infiltration, penetration, subversion) were terms widely used on the American side to define the Soviet–Yugoslav aims regarding Trieste; conversely by mid 1947 the American response was containment, a concept largely dominated by the domino theory. Therefore, the Allied Military Government in Zone A appeared to be 'the last barrier against the infiltration from [the] East into Northern Italy', and firmness, intransigence, and unwillingness to negotiate were the main features of American policy there.[31] Of Yugoslav foreign policy only one motivation was perceived, the expansion of Communism, and the course of American (and British) relations with Yugoslavia were perfectly consistent with such a premiss. In early 1946 the door was slammed in Tito's face when he proposed to make a trip to the US to discuss the conditions of a postwar loan. Such a trip – the Department of State telegraphed to the American ambassador in Belgrade – 'would create an impression in this country totally inconsistent with views towards his [Tito's] regime and Yugoslavia.'[32]

Therefore, in 1946 diplomatic conflict was the most common ingredient of the Yugoslav–US relations. Conflicts arose over several issues: trials against Yugoslav employees of the American embassy in Belgrade on charges of espionage, black market and terrorist activities. The USIS office in Belgrade was closed in September 1946, some diplomatic immunities were broken and the United States were accused of having released suspected war criminals. In August 1946 a USAF transport aeroplane on the way from Vienna to Udine crashed after being forced down by Yugoslav fighters because it had invaded Yugoslav air space. As a response Byrnes and Forrestal, respectively State and Navy secretary, suggested that UNRRA shipments to Yugoslavia should be blocked. Eventually the opinion of the Under-secretary for economic affairs, Clayton, prevailed: 'UNRRA has no responsibility for punitive actions against countries for political misconduct.'[33] In any case the desire to keep the dialogue going with Yugoslavia was so insignificant that from October 1946 to July 1947 there was no American ambassador in Belgrade but only a chargé d'affaires, John Cabot, sent there from a Latin American country.

At any rate Cabot did not let the US–Yugoslav relations go adrift. Several times in the first half of 1947 he proposed a policy of coercion towards the Tito's regime by blocking the Yugoslav assets in the US and even the remittances of Yugoslav emigrants.[34] To Cabot Tito was obviously a Communist leader; at any rate he stressed that the Yugoslav policy was guided much less by the expansion of Communism than by national interest, and in particular by the need for economic reconstruction. Even though he remarked that 'it is a forlorn hope that in this government elements can be found to curb the fanatical Communist drive',[35] Cabot considered Yugoslav Communism basically to be an alternative to inter-ethnic hatred and, therefore, an instrument for national unity, overemphasized 'to the point of fanaticism by the Yugoslav leadership.' The British diplomats tended to concur with such a view.[36] Moreover Cabot was confident that the US would be able to resist the 'revolutionary forays into non-Communist territory.' 'There is good reason to believe [he wrote in July 1947] that our aid to Greece has augmented the Communist jitters.'[37] To sum up, Cabot overemphasized the national interest but conversely de-emphasized the Communist option as the guiding principle of Yugoslav policy, simply reversing the former interpretation of it.

As it happens, if unconventional perspectives are to be commonly accepted they need to be continuously reinforced by hard evidence, and the new ambassador, Cavendish Cannon, did not find anything that could support it. On the contrary he noted that Yugoslav foreign trade in 1947 was much more oriented towards the eastern trading partners than in previous years; moreover commercial agreements with the USSR strengthened this trend, and the Yugoslav lack of interest towards the ERP frustrated Cabot's hopes that the US foreign economic policy could favour the dialogue with Yugoslavia. In fact in September 1947 an economic agreement was reached with Great Britain but a few months later it became a dead letter.[38]

In the end the ambassador drew the conclusion that, as far as Yugoslavia and the USSR were concerned, the division of Europe was in the making. Again, he stressed some more traditional views of Yugoslavia. He wrote in September 1947 'Albania for all practical purposes may be considered the 7th constituent Republic.' And under the influence of the domino theory, he added: 'Yugoslavia offers Russia an outlet to the Adriatic and Mediterranean springboard against Greece, Turkey, Austria and Italy. [...] In general the program of the Soviet bloc, Yugoslav government seems to have chosen to spearhead expansionist movement. [...] Something like a HQ of International Communism seems to be functioning here.'[39] Even though Cannon did not ignore the Yugoslav national interest (as a possible source of conflict with the USSR), he again identified Communism as the guiding force of Yugoslav policy. In January 1948 during a meeting with Tito he denounced the pacts between Yugoslavia and some eastern European countries as the consequence of 'an agreed plan'.[40]

It is such a view of Yugoslavia, much more than an 'intelligence failure', that perplexed both Cannon, and the British ambassador, between March and mid June 1948. Obviously they perceived that Tito's regime was becoming entrenched and exhibiting a certain moderation towards the Western powers; but these were interpreted as symptoms of a conflict within the Yugoslav CP on how to build a Communist society in Yugoslavia. Until early June Cannon's analysis strictly followed this line of interpretation.[41]

Only after mid-June reports from the Belgrade Embassy introduced a new theme: the rift in the Communist bloc, 'the first direct and irrevocable challenge of any satellite to the supreme authority of its Communist overlords in the Kremlin'; moreover the military attachés recommended 'the boldest possible exploitation of this defection.'[42] On the contrary, more conventionally the British Foreign Office tended to think that the dispute was a little more than a family quarrel.[43] At any rate, at this point the Department of State promptly adjusted its policy towards Yugoslavia to the new phenomenon, Tito's heresy. The day after Tito was excommunicated by the Cominform, Kennan, the director of the Policy Planning Staff at the Department of State, finally identified both the dimensions of Tito's project: communism and the national interest. Thus he defined Yugoslavia as 'a communist state resting on the basis of Soviet organizational principles and for the most part on Soviet ideology, and yet independent of Moscow.'[44] If, according to Kennan's views, Tito's heresy undermined the cohesion of the Communist world, this did not turn Yugoslavia from an antagonistic power into an asset for Western security. Rather she should be considered as a grey area between the two blocs; an area that had to remain as such.[45]

Six months later, in January 1949, after ambassador Cannon warned that there was no alternative to Tito but a 'Soviet puppet', the Department of State initiated its new policy towards Yugoslavia: 'keeping Tito afloat'. Accordingly the US began to take charge of Yugoslav security (first economically and in 1951 militarily).[46] In the end Tito's double polarity – Communism and national interest – was able to survive. It was to survive behind a Western security screen.

Notes

1 S. Clissold (ed.), *Yugoslavia and the Soviet Union, 1939–1973. A Documentary Survey* (London: Oxford University Press, 1975); V. Dedijer, *The Battle Stalin Lost. Memoirs of Yugoslavia, 1948–1953* (New York: Viking Press, 1971); M. Djilas, *Memoir of a Revolutionary* (New York: Harcourt Brace Jovanovich, 1973); E. Kardelj, *Reminiscences* (London: 1982).

2 R. M. Blum, 'Surprised by Tito. The Anatomy of an Intelligence Failure', *Diplomatic History*, 12, 1 (1988) pp. 39–57.

3 L. Gibianskii, 'L'Unione Sovietica, la Jugoslavia e Trieste', in G. Valdevit ed., *La crisi di Trieste, maggio–giugno 1945. Una revisione storiografica* (Trieste: Quaderni dell'Istituto Regionale per la Storia del Movimento di Liberazione nel Friuli-Venezia Giulia, 1995) p. 77.

4 G. Procacci ed., G. Adibekov, A. Di Biagio, L. Gibianskii, F. Gori and S. Pons (co-eds), *The Cominform. Minutes of the Three Conferences 1947/1948/1949*, Fondazione Feltrinelli, Annali, XXX (Milan: Feltrinelli, 1994) p. 169.

5 J. Pirjevec, *Il giorno di San Vito. Jugoslavia 1918–1992. Storia di una tragedia* (Torino: Einaudi, 1993) p. 158 ff.; M. Djilas, *Wartime* (New York: Harcourt Brace Jovanovic, 1977).

6 R. Craig Nation, 'A Balkan Union? Southeastern Europe in Soviet Security Policy, 1944–1948', in F. Gori and S. Pons eds, *The Soviet Union and Europe in the Cold War (1943–1953)* (New York: St. Martin's Press, 1996) pp. 128–30.

7 J. Pirjevec, *Il giorno di San Vito*, op. cit., p. 182.

8 G. Valdevit, 'Foibe: l'eredità della sconfitta', in G. Valdevit (ed.), *Foibe. Il peso del passato. Venezia Giulia 1943–1945* (Venice: Marsilio, 1997) pp. 15–32.

9 Craig Nation, 'A Balkan Union?', op. cit., pp. 129–30; G. Valdevit, *La questione di Trieste 1941–1954. Politica internazionale e contesto locale* (Milan: Angeli, 1986), pp. 69–76.

10 L. Gibianskii, 'L'Unione Sovietica, la Jugoslavia e Trieste', op. cit., pp. 48, 57–71.

11 G. Valdevit, *La questione di Trieste 1941–1954*, op. cit., pp. 127–76; L. Gibianskii, 'The Beginning of the Soviet–Yugoslav Conflict', in Procacci ed. *The Cominform*, op. cit., pp. 470–1.

12 A. Di Biagio, 'The Soviet Reaction to the Marshall Plan and the Founding of the Cominform', in Gori and Pons eds, *The Soviet Union and Europe in the Cold War*, op. cit., p. 211 ff.

13 V. Mastny, *The Cold War and Soviet Insecurity. The Stalin Years* (New York: Oxford University Press, 1996), p. 34; Gibianskii, 'The Beginning of the Soviet–Yugoslav Conflict', in Procacci ed, *The Cominform* op. cit., pp. 469–70.

14 V. Mastny, *The Cold War and Soviet Insecurity* op. cit., pp. 32–3; Di Biagio, 'The Soviet Reaction to the Marshall Plan', in Gori and Pons eds, *The Soviet Union and Europe in the Cold War* op. cit., p. 216.

15 L. Gibianskii, 'The Soviet–Yugoslav Conflict and the Soviet Bloc' in Gori and Pons eds, *The Soviet Union and Europe in the Cold War*, op. cit., p. 224.

16 Procacci ed., *The Cominform* op. cit., pp. 171, 175, 297.

17 Ibid., pp. 89, 91.

18 Ibid., pp. 301.

19 G. Swain, 'The Cominform. Tito's International', *Historical Journal*, 35, 3 (1992), pp. 654–5, 663; A. A. Ulanian, 'The Soviet Union and "the Greek Question", 1946–1953: Problems and Appraisals', in Gori and Pons eds, *The Soviet Union and Europe in the Cold War*, op. cit., pp. 150–151; V. Mastny, *The Cold War and Soviet Insecurity* op. cit., p. 35.

20 L. Gibianskii, 'The Soviet–Yugoslav Conflict and the Soviet Bloc' in Gori and Pons eds, *The Soviet Union and Europe in the Cold War* op. cit., p. 231 ff.

21 L. Gibianskii, 'The Beginning of the Soviet–Yugoslav Conflict', op. cit., p. 471; V. Mastny, *The Cold War and Soviet Insecurity* op. cit., p. 37.

22 L. Gibianskii, 'The Beginning of the Soviet–Yugoslav Conflict' op. cit., p. 474. Tito's extremism in the field of foreign policy has been considered as the main reason of the subsequent split with Stalin by I. Banac, *With Stalin against Tito* (Ithaca: Cornell University Press, 1988) and B. Heuser, *Western 'Containment' Policies in the Cold War. The Yugoslav Case, 1948–53* (London: Routledge, 1989), p. 20 ff.

23 V. Mastny, *The Cold War and Soviet Insecurity* op. cit., pp. 40–4; M. M. Narinskii, 'The Soviet Union and the Berlin Crisis, 1948–9', in Gori and Pons eds, *The Soviet Union and Europe in the Cold War* op. cit., p. 62.

24 L. Gibianskii, 'The Beginning of the Soviet–Yugoslav Conflict', in Gori and Pons eds, *The Soviet Union and Europe in the Cold War* op. cit., pp. 474–5.

25 Ibid., p. 476.

26 Ibid., p. 475.

27 Ibid., pp. 476–7.

28 G. Valdevit, *La questione di Trieste 1941–1954* op. cit., pp. 194–6: R. Rabel, *Between East and West. Trieste, the United States, and the Cold War, 1941–1954* (Durham: Duke University Press, 1988), pp. 112–16.

29   L. Gibianskii, 'The Beginning of the Soviet–Yugoslav Conflict', in Gori and Pons eds, *The Soviet Union and Europe in the Cold War* op. cit., p. 478.

30   S. Pons, 'The Twilight of the Cominform', in Procacci ed., *The Cominform* op. cit., p. 503.

31   G. Valdevit, *La questione di Trieste 1941–1954* op. cit., p. 142 ff.; Rabel, *Between East and West*, op. cit., pp. 85–101.

32   The Under-secretary of State Acheson to the Ambassador in Belgrade, 12 January 1948, in FRUS, 1948, vol. 6, p. 868.

33   Byrnes to Clayton, 28 August 1946, Acheson and Clayton to Byrnes, 29 August 1946, in FRUS, 1946, vol. 6, p. 930–3.

34   Cabot to the Secretary of State Marshall, 15 February 1947 and 15 May 1947, in FRUS, 1947, vol. 4, pp. 761–4 and 796–7.

35   Cabot to Marshall, 7 June 1947, in FRUS, 1947, vol. 4, pp. 806–8.

36   Cabot to Marshall, 7 July 1947, FRUS, 1947, vol. 4, pp. 816–21; on the British side see A. Lane, *Britain, the Cold War and Yugoslav Unity, 1941–1949* (Brighton: Sussex Academic Press, 1996), p. 92.

37   Cabot to Marshall, 7 July 1947. FRUS, 1947, vol. 4, pp. 816–21 Cabot to Marshall, 7 July 1947. FRUS, 1947, vol. 4, pp. 816–21.

38   Cannon to Marshall, 7 August 1947, FRUS, 1947, vol. 4, pp. 834–7; Lane, *Britain, the Cold War and Yugoslav Unity* op. cit., pp. 102–3.

39   Cannon to Marshall, 7 September 1947, FRUS, 1947, vol. 4, pp. 840–2; On the domino theory see F. Ninkovich, *Modernity and Power. A History of the Domino Theory in the Twentieth Century* (Chicago: University of Chicago Press, 1994), chapter 5.

40   Cannon to Marshall, 3 January 1948, FRUS, 1948, vol. 4, pp. 1054–6.

41   Cannon to Marshall, 8 June 1948, FRUS, 1948, vol. 4, pp. 1070–2; Blum, *Surprised by Tito* op. cit., pp. 45–8; Lane, *Britain, the Cold War and Yugoslav Unity* op. cit., p. 116.

42   The Chargé d'Affaires Reams to Marshall, 18 June 1948, the military attachés in Belgrade, Partridge and Sweetser, to Marshall, 24 June 1948, FRUS, 1948, vol. 4, pp. 1073 and 1076–7; H. W. Brands, *The Specter of Neutralism. The United States and the Emergence of the Third World* (New York: Columbia University Press, 1989), pp. 145–6.

43   Lane, *Britain, the Cold War and Yugoslav Unity* op. cit., p. 119.

44   PPS 35, 30 June 1948, FRUS, 1948, vol. 4, pp. 1079–81.

45   J. L. Gaddis, *Strategies of Containment. A Critical Appraisal of Postwar American National Security Policy* (New York: Oxford University Press, 1982), p. 65 ff.; W. D. Miscamble, *George F. Kennan and the making of American Foreign Policy, 1947–1950* (Princeton: Princeton University Press, 1992), p. 189 ff.

46   Brands, *The Specter of Neutralism* op. cit., p. 149 ff.; Lane, *Britain, the Cold War and Yugoslav Unity* op. cit., p. 125 ff.

16
Relations Between East European Countries: the Balkan Federation (1942–49)

Stefano Bianchini

The idea of a Balkan integration has been supported by intellectuals of the area since the 16th century, but the defeat of the Hungarian Revolution in 1849 made clear how an extreme interpretation of nationalism could deepen rivalries and affect the attempts at national emancipation and modernization. Since then, the crucial dilemma of war and peace, as a dilemma connected to the geopolitical and institutional adjustment of the area, drove different political movements to include in their programmes a perspective of integration.

Therefore, when the Communists tried to create a Balkan federation, it was not by chance that the British Foreign Office urged the governments in exile of the kingdoms of Greece and Yugoslavia to sign an agreement for a post war union. Indeed, an agreement was signed on 15 January 1942. One week earlier, a 'Committee for planning Eastern and Central Europe' was announced by ministers Sava Kosanović (Yugoslavia), Jan Masaryk (Czechoslovakia), Aristides Dimitratos (Greece) and Jan Sanczyk (Poland).[1] The old dream of the 19th Century – a union from the Baltic to the Aegean sea, as suggested by Mazzini – re-emerged in order to contain Germany and the Soviet Union after the Second World War.

However, these hopes had to face violent disagreements, provoked either by local nationalist claims or by the different behaviour of east European governments towards Nazism and Fascism (as in the Polish–Czech and Albanian–Greek–Yugoslav cases). These contrasts largely contributed to the failure of the integration projects elaborated in exile. More or less simultaneously, Communists outlined similar projects. Convinced as they were they had the ideological support of the 3rd

International, they claimed a Comintern resolution approved at the beginning of July 1924 (at the end of the 5th Congress) when a specific statement included the 'Balkan federation of equal and independent republics of workers and peasants' as a desirable perspective for the peoples of south-east Europe.[2] In addition, Balkan Communists had the advantage in 1943 of the military success of the Yugoslav partisans and Tito's dominant role, which lent strength to their regional integration goals. They perceived how independent they were of the great powers and acquired a new self-confidence due to their own political success.

However, the revolutionary theory and the political practice of the Communists had not overcome the ambiguity of Lenin's 1913–16 statements. At the time, the Bolshevik leader had proclaimed the right of nations to self-determination, and even secession, hoping both to encourage the collapse of the great empires and to open the doors to a Socialist revolution in the world. Nevertheless, Lenin had warned the working class that a consequent enforcement of this right, encouraging the creation of new states with a limited territorial dimension, could affect the economic development of society and the process of modernization. In the end, as is well known, Lenin suggested federal solutions, whereas he never denied how crucial should be the role plaid by the 'democratic centralism'.[3]

This contradictory approach was later conditioned by Stalinist practice which eliminated every kind of autonomy. Furthermore, the trend toward centralization in the Balkans was influenced by the French model of state administration, based on departments, and considered a successful pattern by the emerging independent societies. Yet, the idea of a Balkan union lay in the federalist traditions of revolutionaries, populists and socialists. In sum, a peculiar and rather curious mixture of centralist and federalist ideas, of national pride and an ideological (rather than legal) perception of national self-determination lay behind the Communist attempt at creating a Balkan federation in the 1940s.

Very early this appeared to be inadequate to face both the emotions aroused by nationalism or the categories of 'territory', 'boundaries', 'fatherland' rooted into the popular vision by nationalist claims. Particularly the questions of Kosovo and Macedonia played a crucial role by hindering the integration processes. Even the institutional framework of the union, in other words the alternative between federation and confederation, remained unclear. In addition, the United Kingdom and the Soviet Union sought to influence the project in their own interests. They both encouraged or stopped the Balkan leaders on different occasions, in order to establish their own hegemony and hinder the adversary. Consequently, the risk of destabilizing the area increased.

By contrast, the real dimensions of the geopolitical adjustment that Tito and Dimitrov had in mind when they promoted negotiations with Hoxha or with the EAM–ELAS representatives is difficult to say. Unfortunately, as soon as the archives were opened at the end of the 1980s, they were immediately closed again at the beginning of the Yugoslav war of secession, when history was considered by ethno-nationalists to be a way to a legitimize state power and borders. In this context, any historical document which confirmed past promises or agreements between Communist leaders in order to change borders (as in the Kosovo or Macedonian cases) was considered a lever for new antagonisms and conflicts.

This approach has restricted the field of historical research. However, the available documentation and the chronological comparison of the events makes a study of Communist relations in the Balkans possible, since it is possible to examine when and how they faced the challenge for regional integration.

The Balkan federation in a multilateral dynamic (1942–43)

On 15 November 1942, Tito met Vukmanović Tempo in a train coach near Ostrelj, in Bosnia. During the talk, Tito ordered his general to establish a joint military headquarters with the Albanian, Bulgarian and Greek forces, with the agreement of the Central Committees of their Communist Parties, in order to strengthen the partisan movements in Kosovo and Macedonia.[4] Tempo accepted. He went to Macedonia and started to implement the project. In early summer 1943, when fascism was overthrown in Italy, the situation in the Balkans became uncertain. On 20 June Tempo met Hoxha and a delegate of the Greek party (his name doesn't appear amongst the signatures at the bottom of the 'Conclusions', whose original was written in French). The meeting took place in a still unknown Albanian village. The participants established a political and military co-operation, while the Macedonian question emerged as the most delicate issue. In the end, a Greek proposal was accepted and the fate of the Aegean region of Macedonia was postponed to the end of the war.[5]

Two weeks later, on 2 July, a new meeting took place in Greece when Tempo met Xoxe and V. Samarineos. They agreed that a 'Supreme Headquarters of the Popular Liberation Army in the Balkans' should be created before 10 August under the leadership of four commanders and four political commissars, representing Yugoslavia, Albania, Greece and Bulgaria. In fact, the events of the war made the participation of the Bulgarian Communists in these multilateral meetings impossible, but Tempo had already established bilateral contacts and, subsequently, he obtained their consent.[6] Meanwhile, new controversies arose over the Macedonian question. Tempo supported the claim of the Vardar Macedonians to a 'national Macedonian union in the community framework of the Yugoslav peoples'. By contrast, the Greek Central Committee did not accept the decision of Tempo, Xoxe and Samarineos to send Vardar–Macedonian troops into the Aegean Macedonia. Similar disputes arose between Macedonians and Albanians.

On 23 September, in this context of increasing difficulties, Tito suddenly forced Tempo to interrupt his attempts to create an integrated headquarters. It is unclear why Tito made such a decision, but generally historians agree that, beyond the influence of the different national claims, he was urged to do so by Fitzroy Maclean, because Great Britain opposed the idea of a Balkan federation including countries (such as Bulgaria) which had been defeated during the war and whose fate had still to be discussed at the peace conference. The event provoked a radical turn. Tito in fact changed his strategy. Multilateral negotiations were abandoned, but bilateral negotiations started with Albania and Bulgaria. As Tito made clear in a letter to Tempo on 9 October, the relations 'with Greece and Bulgaria, particularly Bulgaria'[7] had to be strengthened.

The Balkan federation in a bilateral dynamic (1944–47)

During the Second World War, the Serbo-Albanian controversy over Kosovo worsened. In 1941 Italy created a Greater Albania and supported the settlement of Albanian landowners in Kosovo and Çamëria. This event and the concern for new post war arrangements encouraged the Albanian Communists and the liberal/nationalist movement of *Balli in Kombëtar* to search an agreement on the future of Kosova. Nevertheless, the Yugoslav pressures on Hoxha made any compromise impossible and a split between the two organisations arose in Mukaj in 1943.[8] Since then, *Balli in Kombëter* became a pro-German movement and a civil war followed in Albania, while Hoxha urged Tito to maintain the Albanian sovereignty over Kosovo.[9] Riots took place in Kosova when the Yugoslav and Albanian Communist Armies entered the region.[10]

In addition, when the war came to an end, Tito faced the delicate question of Kosova landowners: the Serbs, who had played an active role in the partisan movement, claimed back their farms. New tensions arose. In the end, claiming that the land belonged to those who had cultivated it Tito decided not to reverse the local situation and recognized the *status quo*.[11] Tito believed that the Serbian disappointment would be limited by the reintegration of Kosovo into Serbia, as an autonomous region. Furthermore, if the Albanians forgot their fear of losing their properties, this would open the door to new, better, relations between Belgrade and Tirana, and strengthen the links that had already been established during the war.

In this uncertain situation, on 25 February 1945 two important agreements were signed between the countries. The first was a trade treaty, the second a military alliance against Germany, later transformed into a common defence system against any foreign aggression. The trade agreement gave Yugoslavia the *surplus* of oil products, naphtha and wool, while Albania received via Struga and Ohrid an equivalent value of wheat, maize and sugar.[12] By contrast, the military agreement signed by Tito and Josip Smodlaka for the Yugoslav side, remained secret and the document has not yet been found in the Tito Archives. According to some testimonies, it seems that Tirana accepted Belgrade's help in guaranteeing its independence with the supply of weapons and military and civilian experts. In this way the Albanian leadership sought to overcome its sense of insecurity, provoked by the Greek accusations that the 'Albanian vassals' of Mussolini had taken part in the Italian aggression of October 1940.

In February 1946, the 5th *plenum* of the Central Committee of the Albanian Communist Party approved the proposal to strengthen relations with Yugoslavia. Some months later, from 23 June to 2 July Enver Hoxha visited Belgrade, where he discussed with Tito the bilateral relations and the future of the Balkan federation. The two leaders signed a new agreement of economic co-operation (on 1 July) which provided the conditions for creating joint stock companies. The aim was to encourage the exploitation of raw materials (oil and minerals), the improvement of the railway network, the electrification of the country, the development of export–import relations, the setting up of both steamship companies and a Yugo-Albanian Bank. When Hoxha came back to Tirana, on 6 July, he signed another treaty of friendship and mutual assistance with Yugoslavia, which included the mutual military assistance in case of aggression by a third country (article 3).[13]

Meanwhile, Yugoslavia was preparing a very ambitious five year plan, which had to come into effect at the beginning of 1947. Some weeks before, on 27 November 1946, Boris Kidrić and Nako Spiru signed a new agreement in Belgrade which made the future integration of the planning systems possible. Moreover, the treaty established the conditions for a customs union and joint monetary reform in order to have a single currency within three months.[14]

Nevertheless, the Kosovo issue had a negative influence on bilateral relations. Secret contacts took place, but many events related to them had never been clarified. According to the Albanian leader, Tito had suggested a non-traumatic solution within the framework of the Balkan federation when he met Hoxha in early summer 1946. By contrast, Hoxha sought to consider the problem separately from the idea of a common Yugo-Albanian state. Many years later, in 1989, the Belgrade weekly *NIN* asserted that Hoxha correctly reported the statement of both leaders. It seems that in a record, which was however never published, Tito offered Hoxha the unification of Kosovo, once the Yugo-Albanian federation had been established.[15]

Unfortunately, available diplomatic and political sources are limited. This makes difficult – and sometimes impossible – a reconstruction of the topic. Any serious evaluation seems to be difficult, at the moment, although some speculation is possible when considering Hoxha's radical about-turn against Yugoslavia in 1948. Certainly, he wanted to cancel a tutorship considered too heavy-handed. Also he seized this opportunity to eliminate some political antagonists, as for example Xoxe. Nevertheless, because everybody expected the overthrow of Tito by Stalin, a new geopolitical assessment was a possibility and in such a case Hoxha could hope to receive Kosovo from the Soviet Union in recognition of his loyalty to the Kremlin.

However, Yugo-Albanian relations deteriorated after the second half of 1947 following Hoxha's visit to Moscow in July. The Soviet role in Albania rapidly increased, while the Albanian leadership was involved in a crude political conflict behind the scenes. The Tito–Hoxha correspondence of March–May 1948 – which took place in the same period and on similar topics, and using the same methods and language as between Tito and Stalin – does not help us to understand the 'deep' reasons for the Yugo-Albanian disagreement. As in the Tito–Stalin quarrel, other, more secret reasons eventually provoked the conflict between Belgrade and Tirana. One of these was probably the fate of Kosovo.[16] Indeed, the Tito–Stalin split provoked a similar split between Belgrade and Tirana, and in the 1950s the Albanian population of Kosovo lost its regional autonomy embodied in the Stalinist Yugoslav Constitution of 1946.

The Yugo-Bulgarian bilateral co-operation started in 1944, when Tito – travelling back from Moscow – met two top members of the Bulgarian

Communist Party, Peter Todorov and Dobri Terpesev, in the town of Craiova (Romania) on 5 October. The meeting offered a good opportunity for the signing of a treaty of military co-operation against Germany and a new amity between their countries after a long period of enmity. Nevertheless, three weeks after the Craiova meeting, Tempo sent a dispatch to the Macedonian partisan headquarters as well as to the Macedonian and Bulgarian Central Committees, suggesting the creation of a Macedonian division 'Jane Sandanski' in the Pirin area. He also insisted on establishing an integrated headquarters in order to speed up the unification of Macedonia. On 28 October, Dimitrov reacting from Moscow, sent a telegram to Tito, in which he stressed that the priority of all the partisan movements should be the war against Germany; by contrast, he added, the 'Macedonian Headquarters was regarding Bulgarian Macedonia as an annexed territory', instead of postponing all future arrangements for Macedonia to the postwar period.[17] Crucially, Bulgaria was a defeated country and the Communists had to take care both of the national feeling of the population towards Macedonia and to the possibility of limiting the consequences of defeat, by strengthening the links with Tito's Yugoslavia for geopolitical and ideological reasons.

However, this complex background encouraged the Communists to overcome their difficulties and the bilateral relations improved day by day. On 2 November, the Secretary of the Central Committee, Traichco Kostov, sent a long and friendly letter to Tito in which he stated: 'About the creation of a free Macedonian state within the framework of the new federal Yugoslavia, by which the first step to the achievement of the Macedonian hopes to establish a free and unified Macedonia is accomplished, we would like to inform you that our party and our people warmly support the new Macedonian state. We shall contribute to the strengthening of this attitude in public opinion. [...] We shall contribute to the awakening of national Macedonian consciousness in the Bulgarian Macedonia [...].' Then, he added that the Bulgarians would encourage the cultural and organisational development of the Macedonians.[18]

In conclusion, the Macedonian question and the Yugo-Bulgarian federation were strictly intertwined: the solution of the latter directly depended on the former, and vice-versa. In addition, the issue of Macedonian unification appeared to be even more complicated because it was related to a negotiation with Greece in the broader perspective of a Balkan federation: a perspective which could be discussed only once the Greek civil war had come to an end.

Meanwhile, when difficulties arose between Belgrade and Sofia, they were provoked more by the characteristics of the future federation than by the Macedonian issue. In particular, Yugoslav and Bulgarian delegations could not reach an agreement on the number of the constitutive entities of the union: according to Sofia, they had to be only two (Yugoslavia and Bulgaria), while according to Belgrade, they had to be seven (the six Yugoslav republics plus Bulgaria).

Nine draft treaties were discussed between 1944 and 1947 by both sides. Some of these drafts were very ambitious and they outlined different forms of political, economic and military co-operation. Others were very limited in their aims. During the negotiations, the unresolved territorial issues were also discussed. For instance, the project written on 25 December 1944 introduced a very important innovation. In point 5, the unification of Vardar and Pirin Macedonias was clearly foreseen within the framework of the Yugoslav federation. As far as Yugoslavia was concerned, Belgrade accepted the return to Sofia the districts of Caribrod (Dimitrovgrad) and Bosilgrad, which it had received after the First World War under the Treaty of Neuilly in 1919.[19]

This agreement was advanced when the war had not yet come to an end. The situation drove Churchill to oppose it: he feared that Communism in Belgrade could be strengthened by this union, making a coalition government impossible, despite his agreements with Tito in Italy. A Communist and pro-Soviet Bulgaria would greatly increase Moscow's influence in the Balkans; and Bulgaria had still to be considered to be a defeated country. Probably for these reasons, on 5 December 1944, Anthony Eden wrote a memorandum to halt all Yugo-Bulgarian contacts, which nevertheless were continued secretly. Some months later, in Yalta, the Allies urged the negotiations be interrupted immediately. As a consequence, the project was temporarily postponed. However, Dimitrov, by birth from Pirin Macedonia, promoted a radical change in the Bulgarian national culture by recognizing the special nature of the Macedonian Nation in 1945. In turn, Tito stopped Serbian assimilation in the area between Sar Planina and Gevgelija, considered by Serbian nationalists to be 'Southern Serbia'.[20]

Actually, many Bulgarian Communists genuinely believed that only Bulgarians lived in Macedonia. Nevertheless, they could accept ideologically the idea of an unified Macedonian state as an autonomous state or as a state within the Yugoslav framework because it had been proclaimed by a statement of Comintern in the interwar period.[21] In addition, most of the Bulgarian public opinion hoped that an autonomous Macedonia would establish strong links with Sofia, preparing in a sense for a future unification.

Thanks to these calculations, bilateral contacts increased dramatically. In August 1946, Belgrade and Sofia began to promote close cultural relations in the Macedonian regions of Vardar and Pirin. In August 1947 Tito met Dimitrov on the shores of the Bled lake, in Slovenia. The leaders agreed upon the creation of the federation. They strengthened cultural programmes in the Pirin area, involving intellectuals from the Vardar area. Some months later, on 27 November, Tito and Dimitrov attended a new meeting in Evksinograd (Bulgaria), where they signed a treaty of friendship and mutual aid. However, despite these intentions, new steps for the implementation of the union were not defined.[22]

Apparently, the leaders were trying to seek a solution as to the number of union entities. Meanwhile, the Greek civil war started again. Yugoslavia, Albania and Bulgaria helped the Greek partisans: in some respects a form of multilateral Balkan co-operation had been restored.

Back to a multilateral dimension. The Greek civil war (1946–49)

When the war reignited in Greece, its northern neighbours guaranteed EAM–ELAS mostly food, war hospitals, training areas and weapons in the Vardar area. Although the documentation and the sources currently known to scholars are not complete, it seems impossible to consider this solidarity only in terms of ideological internationalism. Rather, many elements have strengthened the perception that Communists were seeking to implement a Balkan geopolitical adjustment, despite their territorial disputes.[23] By contrast, Great Britain, the United States and the Soviet Union interfered in the Balkans in order to maintain the balance of power or to establish their control over their own camps when the iron curtain divided Europe. Consequently the idea of a Balkan federation came to be involved in a complicated diplomatic game.

On 4 February 1945 Vladimir Popović informed Tito that some days earlier (26 January) the Foreign Office had strongly urged the Sofia government not to sign any agreement with Belgrade, nor to establish any co-operation between Bulgaria and the Hellenic Macedonians.[24] According to Popović, the Foreign Office added that London would support only 'a Balkan federation or confederation in which Albania, Greece and Turkey will also be included'. Although we lack a document confirming Popović's statement, the idea of a larger union is understandable in the light of Britain's attempts at reducing the Communist role: in fact, a coalition centred in Belgrade and involving Athens and Ankara could assure a balance more propitious to British interests, at least at the beginning of 1945.

In turn, Stalin feared the re-establishment of the 'cordon sanitaire'. For this reason he reversed his opinion of October 1943, when he rejected any project of Danubian or Balkan integration supported by the United Kingdom during the Moscow Conference. On the contrary, on 22 November 1944 he warmly supported the idea of a Yugo-Bulgarian federation when he met Edvard Kardelj and Ivan Subašić in Moscow.[25] At the time, a restricted Yugo-Bulgarian agreement seemed to offer the possibility of strengthening Soviet hegemony over the Balkans. It was not by chance that the 7th project of Yugo-Bulgarian union was written in Moscow by Vyshinsky in January 1945. Moreover, this project accepted the Bulgarian point of view of a union of the two states. In conclusion, the issue awoke the very different interests of the great powers and the unstable post war balance explains why the main protagonists frequently reversed their attitudes on the subject.[26]

In addition, Tito pursued his own project, that is to avoid both British and Soviet control. Both the support and sudden stops suddenly imposed by Tito on Tempo in 1943 as well as Tito's distrust when Moscow urged a Yugo-Bulgarian union at the end of 1944 do not give the impression that his project was ill conceived. Rather, difficulties arose because the integration attempt was conditioned by two crucial questions: (1) the project had to receive the support of all the other Balkan partners, and (2) its success depended on the concurrence of the great powers in a period of considerable historical change (1944–47). Tito's efforts in the postwar period were concentrated on achieving these goals, and this can explain why he was so cautious with Stalin. By contrast, Stalin opposed the Balkan union project in 1947: immediately after the Bled meeting he sent a telegram to Tito (12 August 1947) indicating to him and Dimitrov that their idea of union could strengthen the 'reactionary Anglo-American elements' and encouraging their plan to 'invade Yugoslavia and Bulgaria from Greece and Turkey'.[27]

According to Gibianskii, Tito and Dimitrov sent Stalin a draft of a bilateral agreement after the Evksinograd meeting, making it quite clear that similar agreements would be signed with Romania and Hungary before December 1947. Moreover, in accepting one of previous Stalin's criticisms against a Yugo-Bulgarian agreement without an expiry date, Tito and Dimitrov specified that the agreement would last 20 years. In spite of these efforts, when the Tito–Stalin split occurred, a radical change was imposed on Balkan regional relations. After the Communist collapse, Russian scholars suggested that the real reason for this controversy lay in the disagreements between Yugoslavia and the Soviet Union over the Balkan Union.[28] There are many factors which have confirmed such an interpretation.

There is no doubt that Tito supported a geopolitical role for Macedonia: a meeting in Skopje in October 1945 ended with the following words: 'Long live free Macedonia with equal rights within the brotherly community of the peoples of Yugoslavia! I wish you that Macedonia, and all the Macedonians some day will come together in a unified Macedonia!'[29] By contrast, the Greek Communists confirmed the intangibility of the boundaries of their country, when they signed the Varkiza agreement in February 1945. Nevertheless, Hellenic Slavo-Macedonians – who had played a remarkable role during the Resistance – reorganised their military force only a few months later. They were ready to take part in a new phase of the Greek civil war, although at the time, and up until summer 1946, the majority of Greek partisans were uncertain. On the Macedonian issue, opinion was divided: for instance, the General Secretary Nikolaos Zahariades recognized in 1945 the right to self determination for the people of Macedonia, Cyprus, Dodecanese Islands and Northern Epirus, while a few months later Demetrios Partsalides, a member of the Central Committee, rejected the idea that such a right could be applied to the Slavo-Macedonians.

When the civil war exploded again, the Hellenic Slavo-Macedonians rapidly became the backbone of the Communist army. This factor deeply influenced the political evolution of the events: to a certain extent the second phase of the Greek civil war can be considered a war for the unification of Macedonia and, more generally, for the Balkan federation. The help received by ELAS between 1946 and 1947 from Yugoslavia and Bulgaria was by no means marginal: weapons, munitions, radios, money and supplies poured into Hellenic Macedonia from Belgrade. It also seems that, at the beginning of 1948, when the conflict had reached a climax, nearly half of the ELAS Army was made up of Slavo-Macedonians.[30]

On 18 January 1948 Dimitrov visited Bucharest: during a famous press conference he supported the idea of a Balkan federation including Greece. On 29 January *Pravda* criticized Dimitrov's declarations. A few days later, Stalin summoned a meeting with the Yugoslav and Bulgarian leaders, but Tito did not attend. Two months later, the Yugo-Soviet relations worsened. On 28 June Yugoslavia was turned out of the Cominform. Politically divided into two factions (led by General Markos and the General Secretary, Zahariades), the majority of ELAS supported Stalin in the quarrel. The Yugoslav support was lost, while the American support to royalists – announced in 1947 by Truman – became considerable. The military difficulties of ELAS increased and many partisans, particularly Slavo-Macedonians, took refuge in Yugoslavia.[31] In 1949 Tito closed the boundaries with Greece in order to avoid the risk that Greek partisans might enter Yugoslavia and destabilize his power by supporting Stalin's Resolution in Vardar Macedonia. This decision definitely contributed to ending the Greek civil war and ELAS – weakly supported only by Albania and Bulgaria – was forced to yield.

The Yugo-Soviet dispute had a radical influence on both nationalism and Communism. As the Kosova issue affected Yugo-Albanian relations, so Yugo-Bulgarian controversies over Macedonia regularly emerged any time the relations between Yugoslavia and Soviet Union worsened. Even in Greece, despite the pro-Tito orientations that had emerged in 1949 and despite US pressure on Athens to forget its disagreements with Yugoslavia in the 1950s, popular perception on the Macedonia question remained highly sensitive.[32]

The idea of a Balkan union was temporarily abandoned, while an awareness that peace and war in the region strictly depended on the success or the failure of integration processes did not disappear. When the risk of a military attack on Yugoslavia by the Soviet Union vanished and Tito's leadership was strengthened, regional co-operation with Greece and Turkey was restored through the Balkan pact. Potentially, its implementation and the beginning of détente offered a better environment for overcoming both recent and older disputes. New hopes were encouraged, but new difficulties emerged soon.

Notes and references

1 See Federal Ministry of Foreign Affairs, *Dokumenti o spoljnoj politici SFRJ 1941–1947* (Beograd: Jugoslovenski Pregled, 1985), further on DSP, 1941–1945, I, 65, 66 and S. K. Pawlowitch, 'The Balkan Union Agreement of 1942', *Storia delle Relazioni Internazionali*, III, no. 1 (1987) pp. 99–118.

2 A. Agosti, *La Terza Internazionale. Storia documentaria* (Rome, Editori Riuniti: 1976) II, t. I, pp. 159–62. See also Institut za Medjunarodni Radnicki Pokret, *Komunisticka Internacionala. Stenogrami i dokumenti kongresa*, (Gornji Milanovac: Privredna Knjiga, 1982), VII, pp. 996–1002.

3 The article 'Socialist Revolution and the Right of Nations to Self-determination' appeared in *Vorbote*, no. 2, (April 1916). See also Lenin, *Il diritto delle nazioni all'autodeterminazione* (Rome: Newton Compton, 1978).

4 Cf S. V. Tempo, *Revolucija koja tece* (Zagreb: Globus, 1982) vol. II, p. 225 and *Borba za Balkan* (Zagreb: Globus, 1981).

5 DSP, 1941–1945, I, 224.

6 DSP, 1941–1945, I, 228.

7 DSP, 1941–1945, I, 233, 234, e 256. Tempo abandoned the idea of an Integrated Headquarters by order of the 2nd Korpus. A-VII, Fond NOR, sc. 731, 4/ 20–9, in Tito, *Sabrana Djela* (Beograd: Komunist, 1984) vol. XVI, p. 225.

8 See the Vukmanovic Tempo's letter to Haxhi Lleshi, 1 October, in DSP, 1941–1945, I, 251.

9 See Tito's letter to Hoxha, 2 December 1943, in DSP, 1941–1945, vol. II, no. 11.

10 See V. Dedijer, *Novi prilozi za biografiju Josipa Broza Tita* (Beograd: Rad, 1984) III, pp. 180–1; B. Petranović, *Balkanska federacija* (Beograd, Svedocanstva: 1991), p. 99; B. Horvat, *Kosovsko pitanje* (Zagreb, Globus: 1989), p. 77 and S. Djaković, *Sukobi na Kosovu* (Beograd: Narodna Knjiga, 1984).

11 On the question of landowners, see my *Tito, Stalin e i contadini* (Milan: Unicopli, 1988) p. 83. The international dimension is discussed in S. V. Tempo, *Revolucija Kojatece*, op. cit.

12 Archives Josip Broz Tito (hereafter referred to a A JBT), KMJ I-3-6/11. On the military alliance see J. Smodlaka, *Partizanski dnevnik*, (Beograd, 1972) pp. 262–3.

13 DSP, 1946, I, 84, 89.

14 The agreement has been published by *Sluzbeni List FNRJ*, no. 106, 31 December 1946.

15 Cf E. Hoxha, *The Titoistes. Historical Notes*, (Tiranë: ediz. '8 Nëntori', 1982); B. Petranović, *Balkanska federacija*, op. cit. pp. 156 ff. and P. Stojanović, 'Kosovo na poklon', *Nin*, 14 May 1989, pp. 24–7.

16 On Yugo-Albanian relations see B. Petranović, *Balkanska federacija*, op. cit., pp. 164–74; S. Pollo *et al.*, *The History of the Socialist Construction of Albania* (Tiranë, 8 Nëntori: 1988), pp. 96–105 and the Memories of the Albanian vice-minister of Defence (who joined Yugoslavia on 17 May 1957), P. Pljaku, *Nasilje nad albanskom revolucijom*, (Beograd: Narodna Knjiga, 1984), pp. 68–71.

17 DSP, 1941–1945, II, 187 and 190.

18 DSP, 1941–1945, II, 192.

19 The nine projects have been analyzed by Z. Avramovski, 'Devet projekata ugovora o Jugoslovensko–Bugarskom savezu i federaciji 1944–1947', *Istorija XX veka*, no. 2 (1983) pp. 91–124.

20 J. M. Jovanović, *Juzna Srbija od kraja XVIII veka do oslobodjenja* (Beograd: Geca Kon, 1938, *reprint*, Beograd: Tanesi, 1990).

21 See point 1 of the 'Resolution on National Questions in East Central Europe and Balkans', 5th Congress of Comintern, 8 July 1924 in IMPP, *Komunisticka Internacionala. Stenogrami i Dokumenti Kongresa* (Gornji Milanovac, Privredna Knjiga: 1982) vol. VII, p. 998.

22 See the interesting documentation in S. Nesović, *Bledski sporazumi: Tito–Dimitrov 1947* (Zagreb: Globus, 1979).

23 B. Petranović, *Balkanska federacija* op. cit., p. 176 ff.

24 DSP, 1941–1945, II, 222.

25 DSP, 1941–1945, II, 195.

26 M. Ristovic, 'Britanska balkanska politika i jugoslovensko-bugarski pregovori', *Istorija XX veka*, no. 1 (1985) pp. 69–94.

27 L. Gibianskii, 'Ot "Nerusimoj druzbi" k besposcadnoj bor'be: modelj "socija-listiceskogo lagerja" i sovetsko-jugoslavskij konflikt 1948' in L. Gibianskii ed., *U Istikov 'socijalisticeskogo sodruzestva': CCCP u vostocnoevropejskie strany v 1944–1949 gg.,* (Moscow: Nauka, 1995), pp. 186–7.
28 See L. Gibianskii, *Sovetskij Sojuz i novaja Jugoslavija 1941–1947,* (Moscow: Nauka, 1987) and the comments on the Yugoslav–Soviet meetings of historians in Moscow, in *NIN,* nn. 2040–45, (4 February–11 March 1990).
29 B. Petranović, *Balkanska federacija* op. cit., pp. 112–14. Tito's speech in Skopje is in *Sabrana djela* op. cit., XXIX, 1989, pp. 95–103.
30 See E. Kofos, *Nationalism and Communism in Macedonia* (Thessaloniki: Institut for Balkan Studies, 1964) and G. Vaccarino, *La Grecia fra Resistenza e guerra civile 1940–1949* (Milan: Angeli, 1988).
31 New documents on Markos and the Greek Civil War were recently published by D. Kljakić, *Izgubljena pobjeda generala Markosa,* (Beograd: Narodna Knjiga, 1987). On the Soviet opinion see P. J. Stavrakis, *Moscow and Greek Communism 1944–1949* (Ithaca and London: Cornell University Press, 1989).
32 I. Stefanidis, 'United States, Great Britain and the Greek-Yugoslav rapprochement 1949–1950', *Balkan Studies,* no. 2 (1986) pp. 315–43.

17
Some Methodological Questions

Jerzy W. Borejsza

Almost immediately after the collapse of Communism between 1989 and 1991, historians specializing in international relations took advantage of the relatively free access to the archives of the former USSR and Soviet bloc countries and speeded up research into the history of the Cold War. Hundreds of articles, essays and books have been published. Whereas Anglo-Saxon literature predominated up to 1990, it is now unthinkable to write a synthesis of any stage of the Cold War without consulting Russian, German, Polish, Hungarian and Czech publications. They have been appearing in streams, making the studies based on narrow sources outdated.

At the international conference on '*Entstalinisierung in Ostmitteleuropa im Vergleich*' ('Stalinization in East-Central Europe compared'), organized in November 1998 in Poland by the *Deutsches Historisches Institut* of Warsaw, a significant dispute over Imre Nàgy arose between a Russian historian and Hungarian political scientists. The Russian historian attached great importance not only to Nàgy's role as leader of the Hungarian revolution of 1956 but also to his life as an emigré in the USSR from 1930 to 1944. The Hungarians thought that a discussion on Nàgy's role in Stalin's apparatus of terror in the USSR in the 1930s would be absolutely pointless. They stressed the great finale of Nàgy's political career, of his defiance of the USSR at the head of a decisive majority of the Hungarian people in the autumn of 1956, a defiance which earned him the rank of national hero.[1] There are also people who have doubts about the authenticity of the documents brought to light in Russia, for it was common practice for the Russian and Soviet police to set up files with false information on political adversaries or persons who were to be discredited *ex post*.

It is impossible to make proper use of Soviet archival materials if we forget that they were constantly tampered with. Researchers cannot

211

escape the question of whether these materials are authentic and complete. We cannot draw indubitable conclusions on the basis of Soviet archival documents unless we keep the Stalinist terror in mind and remember which of the leading and minor Comintern activists survived the terror and what price they had to pay. This applies to activists such as Imre Nàgy, Josip Broz Tito and Georgij Dimitrov, who as soon as they returned to their home countries ceased to be (though to a different extent) mere tools of Moscow. Among those who openly came out against Stalinism after 1945 were dozens of foreign Communists harshly treated during their stay in the USSR. They wanted their Socialism or communism to be different from Soviet Communism, and cherished illusions of far-reaching autonomy, if not independence. Memory of his own wrongdoing in the 1930s may have induced Imre Nàgy in 1956 to adopt an attitude of desperate opposition to the Kremlin.

Without knowing the realities, the historical climate in which Stalin, Molotov and their subordinates operated in the USSR and Europe, without always keeping this in mind, we shall not come near to the historical truth. We shall not understand it if we forget that in totalitarian and authoritarian systems many decisions were oral and did not leave a trace on paper. In the 1940s, Soviet foreign policy decision making was almost exclusively in the hands of two persons: Stalin and, to some extent, Molotov. The latter had a free hand in questions which were not of key importance and he did launch some initiatives. But Georgi Malenkov and Andrei Zhdanov, who were sent to a conference at Szklarska Poreba in Poland in September 1947 to set up the Cominform, notified Moscow of every step taken.

When considering the chapters by Stefano Bianchini 'Relations between East-European Countries: the Balkan Federation (1942–49)' and by Giampaolo Valdevit 'Yugoslavia between the Two Emerging Blocs 1943–48' we must remember that Stalin agreed to a 'special relationship between Yugoslavia and the USSR' under the pressure of events. He was forced to agree because of the role which Tito, the Yugoslav Communists and, first and foremost, their guerilla army played in the Balkans. Stalin was willing to regard the Yugoslavs as his privileged outpost so long as they were subservient to him. At the same time he tried to back up Bulgaria in order to prevent Belgrade from suppressing Sofia. Honouring his pledge to Churchill, he did his best to hold the Yugoslavs back from getting involved in the Greek civil war. Stalin and Molotov disliked the popularity which Tito and the Yugoslavs enjoyed among European Communists.[2] Any experience that differed from the one Moscow had gained was suspicious in their view. The Yugoslavs had participated in large numbers in the Spanish civil war and easily renewed contacts with their comrades-in-arms of that time. This only increased Moscow's suspicions. Having once rejected the idea of Madrid becoming a new capital of the European Left, Stalin saw no reason why he should tolerate a rival centre in Belgrade. But in the person of Tito he met an adversary who had been given training in his own school.

The USSR's policy in the Balkans was determined by its imperial interests which demanded that the Soviet Union should abandon the Greek Communists and focus attention on an agreement with Turkey, so as to block other powers' access to the Black Sea. It seems that the important factor often escapes the researchers' notice: from the Potsdam Conference to the beginning of 1947 Stalin, disregarding all suggestions, was obsessed with the idea of forcing Turkey to agree to a Soviet base that would control the Straits. This was clearly a return to tsarist Russia's old claims. It is said that his hopes of carrying out this plan were dashed when on 12 March 1947 'Truman asked the US Congress for support of his policy of containment of communism in Greece and Turkey'.[3] It is only recently that scholars have drawn attention to the fact that in the first postwar years the CPSU(b) Central Committee closely linked its Balkan policy with the Turkish question.[4]

Stalin did not want to allow Tito's strong army to dominate the Balkans; even during the war he warned the Yugoslavs not to create the impression that they wanted to swallow up Bulgaria. From the beginning Stalin and Molotov held back from approving the plans for a Yugoslav–Bulgarian federation. At the beginning of January 1945, Stalin warned the Yugoslavs that if they were too tough with the Bulgarians they would push them into the arms of the US, Great Britain and even Turkey. Molotov asserted that even a treaty of friendship and mutual assistance between Yugoslavia and Bulgaria would cause 'confusion in Europe'.[5]

Yugoslavia's territorial ambitions were extensive. At the end of the war the Yugoslavs planned to incorporate Trieste, a part of Carynthia, Greek Macedonia and Salonika into Yugoslavia and hoped to subjugate Albania. They were also considering the incorporation of Timisoara and its environs.[6] Stalin was not too well versed in the Balkan reality; he thought, for instance, that the Albanians were a Slav nation.[7] But he was well experienced in the diplomatic game, and though intoxicated with his victory in the Great Patriotic War, he restrained Tito's expansionism because of Anglo-Saxon pressure.

Giampaolo Valdevit writes that 'Stalin needed Tito as an instrument to test in particular the British intentions in the Balkans.' There is not a shadow of a doubt that Stalin knew about Tito's plans to annex Trieste and the territory of Venezia Giulia but it is doubtful whether he incited the Yugoslav leader. Tito created *faits accomplis*, while Moscow supported or censured him, depending on circumstances. Valdevit rightly points out that Tito sought to expand Yugoslavia's territory to meet the claims of its nationalities, the Slovenes, Croats, Macedonians and Serbs, and to emphasize the achievements of his multinational state. In his latest publications, brought out in 1998, L. I. Gibianskii has supplemented Valdevit's conclusions with a handful of documents concerning Stalin's attitude to 'the first international cold-war crisis', 'the Trieste conflict of 1945'.[8]

The recently published documents from Russian archives show, on the one hand, that not only Tito but also Dimitrov dared to have independent views and make independent enunciations without Moscow's consent. On the other hand, they expose the Machiavellism of the former Commissar for nationality questions in Lenin's government and show how he played off the Yugoslavs against the Albanians, taking advantage of their antagonisms. Similarly, in central European countries Stalin deliberately employed Communists of Jewish descent, assigning them the role of chief executors of his will, in order then to be able to take advantage of anti-Semitic prejudices. His pragmatic political game frequently had nothing in common with the official ideology. Stalin and his team often manifested complete indifference to the national traditions of the countries of their fledgling bloc. They ignored the fact that a Balkan federation had been a long-standing utopia in the Balkan Socialist traditions.[9]

László Borhi's chapter 'Soviet Economic Imperialism and the Sovietization of Hungary' shows that the economic colonization of Hungary, started as early as 1945, preceded political Sovietization. Borhi calls for research into the Soviet bloc countries' economic dependence on the USSR, the network of mutual links and the extent to which the Soviet Union exploited the dependent countries economically. The economic uniformity of the USSR and east central Europe and the uniformity of social structures in the countries of the Soviet bloc are questions awaiting research.

Some final remarks are reserved for the first contribution namely, the weakening of cultural and scientific links and the isolation of east central Europe's culture and science from the Western world. During the first postwar years discussed by Svetla Moussakóva, contacts continued between western Europe and the 'new democracies' recognized as a sphere of Soviet influence in Yalta. But press censorship and police supervision were omnipresent, brought to life by Romain Gary's famous anecdotes, which from the beginning hampered cultural relations.

During the Cold War there were enormous differences in each people's democracy's cultural and scientific contacts with western Europe and the United States. The USSR, Romania, Bulgaria and Czechoslovakia were almost completely isolated from the outside world. Hungary was in a better situation from 1956 on, and Poland's situation was relatively the most favourable. With the exception of the years from 1949 to 1955, the Polish cultural and scientific élite, despite censorship and the authorities' frequent refusal to grant them passports for foreign travels, maintained active contacts with the outside world in many fields and even continued old co-operation provided for by post-First World War agreements. This should be stressed, for the attempts made during the Cold War to obliterate old historical traditions in the people's democracies ended in failure and the Communists did not succeed in making all satellite countries uniform. In examining their history account should, therefore, be taken of the specific character of each country.

Let us also remember that the term 'Cold War', commonly used in Western historiography, was not favoured by Stalin and Molotov. Moreover, even the new Russian historiography frequently emphasizes that the Cold War was initiated by US politicians, that it is they who started 'atomic diplomacy'. A. M. Filitov, a Russian historian, holds the view that up to the middle of 1947 Soviet diplomacy and propaganda were not fully synchronized as far as the Cold War issues were concerned. In Filitov's view it is an open question whether Stalin and his team 'were unable or did not want to try out a non-confrontational development of the postwar world'.[10] Filitov deludes himself into thinking that it was possible to create a zone of neutral countries, of the Finnish type, between the Soviet Union and the Western powers. But these ideas are not borne out by Stalin's plans and activities after 1945. The atmosphere of confrontation, of the arms race and cold war, made it easier for Stalin to terrorize Soviet society once again by totalitarian propaganda. It also made it easier to launch terror in the people's democracies, subordinate their societies and mobilize some social groups to support a Soviet-type system.

Notes

1 W. Musatov, *Predviestniki buri. Politiczeskije krizisy v Vostocznoj Jevropie* (1956–1981) (Moscow: 1996) pp. 265–81. See also: *Sovietskij Sojuz i Viengierskij Krizis 1956 goda. Dokumienty* (Moscow: 1998).

2 In April 1947 Molotov asked Mátyás Rákosi 'is Yugoslavia popular in Hungary?'. 'Even more popular than the Soviet Union' answered Rakosi, 'the

Hungarian people are not afraid of the Yugoslavs, but the traditional fear of the Russians still lingers on.' Quoted in: V. Zubok and C. Pleshakov, *Inside the Kremlin's Cold War. From Stalin to Khruschev* (Cambridge, Mass.: Harward University Press 1996), p. 99.

3 Ibid., p. 93
4 A. Ulunian, 'Grecija i Turcija: Vzgljad iz apparata' CK WKP(b) KPSS 1946–1958, in: *Stalin i holodnaja vojna* (Moscow: 1998), pp. 30–1.
5 *Vostocznaja Jevropa v dokumientach rossijskich archivov 1944–1953*, vol. 1 1944–1948 (Moscow: Novosibirsk, 1997), p. 129.
6 Ibid., p. 127.
7 Ibid., p. 130.
8 *Stalin i holodnaja vojna*, (Moscow: 1998), pp. 44–62.
9 P. Broué, *Rakovsky ou la Révolution dans tous les pays* (Paris: 1996).
10 A. M. Filitov, 'Kak naczinalas "holodnaja vojna"', in *Sovietskaja vniesznjaja politika w gody "holodnoj vojny" (1945–1985)*, p. 65. See also: *Holodnaja vojna. Novyje podchody, novyje dokumienty* (Moscow: 1995).

Part IV
The Partition of Europe 1947–48

18
British Perceptions of the Sovietization of Eastern Europe, 1947–48

Ann Lane

Soviet hegemony in postwar eastern Europe had been accepted in London even before the end of the Second World War as a geopolitical fact and as a consequence of wartime diplomacy. However, Ernest Bevin, Britain's Foreign Secretary, became concerned shortly after taking office about the newly established Soviet sphere and in particular the nature of the political system being established there and what this foretold about Stalin's intentions. Personally distrustful of the Soviet Union, Bevin's perceptions (and those of his senior officials), of the process of Sovietization were critical in shaping British policy elsewhere. Until 1947 Bevin's approach to dealing with the Russians amounted to a combination of seeking co-operation while steadfastly maintaining that firmness, rather than a readiness to, compromise, was the means by which their demands were best met: 'you can never [...] deal with Russians', he once observed, 'if you lie down and let them walk over you'.[1] Indeed, as early as August 1945 he directed the Foreign Office to pursue policies which would enable Britain to maintain footholds in the Soviet sphere, particularly in economic and cultural matters, thereby indicating that he would not simply acquiesce in the imposition of the Stalinist system. However, the obstacles placed in the way of such a policy by Moscow's appointees were, by the spring of 1946, already proving to be insurmountable. The Sovietization process was observed by the British with growing apprehension as being only the first part of a policy designed to spread Soviet influence and the Soviet system beyond the traditional sphere and into areas which the British considered to be properly their areas of interest. This perceived threat to British influence led Bevin, at some indefinable point in the summer of 1947, to abandon hopes of

219

co-operation with Stalin and the adoption of policies designed to both stabilize western Europe and to contain, and even undermine the Soviet bloc. Events in eastern Europe itself were crucial in shaping that decision.

Despite successful completion of the peace treaties with the former enemy satellites early in January 1947, Bevin presented to Cabinet later the same month, a memorandum which argued that the government should be prepared for the possibility that 'the Eastern half of Europe will continue to be excluded from the general free expansion of trade and that the USSR will seek to extend its political and economic influence into Western Europe'.[2] Bevin's Cabinet submission was prepared during the run-up to the Polish elections which were held on 19 January 1947 under anything but 'free and fair' conditions, and resulted in the ousting of remaining 'democratic elements' from the government. Bevin had publicly protested at the methods the Communists were using to attain a monopoly of power in Poland and the episode served mainly to reinforce his existing detestation of Communism.[3] However, in general terms it typified existing problems associated with Western attempts to pursue an effective policy in the region, problems which had largely frustrated British attempts to moderate the nature of the political systems established there shortly after the war. Since the end of 1945, British officials had privately recognized that there was little hope of establishing much influence in eastern Europe; Soviet hegemony quickly came to be understood within the Foreign Office as a total exclusion, political, cultural and economic, of Western influence.[4]

Within the Foreign Office, those charged with defining the British perception of events in eastern Europe had by early 1947 become obsessed by the Marxist fusion of economics and politics; their interpretations of Soviet policy in the 'Orbit', as they called it, were inclined to focus on this already evident process of welding the east European economies into a unit, a policy which the British believed to be designed for essentially political ends. Among the more prominent contributors to this debate was Donald Gainer, Britain's ambassador in Warsaw, who reported on 27 June (that is five days before Molotov exited the Marshall Plan meeting in Paris), that Soviet policy was to dovetail the planned economies of the satellites with each other and with their own economy. The adoption of Five Year Plans in all the satellite states seemed to Gainer to provide adequate evidence. The view that Soviet policy was aimed at ensuring eventual political domination and conformity within the region through completion of the process of transforming the east European political systems into replicas of that of the USSR was widely accepted in the Office by this stage.[5] 'If the measures succeed in improving the economic situation in these countries', Frank Roberts wrote in August, 'they should go a considerable way towards strengthening the Soviet supported governments' leading to regional coalescence and increasing impermeability to Western influences.[6]

These preoccupations are reflected in the directions issued within the Foreign Office to propaganda outlets which were instructed to target the economic weaknesses of Soviet ideology; in May 1947, John Colville, then in the Southern Department, recommended that one or two writers be briefed to develop the thesis that 'communism is not a viable economic theory' and that 'its appeal under a truly democratic regime is not wide and that it can consequently only be imposed on the masses by means of a totalitarian regime.'[7] The question remained, however, as to whether the Soviet Union, once it had made eastern Europe secure, would seek to use this position as a springboard for further expansion into western and southern Europe. In retrospect the possibility of Communist take-overs in western capitals was considerably over-rated, but it was a real preoccupation at the time. The ousting of the Communists in the French government elections of 5 May 1947 provided some respite, and indeed began the process of the marginalization of the left in French politics, but British officials and their ministers were not greatly reassured.

Impressed, then, by the nature of Soviet 'hegemony' in eastern Europe as ideologically driven and totalitarian in style, officials in London noted that the conditions then prevailing in western Europe – economic devastation and institutional and social instability – were precisely those under which Communist parties were best able to take hold. These concerns were linked in British thinking to Soviet policy as expressed in the writings of Soviet economists who since 1945 had been predicting a renewed economic slump in the West. The British economic crisis over the winter of 1946–47, combined with the general failure of Europe to show signs of recovery were, by any standards, signs for those looking for them, that these predictions had some validity. Moreover, such fears were skilfully exploited by European Communists; in the Soviet and east European press, and in official speeches, frequent reference was made during the spring of 1947 to the parallels then being drawn by Soviet economists between the economic conditions currently pertaining with those of 1930 when the Soviet Union was forging ahead with its rapid collectivization and industrialization campaigns, just as the Western democracies were at the brink of world depression.

Since the 1950s, scholars of eastern European politics have been at pains to demonstrate the gradualism of Stalin's policies towards eastern

Europe between 1945 and 1948,[8] and revisionist scholars of Cold War origins have argued that Stalin's decision to consolidate eastern Europe, which became institutionalized by the creation of the Cominform, dated from Marshall's offer of aid to the Europeans.[9] However, recent studies of Soviet policy which draw on evidence from the Moscow archives, suggest that while the Marshall Plan might have accelerated the process of consolidation in the east, it was not in itself the catalyst and that Moscow's actions were indeed determined as much by endogenous factors as by developments outside their sphere.[10] The founding of the Cominform simply marked the beginning of the final phase of Sovietization – the creation of a monolithic bloc through a homogenization of the policies within the Soviet sphere – which was merely part of the essentially linear process of Communist take-over. Indeed, between 1945 and 1947, some diversity within east European politics was observed by British officials and recorded in background briefs and research papers, but British officials, concerned primarily with the way in which Soviet hegemony affected *British* interests, made little concession to this in shaping policy. Indeed, evidence of Moscow's moderation attracted a certain cynicism: Thomas Brimelow among others, who as perhaps the best informed Soviet-watcher within the Office, felt able to argue in June 1947 that the 'present mildness of the Communist Parties in Eastern Europe is nothing more than a tactical deviation from the base line'. Despite the interjections about Soviet security preoccupations from another respected and prolific commentator in the shape of Frank Roberts, recently returned from his posting in Moscow, Brimelow, like his head of department, Robin Hankey, was inclined to see the roots of Soviet foreign policy in expansionist impulses.[11]

While British observers in east European posts were inclined to regard the Marshall Plan as detrimental to Western influence in the region, 'driving these people a step or two back from us',[12] Molotov's abrupt departure from the Marshall Plan Conference at Paris on 2 July fitted the now established British perception of Soviet long-term strategy, with its foundations in Marxist–Leninist ideology and 'Stalinist realism' in which 'American capitalism was the enemy which had to be overthrown'.[13] The political crisis in Hungary, which erupted a few weeks later, provided not confirmation perhaps, but vindication of the belief that Moscow intended to consolidate its own position so firmly that 'even a post-Treaty withdrawal of Soviet troops would not enable Western democrats to regain their influence in the region'.[14]

Foreign Office interpretations of the inaugural meeting of the Cominform at Szklarska Poreba in late September, which are interesting precisely because they emphasized internal factors as determinants of Soviet policy, were, therefore, more perspicacious than has sometimes been acknowledged. This notwithstanding, the real impact lay in the fact of the inclusion of French and Italian Communist Parties which gave it the appearance in the West of a springboard for the further expansion of Soviet influence. Indeed, the Italian and French delegates left Poland with instructions to direct their efforts towards the task of disrupting the European Recovery Programme.[15] This was then unknown in the West, but the Cominform brief to take the lead in resisting plans of imperial expansion and aggression in all spheres raised the question of how far the Communists would indeed push their campaign in countries where they had not yet secured a controlling position.[16]

Interpretations in London of Soviet motives varied: 'The clearest indication yet' of Russian determination to opt out of the international economic system, was how Christopher Warner, then superintending both Southern and Northern Departments, viewed the founding of the Cominform. Drawing an analogy with the 1930s precedents in Stalin's foreign policy, Warner argued that this was simply the end of another 'Popular Front' phase, which was being wound up as cynically as had that of the 1930s, but with the difference that Soviet policy in 1947 was designed to inaugurate an era in which 'there was the opposition of "Communism versus the rest"'.[17]

Bevin had been giving much thought to the problem of how to develop policy in the event that co-operation with the Russians had to be finally ruled out. Frank Roberts, who by late 1947 had become Bevin's Principal Private Secretary, later recalled that 'Soviet attitudes [...] over Eastern Europe in particular' had convinced him that he must build up European strength and unity.[18] The breakdown of the London Council of Foreign Ministers in November was the last straw. During the first week of January 1948 Bevin presented a new policy to the Cabinet to meet the Soviet threat and included his plans for Western Union which he explained as necessary in order to counter the advancing Sovietization of eastern Europe.[19]

Among the accusations against the Soviet Union which appeared in the Foreign Secretary's submissions was the prediction of a *coup d'état* in Czechoslovakia. When this occurred during the third week of February 1948, it was interpreted not as the end of the process of Sovietization, but as the beginning of a further advance: the March edition of the monthly review of Soviet tactics, prepared within the Foreign Office by the Northern Department, explained Soviet consolidation of their zone as preparing 'the way for possible further expansion through the two horns of a crescent pointing to Scandinavia and Italy'.[20] Perhaps the British were particularly susceptible to such a thesis because the Czech crisis occurred at the very moment when the Western powers were fixated with the possibility of a Communist victory in the Italian elections scheduled for 18 April and this conjunction of present and anticipated events probably led to an overvaluation of the dangers of Communist success in Western Europe: 'The Soviet decision to consolidate', so a Northern Department submission to the Russia Committee argued, 'was influenced by expectations that in the forthcoming elections if held under normal conditions, the communists were likely to lose votes'. At the Russia Committee meeting of 11 March, Hankey bleakly projected that 'the Czech tragedy might well be repeated in Italy'. This view, which dominated British thinking at this juncture, appears to have been supported by British Intelligence.[21] Indeed, the possibility of a Communist victory in Italy was apparently taken seriously in the East also: the Italian Communist Party leader, Palmiro Togliatti evidently discussed with the Soviet ambassador in Rome, before the results were known, whether or not he should put himself forward as Prime Minister.[22]

In Yugoslavia, meanwhile, evidence had been accruing that Tito too was under pressure from Moscow. A purge of the Yugoslav government and administration in May 1948 was perceived in London as merely following the pattern typical of the simultaneous purges of left and right which had been witnessed first in Moscow during the 1920s and was accepted as characteristic of Communist-governed states. This interpretation was prepared in London without the benefit of knowledge of the as yet unpublished Tito–Stalin correspondence and the result was a synthesis both of their impressions of the current direction of Soviet policy and their concept of Soviet-style totalitarianism.

The British were surprised, if not startled by the announcement at the end of June of Yugoslavia's expulsion from the Cominform. Yugoslavia had been evaluated by the Foreign Office's Southern Department in early 1948 as 'undoubtedly the prize pupil of east European states within the Soviet orbit'. London believed that the proposal to establish the Cominform headquarters in Belgrade had confirmed Yugoslavia's preeminent status, and that Tito had 'largely been entrusted with the responsibility of consolidating Eastern Europe'.[23]

The Foreign Office analysis of the dispute identified its origins as twofold: the first of these centred on the personality of Tito whose arrogance and independence had unquestionably irritated Stalin to such a degree that a showdown had become inevitable. Indeed, some have argued that it was precisely this, and in particular his evidently growing popularity within Yugoslavia, which provoked Stalin to turn on him.[24] The second concerned the obstacles Tito placed in the way of the Kremlin's foreign policy. Since the announcement of the European Recovery Programme and the creation of Western Union, the Russians had been seeking the closest possible unity in the foreign policy aspect of their sphere. The British conjectured that Yugoslav obduracy regarding the Austrian Treaty and Trieste, (assuming that Moscow had seriously desired to seek a compromise with the West as a factor in their spring 'peace offensive'), as well as their interest in Greece, had played a significant part in shaping current Soviet thinking. Tito was evidently being held personally responsible. In a paper submitted to Bevin as a briefing on the Yugoslav crisis, the Foreign Office concluded that it seemed that 'even if the present differences are composed by some compromise which Western thinking would consider inconceivable, the fear would remain and Tito and his fellow-leaders of Yugoslav communism could never be really accepted back into Moscow's fold. Confidence between them has been destroyed forever'.[25]

This notwithstanding, distrust that the episode was indeed what it seemed, remained largely because of disbelief that the Russians had failed to so-arrange matters that a *coup d'état* could follow immediately upon the issue of the communiqué: 'It seems inconceivable', wrote Geoffrey Wallinger, 'that the Kremlin should have taken a chance in this matter, having regard to the strategic importance to the orbit of Yugoslavia'. Indeed, Anna Pauker, Foreign Minister in Romania, took advantage of the opportunity afforded by the Danube conference held in Belgrade in August, to remark to Peake, with whom she was on particularly good terms, that if Stalin had realized what Tito's reaction would be he would have approached the problem differently.[26] This being so, they reasoned, the Russians must expect Tito, once faced with the condemnation of all his Communist colleagues, to recant or resign.[27]

Bevin was initially unimpressed by the dispute and inclined to regard it as of little significance in policy terms. The Yugoslavs had been the most aggressive of the east European governments in attacking British postwar policy, and he felt that it required more than the publication of an acrimonious exchange of correspondence to constitute convincing evidence of a genuine separating of the ways. A survey of the situation in central and eastern Europe, which Bevin asked the Foreign Office to draft for submission to Attlee at the end of July, and which carried evidence of Bevin's input, concluded in respect to Yugoslavia that 'it would be a mistake to read too much' into the Soviet–Yugoslav dispute which was probably little more than a family quarrel.[28] This paper, which originated in the Southern Department, surveyed British perceptions and policies and argued that the struggle between East and West 'now concentrated with a varying degree of intensity on the principal bastions of the Western line of Europe: Germany, Austria, Trieste, Greece and Turkey'.

However, Bevin's opinion of Yugoslavia's worth to the West had been revised by the autumn, partly as a result of overt and covert information which substantiated Yugoslav assurances that the rift was genuine, but also because it suited the purposes of the more offensive stance which the British were now developing towards perceived Soviet expansionism. Since the beginning of March 1948, Bevin had been guided by the belief that 'Soviet aims were the political domination of Europe and eventually the whole world', a view which had been considerably reinforced by the Soviet blockade of Berlin. During September 1948, the Foreign Office was acting on this, corresponding with the chiefs of staff about the possibility adopting the techniques of psychological warfare in countering the Soviet threat. Similarly, at the Russia Committee Ivone Kirkpatrick, then superintending IRD, promoted the idea of linking offensive propaganda to subversive operations' within the bloc.[29] Moreover, Bevin does not seem to have been overly resistant to the Russia Committee's suggestion in late September that the aim of British policy should now be 'to liberate the countries within the Soviet orbit short of war'.[30] Yugoslavia seemed to suggest a starting point: if Tito could be assisted by discreet aid to maintain his independence from Moscow, this would not only be a strategic advantage for the West, but might also encourage other countries currently in the bloc, once they felt strong enough, to break free. A start could be made with Albania and measures were put in hand to prepare a rising there intended to overthrow the Hoxha regime. A third plank in this strategy was to cajole the Americans into redoubling their efforts to save Greece from Communism.

This policy of 'liberation' was based on a misperception: Yugoslavia was able to survive the rift with the Cominform partly because the Communist government, and Tito in particular, enjoyed genuine popular support, but most of all, because of its geopolitical position at the periphery of the Soviet empire. For the rest of the Soviet sphere, which was organized much more tightly around the Soviet Union's western frontier, independence was not a realistic option so long as the Soviet Union remained prepared to intervene militarily to reimpose its will.

The period between 1945 and 1948 was one in which the Western allies struggled to come to terms with this fact and to interpret its significance for their own interests. The importance of eastern Europe was that Soviet policy there, as it evolved in the immediate postwar years, seemed to confirm the worst fears of Bevin and his officials about the Kremlin's intentions: after the Prague coup and the commencement of the Berlin blockade, Bevin was convinced, in the words of Frank Roberts, 'that containment of the Soviet Union in alliance with the United States was necessarily his first priority'.[31]

Notes

1 H. Thomas, *Armed Truce. The Beginnings of the Cold War 1945–46*, (London: Sceptre, 1986), pp. 295–6. See also G. Warner, 'Bevin and British Foreign Policy', in *The Diplomats 1939–1979*, eds, G. Craig and F. Loewenheim, (Princeton: Princeton University Press, 1994) pp. 106–7.

2 PRO:CAB 129/16, CP(47)35, 18 January 1947.

3 A. Bullock, *Ernest Bevin. Foreign Secretary*, (Oxford: Oxford University Press, 1983) p. 484.

4 See for example L. E. Davis, *The Cold War Begins*, (Princeton: Princeton University Press, 1974); K. Hamilton and A. Lane, 'Power, Status and the Pursuit of Liberty: the Foreign Office and Eastern Europe 1945–1946', in M. Dockrill ed., *Europe Within the Global System 1938–1960*, (Bochum: Universitatsverlag Dr N Brockmeyer, 1995) pp. 31–54.

5 PRO:FO 371 66433 N8714/574/55 Warsaw d. 232, 27 June 1947.

6 PRO:FO 371 66433 N9534/2673/38 Moscow d. 606, 12 August 1947.

7 PRO:FO 371 67360 R5548/24 Colville minute, 1 May 1947.

8 H. Seton Watson, *The Pattern of Communist Revolution*, 2nd edn, (London: Methuen, 1960) pp. 248–70; M. McCauley, *Communist Power in Europe, 1944–49*, (London: Macmillan, 1977) passim; G. Schopflin, *Politics in Eastern Europe*, (Oxford: Blackwell, 1993) pp. 47–51; C. Gati, 'The Democratic Interlude in Post-War Hungary: Eastern Europe before Cominform', *Survey*, vol. 28, (Summer 1984), pp. 99–134.

9 For example, J. and G. Kolko, *The Limits of Power: the World and United States Foreign Policy 1945–54*, (New York: Harper Row, 1973), especially chapter 12; W. LaFeber, *America, Russia and the Cold War 1945–92*, 7th edn, (New York: McGraw Hill, 1993) pp. 60–3.

10 G. Roberts, 'Moscow, the Marshall Plan: politics, ideology and the onset of the Cold War, 1947', *Europe-Asia Studies*, vol. 46, no. 8, (1994) pp. 1371–86; A. Di Biagio, 'The Marshall Plan and the Founding of the Cominform, June–September 1947', in F. Gori and S. Pons eds, *The Soviet Union and Europe in the Cold War 1943–1953*, (London: Macmillan, 1996) pp. 208–21; V. Mastny, *The Cold War and Soviet Insecurity*, (Oxford: Oxford University Press, 1996) p. 40.

11 PRO:FO 371 66433 N6296/2673/38 Brimelow minute, 10 June 1947.

12 PRO:FO 371 67660 R11685/24 Peake letter to Warner, 15 August 1947 and see also G. A. Wallinger minute of 25 September 1947 who shared these doubts.

13   PRO:FO 371 66433 N 8407/2673/38 d. 528 to Moscow, 12 July 1947.
14   PRO:FO 371 66433 N8407/267/38 d. 528 to Moscow, 12 July 1947.
15   E. Reale, *Avec Jacques Duclos au Banc des Accusés a la reunion Constitutive du Kominform*, tr., (Paris: Bonuzzi, 1960); see also S. Pons, 'A Challenge let Drop: Soviet Foreign Policy, the Cominform and the Italian Communist Party, 1947–48', in Gori and Pons eds, *The Soviet Union and Europe in the Cold War* op. cit., pp. 246–63, and V. Zubok and C. Pleshakov, *Inside the Kremlin's Cold War: From Stalin to Khrushchev*, (Cambridge, Mass.: Harvard University Press, 1996), p. 132.
16   A. Bullock, *Ernest Bevin* op. cit., p. 484.
17   PRO:FO 371 66434 N 12662/24, Warner minute, 20 October 1947.
18   F. Roberts, 'Ernest Bevin as Foreign Secretary', in R. Ovendale ed., *The Foreign Policy of the British Labour Governments 1945–51*, (Leicester: Leicester University Press, 1984) p. 29.
19   PRO:CAB 129/23 CP(48)7, 5 January 1948 and CP(48)8, 4 January 1948; *Parl. Debs.*, *HofC*, vol. 446, cols 383–409; V. Mastny, *The Cold War* op. cit., p. 37.
20   PRO:FO 371 71649 N2771/31/38 Monthly review of Soviet tactics, March 1948.
21   PRO:FO 371 71687 N2915/765/38 Minutes of the Russia Committee, 11 March 1948; V. Rothwell, 'Robert Hankey', in J. Zametica ed., *British Officials and British Foreign Policy 1945–50*, (Leicester: Leicester University Press, 1990) p. 171.
22   E. A. Rossi and V. Zaslavsky, 'The Soviet Union and the Italian Communist Party', in *The Soviet Union and Europe in the Cold War*, p. 177.
23   PRO:FO 371 72587 R 413/407/92 Brief concerning the Cominform Headquarters in Belgrade, 10 January 1948.
24   R. Medvedev, *Let History Judge: the origins and consequences of Stalinism*, (London: Macmillan, 1972) p. 475.
25   PRO:FO 371 72583 R 8197/407/92 FO minute, 1 July 1948.
26   PRO:FO 371 77624 N 9737/1052/38 RC/147/49, Russia Committee minutes of 8 November 1948.
27   PRO:FO 371 72583 ibid.
28   A. Bullock, *Ernest Bevin* op. cit., p. 599; PRO:FO 800/502 SU/48/8 PM/48/63 Bevin to Attlee, 28 July 1948.
29   W. S. Lucas and C. J. Morris, 'A Very British Crusade: the Information Research Department and the beginning of the Cold War', in R. Aldrich ed. *British Intelligence, Strategy and the Cold War 1945–51* (London: Routledge, 1992), pp. 99–100.
30   Lucas and Morris, ibid., p. 102.
31   F. Roberts 'Ernest Berin as Foreign Secretary', op. cit., p. 38.

19
The Cultural Policy of France in Eastern Europe

Annie Guénard

To study the cultural policy of France in eastern and central Europe in the immediate context of the division of the continent means to be inside the area where the fracture takes on distinct contours, especially in the field of intellectual and cultural relationships. During the period of postwar transition, that is to say the autumn of 1947 and the whole of 1948, the cultural diplomacy of France faced a situation in which 'it [was] no longer the time to make compromises', as Jean Payard, ambassador in Belgrade, wrote.[1] An often difficult, tense situation, hardened the attitudes of states. Our concern here is to pinpoint some elements of the French choices in cultural strategy abroad. These choices reflected the French perception of evolution in Europe and a precise governmental design.

What exactly was the cultural policy of France in eastern and central Europe at this time? Since 1944–45, it had been the key instrument by which a weakened France sought to regain its influence. In the autumn of 1947, practically all the interwar intellectual and cultural network was reconstituted and even widened, including lycées and Institutes, chairs and lecturers in national universities, and denominational schools, especially in the Balkan zone, the latter a resuscitation of the past. Only the system of friendship associations was far weaker than in the 1930s. *'L'Information française'*, promoted by the government, was part of the French cultural presence in all states. Finally, up to the autumn of 1947, bilateral cultural agreements had been negotiated and signed with Czechoslovakia and Poland. Furthermore, since 1945 France had been working towards its recognition and return in this sphere: it had recognized all the new coalition governments of anti-Fascist and progressive parties, and through its two instruments, information and culture, it had resolutely built up an image of itself as a 'progressive' nation, which indeed it was by the end of the Second World War. France wanted to prove its resemblance with that part of Europe that was carrying out the reconstruction and, between 1945 and 1946, it succeeded to a great extent.

It is certain that the Franco-Soviet diplomatic agreement of December 1944 had strengthened its position in the zone and opened new avenues for cultural influence, in so far as material conditions, sometimes very poor for a long period of time, did not constitute a limit to these activities.

All this helps to explain the importance of the cultural implantation of France in eastern and central Europe in 1947. On the eve of the Cold War, no other ally had so old and so powerful a cultural instrument. Therefore, the people responsible for cultural policy – in Paris, in eastern Europe, and even more so in the Balkan zone – needed to be lucid and realistic, because of successive disappointment and the increasing difficulties encountered in implementing the cultural programme. Sometimes the disappointments occurred very early, for example in 1945 in Romania and in Yugoslavia, though more gradually in the other cases. Without going into further details, these difficulties were linked in several cases to the seizure by Communist parties within coalition governments of strategic ministries for bilateral cultural relationships: information, education and, often associated to the former, fine arts. They were also linked to the existence of state committees dominated by the same parties, which had acquired the monopoly of imports and of the commercial distribution of Western cultural publications (books, reviews, films and so on).[2]

Together with these disillusions, encountered in each country but also during bilateral discussions held in Paris about the reciprocal selection of recipients for university grants, from the spring of 1947 several new elements appeared in the international and French political field, that could modify the perception of France in this area. They are, among others, the expulsion of Communist ministers from the Ramadier government, the Franco-British alliance and, the French acceptance of the offer of American economic assistance.

What was also obvious in eastern Europe, was a deep rooted *'franco-phile'* sympathy in the area. It was to be found among the upper classes, who increasingly shifted to the political opposition, but also within the scientific and university circles and within the whole political class. It was present in governments and even among Communist leaders of political parties which were not yet monolithic. This *'francophilic'* and the subsequent overtures to a France that defined itself as a 'new' or 'progressive' country after the Liberation, largely explain, from the

French point of view, the prudent optimism about the possibilities of cultural and intellectual expansion that determined its activities in the years 1945 and 1946, and the beginning of 1947. It also explained the dreams and illusions of some French foreign policymakers and of a certain number of people responsible for academic missions, until the spring, and more rarely until the summer, of 1947. The dream was two-fold: at the international level, they dreamt of France as a mediator, succeeding in building a bridge between East and West; and at state level, they dreamt of French intellectual and cultural events giving rise to ferments of conciliation between politically and ideologically antag-onistic people. This dream was already shattered by the spring of 1947.

By the winter of 1947–48 – with a varying intensity according to the state – the change which had begun several months before was con-firmed. Everywhere official positions hardened against the unfolding French institutions and the activities of the associations. Even cultural negotiations were interrupted. This was as a result of the direct inter-vention of official Moscow Communist *'moscoutaires'*, or *'staliniens'*, as they were labelled in the Western camp. And until February 1948, Czechoslovakia had been the exception; while the situation was more genial it was not entirely exempt from similar pressures. The officials in charge at the Quai d'Orsay, particularly within the Direction Générale des Relations Culturelles, agreed with those in charge in eastern Europe (diplomats and French Institute directors) on the choices to be made in the face of this new development. Throughout 1948, they decided to base the cultural policy of France behind the iron curtain on the common analysis that when illusions are lost, realism remains.

Two facts underlay the new operational conditions for French cultural policy. From spring 1948, practically everywhere French representatives had to talk to new people. This was the first great change of officials brought about by the dismissal from the scene of the people responsible for ministries and departments during the early postwar period (non-Communists as well as Communists), many of whom were *'Franco-philes'*. The new partners belonged almost systematically to the State ministries in charge of propaganda, generally government information. They proclaimed their personal *'francophile'* feelings and denied they intended to hinder French activity in their country. But their role con-sisted more and more in executing orders from the organs of the Com-munist parties and, sometimes, from specialized committees that were set up within Cominform structures (in Bulgaria the 'Committee of Science, Art and Culture', in Yugoslavia, the 'Committee for Schools and Science' and 'Committee for Culture and Art').[3]

Moreover at the same time, the interventions and requests made by political leaders, including the Communists, demonstrated to French officials that struggles for influence continued within each state, inside the government and even inside the Communist party; struggles that opposed 'national Communists' and *'staliniens'*. Such interventions and requests from the former revealed a desire for links with the West. Two main lines of the action taken since 1945 by the *Direction Générale des Relations Culturelles* were, therefore, maintained and emphasized: the desire to co-operate with governmental and cultural partners as a whole, whatever their political affiliation; and an acknowledgement of the peculiar nature of this regional area. This position differed from the one that Anglo-Saxons seem to have adopted after 1945, in that they kept their distance from representatives and members of Communist parties.

For France, to maintain a bilateral co-operation meant to build intellectual and university partnerships with eastern European states through mixed cultural commissions instituted at an earlier date. This characterized a desire for openness, without making fundamental concessions, for example by accepting a large increase in the number of emissaries with a 'progressive' political profile, but whose scientific fame was indisputable, together with academics and specialists with more diversified political labels.

Therefore, the cultural policy of France was to be one of adaptation to short-term ideological and political constraints which were felt to be in a state of constant evolution. In 1948, several formulas serve to illustrate and clarify this choice: 'To survive, it will be necessary to stick to reality, to listen to its appeals, to satisfy its needs as far as is reasonable'; 'For fear of decay, to adapt with flexibility, prudence, but without hesitation'; 'Flexibility but no docility'; 'It will be necessary to act within the limits of what is possible and to preserve the maximum of our cultural patrimony while presenting it under a particular light.'[4] These formulas show that, for their authors, the very survival of French cultural affirmation was at stake in this uncertain context.

The atmosphere which surrounded the activities of the French cultural and intellectual associations and centres became more and more difficult. In extreme cases verbal threats or even physical violence were used against individuals (French teachers, local *'Francophile'* personalities). The number of activities aimed at the population diminished. French centres in the provinces and French secondary schools which had young nationals as their pupils were required to submit to a minimum of state censorship. The heads of these institutions were very vigilant about excercising control over the themes of public lectures, and ensuring that censored works were removed from the school libraries, but not from those of the French Institutes. They decided to present the major trends of French thought and literature from the 18th and 19th century and to emphasize the writers who had social or realistic themes. These echoed the indictment of 'the bourgeois society' which prevailed in the East, and it appears to have been the first stage of an intellectual *'glaciation'*, before the establishment of 'socialist realism' in the area. The history of the French working-class movement and of trade unionism were also some of the themes touched on in this period. The presentation of French thought and culture was already much reduced.

There was an inward movement towards the Institutes, which were a little less vulnerable and less the subject of censorship and ideological constraints than associations and secondary schools. Here, the French language and literature were still taught but the stress was on science and technology fields. Because of their perceived neutral character, these fields were less likely to be criticized. Besides, being useful to national reconstruction, they made it easier to justify the French policy of an active presence. During 1948, the obstruction of any French cultural expansion increased, initiated by some Communist leaders opposed to an assertive French cultural influence as well as by zealous subordinates. But a close analysis of this trend throughout eastern Europe, reveals a fact which has been underlined by both diplomats and French Institute directors: rather than a policy born from 'national reactions', this restriction is as a result of a global strategy led by Moscow and relayed by agents of the Cominform in the different states, who determined their cultural, intellectual and educational life. For this area as a whole was already entering the time when 'culture is planned, managed and controlled by the State' as Miklós Molnár put it. [5] This was going to become the policy everywhere in the following year.

However, the schedule of this strategy was not exactly the same throughout the region. Encountered much earlier and much more intensely than elsewhere France experienced new forms of obstruction, or even rejection in the Balkans. This foreshadowed what was going to happen in other countries later. An extreme case was that of Romania, which had always been very *'Francophile'*, but was now rigourously controlled by Moscow, and was now the leader in this process: in June 1948, the French Institute in Bucharest and its provincial agencies were told to close and the teaching staff asked to leave the country immediately. At the same time, in the rest of eastern Europe, France negotiated with governments with a view to holding cultural events for national audiences. This was achieved in theatres and through holding exhibitions of art or books and documentaries. France took advantage of greater opportunities than elsewhere in Czechoslovakia (but not for long), in Poland, and in Hungary.

At the time, as the Eastern bloc was in the process of shutting itself off from influences considered to be damaging,[6] the cultural policy devised by France was deficient. Between 1945 and 1947, 'l'Information française à l'étranger', provided support to the cultural and intellectual expansion programme through its ministry, as well as its offices abroad. It disappeared in the autumn of 1947, at a time when emphasis on propaganda abroad could have been fully justified. The Direction Générale des Relations culturelles of the Quai d'Orsay incorporated l'Information à l'étranger into its responsibilities, which proves how closely aligned these two forms of intervention abroad were. But for 'L'Information', the funding was greatly reduced, so that the nature of the documentaries and radio programmes which were offered to national radio stations demonstrated this fusion. Only the Radiodiffusion Française, short wave broadcasts abroad, remained ('EVE', 'Radio Balkans'). However, except for in Poland, its frequency put it at a distinct disadvantage compared with the Anglo-Saxon and the Soviet broadcasts of that time.[7]

A drastic reduction in the commercial circulation of French books was also experienced. The responsibility was largely that of the organs of Cominform in each eastern Europe state, but also the French Trésor Public, as well as French publishers (though to a lesser degree), who did not want to adapt to the specific conditions of the area. Conceived in 1945, the government funded gift of books to teaching and research centres, to universities and National Libraries was supposed to be the continuation of a similar programme set in motion in the last years of the interwar period. Completed in 1947–48, it did not compensate for the interruption to commercial exchanges.

The French position was not devoid of ambivalences, partly due to the fact that the successive governments adopted seemingly contradictory attitudes in their relations with Eastern bloc states. On the one hand France maintained a dialogue with the governments at all costs, through the means of bilateral intellectual and cultural relationships, but on the other hand, it supported emigration and allowed political opposition groups to be established on French territory, and hindered the propaganda of Cominform agents in France. The second ambivalence occurred because government insisted on carrying out its cultural diplomacy without reference to either the evolution of political climate or of international relationships. In February 1948, by first siding with the Anglo-Saxon powers and then acting within the United Nations, France condemned the coup in Prague. However, in the months that followed the government, while moving closer to the centre, continued its active cultural diplomacy based on co-operation in Czechoslovakia and throughout the Eastern bloc. This was manifest in its choice to send representatives. A great many of them were *compagnons de route* or belonged to the Communist party – a political party actively engaged in opposing the French government.

One event was particularly revealing: in mid April 1948, an important academic delegation led by the *Recteur* of the University of Paris, Jean Sarrailh, attended the celebration of the 600th anniversary of the Charles IV University in Prague. During the ceremony, Klément Gottwald, the new head of government was seated next to Edvard Beneš. This choice was very different from that of the Anglo-Saxon powers, who were content with maintaining their presence via their press relations departments, their cultural associations and who boycotted official events. That is why, in April 1948, the United States, the United Kingdom and most north European countries officially turned down the invitation to the celebration of the Jubilee of Prague University to express their disapproval of the events in Prague of February 1948.

France continued to respond to various appeals by sending official delegations. And, before being shown in Warsaw, two exhibitions were held in August 1948 in Wroclaw for the World Congress of Intellectuals for Peace, one of French contemporary printings and tapestry, the other of French books.[8] In a period of tension and crisis as a consequence of the Cold War, these decisions, verging on concessions, could be seen as acts giving some backing to Communist regimes. Yet this risk, as perceived by the officials of the Quai d'Orsay, was preferred to the alternative absence of relations.

What analyses and what objectives underlay this very specific French choice? Clearly, what was at stake was the maintenance of 'observation posts' behind the iron curtain. But studying the archives reveals a determination to avoid the division of Europe. The aim is not to yield to the Stalinist and Soviet domination becoming entrenched at all levels in eastern Europe and, of course, especially in the fields of culture and ideas. French policy was to resist the strategy of weakening French and Western cultural positions as organized by Moscow and to bring its support to all those who wanted to maintain contacts with the West. French officials also refused to countenance the gradual monopoly of bilateral cultural relationships by French Communist militants.

A disquieting situation did develop during 1948. While bilateral official exchanges were taking place, many famous French Communist militants, writers and academics, invited by Communist parties, were making partisan speeches within political associations and trade union structures. Thus, two levels of bilateral cultural relations coexisted. They ignored each other, as Communist regimes systematically kept French diplomats and cultural authorities out of things. Such a reality proves that the assertion of political neutrality by French cultural centres was not acknowledged by national political authorities.

A turning point came in the autumn of 1948, when France was no longer ready to make concessions and hold meetings for 'cultural co-operation'. The atmosphere was tense. Public attendance remained high at the French Institutes, despite the personal risks people were taking, and artistic, cultural and intellectual activities continued there. But in all of eastern Europe, France was beginning to be confronted with a systematic campaign launched against its culture by Zhdanovism. Begun in Romania, in Bulgaria and in Poland, this ideological offensive – one of its slogans qualified Paris as the 'intellectual capital of Western cosmopolitanism condemned by Moscow' – reflected the importance that Moscow attached to the need to eradicate all traces of Western thought and culture, and to achieve the 'normalization' of the states behind the iron curtain.

Notes

1   Archives du Ministère des Affaires Etrangères, Paris (AMAE). Série Z Europe, 1944–60, carton 38. Correspondence from Jean Payard, 2 March 1948.
2   In Belgrad, the Tanjug Agency to which quickly follows Yougoslovenska Kniga, in Wroclav the company Czytelnik, in Praha the Orbis agency (under the control of the ministry of information).
3   AMAE Série Direction Générale des Relations Culturelles (DGRC), Oeuvres diverses, 188, Bulgarie; Série Z Europe, 1944–60, 79, Yougoslavie.
4   AMAE, Séries Z Europe 1944–1960 and DGRC 1945–47, Enseignement; Archives Nationales (AN), Série AJ 16, Chancellerie, Académie de Paris, carton 6955, Tchécoslovaquie, Institut français de Prague, 1920–51: 27 April 1948, extract from the correspondence of Andrè Girard, directeur de l'Institut français de Zagreb, December 1947; 20 October 1948, two extracts of the annual report (1948) written by Marcel Aymonin and addressed to 'le Conseil de Direction de l'Institut français' in Praha; 17 February 1950, two extracts of the report written by Gabriel Beis, director of 'la Maison de France' in Bratislava, addressed to the Consul de France Etienne Manach, 'Statement of two years at "la Maison de France"'.
5   M. Molnár, *La démocratie se lève à l'Est. Société civile et communisme en Europe de l'Est: Pologne et Hongrie* (Paris: Presses Universitaires de France, 1991).

6 AMAE, Série Z Europe, 1944–60, carton 38. Correspondence from Jean Payard, 2 March 1948.
7 AN, Série F 41, Information, cartons 564 and 781; AMAE, DGRC 1945–47. Dossiers généraux, carton 2, Budget 1947.
8 Mondial Congress of Intellectual for Peace, Wroclaw, 25–28 August 1948. AMAE, Série Z Europe 1944–60, carton 80; Fonds de la Direction Générale des Relations Culturelles, 1948–55, Exchanges culturels, dossier 73.

20
'Unpleasant Facts' and Conflicting Responses: US Interpretation of Soviet Policies in East Central Europe, 1943–48

Ronald W. Pruessen

In 1937, a US ambassador described eastern Europe as 'perhaps the least important of all the areas in the world with which the United States has to deal.'[1] During a White House meeting eight years later, held before Germany's surrender ended the Second World War in Europe, Secretary of the Navy James Forrestal vented his frustrations about the workings of the 'Grand Alliance' that was about to bring victory: '[...] for some time the Russians had considered that we would not object if they took over all of Eastern Europe into their power', he said, and 'it was his profound conviction that if the Russians were to be rigid in their attitude we had better have a showdown [...].'[2]

How can such a transformation of attitude be explained? Given limited previous interest, why did the United States come to treat eastern Europe as the earliest arena of the Cold War – important enough, for some at least, to warrant a confrontation with Moscow? Although simple answers would once have been given to these questions, the passage of time and the steady expansion of archival research opportunities has gradually forced a reconsideration. As with so many aspects of international affairs in the initial stages of the Cold War, American policy towards eastern Europe now reveals many previously unappreciated complexities. If Washington deliberations and actions are examined closely, in fact, the 1940s display densely tangled patterns: perceptions or moods shifted regularly, generating steady progressions of distinct responses and initiatives.

Early analysts, and participants, would frequently have painted the story of American policy toward eastern Europe in the stark colours of melodrama. At base, it would have seemed an almost mythic tale in which high and admirable American hopes were mocked by the brutal expansionism of the Soviet Union. The hopes were the product of the idealistic, Wilsonian fervour with which Americans fought the Second World War. The fate of a Poland or a Czechoslovakia, in particular – as victims of Nazi aggression – became important gages of the Grand Alliance's dedication to the motivating concepts of liberty and democracy. As George Kennan put it in his diary in 1944, the handling of something like 'the Polish question' would be 'the touchstone' of the victors' ability to forge 'a decent, humane, and co-operative policy in Europe.'[3]

As Kennan already believed when he wrote these words, however, this touchstone would prove flawed, hopelessly flawed, because of Moscow's essential indifference to democratic ideals. 'The jealous and intolerant eye of the Kremlin can distinguish, in the end, only vassals and enemies', he later explained, 'and the neighbours of Russia, if they do not wish to be the one, must reconcile themselves to being the other.'[4] Other Americans quickly reached the same conclusion. US ambassador Averell Harriman described the situation to Harry Truman, during the new president's first days in the White House:

> In effect what we were faced with was a 'barbarian invasion of Europe', that Soviet control over any foreign country did not mean merely influence on their foreign relations but the extension of the Soviet system with secret police, extinction of freedom of speech, etc. and that we had to decide what should be our attitude in the face of these unpleasant facts.[5]

As far as postwar developments are concerned, the earliest overviews of American perspectives on eastern Europe saw only increasing gloom. Kennan's or Harriman's views became conventional wisdom between 1945 and 1947, with 'unpleasant facts' turning into more deeply disturbing developments. The lofty pledges of Yalta's Declaration on Liberated Europe came to seem more and more hollow as political routines were manipulated in Poland and elsewhere and as Allied Control Commissions dominated by the Soviets kept a tight rein on the affairs of former belligerents like Hungary, Romania and Bulgaria. Disappointment and distaste began to move toward fiery anger as the Kremlin's campaign to build a tight satellite structure reached its crescendo in

1947 and 1948. A first sign that the situation was going from bad to worse was the way Moscow crudely restrained restless 'vassals' from participating in Marshall Plan negotiations. In words that Washington policy makers would have sadly appreciated, Czechoslovakia's Jan Masaryk summed up his bitter session in the Kremlin at this time as 'a new Munich. I left for Moscow as Minister of Foreign Affairs of a sovereign state. I am returning as Stalin's stooge.'[6] Although a final clamp down took place throughout eastern Europe in succeeding months, it was widely felt that a shocking lowpoint came with the brutal suppression of the even mildly independent political forces in Prague – in February and March 1948. The death of wartime dreams was all too fittingly seen as symbolized at this point by the suicide, or execution, of the bitterly depressed Jan Masaryk.

The evolution of scholarly work has made it clear that the earliest overviews of US approaches to eastern Europe were greatly oversimplified. Sagas in which good struggled steadfastly against evil have been replaced: both drama and tragedy remain, but they are coloured by nuances and complexities only rarely considered during the earlier years of the Cold War. It is now apparent, for example, that this drama was actually comprised of a succession of quite separate 'acts'. At least three times in the mid 1940s alone, American perceptions of eastern European developments and opportunities underwent notable shifts. Because of this, both the mood of policy makers and the nature of their initiatives went through clearly identifiable stages. Yet further complexity emerges from the fact that none of the 'acts' of US policy-making was totally dominated by a single mood or programme. Washington deliberations about eastern Europe revealed constant debate, indecision and ambivalence between 1943 and 1948 – so much so that both contemporaries and later historians might be forgiven for some measure of confusion concerning the essential thrust of policy.

The period from early 1943 through April 1945 might be seen as Act 1. During months of intense planning for the 'postwar world', there was a clear level of American concern for the future of eastern Europe – but an equally clear tendency to limit the active impact or intensity of this concern. In the abstract, Washington evidenced sympathetic support for the notion of democracy and self determination. In part, this was the result of wartime idealism, of the kind that led Harry Hopkins to proclaim that 'We should not be timid about blazoning to the world our desire for the right of all peoples to have genuine civil liberty. We believe our dynamic democracy is the best in the world.'[7] In part, the desire to blazon had a more sophisticated source as well: the conviction that old-fashioned and dangerous 'spheres of influence' should give way to a more open and presumably more peaceful international system. Cordell Hull was one of the great articulators of this 'universalist' philosophy and was quite prepared to apply it to the specifics of the eastern European situation. In a 1943 address to Congress, the Secretary of State enthusiastically sketched his vision of a future in which 'there will no longer be need for spheres of influence, for alliances, for balance of power, or any other of the special arrangements through which, in the unhappy past, the nations strove to safeguard their security or to promote their interests.'[8]

If hopes glowed brightly, however, they tended to have only limited substantive impact on US policies toward the specific region of eastern Europe. Under Franklin D. Roosevelt's leadership, in particular, the maintenance of a co-operative working relationship with Moscow took precedence – even if this meant recognizing the creation of a Soviet sphere of influence. On one hand, the President would have argued, Stalin was too important to victory over Germany (and Japan) to risk alienation on behalf of smaller states so far from North America. On the other hand, Roosevelt recognized the relevance of the fact that those smaller states were not at all far from the Soviet Union itself. Inevitably, he concluded, great powers exercised a measure of control over bordering territories: it was only realistic to assume that the Soviets would behave in their backyard just as the United States did in its own. Representatives of the pressing London Poles, for example, were told that Washington's 'principal concern' was 'to avoid having this dispute enlarge into an issue which would imperil the newly formed association between Great Britain, the United States, and the Soviet Union.'[9] And the President told Senate leaders, in January 1945, that 'the Russians had the power in Eastern Europe, that it was obviously impossible to have a break with them and that, therefore, the only practicable course was to use what influence we had to ameliorate the situation.'[10]

There is debate about how much 'amelioration' was anticipated by American policy-makers. Before the end of the war, at the least, Roosevelt was personally unwilling to strenuously press Stalin regarding Polish or other eastern European issues. Nor do the broader contours of US policies in this period suggest that he would automatically have shifted into some higher gear once victory had been achieved. Roosevelt's interest in the special role of the 'Four Policemen' in a new international organization, for example, suggests quite fundamental attachment to the logic of power politics. So do other developments:

the Italian model for dealing with occupation responsibilities (and opportunities) in liberated or defeated countries – or Roosevelt's willingness to avoid creating any kind of enforcement mechanism for the abstract Declaration on Liberated Europe that emerged from the Yalta conference.[11] Other policy makers, however, including any number who would remain influential after Roosevelt's death, had higher hopes for the impact of US desires on the fate of eastern Europe. Historian Eduard Mark has convincingly demonstrated the way in which some Americans looked forward to Moscow's acceptance of what could be labelled an 'open' sphere of influence. This would have translated into a Latin American-like pattern in which weaker states would 'accept some degree of Soviet supervision in foreign affairs' while still enjoying the ability 'to conduct their domestic affairs without interference.'[12]

Mixed messages continued to figure in Act 2 of the US–eastern Europe drama, which can be seen as extending from approximately April 1945 to March 1947. The mood of the mix shifted, however, with a relatively relaxed combination of concern and realism giving way to a pairing of anger and frustrated acceptance.

Anger is a familiar feature of virtually every narrative of the early postwar period. Well before George Kennan's acerbic 'Long Telegram' from Moscow, US policy-makers were trying less and less hard to hide their intense displeasure at the course of Soviet behaviour. While elaborate lists of grievances included criticisms of Kremlin manoeuvres in Germany, Iran, Turkey and China, there was also prominent emphasis on Poland, Hungary, Czechoslovakia, Bulgaria and Romania. In a famous early episode, Harry Truman was barely installed in the White House before he was tearing a strip off the Soviet foreign minister. Discussing developments in Poland, the President recalled, 'I gave it to him straight one–two to the jaw': Washington would not tolerate 'a one-way street' approach to US–Soviet co-operation and previous agreements on eastern Europe would have to be honoured.[13] Truman's advisers regularly echoed his words and mood as well. As he departed for May 1946 negotiations on peace treaties with Hungary, Bulgaria and Romania, for example, Secretary of State James Byrnes told a national radio audience that 'We must take the offensive for peace as we took the offensive for war: there is no iron curtain that the aggregate sentiments of mankind cannot penetrate.'[14]

But Byrnes' words were far braver than American actions. In an overall sense, US policies took on a steadily tougher quality during the second year of Truman's presidency. 'Containment' logic and determination, for example, generated a firm response to the Iranian crisis and then the dramatic, open-ended rhetoric of the Truman Doctrine. But when it came to resisting Soviet moves in eastern Europe, Washington consistently followed angry protests with accommodating acts. For all of the heat evident in communiqués to Moscow concerning elections and the composition of political coalitions in Warsaw, for example, the United States recognized the Polish government after minimal concessions. Byrnes' efforts to combine tact and toughness in negotiating the treaties for Hungary, Romania and Bulgaria eventually moved in the same direction: though Molotov was told at one point that there was 'no hope for agreement', Byrnes and feisty associates like Senator Arthur H. Vandenberg ended up signing the treaties.[15] Truman's words on delivering them to the Senate caught the element of resignation that was common in thoughts about eastern Europe at this point: he did 'not regard the treaties as completely satisfactory', he said, but 'whatever their defects [...] I am convinced that they are as good as we can hope to obtain by agreement among the principal wartime Allies. Further dispute and delay would gravely jeopardize political stability in the countries concerned for many years.'[16]

During Act 3 (March 1947–March 1948), an already complex American approach to eastern European developments became even more so: anger and resigned accommodation continued, but the frustrations inherent in such a combination generated increasing speculation about ways in which Soviet power over its neighbours might yet be diminished. This year of Truman's presidency is almost invariably painted in vibrant colours, thanks to dramatic initiatives like the Truman Doctrine, the Marshall Plan and NATO. While most of these milestone enterprises were aimed at problems outside eastern Europe, they also eventually involved or contributed to shifts in the US approach to this region.

The nature of the impact is probably most easily seen in the evolution of the Marshall Plan. Though aimed primarily at the reconstruction of western and central European economies, that is, thoughts of the other half of the continent were never absent. For some, the prod in this direction was economic history – appreciation for the traditional ties between regions and the potential difficulties of engendering industrial recuperation in the West without some access to the food and fuel of the East. For others, such calculations took on an appealing reverse implication. Might American aid become a powerful force in Warsaw, Budapest and Prague? Could hunger for solutions to profound economic difficulties overpower fears of displeasing Moscow? And would a restoration of historical trade patterns then reverse the trend toward Soviet domination in the East? This was a policy manoeuvre which George Kennan referred to at the time as 'a squeeze play' on Moscow – and it was one which Ernest Bevin and US Under-Secretary of State Will Clayton discussed as early as June 1947.[17]

The 'squeeze play' did not work, of course. Although Moscow itself was initially interested in participating in a US aid program, the nature of the package developed in Paris negotiations proved to be unacceptable. And as Moscow moved in July 1947, so did the governments in eastern Europe: whatever the complex deliberations in each separate capital, the end result was a hasty retreat from early explorations of possibilities with the West. Some American policy-makers were outraged by this development: Walter Bedell Smith, the US ambassador in Moscow, castigated what he described as 'nothing less than a declaration of war by the Soviet Union on the immediate issue of the control of Europe.'[18] Others, like Kennan, were not at all surprised. He had expected a 'baring of the fangs' by Moscow in the wake of Marshall's initiatives and, as he wrote at the time, the 'sweeping away of democratic institutions' in eastern Europe was an almost inevitable by-product.[19]

Whether shocked or not, however, American policy-makers adjusted to the Soviet clamp-down on eastern Europe by escalating the hints of 'rollback' or 'liberation' thinking which some had seen as a feature of Marshall Plan enticements in the first place. Kennan speculated about the way in which the tensions inherent in Moscow's crudely constructed empire could be encouraged: as he put it in his famous Mr X article in *Foreign Affairs*,

the United States has it in its power to increase enormously the strains under which Soviet policy must operate, to force upon the Kremlin a far greater degree of moderation than it has had to observe in recent years, and in this way to promote tendencies which must eventually find their outlet in either the break-up or the gradual mellowing of Soviet power.[20]

Others in Washington were quick to devise specific techniques for hastening such a broadly-sketched process. By early 1948, such policy pronouncements as NSC 7 had begun to delineate the whole range of covert operation possibilities that would figure in US approaches to eastern Europe for at least the next decade.[21]

Why did US policies concerning eastern Europe go through several stages between 1943 and 1948 – and why did shifting policies always carry mixed messages within them? What were the sources of conflicting American impulses? One particular wellspring seems to have been especially significant, though in keeping with the attitudes and actions it helped to generate, it was a wellspring of considerable complexity in its own right. On the one hand, that is, American ambivalence toward eastern Europe owed much to the *Realpolitik* heart that beat at the core of American foreign policy. On the other hand, however, that heart could quite regularly race because of adrenaline bursts produced by idealism, or appetite.

Realpolitik was certainly the predominant impulse. The US had thoroughly global interests by the mid 1940s – and American leaders revealed passionate conviction when it came to serving them. But a globalized agenda did not mean that every quarter was of equal importance and there was little doubt that eastern Europe was relatively far down Washington's agenda of priorities. Although Franklin Roosevelt could zestfully speculate about the way the US would be one of the 'Four Policemen' monitoring world affairs after the Axis powers were defeated, for example, his blueprint intrinsically delegated major responsibilities for some regions to others.[22] By 1947, Assistant Secretary of State Will Clayton could ruminate about the way 'the reins of world leadership are fast slipping from Britain's competent hands' – and the concomitant need for the United States to step into the breach.[23] When it was time to transform abstraction into reality, however, Clayton and his Washington associates were likely to sharpen their focus: the milestone Marshall Plan of this period was overwhelmingly conceptualized with the economic and political problems of western and central Europe in mind, for instance, in contrast to the marginal efforts directed to the eastern part of the continent.

American ambivalence toward eastern Europe emerged in substantial part from this readiness to prioritize among wide-ranging interests: there was *anger* or distress about what was happening in the region, but *resignation* because of a recognition of the limits to US capabilities and resources. Significantly, however, ambivalence became an essentially permanent characteristic of American behaviour. It was not just momentarily confined to the period of adjustment that would inevitably have followed a major conflict. *Realpolitik* did *restrain* American actions in eastern Europe from Act 1 through to Act 3 of the period being considered here, but a determination to work at undercutting Soviet power was actually more evident in 1948 than in 1943. The possibility of using Marshall Plan aid to entice Warsaw or Prague, the development of covert operations capabilities that might eventually bring 'liberation' or 'rollback', and so on: these components of the US approach suggest that the region was still very much *on* the agenda of foreign policy concerns even if it was in a relatively low position *within* it.

The staying power of US expectations for eastern Europe is an important example of the complexity built into the US policies of the mid 1940s. It also has great relevance to subsequent developments. Dwight Eisenhower and John Foster Dulles, for example, certainly displayed the same mixture of cool calculation and more hot-headed appetite. As a result, they made their own ambivalent and problematic contributions to the volatility that characterized eastern Europe at dramatic moments in 1953 and 1956.[24] Indeed, the longer-term consistency of US attitudes toward eastern Europe are particularly helpful in illuminating an important overall characteristic of Cold War American foreign policy: the difficulties experienced by Washington leaders in backing off or giving up, even when they recognized that circumstances or competing priorities suggested it would be logical to do so.[25]

Appreciation for the complexity of US policies – and for the complexity of their sources – can contribute to an understanding of the overall dynamics of eastern European developments in the mid 1940s. Delineation of nuance and intricacy highlights the fundamental relevance of *process*, for instance, and also illuminates some of the elements which figured in the *specific* processes of this particular period. It never hurts to be reminded of history's capacity for messiness, of course, or of its tendency to avoid neat paths and straight lines. The experience of any moment almost inevitably comprise just one additional segment of a layer by layer progression – a progression in which each layer affects to some degree the ones which follow. The relatively distinctive 'acts' of US policy between 1943 and 1948 certainly suggest this pattern. If it had not been for early idealism in US thinking about eastern Europe, for example, would anger have been increasingly expressed after May 1945? But if there had not also been a history of more hard-headed 'realism', would the anger have been as controlled as it was during what were seen as the crisis months of 1947–48?

If US policies are representative of overarching historical processes, they are also useful for what they tell us about the specific dynamics of the mid 1940s. In particular, the complex reactions of American leaders must be seen as a factor which affected the particular ways in which eastern Europe evolved in this period. As American leaders struggled to sort out the balance between their *Realpolitik* analysis and their great power ambitions, for example, they generated 'mixed messages' which affected all of the other players in this drama. Moscow certainly tried to decipher the nature and import of US moves – as did eastern European governments and populations.

In neither case do we have as much information as we would like about the specifics of the interaction process, to be sure. Still limited archival research opportunities allow only preliminary sketches concerning the Kremlin's interpretations of US behaviour, or of the relative weight of this behaviour in shaping Soviet policy.[26] It is true that research in eastern European archives has been deeper and denser, but there are still many complexities involving US actions in the region which require exploration: 'grassroots' perceptions of American covert operations – and of the potential for American covert operations – is an important example, with relevance to both the mid 1940s and subsequent years. To point out incomplete information is not to minimize the importance of the issues, however it serves only to underline the need for further research.

Notes

1 Quoted in E. Mark, 'American Policy Toward Eastern Europe and the Origins of the Cold War, 1941–1946: An Alternative Interpretation', *Journal of American History*, 68 (September 1981) p. 332.

2 Quoted in W. Millis, ed., *The Forrestal Diaries* (New York: Viking Press, 1951) p. 50.

3 G. F. Kennan, *Memoirs, 1925–1950* (Boston: Little, Brown and Co., 1967) p. 204.

4 Ibid., p. 209.

5 *Foreign Relations of the United States, 1945*, (Washington DC: US Government Printing Office) vol. V, p. 232.

6 Quoted in B. Kovrig, *Of Walls and Bridges: The United States and Eastern Europe* (New York: New York University Press, 1991) p. 29.

7 Quoted in D. Reynolds, 'The "Big Three" and the Division of Europe, 1945–48: An Overview', *Diplomacy & Statecraft*, 1:2 (1990) pp. 127–8.

8 C. Hull, *The Memoirs of Cordell Hull* (New York: 1948), Volume II, pp. 1314–15.

9 Quoted in Mark, 'American Policy Toward Eastern Europe' op. cit., p. 214.

10 T. M. Campbell and G. C. Herring, eds, *The Diaries of Edward R. Stettinius, Jr., 1943–1946* (New York: New Viewpoints, 1975) p. 214.

11 See R. Dallek, *Franklin D. Roosevelt and American Foreign Policy* (New York: Oxford University Press, 1979) and W. F. Kimball, *The Juggler: Franklin D. Roosevelt as Wartime Statesman* (Princeton: Princeton University Press, 1991).

12 See Mark, 'American Policy Toward Eastern Europe', op. cit., passim and 319; Reynolds, 'The "Big Three" and the Division of Europe' op. cit., passim and pp. 116–17.

13 H. S. Truman, *1945: Year of Decisions* (New York: Signet Books, 1955) p. 99. See also J. L. Gaddis, *The United States and the Origins of the Cold War, 1941–1947* (New York: Columbia University Press, 1972) p. 205.

14   J. F. Byrnes, *Speaking Frankly* (New York: Harper & Brothers, 1947) pp. 130–1.
15   Ibid., pp. 152–3.
16   Quoted in Kovrig, *Of Walls and Bridges* op. cit., p. 25. The standard fuller survey of ultimate US accommodations with eastern European developments in this period can be found in G. Lundestad, *The American Non-Policy Towards Eastern Europe, 1943–1947* (Tromso: Universitetsforlaget, 1978).
17   Quoted in M. P. Leffler, *A Preponderance of Power: National Security, the Truman Administration, and the Cold War* (Stanford: Stanford University Press, 1992) pp. 183, 190.
18   *Foreign Relations of the United States: 1947* op. cit., vol. 3, p. 327.
19   Kennan, *Memoirs* op. cit., pp. 378, 402.
20   Kennan, *Memoirs* op. cit., pp. 357–8.
21   NSC 7, 'The Position of the United States with Respect to Soviet Directed World Communism' (March 1948) and NSC 20/1, 'U.S. Objectives with Respect to Russia', (August 1948) are both reprinted in J. L. Gaddis and T. Etzold eds, *Containment: Documents on American Policy and strategy, 1945–1950* (New York: Columbia University Press, 1978).
22   *Foreign Relations of the United States: The Conferences at Cairo and Tehran, 1943* (Washington DC: United States Government Printing Office, 1961), pp. 594–5.
23   Quoted in Leffler, *A Preponderance of Power* op. cit., p. 143.
24   See, for example, R. W. Pruessen, 'Beyond the Cold War – Again: 1955 and the 1990s', *Political Science Quarterly*, Spring 1993.
25   See, for example, my discussion of 'intellectual brinkmanship' in 'John Foster Dulles and the Predicaments of Power', in R. Immerman ed., *John Foster Dulles and the Diplomacy of the Cold War* (Princeton: Princeton University Press, 1989).
26   See for example, V. O. Pechatnov, 'The Big Three After World War II: New Documents on Soviet Thinking About Post War Relations with the United States and Great Britain', *Cold War International History Project Working Paper No. 13* (Washington: Woodrow Wilson Center, 1995); M. Narinskii and S. D. Parrish, 'New Evidence on the Soviet Rejection of the Marshall Plan, 1947: Two Reports', *Cold War International History Project Working Paper* No. 9 (Washington: Woodrow Wilson Center, 1994).

21
The Art of Failure: British and French Policies towards Germany and the Council of Foreign Ministers, 1947

Martina Kessel

The Council of Foreign Ministers, set up at the Potsdam conference, was supposed to find a peaceful solution for the 'German question'. It was a daunting task. The foreign ministers of the four occupying powers, the United States, the Soviet Union, Great Britain and France met five times between September 1945 and December 1947, devoting the last two conferences in Moscow in March and April 1947 and in London in November and December 1947 almost entirely to this problem. They discussed every major issue associated with it: demilitarization and democratization, economic and political unity, reparations and the level of industry, the control of German heavy industry and of its political structure, boundaries and the Saar question. At bottom, though, they had to solve the basic clash between Soviet and Western notions of democracy in this pivotal European country.

The failure of the Moscow conference in the spring of 1947, which marked the end of the four-power system in Germany, was not entirely the result of an inability to agree on details. In thinking about what kind of *Realpolitik* was possible in the presence of another new superpower with an expansionist ideology, British diplomats were quick to perceive a balance between fears and weaknesses in East and West that could be used to their advantage. The Potsdam protocol, which formed the basis both for the occupation policies and the ministers' discussions, was ambivalent; it demanded economic and political unity but allowed for independent zones and reparation policies. Still, the conferences' failure was not a foregone conclusion, but rather the result of active diplomacy.

The developments of 1945/46 had in French and British eyes already mapped out the future political and ideological landscape of Europe with an inner border running through Germany even before the conference started. The Foreign Office regarded the 'failure' of these peace talks as a precondition for achieving peace on Western terms. A clear separation of the spheres of influence in Europe seemed the best way to *prevent* a cold war, or even another hot war, instead of creating a battle ground in the middle of the continent that the two ideologically opposed sides could argue about endlessly, which, once more, would benefit Germany.[1]

Containment and division

Some general remarks may help to clarify a tangled picture in which diplomats played a major and often decisive role, but were not alone – the respective governments and political coalitions at home, the members of the various institutions of the Control Commission in Germany, economic considerations and the needling issues of imperial politics, all these levels influenced policy making toward Germany. On each side, different people in various positions interpreted the German or Soviet threat differently, and their aims often conflicted. Policy making was not only in France a *'processus hésitant, marqué de reculs et de poussées'*.[2] These conflicting levels have to be kept in mind, even when studying primarily the diplomacy of the Foreign Office and the Quai d'Orsay.

Furthermore, these events can only be understood in the light of longer-term perceptions of the future of the German question within the framework of European politics, the combined German and Soviet threat and the unstable relations with the new superpowers. Thus, the question was not and is not: who divided Germany? or who wanted to divide Germany? Not only is it impossible to personalize these complex issues. The division was never a goal in itself but a means towards a larger political goal.[3] Memories played an equally important role: memories of the failure of the interwar system to stop German expansionism with treaties alone, memories of the powerful German military–industrial complex and – a decisive aspect of the French collective memory – memories of defining oneself as a great power without having the power to defend that status.

Looking for motives and perceptions on the British and French side, therefore, does *not* mean to push back the origins of the Cold War or to saddle any side with moral blame. It is hard to see why any country should have taken pains to preserve German unity unless it served their own goals or helped to keep options open. The question was rather: how many problems for British or French foreign policy could a united Germany solve and how many new ones could it possibly create? The answer to this question was never one-sided even though the possibility of division had been contemplated at least by leading British diplomats since late 1945. But again, and this is a decisive point, it was never a question simply of 'division or no division'. The overriding issue after the end of the war was the *control* of Germany and its heavy industry and the desire to prevent any further aggression. All the European countries shared this desire for control, and this specific and important worry brought them closer together, despite all the differences regarding both details and the basic definition of 'democracy'.

The issue of control and the possibility of a division formed a threatening knot in the perception of those western European diplomats who already anticipated the breakdown of the four-power system. They feared that German (economic) power was only temporarily paralyzed, and they were also aware (an awareness that fuelled their fears) that the only country that might definitely profit from a conflict between East and West was Germany. Both British and French diplomats worried about what would happen if the western European powers demanded economic and political controls in Germany at the very moment when the division was revealed to the German population, while the Soviet Union posed as the defender of German unity.

There was never a 'red scare' wave that shook the whole Foreign Office or Quai d'Orsay. Very few planners put forward wholeheartedly the hypothesis of a united Germany going Communist. But French and British diplomats accepted the role of the Soviet Union as a new super-power and its predominance in eastern Europe. And when thinking of a divided Germany forced to accept international control of its economy, most officials feared a German *revanchisme* that would *then* turn against the West and move toward the Soviet Union. During the Moscow conference the French representative in Stuttgart and Tübingen, Pierre d'Huart, summed up some of those fears when he warned that the choice *Germany* would make at a given moment in the future would depend on the power of its partners.[4] Thereby, he reminded his colleagues, on the one hand, of the French traumatic discovery after defeat and occupation that in order to be a power you had to be accepted as one, and on the other hand, that Germany would be able to *make* a choice.

By 'power' they meant a combination of economic and military capacity that seemed to be necessary to make Germany accept a specific political system. During the conferences, the question of economic unity and reparations always took up a large amount of time, and most speakers presented it as the major stumbling block.[5] But this question was not only an economic issue but also a problem of ideology and security. Both British and French diplomats assumed that, in order to convince the German population in their respective zones of the effectiveness of Western democracy, it must be shown to pay off economically. The rise of National Socialism had proven, in their eyes, that the majority of the German population would opt for a totalitarian solution in times of economic crisis and social turmoil. Communist ideology presented the West as being in crisis after the war. The huge deficit in the British zone did little to disprove that, and it was highly visible, whereas it was very difficult for the Western powers and the German population in the Western zones to estimate the economic situation in the Soviet zone. This was a second reason why British planners at least worried about German reactions if they opted for heavy handed control while at the same time not being able to balance the budget.

Perceptions and policies: on the road to Moscow

While generally agreeing on the necessity for control, British and French plans for Germany and Europe were at odds. Basically, the British Foreign Minister Ernest Bevin used the conferences as a means for 'dual containment' (Wolfram Hanrieder), whereas the French tried to achieve a Western agreement for the control of the Ruhr industry as long as the four-power system lasted. As long ago as the autumn of 1945 British scepticism regarding Soviet aims had been translated into carefully crafted diplomatic language that paved the way for future action at the meetings. At the first Council of Foreign Ministers in London in September 1945, Bevin introduced the formula he would never abandon until the Council of Four had definitely failed: he said he would not accept an agreement on any single issue until a solution for 'Germany as a whole' had been found.[6]

The notion of a 'general settlement' had originally been discredited because of the failure of appeasement. This failure raised the basic question of how to deal with non-democratic countries that followed an expansionist ideology. After the war, the same formula allowed the West to play for time to find out more about Soviet aims and to develop its own plans. Moving from one issue to the next while insisting on a definition of 'democracy' at large as the necessary precondition for a 'general settlement' – this notion could now be used to delay any agreement.

In the month before the founding of the *Sozialistische Einheitspartei*, March 1946, the forced unification of the Social Democratic and the Communist Party in the Soviet zone, the Foreign Office decided not to run the risk of a united Germany susceptible to Soviet influence. With 1938 in mind, they chose to build up Western democracy behind the 'protective zonal barrier'.[7] The FO differed slightly from Sir Brian Robertson, the British commander-in-chief in the zone, who also saw no common ground beyond the economic realm but who favoured zonal co-operation in order to ease the economic crisis.

Moving from apprehension to decisiveness, the Foreign Office was not swept by a 'red scare'. In particular Frank Roberts, member of the British embassy in Moscow, argued very carefully that the Soviet Union seemed economically as weak as Britain, and that British politics had to turn this parity of weakness and of fear to Britain's advantage. In an extremely farsighted analysis of later developments, he envisioned in September 1946 two spheres of influence in a peaceful Europe, trading across the frontier between two saturated German states, partners respectively in a western and an eastern bloc.[8] In general, the Foreign Office used a language of artificially heightened 'threat perceptions' in order to create a defence barrier while the Soviet Union seemed to be as weak as the West.[9] Germany had to be the pivotal frontier separating the spheres in Europe, but Roberts also emphasized that the Western zones needed to be offered attractive moral and especially economic conditions in order to accept this system.

British diplomats achieved their goal of Anglo-American co-operation in Germany at the Paris conference in the summer of 1946, when American Secretary of State James Byrnes dropped his piecemeal approach to the German problem, and like Bevin demanded a solution of the general principles of the occupation policy before details were discussed, and finally offered the fusion of the British and American zones.[10] In Paris, the British officials decided not to push harder in order not to be left in isolation if the 'point of splitting Germany' should arise.[11] But the careful British diplomacy from 1945 and 1946 resulted in a triumphant note of January 1947 that with the setting up of the bizone it would be Britain and not the Soviet Union that could best afford to deal slowly with the German problem,[12] thus also refuting the thesis that Britain had acted under the pressure of events.[13]

The means for controlling the process were written into the conditions for joining the bizone.[14] These in turn were included in the

'Revised Potsdam Agreement' which formed the basis for the British position in 1947. The bizone was defined as the first step towards economic and political unity. The Foreign Office was quite sure that the Soviet Union would not accept this unity because the Russians would have to open up their zone *and* help reduce the already existing deficit in order to join. The Potsdam protocol did not provide explicitly for the latter but stated that the export surplus of one zone could be used to balance the deficit of another. The Soviets refused to accept this reading because they had received less in the form of reparations from the West than they had demanded, and the Americans in turn refused reparations as long as they could not assess developments in the Soviet zone.[15] British diplomats acknowledged that both sides had equally valid arguments; therefore, procedural questions became very important. The British clung to their idea of an all-inclusive solution, whereas the French and the Soviets followed a piecemeal strategy. Besides a traditional reluctance to get involved on the continent, it was due to these worries and their anxiety about German opinion that the Foreign Office diplomats refused to support any detailed French plans to control German heavy industry, beyond a general endorsement.

But by solving the Soviet problem in Germany, Bevin had to ignore some irritation at home. First of all, while refusing the Soviet claim for reparations, he was confronted with similar claims in his own country. Therefore, he carefully never ruled out reparations in general, only on Soviet terms. Second, the FO wanted control of German political and economic developments, just like the other Europeans. As long as the four-power system lasted, though, Bevin did not push for this publicly. Only during and after the Moscow conference did he try, unsuccessfully by then, to secure US support for a slow and controlled development in Germany, something the French had demanded since 1945. The American commander-in-chief Lucius D. Clay had always suggested that an agreement with Moscow was possible, and the US delegation in Moscow toyed with the idea of a 'rapprochement' on reparations. To my mind, Marshall did not really want an agreement but used this ambivalent approach to silence the British and French. A third problem was that both British and French planners were convinced that democracy in Germany needed an efficient economic basis. Yet they feared both the centralization that would be necessary for improvement in the economy and a backlash of German nationalism against *Western* control in a divided country. Shuttling between the German desire for unity and the Allied insistence on security, British policy was criticized both at home and in Germany.

John Kent summed up Britain's imperial strategy explaining that the goals of its policy were set in terms of great power status and equality with the United States and the Soviet Union. British policy-makers did not refuse to recognize Britain's postwar weakness, but refused to accept that it could not be overcome.[16] This analysis applies to some extent also to the French position. France wanted security and the restoration of its former power. But haunted by their recent memories of defeat, occupation, collaboration and dependency on the Western allies, French planners were less certain than the British about their position in *German* eyes.

The French situation was even more complicated, the views in Paris, in Berlin and in the zone, even more diverse than on the British side and certainly less co-ordinated.[17] French policies resulted from a complex mixture of the desire for security, the wish to reinstate French standing in Europe and elsewhere, an apprehensive fascination with Germany's military–industrial complex, and the strong will not to be entirely dominated by the United States in a future Western alliance.[18] With respect to their status both in the West and in German eyes, most French planners harboured few illusions; their plans betrayed a burning awareness first to having lost the peace and then to *not* having won the war on their own account.

French German policy rested on three premiss. First of all, planners assumed that only an agreement with Germany could secure peace in the long run. Second, they expected the German population to opt for the West (or France) only if France proved to be firm, the more so in a bipolar world. The 'German choice' was a recurring phrase. Paradoxically enough, clinging to the *'thèses françaises'* could be interpreted as a way to prove French steadfastness. Third, French planners realized early on that international control of German heavy industry would only be possible within a tripartite coalition. Due to his permanent contacts with the British and his unsuccessful attempts since 1945 to organize an effective alliance, the Minister of Foreign Affairs Georges Bidault (who as the former leader of the Résistance in France had experienced the German occupation) was aware that the four-power system would not last long. And in the Western group, Paris would certainly be the weakest partner.

Instead of supporting the idea of a 'general settlement', the French tried to reach a step-by-step agreement for measures of control before the four-power system collapsed. As they did not expect the German economy to be cast down for long, they argued for a precise assessment of the German economy instead of endless conference rhetoric. Various plans for economic integration had surfaced since 1944/45, based on the lessons of German occupation: in order to control a country, you have to control (or integrate) its economy. Bidault shared the British conviction that the German economy needed to be improved in order to appease German public opinion, and he proved quite flexible in discussions about the acceptable level of industrialization. Regarding the political structure, the Quai d'Orsay insisted on a successive development that could be controlled easily, but most plans aimed at a federal system instead of a confederation of states. Already in 1946 French planners drew up plans for a federal Germany,[19] and in 1947 France was the only occupying power to present a detailed plan for the future political system.[20]

These actions do not bear out an often alleged inflexibility. In particular, French ideas about control via co-operation refute the thesis that France accepted the development of a West German state only under severe pressure from the USA in 1948. The infamous *'thèses françaises'* (the exclusion of parts of the Rhineland and the Saar from German control and a strong decentralization) were more tactical than genuine; Bidault needed something to concede in talks with the Western powers. At the same time, Bidault was very sensitive about having to follow the British lead, whereas internal critics quite correctly pointed out that it was the lack of a clear foreign policy that forced France to compromise with the British.[21]

Both National Socialist Germany and Communist Russia confronted the Western allies with (seemingly) successful ways to organize mass societies and run them efficiently. In France, an eye permanently on the East probably fuelled the *'mentalité productiviste'* that characterized the *'trentes glorieuses'*, the three decades of economic improvement after the war.[22] The French military warned again and again *not* to repeat the mistakes of Versailles, that is either to replace France's own economic rearmament with demands for German reparations, or to try to guarantee peace with a system of alliances that excluded Germany. Instead, they demanded an active foreign policy based on French initiatives in order not to present Germany anew with the picture of France as the weakest Western ally.[23]

In general, planners on both sides of the Channel developed ideas that in the long run became central to the representation of West Germany as a state and to the development of its political mentality. What became known in the Federal Republic as Adenauer's 'magnet theory' was clearly visible in British thinking: economically strong Western zones should serve as an attractive model of efficient democracy, making sure that the anticipated fervour for national unity in Germany would function on Western terms and would be inclined toward Western democracy. The 'politics of productivity' (Charles Maier) were not only an American idea. In France, several suggestions were developed – behind the shield of the *'thèses françaises'* – on how to integrate the German economy into western Europe, allowing for control by co-operation. Both concepts were fuelled by the desire never again to underestimate the relevance of economic power in international relations, although only France translated this awareness into a programme for itself. In Britain, success at the conferences on Germany may well have hindered deeper reflections on the relation between means and goals in imperial and internal politics.[24]

The Byzantine round: conference diplomacy

At the Council of Foreign Ministers in Moscow from 10 March to 25 April 1947, more than six long weeks of discussion produced more paper than decisions of substantial value – except for the basic result that an agreement concerning all four zones was put off.[25] After the first round in which all sides presented their views, the following discussion of economic problems in late March and early April ended with a disagreement on reparations. The breaking point came on 1 April. Once again Bevin refused reparations from current production as long as one zone carried a financial deficit, and demanded instead a general share in the deficit of the bizone. Marshall suggested a limited amount of reparations from current production, instead of capital equipment but also demanded firmly the opening of all zonal borders, in order to achieve real economic unity. Molotov insisted that both reparations from current production and delivery of capital equipment were possible with a higher level of industrial production (a position the Foreign Office agreed with internally). At this point and with three more weeks to go, Bevin had everybody agree that no single issue would be decided unless they reached a decision on 'Germany as a whole' first. Due to the Anglo-American connection between political and economic aspects, the following agreements regarding the political organization of Germany were quite useless. The British team enjoyed the triumph of its 'comprehensive method of approach'.[26]

At the conference table, Britain and France moved between the Soviet demand for a central government and the American inclination to go fast in Germany in order to stop the European economic crisis. Using the same strategy as Bidault, Molotov tried to keep the four-power system going. Norman Naimark has pointed out that Soviet policy included three options: a 'neutral', demilitarized Germany, which became increasingly unlikely throughout 1945/46; a united Germany under the leadership of the SED, or at least susceptible to Soviet influence; and third, the separate establishment of an Eastern zone. According to Naimark, even in 1949 Molotov might have been willing to work for the solution of a united Germany.[27]

Judging from the conference records, Molotov did indeed try throughout the conference to prolong the four-power system, in order to keep at least the last two options open. He slowly began to compromise on important issues. The Soviet Foreign Minister also tried to avoid being held responsible for the division of Germany. He emphasized explicitly those points where the Soviet position resembled western European ideas, for example how similar they were on the level of steel production, the establishment of central administrations and the need for higher German exports. Molotov also suggested the reparation period should be lengthened from ten to 20 years in order to lighten the immediate burden on the German economy.

Three factors especially highlight the complex interactions not only between East and West, but also between the Western allies. First of all, the most vexing problem for Bevin in Moscow was less the Soviet demand for reparations than the Soviet compromises on this issue. Molotov kept insisting on a total of US\$ 10 billion. But on 19 March he started to give some information about the reparations the Soviets had taken from their own zone up to that point, a concession the British had required before talking seriously about reparations. Furthermore, he promised to give all the relevant information. The British minister countered this with his idea of 'Germany as a whole'.

Second, however, this dilemma intensified the tensions between the western Europeans and the United States. The US Secretary of State George Marshall showed little inclination to agree with Molotov on reparations. But he played with the idea of a Soviet–American rapprochement in order to silence western European demands for control mechanisms in Germany. At least he always raised this possibility whenever his French and British colleagues started to debate institutionalized means of control in Germany. And he pushed the idea more, when an agreement with Molotov became less likely. This aspect, evident not only in Moscow, but particularly prevalent during those meetings, foreshadowed the perennial western European dilemma after the Second World War, of being dependent economically and militarily on the United States and wanting its commitment, but not wanting to have their policies influenced by Washington.

Third, all three Europeans harboured similar hopes for controlling Germany without ruining it economically. In particular the final discussions about the Ruhr area, the boundaries and a German peace treaty showed how close they actually were. France and the Soviet Union both demanded the control of the Ruhr, but differed on how to organize the German government. London and Moscow, on the other hand, had closer views regarding Germany's political organization. Furthermore, all agreed the level of industry should be revized and exports raised. Molotov emphasized these similarities in order to highlight the possibilities of an agreement in the eyes of the public. When Marshall discussed these issues with Bevin, he was less of a cold warrior than when he talked to Truman. Although Bevin never specified any possible restrictions (reflecting the rather vague planning at home), Marshall brought up the question of saving American expenditure if the Soviet Union played straight on economic unity.

For French foreign policy, the Moscow conference was not a big turning point in terms of planning, only in terms of public opinion which, as Wilfried Loth has pointed out, was still not prepared to accept the division of Europe.[28] The Quai d'Orsay had not expected an agreement between the superpowers – '*rien ne sera réglé à Moscou*'[29] – and Bidault was already looking beyond, not debating a federal West German government in principle but only the details of its structure, development and control. Intensive talks with Washington and London before the conference had confirmed what the Quai d'Orsay had suspected, that is that any policy could only be managed with the US and Britain and definite arrangements for the Ruhr could be made only after the Council's failure. But Paris hoped to sell the tripartite agreement as dearly as possible. Against the wishes of the Ramadier government, Bidault stuck to his demand for taking one problem at a time. He managed to annoy both Marshall and Bevin most of the time, but he also ensured coal deliveries to France. Molotov's refusal to agree on the Saar question offered a welcome argument to convince the French public of the need for a split.

In the thorny debate about reparations, Bidault left the field mostly to his British and Soviet colleagues. Molotov tried to involve him in the debate on political principles, touching on the relationship between the *Länder* (states) and the federal government, so central in French plans, or talking about who should head central administrations, but with little success. Bidault was more specific about security controls, and he emphasized this point again and again for the benefit of Western ears. The Moscow conference foreshadowed the complexity of dealing exclusively with the United States. Not only French, but European interests in general, could always be threatened both by a separate agreement between the superpowers (an idea Marshall played with superbly) and a hot cold war that would make an independent policy within or without a Western alliance illusory.

Regarding the political structure of Germany and its establishment, the alliances were curiously reversed. Bevin and Molotov both opted for a provisional government on the basis of a provisional constitution. Marshall wanted to appoint as soon as possible a government formed by state representatives to work out a permanent constitution. Bidault insisted, like Marshall, on a government formed by state representatives, but also on a provisional constitution like his European colleagues. The Western countries sorted out their differences about the political system on 4 and 5 April, at least for the time being, and foreclosed the conference. More specifically, Bevin and Marshall backed Bidault's demand to let bodies of state representatives, instead of permanent secretaries, supervize the central administrations, as the Potsdam protocol and Molotov had demanded. Marshall and Bevin decided on 8 April that the conference was over, and even Molotov's acceptance, a week later, of former Secretary of State Byrnes' ideas about demilitarization as a basis for a future peace treaty did not help. The deputy ministers, who were to continue the Allied discussions after the Moscow Conference, were not entitled to discuss economic principles, thereby safeguarding the Anglo-American position.

The last 'Council of Four' in London from 25 November to 15 December 1947, took place after the Marshall Plan had been launched during the summer. It was supposed to clear the way for the development of the western zones on a democratic free-market basis, but without holding the Western powers responsible for the division of Germany. At least the British delegation knew well that it was impossible 'to choose any one point about which we are so right and the Russians are so wrong that a break can be justified in the eyes of the world'.[30]

In the light of this policy development, the last meeting of the Foreign Ministers in London does not look like the 'conference of the last chance',[31] only in the eyes of the public. It was little more than a nervous affair of how to seal the end of the four-power system in Germany without setting a new date for another fruitless meeting and without being saddled with the responsibility for failure. Concerning East–West relations, especially the French harboured the same hopes that Frank Roberts had formulated in his 'long telegram' of September 1946, the hope that once the bitter feelings of the immediate postwar period had died down, it would be possible to enter a policy of détente with Moscow without too much ideological encumbrance. The French wanted to end the talks with the Soviets about Germany without giving up the possibility to deal with them on other matters. Up to the very last day of the four-power conferences, Bidault, therefore, was extremely careful to let differences crystallize only on concrete issues, not on general principles and without much ideological fighting. While the British also hoped for clear-cut spheres of influence in Europe and a policy of détente across the ideological borders, they never spelled out in detail how a policy of confrontation could be turned into co-operation between systems. While Roberts had mapped out the policy of détente that would be started 20 years later, Bevin proved once more extremely apt in tactics but refrained from offering precise concepts for Germany or the framework of European politics.

Given the events of the summer, Molotov tried even more intensely to keep the four-power system in place by strongly pushing for a central government. It proved therefore the most important point for the Western diplomats to avoid an agreement on. It would have left things as they were, and it would have brought out Western differences about the German federal structure. Bidault saved this most dangerous situation by steering the discussion back to the agenda when Marshall was drawn out by Molotov and had demanded the quick establishment of a provisional government. Bidault, who like Marshall was addressing Western listeners, pointed again toward a slow and piecemeal solution of all problems. He also managed to secure the Americans' agreement to prevent the revival of German industry at a faster pace than that of the other democratic countries in Europe.

After 2 December, Marshall and Bevin tried to cut the conference short. Yet, they had several other meetings during which Molotov attacked exactly those points that the Foreign Office also thought to be the weakest aspects of Western policy. On the one hand, the Soviet foreign minister pointed to the low rates of production in the bizone. On the other hand, he complained about Western negligence of German public opinion regarding a separate development of the western zones, a worrisome point also in Western eyes. In terms of compromise, Molotov went as far as to call for agreement on reparations that was a preliminary condition for economic unity; he proposed to do both at the same moment. But Molotov's offers were as carefully devised as Bevin's; even his latest proposal included a free hand for the commanders-in-chief of the zones. Neither side tested the seriousness of the other's efforts at compromise. After even Marshall admitted, on 10 December, that Molotov's 'almost desperate attempts' to continue the talks could be embarrassing in developing the western zones, he demanded a comprehensive solution of all the critical points.[32] Marshall achieved the adjournment without setting a new date for another meeting.

Conclusion

The failure of the Council of Foreign Ministers to agree on Germany to my mind does not necessarily prove that such a council was in the first place the wrong way to deal with this important question, as Ann Deighton suggests.[33] It was rather a deliberate choice not to take the road of private diplomatic talks with Moscow as there had been between all three western Allies. The conference talks repeatedly reached a point where compromises could have been possible, as not only the American and the British commanders-in-chief in Germany but also the Foreign Office was quick to point out. But Bevin's fine art of diplomacy included the art of failure, using the Council of Foreign Ministers successfully as a means of containment – of two countries.

Bidault tried to use the conferences to put pressure on his Western allies, to gain their assent for control measures in Germany, for a French solution to the Saar question, for coal exports and for the basic desire not to let the German economy recover more quickly than that of the democratic Allies. After the Council of Foreign Ministers at the end of 1947, the most fascinating aspects of French planning since 1944/45 surfaced. One of the central features of postwar co-operation between France and West Germany, the Schuman Plan, reflected their primary goal of tying the German economy closely to the rest of the French and the European economy, hoping on the one hand, that economic efficiency and the doctrine of European integration would supplant the violent aggressiveness of German nationalism, and, on the other hand, to ensure a French position independent of *both* Soviet Communism and American power.

The western Europeans realized again and again, that getting closer to the desired 'special relationship' with the United States created its own problems. A steadier US foreign policy did not necessarily make this relationship any easier, either for London or for Paris. The 'German question' always included the double worry about the strength of German nationalism and the problem of not letting all international relations be burdened by the German question. In general, the conferences were as important for Britain and France in trying to carve out a good place in an alliance with the United States as they were with regard to the four-power system. Whereas British planners formulated some aspects of a détente policy, via trade and other economic relations, that would only be implemented more than two decades later by the Nixon administration, French diplomats and military personnel indicated, in their overriding desire to be independent from all sides, their later distance from NATO.

Underlying the heated atmosphere of the year 1947, British and French planning reflected, beyond all wavering and hesitation, a surprising sense of realism, regarding both the presence of a new superpower in Europe and the difficult question of setting up an economically strong, but peaceful and non-Communist Germany. Next to the overriding influence of the United States in western European culture and politics after 1949[34] one should, on the one hand, minimize neither French nor British influence on the complex bundle of economic, ideological and political factors and mentalities that made up the rationale of the Federal Republic. On the other hand, fears of a united Germany never subsided totally in western Europe. In 1989, François Mitterrand explained to Gorbachev that it would be the four powers that would have to secure the balance of power in Europe, and Margaret Thatcher was even willing to leave Soviet troops in Germany.[35] The history of the years in between is, as always, not just a history of diplomats and conferences. It is a history of fears, of pride and of anger, translating into images, metaphors and memories that in turn influenced international relations after the Second World War, a history of '*l'imaginaire*' that spreads beyond the boundaries of 1945 *and* 1989.

Notes

1 M. Kessel, *Westeuropa und die deutsche Teilung. Englische und französische Deutschlandpolitik auf den Auaenministerkonferenzen 1945 bis 1947* (München: R. Oldenbarg 1989) p. 297. A. Deighton, *The Impossible Peace. Britain, The Division of Germany and the Origins of the Cold War* (Oxford: Clarendon Press, 1990) reaches similar conclusions regarding the British side. See also: M. Kessel, ' "L'Empêcheur de la danse en ronde": Französische Deutschlandpolitik 1945–1947', in S. Martens ed., *Vom 'Erbfeind' zum 'Erneuerer'. Aspekte und Motive der französischen Deutschlandpolitik nach dem Zweiten Weltkrieg* (Sigmaringen: Thorbecke, 1993) pp. 65–85. Further literature in W. Loth ed., *Die deutsche Frage in der Nachkriegszeit* (Berlin: Akad Verlag, 1994).

2 G. Soutou, *Les dirigeants français et l'entrée en Guerre Froide: un processus de décision hésitant (1944–1950)*, in G. Schmidt ed., *Ost–West–Beziehungen: Konfrontation und Détente 1945–1989*, Bd. 1 (Bochum: Brockmeyer, 1993) pp. 256–69 in particular 256.

3 Kessel, *Westeuropa* op. cit., p. 9. For the following see esp. ibid. pp. 295–305.

4   Kessel, *Westeuropa* op. cit., p. 241.
5   Cf J. Fisch, *Reparationen nach dem Zweiten Weltkrieg* (München: Beck, 1992) pp. 69 ff., pp. 92–104; see esp. the careful discussion of the change in US reparations policy by W. Mausbach, *Zwischen Morgenthau und Marshall: Das wirtschaftspolitische Deutschlandkonzept der USA, 1944–1947*, (Düsseldorf: Droster, 1996).
6   Kessel, *Westeuropa* op. cit., p. 35. For the personal dislike between Bevin and Molotov see Deighton, *The Impossible Peace* op. cit., p. 47 ff.
7   Kessel, *Westeuropa* op. cit., p. 52 ff., esp. p. 55 ff.; for an insider's view see N. Annan, *Changing Enemies. The Defeat and Regeneration of Germany* (London: HarperCollins, 1995), who organized a referendum in the Western sectors of Berlin on the unification. J. Farquharson, 'From Unity to Division: What Prompted Britain to Change its Policy in Germany in 1946?' *European History Quarterly* 26 (1996), pp. 81–123, sees a change only in the winter of 1946 on economic grounds. I would emphasize wider political and ideological considerations instead.
8   Kessel, *Westeuropa* op. cit., pp. 38, 56, for his 'long telegram' in September p. 107 ff. See also S. Greenwood, 'Frank Roberts and the "other" Long Telegram. The view from the British embassy in Moscow', *Journal of Contemporary History* 25 (1990) pp. 103–22.
9   F. S. Northedge and A. Wells, *Britain and Soviet Communism. The Impact of a Revolution* (London: Macmillan, 1982) p. 122.
10   The latest revisionist account is offered by C. W. Eisenberg, *Drawing the Line: The American Decision to divide Germany, 1944–1949* (Cambridge: Cambridge University Press,1996).
11   Kessel, *Westeuropa* op. cit., p. 90.
12   Kessel, *Westeuropa*, p. 161.
13   A. Deighton, 'Towards a Western Strategy: The Making of British Policy towards Germany 1945–1946', in A. Deighton ed., *Britain and the First Cold War* (New York: St. Martin's Press, 1990) pp. 53–70.
14   Kessel, *Westeuropa* op. cit., p. 121 ff.
15   Mausbach, *Zwischen Morgenthau und Marshall-Plan*, traces the conflict in US policy over how to use reparations as a tool for securing a peaceful Germany. The options were either to disarm Germany economically by dismantling capital equipment, or to use its economy for the economic recovery of the rest of Europe through reparations from current production.
16   J. Kent, *British imperial strategy and the origins of the Cold War, 1945–1949* (Leicester: Leicester University Press, 1993) p. 214.
17   Kessel, *Westeuropa* op. cit., pp. 15–24 and 60 ff.; for the latest account see D. Hüser, *Frankreichs 'doppelte Deutschlandpolitik': Dynamik aus der Defensive – Planen, Entscheiden, Umsetzen in gesellschaftlichen und wirtschaftlichen, innen- und auaenpolitischen Krisenzeiten 1944–50* (Berlin: Duncker & Humblot, 1996).
18   For US–French relations, see F. Costigliola, *France and the United States. The Cold Alliance since World War Two* (New York: Twayne Publishers, 1992).
19   Kessel, *Westeuropa* op. cit., p. 133 ff.
20   F. R. Pfetsch, *Ursprünge der Zweiten Republik. Prozesse der Verfassunggebung in den Westzonen und der Bundesrepublik* (Opladen: Westdeutscher Verlag, 1990) p. 228.
21   Kessel, *Westeuropa* op. cit., p. 66 ff.

22 R. Frank, *Les Français et la deuxième Guerre Mondiale depuis 1945: Lectures et interpretations*, in R. Frank *Histoire et temps présent* (Paris, Institut d'histoire du Temps: 1981) pp. 25–40.

23 For example Kessel, *Westeuropa* op. cit., p. 97 ff.

24 C. Barnett, *The Lost Victory. British Dreams, British Realities 1945–1950* (London: 1995) criticizes the Labour government for losing the peace during those years. On foreign policy attitudes, a similar critique by M. Blackwell, *Clinging to Grandeur. British attitudes and foreign policy in the aftermath of the second world war* (Westport, Conn.: Greenwood, 1993).

25 For a detailed account see Kessel, *Westeuropa* op. cit., pp. 210–56.

26 Kessel, *Westeuropa* op. cit., p. 232 ff.

27 N. M. Naimark, *Die Russen in Deutschland. Die sowjetische Besatzungszone 1945 bis 1949* (Berlin: Ullstein, 1997), p. 584; N. M. Naimark, 'Die Sowjetische Militäradministration in Deutschland und die Frage des Stalinismus. Veränderte Sichtweisen auf der Grundlage neuer Quellen aus den russischen Archiven', *Zeitschrift für Geschichtswissenschaft* 43 (1995) pp. 293–307.

28 W. Loth, *Stalins ungeliebtes Kind. Warum Moskau die DDR nicht wollte* (Berlin: Rowohlt, 1994) p. 88.

29 Archives du Ministère des Affaires Extérieures, Paris, Série Y 1944/1949, Internationales, 378–55–1/3, Secrétaire Générale, MAE, note 8 March 1947.

30 Kessel, *Westeuropa* op. cit., p. 293; for an account of the conference, ibid. pp. 282–94.

31 This is the view of C. Buffet, *Mourir pour Berlin: la France et l'Allemagne 1945–1949* (Paris: Colin, 1991) p. 55.

32 Kessel, *Westeuropa* op. cit., p. 292.

33 Deighton, *The Impossible Peace* op. cit., p. 233.

34 Some recent literature in D. Reynolds, 'Review Essay: America's Europe, Europe's America: Image, Influence, and Interaction, 1933–1958', *Diplomatic History* 20 (1996) pp. 651–61.

35 P. Zelikow and C. Rice, *Germany Unified and Europe Transformed. A Study in Statecraft* (Cambridge, Mass.: Harvard University Press, 1995).

22
The Partition of Europe 1947–48: an Overview

Saki Dockrill

The dominant feature of this period was the breakdown of the wartime alliance between the United States, Great Britain and the USSR and the beginning of the East–West confrontation. The turning point was the failure of the London Conference of the Council of Foreign Ministers in December 1947. *Before* the meeting, there had been much uncertainty about the nature and the scale of the American commitment to postwar Europe. The situation had also been fluid as the postwar peace settlements became intertwined with emerging Cold War pressures in Europe. These developments were magnified in drafting of the peace treaties with Italy, Hungary, Romania, Bulgaria and Finland, which were signed in February 1947. The Soviet Union wanted to conclude peace treaties with the eastern European countries quickly in order to consolidate its bloc. The peace treaty with Italy gave it much less than the Rome government wanted, since it did not resolve the problem of Trieste or the status of Italy's former African colonies. However, given the emerging Cold War pressures, Italy decided to ratify the treaty. There was also serious concern in the major western European capitals about the subordination of their political interests to those of the United States. In the autumn of 1947, France and Britain were discussing the creation of an independent western Europe as a 'third force', by utilizing the resources of Europe's colonial possessions in Africa and in the Middle and Far East. They hoped that such a power bloc might become strong enough to withstand the Soviet monolith.[1]

However, *after* the collapse of the London Conference of the Council of Foreign Ministers in 1947, Britain, France and the United States felt able, for the first time since the end of the Second World War, to co-operate overtly in consolidating western Europe in opposing the Soviet Union – a remarkable shift in postwar European history. For instance,

France decided to adopt a more constructive approach towards the defence of western Europe and also towards the formation of trizonia in Germany. In January 1948, Ernest Bevin, the Foreign Secretary, circulated to the Cabinet two memoranda which were the clearest exposition so far of Britain's policy towards the Cold War. Bevin accused the Soviet government of having made 'a mockery of their many pledges about free elections etc., in the Yalta and Potsdam Agreements' by having 'ruthlessly consolidated their position within their orbit and in eastern Europe'. He called for the creation of a Western Union 'backed by the American and the Dominions.'[2] The failure of the London Conference was received by Washington with 'a sigh of relief'. The Americans believed that 'Now, finally, they could move forward on matters they deemed critically important.'[3]

Thus by the end of 1948, the wartime great power alliance had become a thing of the past. Despite the increasing number of studies of Soviet foreign policy based on Russian archives, so far there has been little explanation of why the Soviet Union suffered so many diplomatic setbacks in Europe in 1947 and 1948. This was even more remarkable given that the Kremlin knew a lot about Western policies through its excellent intelligence sources, for example its British agents in the Foreign Office. The Soviet Union was determined to exercise tight control over eastern Europe at all costs, while it also wanted the whole of Germany to be 'friendly' towards Moscow.[4] In January 1944, one of the two deputies of V. M. Molotov in the Commissariat of Foreign Affairs, Ivan Maisky, had written to Molotov rather optimistically that, after the war, the Soviet Union would become the 'centre of gravity for all truly democratic medium-sized and small countries, particularly in Europe.' *Inter alia*, France, Belgium, Italy and Norway would come under some form of Soviet influence.[5] It all went terribly wrong.

Both the Soviet refusal to join the Marshall Plan, and its subsequent pressure on other east Europeans (especially the Czechs and the Poles) to follow suit made the Marshall Plan a much more definitive Cold War initiative in the division of Europe, and of Germany, than when it had originally been conceived. The Soviet Union countered the Marshall Plan with the less than imaginative idea of rehabilitating the dissolved Comintern under the new name of the Cominform, which was established in autumn 1947. The Cominform turned out to be totally inadequate as a means of frustrating the Marshall Plan nor did it help to enhance the solidarity of Moscow's eastern satellites when an independent and defiant Yugoslavia seceded from the Cominform in June 1948. The Soviet position in Germany went from bad to worse: Stalin failed not only to dominate the whole of Germany, but his confrontational approach towards Berlin after the spring of 1948 encouraged the United States to intervene more actively in European affairs.

The other side of the coin was that Western leaders had failed to exert much influence in the area east of the iron curtain. The Soviet Union tightened its already firm grip on the eastern European countries in 1948, when the Czechoslovakian coup resulted in the replacement of the last eastern European coalition government by a Communist government. Ann Lane explains that Britain's policy towards eastern Europe had been more or less decided by the end of 1945. Britain's suspicions about Russia's motives were deep rooted, the wartime alliance did not in any way help to restore Britain's confidence in the Soviet Union. In 1941, the Soviet Union annexed the Baltic states and, in early 1942, demanded that Britain recognize this annexation. In the same year, the Foreign Office reluctantly accepted that the Soviet Union could dominate the Balkans at the end of the war. By spring 1945, the Red Army had in any case occupied most of eastern Europe. Lane takes the view that Britain's *Realpolitik* approach prevailed: by early 1946, Britain conceded the dominance of eastern Europe to the Soviet Union and thereafter eastern Europe became a 'sounding board for British diplomats searching for evidence of Soviet intentions in the medium and long term.' Similarly Ronald Pruessen shows that, after the death of Roosevelt, the Americans became more impatient about Soviet behaviour in eastern and central Europe, but there was nothing that they could do to reverse the trend. However, after March 1947, the United States began to search for ways in which it might reduce Soviet power in eastern Europe without the risk of war. Pruessen argues that the American invitation to the eastern and central European states to join the Marshall Plan can be seen as the first, albeit unsuccessful, initiative in American's roll-back policy. Nevertheless, both Lane and Pruessen agree that neither Britain nor the United States gave any priority to eastern Europe, as the development of the Cold War made the integration of western Europe under American leadership a much more urgent task.

France was more concerned about eastern Europe than Britain or the United States, and sought to exert influence through its cultural legacy there as a means both of reasserting France's power on the continent and of keeping eastern Europe open to the West. Annie Guénard's study shows how France's initial aspiration to restore its status as a European great power was severely undermined by the division of Europe and by its increasing reliance on the United States for France's economic recovery. After the Franco-Soviet treaty of 1944, France's cultural influence was initially accepted by the eastern Europeans, but by 1948 France's cultural institutions in eastern and central Europe began to suffer from the hard line attitudes adopted by Communist officials, who now imposed restrictions on French cultural activities. Nevertheless, France continued to try to maintain a cultural dialogue with the eastern European countries, which, as Guénard argues, contrasted with the attitudes of the Anglo-Americans, who were apparently resigned to Soviet dominance of that region.

Western leaders were more successful in resisting further Soviet encroachments into the Western bloc between 1947 and 1948. Britain's decision to withdraw from Greece and Turkey was followed swiftly by the Truman Doctrine, which allowed for American financial and political support for these Mediterranean countries. The Marshall Plan helped to stabilize western Europe, and the conclusion of the Brussels Treaty in March 1948 established the 'nucleus' of a western European collective security system which comprised Great Britain, France, Belgium, the Netherlands, and Luxembourg.[6] In May 1947, Communist ministers were expelled from the French and Italian Cabinets. In April 1948, the Italian Communist Party was defeated in the Italian general elections, and, despite lingering sympathies towards neutrality, Italy began to establish friendly relations with the western democratic countries by participating in the Paris conference of the Marshall Plan in 1947, and nearly eighteen months later by joining in the North Atlantic Treaty. More ominously for the Soviet Union was the growing cooperation between the Western occupation powers in Germany, thus dividing Germany further between East and West.

The defeat of Germany posed problems for western policy-makers, too. France, which had been invaded three times in 70 years, found it difficult to come to terms with a defeated Germany, while the British remained generally more suspicious than their American counterparts about the possible resurgence of Germany once the occupation ended and Allied troops withdrew from the country. The problem of Germany's future was also complicated by the fact that the Russian wanted a pacified and weak Germany under their influence. Martina Kessel discusses the difficulties the British and French encountered in formulating an agreed solution to the German question which would satisfy their own national interests as well as those of the other occupying powers. The successive failure to reach agreement on Germany at the Council of Foreign Ministers in Moscow and London in 1947 finally persuaded France, who was most opposed to the creation of a centralized and economically strong Germany, to accept the need for consolidating the three Western occupation zones economically and politically. Consequently, the London talks on Germany between the three Western powers in spring 1948 laid the foundations for the establishment of a federal government in western Germany. On 16 March 1948, the western zones of German were invited to join the European Recovery Programme (or the Marshall Plan). This move towards setting up a western German government was the final blow to Stalin. Instead of admitting the defeat of his policy towards Germany and searching for a peaceful alternative, Stalin opted for confrontation with the West[7] and the outcome was the Berlin crisis which finally demonstrated to the world that East–West relations had irretrievably broken down.

Between 1947 and 1948, the Soviet Union realized that its expansionist policy in Europe had been steadily undermined by western resistance and, this in turn resulted in the opening of the 'unwanted Cold War'.[8] Western Europeans also lost any opportunity they might have had to build a peaceful and united Europe by themselves. Napoleon I prophezied during his last days on St Helena that 'a hundred years after his death, Europe would be either Americanized or Cossack.'[9] He was partially right. After 1948 the continent witnessed the establishment of an iron curtain through the middle of Europe, dividing it between Moscow and Washington.

Notes

1 J. Young, *France, the Cold War and the Western Alliance, 1944–1949*, (Leicester: Leicester University Press, 1990) pp. 168–9.
2 Bevin's minute 'The First Aim of British Foreign Policy', 4 January 1948, CP(48)6 and Bevin's minute 'Review of Soviet Policy', CP(48)7, 5 January 1948, both in PRO:CAB 129/23.
3 M. P. Leffler, *A Preponderance of Power: National Security, the Truman Administration, and the Cold War* (Stanford: Stanford University Press, 1992) p. 199.
4 V. Mastny, *The Cold War and Soviet Insecurity: The Stalin Years* (New York: Oxford University Press, 1996) pp. 11–29 ff., V. Zubok and C. Pleshakov, *Inside the Kremlin's Cold War: From Stalin to Khrushchev* (Cambridge, Mass: Harvard University Press, 1996) pp. 36–48.
5 Zhubok and Pleshakov, *Inside the Kremlin's Cold War* op. cit., p. 29; V. L. Pechatnov, 'The Big Three after World War II: New Documents on Soviet Thinking about Post War Relations with the United States and Great Britain', *Cold War International History Project, Working Paper no. 13*, (Washington DC: The Woodrow Wilson Center, 1995) pp. 2–6.
6 A. Toynbee, 'Introduction' in P. Calvocoressi, *Survey of International Affairs, 1947–1948* (London: Oxford University Press, 1952) p. 4.

7 Mastny, *The Cold War and Soviet Insecurity* op. cit., pp. 47–53 ff.; Zubok and Pleshakov, *Inside the Kremlin's Cold War* op. cit., p. 51.
8 Mastny, *The Cold War and Soviet Insecurity* op. cit., p. 23.
9 M. Charlton, *The Price of Victory* (London: British Broadcasting Corporation, 1983) p. 66.

Part V
The Setting-In of the Cold War

23
The Soviet Union
and the Marshall Plan

Mikhail M. Narinskii

In the spring of 1947 the atmosphere in Europe was unstable and tense. The Soviet Union was steadily tightening its control over eastern Europe and its newly established people's democracies. The signs of an imminent crisis were evident throughout western Europe, fraught with mounting social tensions. Millions lost their jobs and eked out a miserable existence on the verge of starvation during the austere winter of 1946–47. The growing economic difficulties fed hopelessness and despair. In May, as US government agencies explored opportunities to render assistance to Europe, Under Secretary of State Dean G. Acheson made a public statement about the need for urgent American aid in order to promote the unification of European states, which would also take their own steps toward their rehabilitation. 'It is necessary if we are to preserve our own freedoms and our own democratic institutions' Acheson stressed. 'It is necessary for our national security.'[1] On 5 June 1947, Secretary of State George C. Marshall made a programmatic speech at Harvard University which served as a point of departure for the realization of a set of economic and political measures which became widely known as the Marshall Plan.

I accept the viewpoint, expressed by my colleague Melvyn P. Leffler, that the Marshall Plan was essentially designed to stabilize the sociopolitical situation in western Europe, to speed the incorporation of western Germany into the Western bloc, and to reduce Soviet influence in eastern Europe.[2] In regard to this last aim, it was decided at a meeting held by Secretary of State Marshall that the east European countries would take part in the rehabilitation programme on the condition that they alter their almost exclusive pro-Soviet economic orientation in favour of broad European integration.[3] The Marshall Plan proposed to exploit east European raw material resources for the rehabilitation of western Europe. In fact, the Plan's terms were such that from the outset it seemed quite doubtful that the Soviet Union and east European countries would accept it.

The British and French Foreign Ministers, Ernest Bevin and Georges Bidault, played a decisive role in discussing Marshall's offer with the Soviet Union. They offered to hold a meeting of the foreign ministers of the three principal European powers – Britain, France and the Soviet Union – in Paris on 27 June 1947 to discuss Marshall's proposals. There is every reason to assert now that Bevin and Bidault were playing a double game: claiming in public that they favoured Soviet participation in the implementation of the Marshall Plan, while assuring the US ambassador in Paris, Jefferson Caffery, 'that they hope the Soviets will refuse to co-operate, and that in any event they will be prepared to go ahead with full steam even if the Soviets refuse to do so.'[4]

Initially, Moscow received with interest Marshall's proposal, regarding it as an opportunity to obtain US credits for the postwar recovery of Europe and the USSR. Soviet Foreign Minister V. M. Molotov gave instructions for serious preparations to be made for the Marshall Plan discussions. On 21 June 1947 the Politburo CPSU(b) Central Committee (CC) endorsed the Soviet government's positive reply to the notes of the British and French governments proposing the meeting of the foreign ministers in Paris.[5]

The cables sent on 22 June 1947 to Soviet ambassadors in Warsaw, Prague and Belgrade confirm that the Soviet Union took the matter quite seriously. The ambassadors were instructed to tell Bolesław Bierut, Klement Gottwald and Jozip Broz Tito – the Communist leaders of, respectively, Poland, Czechoslovakia and Yugoslavia – the following: 'We consider it desirable that the friendly allied countries should, for their part, make a corresponding initiative to ensure their own participation in the elaboration of the economic measures under consideration and make their own claims in view of the fact that some European countries (Holland and Belgium) have already stated such desires.'[6]

At the same time distrust and warnings were constantly expressed inside Soviet official circles. For instance, the economist Yevgeny Varga asserted in a report to Molotov dated 24 June: 'The US economic position was of decisive importance in proposing the Marshall Plan. The Marshall Plan was meant primarily to be instrumental in resolving the imminent economic crisis, the approach of which no one in the USA denies. Thus, the USA, in its own interests, *must grant much greater credits than it has done heretofore – just to rid itself of surplus goods at home*, even if it knows in advance that part of those credits will never be repaid [. . .].

In this context, the Marshall Plan's aim was this: if it is necessary for the USA, in its own interests, to send abroad American goods worth billions of dollars on credit to unreliable debtors, then it is necessary to try to squeeze the maximum political advantages from this.'[7]

The Soviet ambassador to the United States, Nikolai V. Novikov, emphasized the political aspects of the Marshall Plan in a telegram to Molotov on 24 June:

> In this context, the main goals of US foreign policy, the essence of the 'Truman doctrine', – to check the process of democratization in European countries, to stimulate forces hostile to the Soviet Union and to create conditions for the buttressing of the positions of American capital in Europe and Asia – remain without any substantial changes. A thorough analysis of the 'Marshall Plan' shows that, in the final analysis, it is directed toward the establishment of a West European bloc as an instrument of American policy. [. . .] Thus, instead of the haphazard actions of the past, which were aimed at economic and political subjugation of European countries to American capital and to the establishment of anti-Soviet groupings, the 'Marshall Plan' envisages a wider-scale action, designed to solve the problem more effectively.[8]

In that situation, the Soviet leadership sought to prevent the United States from obtaining any economic and political advantages through the implementation of the Marshall Plan. The Soviet Union resolutely rejected any form of US control over the economy of the USSR and the east European countries. At the same time, the Soviet Union had a stake in obtaining US credits for its postwar rehabilitation. Ambassador V. I. Yerofeyev, a former staff member in Molotov's secretariat, defined the Soviet government's stand thus:

> The test plan was to accept that proposal and make an attempt, if not to eliminate, as least to minimize its negative aspects and ensure that they should not impose any conditions on us. In a word, it should be something like Lend-Lease. Comrade Molotov was, in fact, a supporter of just this kind of approach.[9]

However, American officials found such an approach entirely unacceptable, and in fact, Will L. Clayton, the Under Secretary of State for Economic Affairs, during negotiations with British leaders on 25 June 1947, specifically rejected any reference to the term 'Lend-Lease' in the memorandum which was in preparation.[10]

Grounded in scepticism toward US intentions and a desire to shape the emerging aid proposals in a form reflecting Soviet interests, the Kremlin's instructions to the Soviet delegation to the Paris meeting of foreign ministers emphasized the importance of obtaining information 'on the nature and terms of the proposed economic assistance to Europe. 'In particular', the instructions stressed, 'the Soviet delegation should clarify the following points: the forms, possible dimensions and conditions under which this assistance will be offered'. The Soviet delegation was to initiate from the fact that

> US economic assistance should be seen not as an economic program for European countries but rather as a means to expose their economic need for US assistance (credits, deliveries of goods), with European countries themselves making the demands. In this regard the delegation should not allow the meeting of Ministers to take the course of evaluating and confirming the European countries' resources rather, deflecting such a formulation of the question by insisting that the meeting's task is to elucidate the requirements of the European countries and to find out whether or not the USA can satisfy them, rather than to draft economic plans for the European countries.

In particular, the instruction stressed the following: 'In discussing any concrete proposals bearing on US assistance to Europe, the Soviet delegation must object to terms of assistance, which could entail any limitation on countries' sovereignty, or violation of their economic independence.'[11]

The Soviet delegation at the Paris meeting of the three powers' foreign ministers was consistently guided by those instructions, so it was impossible for it to accept the Western proposals for a co-ordinated European effort to rehabilitate the continent's economy. The fact that the Soviet leadership ruled out in advance the possibility of evaluating and confirming the European countries' resources, made it impossible to reach mutually acceptable agreements in Paris. The Soviet proposals, which confined themselves to determining the individual European countries' requirements and to sending the respective applications in a package request to the United States, were unacceptable to the West. The Paris meeting showed that it was impossible to reconcile those mutually exclusive positions.

In the course of the Paris meeting the French delegation, led by Bidault, showed the greatest zeal in search of a mutually acceptable compromise. Molotov, however, stressed in a coded telegram message from Paris to Moscow, sent after the second meeting, that the Soviet and French proposals differed fundamentally. 'To [Bidault] I answered', Molotov wrote,

> that such a difference exists and it boils down to the fact that the Soviet project limits the tasks of the meeting and committees, which may be set up, exclusively to the discussion of the issues which are directly related to the American economic assistance to Europe, whereas the French project envisages also the design of economic programmes which encompass both the domestic economies of European countries and issues concerning economic relations between them.[12]

Early in the morning of 30 June, Molotov received important information, which showed the Western powers' position in an extremely disadvantageous light, in a ciphered cable sent by Soviet Deputy Foreign Minister Andrei Vyshinsky. The information had been supplied through the channels of the Soviet intelligence service. The cable, alluding to London sources, informed Molotov that as a result of meetings between US Under Secretary of State Clayton and British ministers, an agreement was reached on the following:

> a) Britain and the USA agreed that the Marshall Plan should be regarded as a plan for the reconstruction of Europe, not as assistance to Europe, and that it should not be a continuation of UNRRA (United Nations Relief and Rehabilitation Administration).
> b) Britain and the USA agreed that the reconstruction of Europe may be achieved by setting up a series of functional committees for coal, steel, transport, agriculture and food, under the leadership of one-man committees.
> c) Any organization set up for the realization of the Marshall Plan should operate outside the United Nations framework. [...] That is explained by the fact that Germany is not a member of the United Nations Organization.
> d) Britain and the USA believe that Germany is still the key to the European economy. Therefore it is, in fact, one of the bases of any plan for rehabilitation of the continent.
> e) [...] Britain and America will oppose payment of (German) reparations to the Soviet Union from the current production.[13]

Throughout this period the Soviet leadership had well-placed informants of a special nature in the British Foreign Office. Thus Moscow's privileged information from these espionage sources about the principal results of Clayton's London conversations was accurate. During his first meeting with British Cabinet ministers, according to later declassified official western records,

> Mr Clayton described the idea presented by Secretary Marshall as involving a really big problem. The US Administration wanted information from all of the interested European countries as to why recovery in Europe has been so slow, what Europe could do to help itself, and how long it might take, with a minimum of assistance from the United States, for Europe to get back on its own feet.[14]

In fact, during Clayton's visit the US and British officials decided to implement the Marshall Plan without Soviet participation. An *aide-mémoire* by the British Foreign Office summing up the Anglo-American agreement noted: 'It is understood that, while it is hoped that the scheme will cover Europe as a whole, the US Administration would be satisfied if it could be started with the Western countries of Europe as a nucleus, on the understanding that the scheme would be open to other countries if they so desired.'[15] Indeed, the US and British officials hoped for the participation of eastern European countries in the Marshall Plan even if the Soviets refused – as Foreign Minister Bevin said: '[...] Russia cannot hold its satellites against the attraction of fundamental help toward economic revival in Europe.'[16]

In the light of the information from Moscow, Molotov's talks in Paris seemed quite futile and ambiguous. As it happened, the US and British leaders had already decided everything in advance, and were using the Paris talks to hide their duplicitous game. One should also take into account how morbidly Moscow reacted to any attempts to shove the Soviet Union aside in the settlement of the German issue or to infringe upon its rights as a victorious power, especially regarding reparations. It is no accident that the instructions to the Soviet delegation specified that it should 'object to any discussion at the meeting of Foreign Ministers on the issue of the utilization of German economic resources to meet the requirements of European countries and to the discussion of the issue of economic assistance to Germany from the USA.[...].'[17]

The message from Moscow made the Soviet Foreign Minister take more resolute steps to rebuff the 'behind-the-scenes collusion of the

USA and Great Britain' against the Soviet Union. Therefore, in his address at the 30 June meeting, Molotov stressed that the task of the conference 'does not include the drafting of an all-round program for European countries' and that 'the German issue is subject to discussion by the four powers: Great Britain, France, the USSR and the USA.'[18]

It became clear at that meeting that it would be impossible to adopt co-ordinated positive decisions. In assessing the work of the conference, Molotov telegraphed to Stalin: 'Since our stand differs in its essence from the Anglo-French position, we are not counting on any joint decisions on the substance of the issue in question.'[19] And by then, Bidault's last-ditch diplomatic efforts could not change anything. On 2 July, the Paris meeting of the three foreign ministers ended with the Soviet delegation's refusal to take part in the Marshall Plan's implementation. In this way, ironically, Soviet foreign policy played into the hands of the Plan's organizers. That was, I believe, a serious diplomatic blunder. In September 1947, in conversation with former US Secretary of State James F. Byrnes, Bidault similarly evaluated Molotov's actions:

> I admit, I could never figure out why Molotov had acted like that – either he had hoped to profit partially from it, or, if the whole thing had ended in failure, that would have succeeded because no one would have gained anything from it, for if he had continued to side with us, he could not have lost anything in any case, but he had chosen the only way to lose for sure.[20]

Nevertheless, there was a certain logic in the Soviet leadership's policy. The unbending and unconstructive stand taken by the Soviet delegation in Paris was largely attributable to the desire to prevent the West from gaining a foothold in eastern Europe, which Moscow regarded as its sphere of influence. Approaching international relations as a zero-sum game required them to exert maximum effort to thwart the US plans to increase its influence in Europe. In a message to Stalin on the night of 30 June, Molotov summed up his impressions of the Paris meeting:

> Both Britain and France are now in dire straits and they do not have at their disposal any serious levers to overcome their economic difficulties. Their only hope is the United States, which demands that Britain and France set up some kind of European body to facilitate US interference in the economic and political affairs of European countries. Great Britain and – to some extent – France count on using this body to promote their own interests.[21]

On the concluding day of the Paris meeting, Bevin and Bidault published a joint communiqué on behalf of the government of Great Britain and France inviting all European countries (with the temporary exception of Spain) to take part in an economic conference to set up a provisional organization to draw up speedily a programme of European reconstruction which would co-ordinate the resources and requirements of each state. On 4 July, official invitations were sent to the governments of 22 European countries to attend the conference, which was scheduled to open in Paris on 12 July 1947.

The Soviet Union refused to attend that conference and took steps to prevent its success, yet showed hesitation and uncertainty as to the best means of doing so, particularly on the sensitive question of whether Soviet-aligned states in eastern Europe should attend at least the conference's early stages. On the morning of 5 July, Soviet ambassadors in several European capitals received instructions from Moscow to relay a statement with a negative assessment of Marshall's proposals to the respective host countries' foreign ministers. The statement said, in particular: 'The Soviet delegation saw in those claims a desire to interfere in the European states' internal affairs by imposing its own programme and making it difficult for them to export their goods where they would wish and in this way forcing those countries' economies into dependence on the interests of the USA.'[22] The Kremlin assigned a special role to its east European allies, as explained, precisely and with great clarity, in Molotov's 5 July telegram to the Soviet ambassador in Belgrade. In the name of the CPSU(b) CC the ambassador was to tell Tito:

> We have received a message about the Yugoslavian government's intention not to attend the Paris conference convened for 12 July by the British and French. We are gratified that you are standing firm on the issue of the US credits, which are intended to enslave you. However, we believe that it would be better for you to take part in that conference, sending your delegation there and giving a rebuff to America and its satellites, Britain and France, in order to prevent the Americans from unanimously pushing through the plan, and then leaving the conference, taking with you as many delegations of other countries.[23]

In a more diplomatic and milder form, that CPSU(b) CC stand was communicated to party leaders Bolesław Bierut (Poland), Klement Gottwald (Czechoslovakia), Gheorghe Gheorghiu-Dej (Romania), Georgi

Dimitrov (Bulgaria), Mátyás Rákosi (Hungary), Enver Hoxha (Albania), and Hertta Kuusinen, the leader of the Finnish Communists.

The head of the Bulgarian government, Dimitrov, had already gone on record favouring the stand adopted in Moscow, that is that east European countries should attend the Paris conference and at it uphold the Soviet concept of European reconstruction. At a reception held by the American political representative in Sofia on 4 July, Dimitrov pointed out in a conversation with Soviet ambassador Kirsanov that 'refusal to attend the conference by such countries as Bulgaria would have given grounds to accuse them of a lack of political independence.'[24] Accordingly, on the evening of 6 July, Molotov cabled instructions to Soviet ambassadors in Warsaw and Belgrade to tell Bierut and Tito that an unofficial visit of their envoys to Moscow would be desirable 'in order to adopt a co-ordinated stand on the Paris conference and avoid unnecessary difficulties during that conference.'[25] However, just a few hours later, Moscow beat a retreat. On the night of 6 July, messages were sent to Soviet ambassadors in Belgrade, Budapest, Bucharest, Warsaw, Prague, Sofia, Tirana and Helsinki with instructions to inform Bierut, Gottwald, Gheorghiu-Dej, Dimitrov, Rákosi, Tito, Hoxha and Kuusinen that 'the CPSU(b) does not advise them to give any reply to the British and French until 10 July, for in some countries the friends [that is, leaders of Communist parties] were against participation in the conference which is to be held on 12 July, since the USSR was not going to attend it.'[26]

The Stalinist leadership vacillated. On the one hand, it wished not only to refuse to attend the conference but also to spoil all the plans of its sponsors, that is, to leave the stage by 'slamming the door' after kicking up a row. On the other hand, they realized that the temptation of US economic aid might prove too alluring for the governments of some East European countries. If one takes into account the coalition nature of the governments of Czechoslovakia and Poland, with no absolute Communist control over the diplomatic services of those countries, Moscow would have been hard pressed to bend their representatives to its *diktat* at the Paris conference in specific cases. For instance, Czechoslovakia was supposed to be represented at the conference by its ambassador in France, Jiri Nosek. In view of this, the Soviet ambassador in France, A. Bogomolov, drew the attention of the Soviet leadership 'to the fact that Ambassador Nosek is well known as a conservative in domestic policy and as an advocate of a pro-Western orientation in foreign policy.'[27] Moreover, participation by the people's democracies in the Paris conference would seriously hamper the propaganda campaign launched by western European Communist parties against the Marshall Plan.

Finally, all those apprehensions took the upper hand. On the night of 7 July, Soviet envoys in Belgrade, Budapest, Bucharest, Warsaw, Prague, Sofia, Tirana and Helsinki received messages with instructions immediately to hand deliver to Bierut, Gottwald, Gheorghiu-Dej, Dimitrov, Rakosi, Tito, Hoxha and Kuusinen the following CPSU(b) CC message:

> The latest information received by the Soviet Government about the July 12 Paris meeting revealed two facts. First, the sponsors of the conference, the British and the French, have no intention of introducing any changes in their plans for the economic revival of Europe, without taking into account the interests of sovereignty and economic independence of small countries. Second, under the guise of drafting plans for the revival of Europe, the sponsors of the conference in fact are planning to set up a Western bloc which includes West Germany. In view of those facts, the CC CPSU(B) cancels its message of July 5 and suggests refusing to participate in the conference, that is, not sending your delegations to the conference. Each side may present its own reasons for its refusal.[28]

However, the Kremlin's vacillations between 4 and 7 July had complicated the situation. The governments of Albania, Bulgaria, Hungary, Poland, Romania, Yugoslavia and Finland acted in compliance with the instruction, but difficulties arose in Prague. When M. Bodrov, the acting Soviet Charge d'Affaires in Czechoslovakia, on 8 July visited Gottwald, the head of the Czechoslovak government, and handed over the message to him, the latter said that it was impossible to change the Czechoslovak government's decision to attend the Paris conference, for 'the government will not support us (Communists).' Gottwald was supported by Communist V. Clementis, the State Secretary for Foreign Affairs, who told Bodrov 'that they will not be able to change anything now, for they have already taken the necessary steps, the British and French have been informed of their decision, and it has been carried by the press, Nosek in Paris has received instructions to the effect that he is entrusted with the task of attending the conference.'[29]

An enraged Stalin demanded that a Czechoslovak government delegation immediately visit Moscow, and on the morning of 9 July, a delegation led by Gottwald duly flew to the Soviet capital. At first Stalin received only Gottwald, and according to the latter, furiously demanded that the Czechoslovak government immediately cancel its decision to attend the Paris conference. About five hours later Gottwald rejoined his colleagues, having promised that Stalin's demand would be fulfilled. When Stalin received the entire Czechoslovak delegation at 11:00 hrs he was in a more placid mood. He asserted that, according to the information received by the Soviet government, the Paris conference was intended to become a part of a large-scale Western plan to isolate the Soviet Union. And he stressed the West's stake in the rehabilitation of the German economy, notably of the Ruhr Basin, which was to become the industrial core of the Western bloc. Sweeping aside mild protests by the Czechoslovak ministers, Stalin declared:

> Participation in that conference will present you in a false light. This 'breaking of the front-line' would be a success for the Western powers. Switzerland and Sweden are still vacillating, and your participation would influence their decision. We know that you're our friends, none of us doubts this fact. But if you participate in the Paris Conference you would give them a chance to use you as a tool against the USSR. Neither the Soviet Union nor its government could allow it.[30]

Before the Czechoslovak delegation returned to Prague, on 10 July, an extraordinary meeting of the Czechoslovak government was held, lasting for almost a whole day. In closing the meeting, Viliam Široký, the Deputy Head of Government, read out a new decision: the government unanimously cancelled its decision to attend the Paris conference on the Marshall Plan. Czechoslovak Foreign Minister Jan Masaryk is said to have told friends: 'I went to Moscow as the foreign minister of an independent sovereign state; I returned as a lackey of the Soviet government.'[31]

An analysis of the Soviet stand on the Marshall Plan leads one to the conclusion that the establishment and consolidation of Soviet control over the countries of eastern Europe was the first priority of Moscow's foreign policy strategy. Stalin considered the Soviet zone of influence to be the most important legacy of the Second World War. He was not going to make any concessions to the West in that region, for at that time the Soviet government regarded control over that sphere of its influence as essential for imperial, geopolitical and ideological considerations. The Soviet leadership saw the US as its main rival in the international arena and made every effort to prevent the US from expanding its influence in Europe. Any attempt to set up a Western bloc, dominated by the United States, was simply intolerable to Moscow.

Paradoxically enough, implementation of the Marshall Plan without Soviet participation and with strong opposition from the USSR to a certain extent suited both sides. The Soviet Union retained and consolidated its influence in the countries of eastern Europe, whereas the US and its partners in the Marshall Plan had an opportunity to carry out a set of measures to stabilize the socio-political situation in Western Europe and, later, to set up a military–political Western alliance. The actual realization of the Marshall Plan and the sharply negative Soviet reaction to it marked an important turning point on the way to the splitting of Europe into two. The concept of Europe's division into spheres of influence – to which the US ruling circles had earlier been opposed – triumphed.

Notes

1 See D. G. Acheson, *Present at the Creation: My Years in the State Department* (New York: Norton & Co., 1969) p. 229.

2 See M. P. Leffler, 'The United States and the Strategic Dimensions of the Marshall Plan', *Diplomatic History* 12:3 (Summer 1988), p. 283; see also M. P. Leffler, *A Preponderance of Power. National Security, the Truman Administration, and the Cold War* (Stanford, CA: Stanford University Press, 1992) esp. pp. 1 and 5–86.

3 M. J. Hogan, 'One World into Two: American Economic Diplomacy from Bretton Woods to the Marshall Plan', unpublished paper presented at the Soviet Academy of Sciences, Moscow, 28 June 1987. Paper in possession of the author.

4 US Department of State, *Foreign Relations of the United States, 1947*, (Washington DC: US Government Printing Office) vol. 3, p. 260 (hereafter referred to as *FR* with year, volume, and page numbers), J. Caffery to Secretary of State, 18 June 1947.

5 Decision of the CPSU CC Politburo, 21 June 1947, Archives of the President of the Russian Federation (APRF), fund 3, inventory 63, case 270, list 12.

6 Molotov to Soviet ambassadors in Warsaw, Prague, Belgrade, telegram, 22 June 1947, Foreign Policy Archives of the Russian Federation (FPARF). f.6, i.9, p.c.18, c.214, l.19.

7 E. Varga to Molotov, note, 'The Marshall Plan and the US economic situation', 24 June 1947, ibid., c.213, l.24.

8 N. Novikov to Molotov, telegram, 24 June 1947, quoted in G. Takhnenko, 'An Anatomy of a Political Decision: Documents', *Mezhdunarodnaya zhizn*, 5 (May 1992) p. 121.

9 Author's interview with V. l. Yerofeyev, 15 October 1992.

10 *FR*:1947, 3:283, Peterson, memorandum of conversation, 25–26 June 1947.

11 Directives for Soviet delegation, 25 June 47, FPARF, f.6, i.9, p.c.l 8, c.214, 1.4–6.

12 Molotov to Moscow, cipher telegram, 29 June 1947, APRF, f.3, i.63, c.270, l.54.

13 A. Vyshinsky to Molotov, cipher telegram, 30 June 1947, ibid., 1.59–60.
14 *FR*: 1947, 3:273, Peterson, memorandum of conversation, 24 June 1947.
15 *FR*: 1947, 3:268, Bevin aide-memoire, 25 June 1947.
16 *FR*:1947, 3:268, Peterson, memorandum of conversation, 24 June 1947.
17 Directives for Soviet delegation, 25 June 1947, FPARF, f.3, i.63, c.270, 1.64–65.
18 Molotov to Moscow, telegram, 30 June 1947, APRF, f. 3, i.63, c.270, 1.65–66.
19 Molotov to Stalin, cipher telegram, 1 July 1947, ibid., 1.70–71.
20 'Entretien de M. Bidault avec M. Byrnes du 23 septembre 1947', Archives Nationales (Paris), Section contemporaine, Papiers privées de M. Georges Bidault, AP-80, 7354, p. 6.
21 Molotov to Stalin, cipher telegram, 1 July 1947, APRF, f.3, i.63, c.270, 1.71.
22 Molotov to Soviet ambassadors, telegram, 5 July 1947, ibid., 1.93–94.
23 Molotov to Soviet ambassador in Belgrade, cipher telegram, 5 July 1947, ibid., 1.96.
24 Kirsanov to Moscow, cipher telegram, 6 July 1947, ibid., 1.118.
25 Molotov to ambassador Lebedev, cipher telegram, 6 July 1947, ibid., 1.135.
26 Molotov to Lebedev, cipher telegram, 7 July 1947, ibid., 1.142.
27 Bogomolov to Moscow, cipher telegram, 10 July 1947, ibid., 1.201.
28 Molotov to Lebedev, cipher telegram, 8 July 1947, ibid., 1.158.
29 Chargé d'Affaires M. Bodrov to Molotov, cipher telegram, 9 July 1947, ibid., 1.183–84.
30 Quoted in *Izvestia*, 9 January 1992.
31 R. H. B. Lockhart, *Jan Masaryk, A Personal Memoir* (New York: Philosophical Library, 1951) p. 66.

24
The United States, Europe and the Marshall Plan

Ennio Di Nolfo

In 1964 a well known British economic historian of the Soviet Union, Alec Nove, wrote a seminal book *Was Stalin Really Necessary?* Through a careful extrapolation of statistical data, Nove was able to prove that if the Russian take-off of the last decade of the 19th century had not been interrupted by the war and, worse, by Stalinism, the Russian economy would have entered an age of stabilized growth somewhat earlier; industrialization and political power would have been achieved at a much lower social cost.[1] Twenty years later, in a controversial but important book, Alan Milward wrote his *Reconstruction of Western Europe, 1945–1951*, in which he maintained that the Marshall Plan 'was never the critical intervention it is almost always considered to have been'.[2] Some five years later Milward echoed the title of Alec Nove in a well-known article which asked: 'Was the Marshall Plan Necessary?'[3] The economic emergency detected by American officials was, he says, no more than a payment crisis determined by high demand for import items for reconstruction – a demand often fuelled by high public investment. As a consequence Milward deems massive American aid to have been unnecessary: the Western countries would have recovered even without American aid by curtailing domestic demand, consumption and imports. At the same time, European governments could have redressed their balance of payments deficits by forceful stimulation of the export sectors, especially if directed toward the acquisition of badly needed dollars.[4]

I have referred to the work of these two authors, not to discuss from any of the opinions expressed by Milward or by others, but only as a form of method. Neither Nove nor Milward deny the achievements of Stalinism or of the Marshall Plan. What they discuss is the question of 'necessity'. On this point, Nove carefully differentiated the term 'necessary' from the term 'inevitable'.[5] This leads to a preliminary point, which seems to be unavoidable. When one accepts the difference between necessary and inevitable one enters the historical field. The Marshall Plan may have been unnecessary, however it is a fact of history. Paradoxically one could wonder, was the Second World War really necessary? In fact the war took place even though some might be ready to admit that Hitler himself did not want it in 1939. Maybe the Marshall Plan was not necessary; however it was one of the crucial events of the Cold War years and it is inevitable that we must understand it within this framework. Seminal discussions, like Milward's, take for granted that history should be dealt with only from one point of view. However history refuses to adapt itself to the schemes that historians and politicians craftily devise for it. It is possible, sometimes useful, to isolate one of the many variables of a multifaceted process, so that more light is cast upon it. It is much more of a limitation to eliminate all other variables from the picture. This gives a picture that is simplified, by offering us the sight of only one of the sides of the polygon.

It is impossible to simplify the interpretation of the Marshall Plan. In the huge number of historical books which until now have dealt with this matter, even those who try, like Milward, to identify the central feature of the plan tend to admit to the complexity of the question. Broadly speaking we can identify two schools of thought: the 'realistic' or 'systemic' interpretation and the 'corporatist' one. From a European point of view this division, which has become usual in Anglo-Saxon literature, could be better understood with a slight but significant change of terms. Rather than speaking of realism one should speak of 'power politics'; rather than speaking of corporatism – a term which is too reminiscent of Italian corporativism – one suggests these different approaches be unified under the term 'structuralism', or sometimes that of 'economic determinism'. Whatever the definition, it is necessary to recognize that after the first phase of this debate much water has been poured into each other's wine and clear-cut positions have become rather rare.

'Structuralism' might suggest a sort of continuity in American foreign policy. The Marshall Plan was one of the aspects of this policy, whose roots can be traced back to before the First World War. Charles Maier has written that

as a system of supranational co-ordination, American ascendancy rested in large part upon an international economic order. Such co-ordination required explicit consultation, debate and political decision. But it also rested on the effectively self-regulating, or cybernetic, controls exerted by the international economy, such that co-ordination would be achieved without conscious effort but by the suasion of so-called market laws. American ascendancy, in a word, relied on its invisible hand [...] the invisible hand, however, depended in turn upon relative monetary convertibility – the free exchange among currencies and goods..., and this required price stability.

The intense trading of 1913 never recovered its robustness after the onset of the First World War. 'Whatever degree of recovery in the late 1920s that the depression had not disrupted, the Second World War certainly did.'[6] The Second World War gave an enormous impulse to the problem of reconstruction, which mostly meant, to American eyes, 'escaping the traditional nature of politics as necessity/scarcity by means of constant growth'. It is the concept of productivity that Maier himself has rethought as the conceptual framework within which to understand both postwar epochs. 'For Maier, productivity was the essential element in American post-war strategy to eliminate ideology from politics, since it turned the latter into a question of economic growth.'[7]

The Cold War fits into this interpretation only in a secondary manner. This is particularly true in the context of the well-known book by Michael Hogan on the Marshall Plan.[8] Hogan sought to explain the Marshall Plan 'in the context of America's twentieth century search for a new economic order at home and abroad.' Marshall aid, then, aimed at 'economic growth, modest social programs, and a more equitable distribution of production', which would 'immunize participating countries against Communist subversion while generating the resources and mobilizing the public support necessary to sustain a major rearmament program'. Ellwood has summarized this viewpoint in a meaningful sentence:

> To substitute the fear-based security obsessions which had dragged Europe into the abyss in 1914 and 1939, the Marshall Plan offered individual Europeans and their families the promise of ever-greater prosperity. An 'economic United States of Europe' would emerge, in which the American dream could be dreamt without leaving home: 'you too can be like us!', that was the promise of the Marshall Plan.[9]

The realist school, which maybe we should call 'traditionally diplomatic', is well represented by Melwyn P. Leffler, who sees American foreign policy in the Cold War as primarily motivated by the problems of national security from a potential Soviet threat:

> Although American officials hoped the Marshall Plan would benefit the American economy, they also wanted to redress the European balance of power and to enhance American national security. By national security, American officials meant the control of the raw materials, industrial infrastructures, skilled manpower, and military bases. And from their viewpoint, the most fundamental strategic interest of the United States was to prevent any potential adversary or coalition of adversaries from mobilizing the resources and eco- nomic–military potential of Europe for war-making purposes against the United States.[10]

A lot of other sentences could be added to this quotation, written before the polemics among orthodox and revisionist historians, since it is evident that the orthodox school (if one may call it so) was mostly concerned with the Soviet danger and it was, therefore, profoundly realistic, while the revisionists, who were looking for the internal roots of American foreign policy, following the teaching of William Appleton Williams, were mostly Marxist and tendentially 'corporatist'. I cannot enter here into details about these problems. I have only raised them to establish the point at which the matter has arrived. I cannot however conceal one impression: the more the Cold War enters the kingdom of oblivion, the less historians are willing to remember that the Cold War was not only a competition between opposing development models but also a political struggle around the future of power politics. It is true that many major issues had been settled by the big summits of the war but it is also true that some things had been left open in the political and diplomatic field: the peace treaties of 1947; the German question; the nuclear question (which was by no means a problem of corporatism); the Korean question. Only in the mid 1950s, when decolonization became the central issue of world politics, were political problems ob- scured by financial and economic ones. This does not imply forgetting that 1947 was a year of economic crisis. It only means that this crisis cannot be intimately separated from the Cold War climate. One book seems to be at a midway point between the two above-mentioned schools. In 1973 David Calleo and Benjamin Rowland wrote:

> America's euphoric sense of omnipotence and vast vision of a new international order had confronted, in Stalin's Russia and later Mao's

China, obstacles infinitely more contrary than Attlee's Britain. The family quarrel over money was overtaken by the Cold War. The American liberal universe, discovering Communism, became finite. The universalism of the UN and IMF shrank to the Atlanticism of NATO and the OEEC.

Therefore,

> free trade was not the link which actually brought together post-war America and Europe. On the contrary it was the issue that divide them [...]. The post-war Atlantic community came into being only after the United States, prompted by its fear of Russian and domestic European Communism, suppressed its liberal economic scruples in the interest of 'mutual security' and Europe's rapid recovery [...]. Economy was subordinated to politics. Trade took directions from the flag. And American's hegemony over Europe took a more visible form than free trade imperialism, and also a form more useful and acceptable to the Europeans.[11]

Neither the 'realist' nor the 'corporatist' overviews of the Marshall Plan are fully persuasive. It is even too easy to point out that both of them tend to explain one side of the same coin. No one can seriously debate the pervasive nature and structure of the American economic system, neither is it possible to deny that economic internationalism took the initiative even in the worst years of American isolationism, like the early 1920s, before the depression. When Roosevelt was elected president of the United States and Hull became his Secretary of State the open door doctrine became one of the pillars of the New Deal. It was also going to become one of the pillars of Roosevelt's Grand Design, during the Second World War. Economic internationalism was going to interact with political internationalism. Sometimes one tends to interpret the Lend-Lease Act as the first step of the fight against British protectionism and an expression of economic internationalism. It is probably more correct to reverse the order: the Lend-Lease Act was the first expression of the rebirth of political internationalism, which met an already existing economic internationalism. The hostile power was then the preferential system in British trade. However, this was a mere detail: undoubtedly an important one, but a logical detail, within the much broader frame resulting from the combination of political and economic internationalism. Thus the United States were bound to be involved in the European war just for fostering this connection. For a time Roosevelt thought he would be able to involve even the Soviet Union in his design. He was mistaken, as postwar events were going to prove. However the Marshall Plan was exactly the moment when the link between political and economic internationalism became fully apparent. Historians have individual interests. However, when these interests fail to take into account important factors in the sequence of events, they become rather unsatisfactory.

A young Italian historian has recently remarked that the quarrel between the two different interpretations of the Marshall Plan derive mainly from the fact that they start by posing specific questions: 'what was the actual impact of the ERP? Did the United States manage effectively to influence the course of French and Italian economic policies?' Her sound conclusions are the following:

> America achieved little that the French and the Italians did not already want to achieve themselves, and both governments did indeed use the ERP to implement their own national economic agendas. However, the American, French and Italian governments shared with the Truman administration all-important strategic–ideological goals, and as a consequence the Marshall Plan did reach its principal targets.[12]

When the ERP is considered from such a point of view, one can no longer ignore the extreme difference of the American intervention in the various countries. This presupposes that if there was a corporatist programme it was at least a multifaceted one: it is difficult to export one economic model to different economic realities, simply because they can react in an unforeseen way to such a challenge.

This is a main reason why the contribution of Chiarella Esposito, the young Italian historian mentioned, fills a gap in the historiography of the Marshall Plan. Or, rather, it adds a careful interpretation to the new wave of studies on the ERP that have been published in recent years. What I mean is that the time has come to return to the very origins of the ERP and, rather than working on general issues, to verify the interaction between the ERP, the ECA and national authorities. This new approach could contribute, maybe from below, to a better understanding of the actual consequences of the Marshall Plan, even without falling into the trap prepared by John Gimbel, who connected two political problems – the future of Germany and the future of American politics in Europe.

Some steps have already been taken in this direction. John Harper has given a confused but interesting picture of Italy,[13] which however deals with the subject only until 1948, when the ERP actually began to take effect; Zamagni has also written extensively on Italy.[14] Gérard Bossuat has recently shown how Jean Monnet conceived the ERP as a positive way to push his 'Plan de modernization', and he also added much to our knowledge of French reactions to the ERP.[15] However, in producing this personal contribution to the new wave of history on the Marshall Plan, I think that two steps may be useful.

If we go back to the law which in April 1948 enacted the Economic Co-operation Administration, we can see that the two aspects already mentioned are *de facto* closely interwoven. The law said:

> Mindful of the advantages which the United States has enjoyed through the existence of a large domestic market with no internal barriers, and believing that similar advantages can accrue to the countries of Europe, it is declared to be the policy of the people of the United States to encourage these countries through a joint organization to exert sustained common efforts [...] which will speedily achieve that economic co-operation in Europe which is essential for lasting peace and prosperity.

This section of the law anticipates a corporatist interpretation. However, if we enter into a more detailed analysis of the same law we can see that the creation of the ECA administrator and that of US special representatives abroad diluted this general approach. Each representative was actually given the power to ensure that the activities of the American mission in each country were not only consistent with the general aims of American foreign policy, but also for those special adjustments which were deemed to be necessary for the special situation of each country.[16] Each country was to have a special ECA commission and its head was to receive the formal grade of ambassador. This means that each country was considered to be a different reality, ranging from underdeveloped Portugal to Britain and Western Germany and Italy: different countries requiring different economic policies.

When looking more carefully at the Italian case – just to mention my own interpretation in a few words – one cannot avoid the consideration that there were as many lines of interaction as American authorities involved in the policy making process. From a historiographical point of view, we are used to seeing Italy as a special case. The 1949 ECA Country study was taken for granted by many historians in order to criticize the use made by the Italians of American assistance: not to increase productivity, but to adjust a deficit budget.[17] This, however, is a misperception. There were close links between American economic authorities, American experts on Italian economy and the Italian government. The chief adviser of the US government on the matter was Professor Mario Einaudi of Cornell University. He was surrounded by a group of ethnic Italian experts and by sympathetic people, like Albert Hirshman. The main interlocutor of Mario Einaudi's was his father, Luigi Einaudi, the Minister for the Budget and the architect of the economic choices of the reconstruction. Luigi Einaudi, who had been the governor of the Bank of Italy before entering the government, had close links with his successors, like Donato Menichella and Paolo Baffi, both of whom have written extensively on the matter. From this correspondence and the political attitude of the US government what emerges is that the sharply critical Country study of 1949 had little echo in Washington.[18] In Rome, Esposito wrote,

> the Americans consistently supported a government whose economic policy did little to address the need of workers and create the 'prosperity for all' that formed the basis of New Deal ideology. The Italian government appeared as the safest pro-American regime that could be secured in Italy [...] despite its unsavoury economic policies.[19]

While it would be unwise to draw generalizations from a very special case, I conclude my study with this note: progress toward an understanding of the effects of ERP can be obtained from many perspectives and I believe that an attempt to understand the mechanism of its day-to-day activities may offer important insight to provide for a more realistic and less aprioristic general approach.

Notes

1 A. Nove, *Was Stalin Really Necessary? Some Problems of Soviet Political Economy* (London: Allen & Unwin, 1964) p. 21.

2 A. S. Milward, *The Reconstruction of Western Europe, 1945–1951* (London: Methuen, 1964), chap. 3; see also: A. Stephanson, *The United States*, in the vol. *The Origins of the Cold War in Europe. International Perspectives*, D. Reynolds ed. (London: Yale University Press, 1994) p. 43.

3 A. S. Milward, 'Was the Marshall Plan Necessary?', *Diplomatic History*, 1989, pp. 231–53.

4 These considerations have been suggested by: C. Esposito, *America's Feeble Weapon. Funding the Marshall Plan in France and Italy 1948–1950* (Westport: Greenwood Press, 1994) pp. XXI–XXII.

5 A. Nove, *op. cit.*, pp. 19–20.

6   C. S. Maier, 'The Making of "Pax Americana"', in *The Quest for Stability. Problems of Western European Security 1918–1957*, ed. by R. Ahmann, M. Birke and M. Howard (London: Macmillan, 1993) p. 404.

7   A. Stephanson, *op. cit.*, pp. 41–2.

8   M. Hogan, *The Marshall Plan: America, Britain and the Reconstruction of Western Europe, 1947–1952* (New York: Cambridge University Press, 1987).

9   M. Hogan, *op. cit.*, pp. 427, 429, 443; see also in the same sense D. W. Ellwood, *Rebuilding Europe. Western Europe, America and Postwar Reconstruction* (London: Longman, 1992) pp. 88–9.

10   M. L. Leffler, 'The United States and the Strategic Dimension of the Marshall Plan', *Diplomatic History*, 1988, p. 277.

11   D. P. Calleo and B. M. Rowland, *America and the World Political Economy. Atlantic Dreams and National Realities* (Bloomington: Indiana University Press, 1973, 2nd printing) pp. 42–3.

12   Esposito, *op. cit.*, pp. XXIII–XXV.

13   J. L. Harper, *America and the Reconstruction of Italy 1945–1948* (Cambridge: Cambridge University Press, 1986).

14   V. Zamagni, 'Betting on the Future: the Reconstruction of Italian Industry 1946–1952', in J. Becker and F. Knipping eds, *Power in Europe? Great Britain, France, Italy and Germany in a Postwar World 1945–1950* (Berlin: de Gruyter, 1986) pp. 293–300.

15   G. Bossuat, *La France, l'aide américaine et la construction européenne 1944–1954* 2 vols. (Paris: Comité pour l'histoire économique et financière de la France, 1992) vol. II, pp. 624 and 624–30.

16   *Foreign Relief Assistance Act of 1948. Hearings held in Executive session before the Committee on Foreign Relations. United States Senate, Eightieth Congress* (Washington DC: US Government Printing Office, 1973) pp. 789, 782, 784.

17   See on this: C. Daneo, *La politica economica della ricostruzione 1945–1949* (Turin: Einaudi, 1975); P. P. D'Attorre 'Aspetti dell'attuazione del Piano Marshall in Italia' in E. Agarossi ed., *Il Piano Marshall e l'Italia* (Rome: Istituto dell'Enciclopedia italiana, 1983) pp. 163–80; M. Salvati, *Stato e industria nella ricostruzione* (Milan: Feltrinelli, 1982).

18   On this see: E. Di Nolfo, 'Il ruolo di Mario Einaudi nell'esportazione di modelli economici per la ricostruzione italiana', in *Mario Einaudi (1904–1994) Intellettuale, storico e organizzatore culturale tra America e Europa* (Turin: Einaudi, 1995) pp. 133–45.

19   Esposito, *op. cit.*, p. XXV.

25
The Cominform as the Soviet Response to the Marshall Plan

Anna Di Biagio

The main aim of this chapter is first of all to examine briefly the most recent historical contributions on the role played by the Marshall Plan in the decision to set up a new Communist European organization, the 'Information Bureau' (Cominform). Second, I will attempt to indicate, by means of a brief analysis of the most significant new evidence, the hypotheses that we can now advance on the objectives formulated by the Soviet leadership for Cominform. Some preliminary considerations are necessary of the documentation concerning the setting up of Cominform and its prehistory. Despite progress in the accessibility of the archival documentation, it is important to point out that foreign scholars are not yet permitted to consult the sources held in the Archives of the President of the Russian Federation. This means that we are still unable to gain access to information at the decision-making level. Thus, with respect to the reconstruction of the actual motivations and the formulation of goals of the Soviet leadership, we can only proceed by advancing plausible hypotheses. Furthermore, the available documentation is in crucial respects fragmentary. Finally, one must also remember that the official collection of diplomatic documents available on the post Second World War period is not yet quantitatively comparable to the collection in existence for the prewar period.

Nevertheless, scholars have embarked upon a reappraisal of the history of the partition of Europe, utilizing the new sources of information and evaluation. The most recent work on the Soviet reaction to the Marshall Plan and on the establishment of Cominform, gives the impression that the general terms of the historiographical controversy have not changed in a substantial way. In other words, at the centre of the debate among scholars the question remains as to whether the Soviet leadership's decisions in the area of foreign policy should be understood as responses to Western initiatives, particularly those of the United States; or whether the role of the West in influencing Soviet foreign policy should be considered secondary, given that the formulation of strategies in the international arena on the part of the Soviet leadership did not reflect in any way the actions and declarations of the West.[1]

In fact, in his substantial and well-documented study on the Soviet reaction to the Marshall Plan, Scott D. Parrish did not shift from the earlier interpretation, drawing the conclusion that Stalin and Zhdanov 'designed the meeting [of the first Conference of Cominform], its agenda, and the organization which emerged from it, primarily as a response to the perceived threat presented by the Marshall Plan'. Within this perspective, the Cominform was to take the form of 'the institutional expression of the shift in Soviet grand strategy', which occurred as a consequence of the Marshall Plan, and would thus prove the Soviet leadership's abandonment of any further attempts to work out a compromise settlement with the West.[2]

L. Gibianskii, on the other hand, adopted a different approach in his study on the origins of Cominform. His archival research may be considered a fundamentally important contribution from the point of view of a plausible, albeit still incomplete, reconstruction of the immediate events leading to the establishment of Cominform. His assessment of the new information leads him to underline in particular the relations between Moscow and the countries of the Eastern bloc. He thus maintains that right from June 1946, the Information Bureau was conceived as the pivotal point in the political structure of the Socialist camp. In Gibianskii's interpretation, one essentially senses the tendency to consider Cominform above all as a tool to strengthen the Eastern bloc and determine the definitive Sovietization of eastern Europe. Furthermore, according to this reading, the basis for the plan lay in the internal logic of the Stalinist system: its realization was thus not conditioned by what the US did.[3]

From this brief and sketchy outline of the most recent analyses of the role assigned to Cominform by the Soviet leadership, one easily realizes how crucial it is, in order to develop a clearer understanding of the question, to determine in chronological terms when the idea of creating a new Communist organization actually emerged; second, what its objectives were; and third, to what extent did those original objectives underwent changes due to the influence of the international situation.

The documentation available at present does not allow these questions to be dealt with exhaustively. Archival investigations, however, have confirmed the fact that the establishment of an Information Bureau was examined in Moscow as early as June 1946 on the occasion of Tito's visit to the Soviet capital. Among the tasks set for this inter-party office and among the general political objectives outlined during the course of these discussions, there was no indication that the decisions taken would be binding on member parties, as had been the case for the dissolved Comintern, while it was recommended that the new organ should 'take into account the specificity of the individual countries'.[4] During this meeting, Stalin declared his desire not to recreate the old type of Communist International. This reassurance, however, takes on a different light if we consider that the dissolution of Comintern had not entailed the dissolution of its central apparatus as well. Indeed, it continued to operate, under the direction of Dimitrov, as an integral part of the apparatus of the CC of the VKP(B). After the end of the Second World War, a restructuring process was initiated. This gave rise to the Foreign Policy Department (FPD), which started operating actively in April 1946, under the direction of Suslov. FPD policy was based on the propaganda of Marxist–Leninist ideas, and the use of national Communist movements to promote the interests of the Soviet Union.[5] It is possible that the initial proposals for an Information Bureau were part of a more general plan to strengthen the bureaucratic apparatus of the CC, which handled the network connecting the VKP(B) with the European Communist parties.

The data in our possession are not sufficient to enable us to reconstruct a detailed and complete picture of the relations between the VKP(B) and the European Communist parties after the dissolution of Comintern. Some available evidence, however, suggest that the relations between Moscow and the parties of the East were closer and more regular than those between Moscow and the Western parties. With regard to the latter, the contents of a letter sent by Zhdanov to Thorez on 2 June 1947, following the exclusion of the PCF from the government, may be revelatory. 'Many people think', wrote Zhdanov, 'that the French communists concerted their action with the CC of the VKP(B). You yourselves know that this is not true, that as far as the CC of the VKP(B) is concerned the steps you have taken were totally unexpected.'[6]

A document sent by the deputy head of the FPD (L. S. Baranov) to Zhdanov and Suslov on 2 September 1947 concerning the 'International Links of the VKP(B)' throws light on the fact that right from the dissolution of Comintern 'contacts of a constructive character on the fundamental questions of strategy and tactics as well as on the co-ordination of activities' had been established with the main countries falling within the sphere of Soviet influence. This co-ordination concentrated in particular on collaboration by the VKP(B) in the 'drawing-up of programmes, political platforms, and the most important laws concerning the general formation of democratic governments' in eastern Europe.[7]

The reconstructions now available on Soviet reactions to the Marshall Plan have demonstrated the existence of a diplomatic channel linking Moscow and the countries of eastern Europe, through which directives were sent to the Communist leaders of those countries on matters relating to foreign policy.[8] This, however, did not mean that Moscow exercised absolute control over the governments and Communist parties of the eastern countries at that time, nor does it mean that their subordination was unconditional.

We now know that with regard to the invitation extended by Bevin and Bidault to all the European governments to participate in the Paris Conference, which was to meet on 12 July, there were significant divergences in the positions of the eastern Communist leaders, even after Moscow had invited them to take part in the conference. Moscow's objective then was stated explicitly in the telegram that Molotov sent on 5 July to all the eastern Communist leaders: it was necessary to send delegates 'in order to show at the conference itself the unacceptability of the Anglo-French plan, not to allow the unanimous adoption of this plan and then to withdraw from the meeting, taking with them as many delegates from other countries as possible'.[9] In other words, Moscow had decided to have the governments of eastern Europe attend the conference to boycott the American aid plan and defend the sovereignty and national independence of the European countries. This directive was not unanimously accepted: while the Czechoslovak government immediately accepted the invitation to take part in the Anglo-French conference, this was not the case for the Yugoslav government. Tito's opposition to the invitation led Moscow to intervene in Belgrade and to exert pressure to make the Yugoslav leader change his position.[10]

It is possible to ascertain with a fair degree of certainty that the difficulties encountered in achieving a united stand on the Anglo-French conference proved to be one of the reasons leading Moscow, a few days later, to revoke the 5 July order and to propose instead that no delegation should be sent. This decision, in turn, created new complications for those governments that had accepted the first directive issued by Moscow. This was particularly the case for the Czechoslovak government which, as is well-known, was subjected to Stalin's diktat during a meeting between the head of the Kremlin and the delegation headed by Gottwald in Moscow during the night between 9 and 10 July.[11]

There is no reason to doubt that the difficulties encountered by the Soviet leadership in imposing its will on the Communist leaders of the eastern European countries led Moscow to carry out a plan which until then had remained in an embryonic state: to establish an inter-party institution which would act as a co-ordination centre and as a tool to synchronize the political actions of the European Communist parties. Thus steps were taken, transforming an informal initiative agreed between Stalin and Gomułka in the spring of 1947 into a conference which would give formal approval to the founding of Cominform. The way in which Moscow contrived, during the preparatory phases of the work for the conference, to conceal its real objectives from the delegates can be explained by the probable opposition to the idea of reconstituting a new Comintern, fostered in particular by the very Polish Communist leaders who had been given the task of promoting the initiative.[12]

The Foreign Policy Department was given the job of preparing all the preliminary phases of the conference. The dossiers put together by the department's officials on the Communist parties invited to attend the conference offer a useful picture of how they were viewed by Moscow. The most striking feature is the fact that the parties of the East were subjected to criticism particularly in relation to their actions, in support of their domestic policy. The general drift of this criticism may be summed up in the accusation, aimed at the supporters of the 'national road to socialism', of demonstrating a 'national limitedness'. Significant criticism along the same lines was addressed to the Yugoslav party for its orientation in foreign policy. It is worth underlining here that these criticisms were not at all related to the Marshall Plan, towards which, as we have seen, Tito had immediately assumed a position of uncompromising rejection. The object of Moscow's disapproval was the aspiration on the part of the Yugoslav party to a 'leadership role in the Balkans' and to thus display a tendency to ignore 'the general interests of the democratic forces'.[13]

In other words, on the whole the criticisms contained in these dossiers reveal Moscow's intention to accelerate the transition of the eastern European countries from 'new democracy' regimes, to use Varga's well-known definition, to socialist regimes, accepting the 'Soviet way'. The fact that these dossiers were drafted after the Soviet rejection of the Marshall Plan does not, however, allow us to assert that the American initiative was the only, or the main, cause of Moscow's sudden decision to assume complete control over its sphere of influence. Within this sphere, there were also strong centrifugal drives, particularly Tito's attempt to create a centre for regional integration in the Balkan area, which Moscow viewed as a threat to its hegemony over the entire area of the East.[14]

For our purposes, it is also important to point out that the criticisms of the eastern parties were not made public, nor were they examined by the founding Conference of Cominform. Instead, the conference was only called upon to make a statement on the 'mistakes made by certain Communist Parties, especially the mistakes of the French and Italian CPs'.[15] A list of these 'mistakes' may be found in the substantial dossier which was compiled for Zhdanov for his speech. The striking feature of this list is the absence of any reference to the foreign policy orientation of the Western parties, much less to their positions regarding the Marshall Plan.[16]

During the conference, in the reports given by delegates prior to Zhdanov's report, little interest was expressed in relation to the Marshall Plan. The Soviet delegate, Malenkov, dedicated only a few lines to it, and judged it, together with the 'Truman Plan', to be 'the plainest and most concrete expression' of American expansionist tendencies.[17] Gomułka recalled the 'negative attitude' assumed by his party towards the Marshall Plan, but at the same time did not exclude the possibility 'of utilizing American credits' if they were to be offered with conditions less injurious to the sovereignty of his country.[18] Essentially, the delegates' interest in the Marshall Plan during this first phase of the conference was undoubtedly secondary to another topic which, moreover, had been the subject of criticism by Moscow prior to the conference: Yugoslav policy in the Balkan area.[19]

Greater space was given, however, to the Marshall Plan in the reports given by the two Western delegates. Duclos, in particular, formally proposed that the conference put this topic on the agenda, dividing it into two distinct questions: how to organize a campaign 'to show the real significance of the "Marshall Plan"', and second the thornier and more controversial question: according to the French delegate, to 'unmask' the Marshall Plan effectively it would be necessary to demonstrate to the French masses 'that the countries of Europe were perfectly capable of restoring their economies by themselves, even without help from the USA.'[20] Zhdanov did not miss the significance of this statement. As he pointed out in a telegram sent that day to Stalin, Duclos had intended to suggest that it would be possible to reject the American offer of aid only if the USSR and the new democracies displayed a willingness to offer their help instead.[21] Like Gomułka, Luigi Longo, vice-secretary of the PCI, suggested they could 'negotiate with America on equal terms' about the economic aid and then made a statement which was shortly afterwards to sound like a heresy: 'We are for friendship with both the US and the USSR.'[22]

The report that Zhdanov read during the second part of the conference is generally viewed as the formal act by which the Soviet leadership recognized the definitive end of the phase of a search for multilateral solutions to its own security problems with its wartime allies and the development of a rigid bipolar conception of the postwar world. 'The American plan for the enslavement of Europe' was placed at the centre of the Zhdanovian analysis. Central to his argument was the accusation against 'American imperialism' for aspiring to 'world domination' and the need to form a 'democratic and anti-imperialist camp' to counter the 'Western bloc' led by the US. The position adopted by the two western parties on the Marshall Plan thus came to form the basic motivation for Zhdanov's criticism of them at this time. It was upon this basis that the Soviet leader formulated precise guidelines, aiming to enlist the support of the PCF and the PCI in boycotting the American plan, by using the new bone of contention by which to divide the countries of Europe: the fears – harboured mainly by France – of a rebirth of German power. Furthermore, the western Communists were assigned

> a special historical role – to head the resistance to the American plan for the enslavement of Europe, to expose courageously all the internal accomplices of American imperialism. At the same time, the Communists must support all truly patriotic elements who do not want their country dishonoured, and who want to fight against the enslavement of their motherland by foreign capital, and in support of their national sovereignty.[23]

With these words, Zhdanov imposed a considerable shift in the political line followed until then by the two western parties: to end the alliance with the Socialists, now openly denounced as 'agents of the imperialist circles of the USA'[24] and search for new supporters among the nationalist and patriotic forces sensitive to the 'defence of the motherland's honour and independence'.

All those who took part in the debate on Zhdanov's report grasped the importance of this 'serious reorientation' imposed on the two western parties, although they drew different implications from it. The Bulgarian, A. Pauker, pointed out to the PCF and the PCI the example of the

Greek party and its fight against 'American aid'. She responded to the question raised by Duclos by recalling 'the heroic example of the USSR, which restored its economy under conditions of blockade by a hostile encirclement' and thus 'by relying, in the first place, on its own forces'.[25] Quite different in tone was the intervention by Gomułka, who raised a crucial question: in the battle against American imperialism, 'who, in the first place, can be our ally?' This question, in actual fact, served to advance serious and well-founded doubts on the efficacy of a political line which foresaw the abandonment of collaboration with the Social Democratic parties which 'still enjoy serious influence in the working class in certain countries. And, after all, it is only the working class that can lead the people in this fight.'[26]

In his concluding remarks, Zhdanov was even more explicit in pointing to the general implications in the 'turning-point' he had outlined in his report: 'It must not be supposed that the front of resistance to American imperialism will be drawn along the same line as the front of the struggle against German imperialism. Such thinking would be dangerous schematism.'[27] With these words, Zhdanov declared a close to the season of national fronts, both in the West and in the East.

The newly-available material on the founding of Cominform does not provide us with explicit indications on the line that the Communist parties of the East were to adopt in order to contribute to the battle against the expansionist plans of the United States. If 'lessons' were also drawn by the Communists of the East from Zhdanov's indictment of the two western parties, this took place elsewhere. This prevents us from being able to give a complete answer to the question raised by historical research on the goals pursued by the Soviet leadership after deciding to create Cominform. It remains an open question. The new sources of information, however, do enable us to grasp the insufficient nature of those interpretations that tend to relate the Soviet decision to establish Cominform exclusively to the need to come up with an answer to the American initiative of economic aid for the reconstruction of Europe.

Notes

1 Most representative of this historiographical position is G. D. Ra'anan, *International Policy Formation in the USSR. Factional 'Debates' during the Zhdanovshchina* (Hamden, Conn: Archon Books, 1983).

2 S. D. Parrish, 'The Turn to Confrontation: The Soviet Reaction to the Marshall Plan, 1947', in *New Evidence on the Soviet Rejection of the Marshall Plan, 1947: Two Reports*, Working Paper, no. 9, Cold War International History Project (March 1994) p. 32; this interpretation was largely taken up by G. Roberts in

'Moscow and the Marshall Plan: Politics, Ideology and the Onset of the Cold War, 1947', *Europe-Asia Studies*, vol. 46, no. 8 (1994) 1371–86.

3   L. Ya. Gibianskii, 'Kak voznik Cominform. Po novym arkhivnym materialam', *Novaya i Noveishaya Istorya*, 4 (1994) p. 134–44.
4   Ibid., p. 135.
5   N. I. Yegorova, 'From the Comintern to the Cominform: Ideological Dimension of the Cold War Origins (1945–1948)', paper presented at the conference *New Documents on the History of the Cold War* (Moscow, 12–15 January 1994); G. M. Adibekov, *Cominform i poslevoennaja Evropa, 1947–1956 gg.*, (Moscow: 1994) pp. 6–14.
6   RTsKhIDNI, f.77, op.3, d.89,1.7.
7   RTsKhIDNI, f.575, op.1, d.3,1.17–18.
8   G. Takhnenko, 'Anatomiya Odnogo Politicheskogo Resheniya (K 45-letiyu plana Marshalla)', *Mezhdunarodnaya zhizn*, 5 (May 1992) pp. 113–27; M. M. Narinskii, 'SSSR i plan Marshalla: Po Materialam Arkhiva Prezidenta RF', *Novaya i Noveishaya Istoriya*, 4 (April 1993) pp. 11–19.
9   Takhnenko, p. 125.
10 Narinskii, pp. 16–17.
11 Ibid., pp. 17–19.
12 Gibianskii, pp. 138–40.
13 RTsKhIDNI, f.575, op.1, d.41, 1.22–3; for a more detailed analysis of the preparatory materials for the conference see A. Di Biagio, 'The Establishment of the Cominform', in *The Cominform. Minutes of the Three Conferences, 1947/1948/1949*, Fondazione G. Feltrinelli, Annali, a. XXX (Milan: Fondazione Feltrinelli, 1994) pp. 12–25.
14 L. Gibianskii, 'The Beginning of the Soviet–Yugoslav Conflict and the Cominform', in *The Cominform*, pp. 469–70.
15 Memorandum from Zhdanov to Stalin on the eve of the conference (RTsKhIDNI, f.77, op.3, d.90, 1.10).
16 RTsKhIDNI, f.575, op.1, d.3, 1.74–5.
17 Di Bagio *The Cominform* op. cit., p. 89.
18 Ibid., p. 63.
19 Di Biagio *The Cominform* op. cit., p. 31.
20 Ibid p. 123.
21 RTsKhIDNI, f.77, op.3, d.92, 1.8.
22 Di Bagio *The Cominform* op. cit., p. 195.
23 Ibid., p. 457.
24 Ibid., p. 455.
25 Ibid., p. 267.
26 Ibid., p. 339.
27 Ibid., p. 353.

26
First Budapest, then Prague and Berlin, why not Vienna? Austria and the Origins of the Cold War 1947–48

Oliver Rathkolb

Austria – special case or another object of the Cold War?

Recent historiography of Austria after 1945 concludes that, despite or maybe because of the geopolitical situation between the two emerging post-Second World War power blocs, this small country was only freed in 1955 from allied administration in general and from Soviet control of the eastern parts and Vienna in particular.[1] This chapter examines *whether* Austria was a 'special case' and geopolitical conditions alone and/or Western containment hindered the execution of Stalin's alleged master plan for a complete political and economic domination and integration of central Europe, *or whether* Austria was not in fact part of the Soviet plan after 1945. A third option is the 'approaches policy' (*Vorfeldpolitik*) – or 'outer circle policy' – which means that Soviet policy had clearly defined limited intervention in a partly occupied territory on the periphery of the belt of 'fully occupied' states of eastern and south-eastern central Europe.[2]

There are a few central points in Austria's postwar history in 1945–46, which make the Austrian example more easily comparable with Soviet policies in other liberated and occupied territories. Eastern Austria and the capital Vienna was liberated from German troops and occupied by Soviet troops in April 1945; on 27 April 1945 a Provisional Government under the old socialdemocrat Karl Renner with a three-party structure (Socialdemocrats, Conservatives and Communists) had been set up and accepted by Stalin.[3] All German assets had been seized as war booty;

negotiations to form joint Soviet–Austrian companies embracing the Danube Shipping Company and oil assets had been turned down in September 1945 after British and US pressure and the resistance of part of the Austrian government; in the Austrian national elections of 25 November 1945 the Communist Party was reduced to 5.41 per cent of the total vote with only four seats in parliament, whereas the Peoples Party won 85 seats and the Socialdemocrats 76. Any hope for the Communists, who had paid the highest price in the resistance against the Nazi regime, of gaining more votes were ended by the behaviour (especially the raping and plundering) of the Soviet occupying forces and the economic exploitation at any price to compensate for the destruction of the Soviet economy and industry during the Second World War. During February to April 1946 the Soviet administration continued to confiscate German assets on a massive scale.

Despite the fact that already in February 1946 the Cold War was affecting the Allied media in Austria – pulling all previous anti-Hitler coalition stops out –,[4] in April 1947 the Austrian case on the agenda of the Foreign Ministers Conference seemed not to be so hopeless compared with the case of Germany. The main obstacle for an agreement over the Austrian State Treaty was that since early 1946 General Mark W. Clark, the US High Commissioner, had become a staunch cold warrior. Together with his staff he convinced the newly appointed Secretary of State, George C. Marshall, that the Soviet offers to accept an economic ransom for the confiscated German property as the price for the end of occupation were only meant to provoke a social crisis and in the long run would destabilize the weak Austrian economy and lead to the overthrow of the anti-Communist government and turn Austria into a Soviet satellite state. State Department officials in Austria opposed this view only half-heartedly.[5]

Rakosi's 'salami tactics' in Austria reconsidered: 1947 and the economic integration of the Marshall Plan

General Clark's fears of an economic crisis as a prerequisite for a Communist *coup d'état* seemed to have been proven when, after the failure of the Moscow conference, the Communists organized 'hunger demonstrations' against the Austrian government and even besieged the Federal Chancellery on 5 May. Only a few weeks later the Hungarian Prime Minister Ferenc Nagy was forced to resign.[6] Even today US historians, like Audrey Kurth Cronin, argue that 'numerous signs pointed to Russian hopes of turning Austria into an Eastern bloc country'[7] thus completing Stalin's alleged 'Master-Plan' for the complete domination of central Europe including large parts of western Europe.

This war of nerves became more intense when in early July the Austrian government voted unanimously – that is including the vote of the only Communist minister – to accept the invitation to participate in the European Recovery Program (the Marshall Plan).[8] It took the Austrian Communist Party and the Soviet administration in Austria ten days to react. The Soviets intensified the pressure on the Austrian government and many rumours of a Communist putsch circulated in July and August as a consequence of the Marshall Plan debate.[9] However, this suspected instrument for the partitioning of Austria was neutralized when food supplies were transferred into the Soviet zone of occupation, passing through Vienna. After March 1946 President Karl Renner already had reported several times to US diplomats on the danger of a Russian take-over and the geopolitical need for Western Allied military presence in Austria: '[...] Czechoslovakia was already lost to the Russians [...]. If Vienna and Austria were likewise to fall within the Russian orbit, then Western Europe would effectively be severed from Eastern Europe. There would be a Chinese wall from the North to the Adriatic Sea [...]'.[10] In March 1947 he focused on the alleged policy of the Russian Commanders, who were depositing hidden stores of weapons in the industrial establishments administered by the Soviets in Lower Austria. Renner feared that these weapons had been earmarked for uprisings against the government after the Allied withdrawal.[11] He, too, now advocated the 'security first' policy over the 'liberation first' target.

The inner circle of the government even worked out plans for 'permission' to form an Austrian government in exile with members of the government in France or the US. To obtain the necessary financial means for the project an exhibition of the treasures from the Vienna Museum of Arts, planned to be shown in the USA, was earmarked to be sold off in case there was a Soviet or Communist overthrow of the government (the exhibition continued to travel abroad – despite the protests of Austrian art experts – until 1952).[12]

In fact neither Soviet nor US policies deriving from the Marshall Plan debate, were ever meant to move the iron curtain westward. The Soviets were interested in continuing the economic exploitation of their empire the USIA, the confiscated German property, the US diplomats and military people even changed the political will of US Congress in 1948 and later, when they turned down investigations of ERP-aid to Soviet managed firms in Austria.[13]

It should be noted here that in internal memoranda US military experts conceded that, if Austria were next on the list of the Soviet Union, the Western occupying powers could do little if confronted with a *fait accompli* in eastern Austria alone. Tactical plans for the withdrawal of US forces to Germany and, later in 1949, to northern Italy, had already been approved.[14]

'Prague was west of Vienna' and the beginning of the Western build up of Austrian security forces

With these words, Austrian Foreign Minister Karl Gruber expressed deep concern in March 1948 when he summarized his impressions of the *coup* and the Communist take-over in Prague.[15] On the day the *coup* started, 20 February, he even suggested in a conversation with a British diplomat that Austria should join the Western Union in order to maintain its independence – a proposal which Foreign Minister Ernest Bevin turned down immediately.[16] At the same time these trends in the Austrian political decision-making élite – to seek internal and external military security more than full sovereignty through the Austrian State Treaty – strengthened and coincided with the strategic planning of the US military establishment. The joint chiefs-of-staff pressed for an organized army within the regulations of the State Treaty to prevent either a 'Yugoslav scenario' (defending itself against border raids), or a 'Czech scenario' (overthrow of the government by Communist infiltration and subversion).[17] Indeed this view was included in the State Treaty negotiations and, after late 1949, the military build up of an Austrian army (under US guidance) became a US precondition for approval of the treaty.[18]

As a short-term action the Austrian government asked the US in April 1948 to establish a stock of weapons, equipment and ammunition for the purpose, should there be an emergency, of arming and strengthening the Austrian police and gendarmerie under US control and custody. Until 31 December 1948, 2750 Austrians had been instructed in the use of these small arms and the total number of the Austrian police and gendarmerie forces was about 26 000.[19] The military power of the Communists, however, was extremely weak; the '*Werkschutz*', a troop of guards for the oil installations confiscated by the Soviet Union, was only about 1000-strong. The Communist influence among the police officer corps was strong in Vienna (12 out of 26 Viennese district police chiefs were Communists), but the Socialdemocratic Minister of the Interior was already convinced that in case of crisis these could be 'neutralized' and during 1947–48 he carried out a strict anti-Communist purge of the police force.[20]

For his Harvard Ph.D. thesis Günter Bischof unearthed a document, written in German, in the French archives: a 40 page *'Aktionsplan'* allegedly drafted by the former Vienna state police chief Dürmayer and two other Communist functionaries, Umschweif and Marek. According to this plan, 17 000 Communist activists were ready to take power in Vienna and arrest the leading politicians of the Grand Coalition (Chancellor Figl, Foreign Minister Gruber and Vice-chancellor Gruber).[21] However, a brief formal analysis of this document seems to prove that this was a rather unprofessional forgery since the special committee cited did not exist in the Communist decision-making structure.[22] To this day we do not know exactly how this document ended up in the French archives, whether it is a fake or if it was indeed a putsch plan. US intelligence could only report rumours that in the Soviet headquarters a card index with the names of 17 000 Austrians representing the total Communist military potential did exist and could not verify these rumours, but very much doubted the number quoted.[23] To put it bluntly, even if it were true, it did not correspond to the military power of the Communists (*Werkschutz*) and the Western allied military presence in Vienna. At the same time the demonstrations against the wages and price agreement of September–October 1950 – heavily influenced and partly controlled by the Austrian Communists – showed that the Soviet occupation forces had received no orders to use military force in concert with the Communist stormtroopers![24]

Nevertheless at that time all Austrian and some western political decision-makers and experts feared that Vienna might be blocked like Berlin, since all the transit roots ran through Soviet-controlled territories. Therefore, in two separate operations (codenamed Squirrel Cage and Jackpot) food sufficient for 84 days was stored in Vienna (which in the long run proved to be a feast for rats!)[25] Behind the political scenes US observers made it quite clear that the situation in Berlin was different from Vienna, since a blockade of Vienna would mean partitioning the small country into two halves.[26] The Austrian population and some policy leaders, however, had sometimes 'feelings of near panic' in July 1948. Intelligence evaluations, both from the CIA and the military establishment, conclude that even after the Prague putsch and the Berlin crisis the 'USSR [... had] not embarked' on a forced partition of Austria.[27] Nevertheless the US forces prepared special evacuation plans for US personnel and, according to a priority list (along the lines of three categories), for the Austrian President, Chancellor and other members of the Austrian government, as well as the president and vice-president of the Trade Unions and the director general of the largest bank, the *Creditanstalt Bankverein*.[28] They were to constitute an Austrian government in exile.

Austrian social democracy on its way into the 'Western camp'

The political power of the Communist Party was steadily declining and even in the Trade Unions the Communist membership was limited to 15 per cent, with a dominant overall social democratic majority which since 1947 had been drawn, in an ideological sense, into the Western camp.[29] In the orthodox historiography on the Cold War the trend to form 'front' organizations in order to include non-Communist parties and bring them under communist domination, has been repeated in Austria too, but was, to cite William Lloyd Stearman, 'frustrated by the steadfast refusal of the two non-communist parties to co-operate in this scheme.'[30] Although there did exist a Socialist–Communist liaison committee in Austria in 1945, which held several meetings up until the poor general election results, despite the fact that the party election platform of the Socialdemocrats was strongly dominated by the left wing. Maybe it was because of the Marxist rhetoric that the leftist group in the Socialist Party did not proceed to form a 'common front' with the Communists.

One, however, should keep in mind that in 1945 and especially 1946 within the Social Democratic Party one strong wing advocated a 'Third Force' in the nascent geopolitical confrontation between the East and West – preferably dominated by European Social Democrats. This official party policy which wanted to create a 'democratic socialism' between 'capitalism and socialism' was simply formulated by the French Socialist leader Léon Blum: 'We should become neither Soviet nor American.'[31] On the other hand the conservative Austrian People's Party – the dominating factor in the Coalition after the elections of 1945 – in 1946 had already focused on a hard line, openly anti-Soviet foreign policy course. Foreign Minister Karl Gruber sometimes went so far as to use 'the threat of Eastern European Communism to frighten Americans into treating Austria more generously'.[32] In the depressing political atmosphere after the Moscow conference of April 1947 and the announcement of the ERP, the Socialists changed their 'neutral' policy of 'equidistance' and became openly pro-American (a change already advocated in part by the Austrian President Renner in March 1946 and by Vice-chancellor Figl). On 19 June 1947 Schärf opined that his party was now 'in the

American camp', whereas at the beginning of the occupation the Socialist party had been more interested in establishing friendly relations with the Soviet Union.[33] In November 1947, the bipartisan Austrian anti-Soviet foreign policy was so strong that Schärf even turned against personal confidants like his man in the Austrian legation in London, Walter Wodak, urging him to renounce his pro-Russian policy immediately, otherwise the party would turn against him.[34]

Adolf Schärf, who led the inner party faction against the left wing, grouped around the Party Secretary Erwin Schärf, during August–September 1945, under pressure from the British and the Americans, had already overruled the then Chancellor Renner and many of his cabinet colleagues when they discussed a Soviet–Austrian treaty on co-operation in the exploitation of oil fields under Soviet control in eastern Austria.[35] 'Russian economic influence' certainly increased in Austria, partly as a result of economic necessity (loans, food aid and so on) and the extreme *de facto* reparations policy before and after the conference of Potsdam, when the Soviet Union gained legal title to confiscate so-called German property (*Deutsches Eigentum*) – which literally meant that all firms and properties under German control between 1938 and 1944–45 (even those that had been 'Aryanized' by the Nazis expropriating them from their Jewish owners) were considered as *de facto* war booty.

In the special case of oil in Lower Austria (which included former Western allied or foreign property) the Soviets had negotiated since August 1945 to form a joint stock company to exploit the oil fields and to distribute the oil products. Within five years the Austrians were to raise 13 million dollars to complete their half of the investment, the other half – the Soviet share – being valued at 12 million dollars including the oil fields claimed by the Soviets.[36]

Although the deal, which was intended to coincide with a desperately needed comprehensive trade agreement, was blocked by the Western Allies for geopolitical reasons, both Renner and one of the strong men in the People's Party, Julius Raab, had already agreed in principle to sign an agreement on the oil fields in order to get at least part of the oil back into Austrian economy – against stiff opposition from the Socialist Schärf.[37] In retrospect Austria was obliged to pay reparations in oil till the end of the 1950s, which after the State Treaty of 1955 were reduced. In 1955 the yearly production due to overextensive exploitation had reached 3.7 million tons (in total Austria paid 6 million tons in oil worth 2.7 billion Austrian shillings (equal to US\$ 108 000 000). In 1945 the Soviets were prepared to share the profit 50:50, although at the beginning a lot of money would have been invested into the so-called joint investment fund. The net profit for the Austrian economy would have been higher, if we take US$ 18 million as the average price for 1 million tons of oil.[38]

Soviet versus local Communist political aims and priorities in Austria (1945–48)

From the very beginning the Soviet political officers had major differences of opinion with their Austrian 'comrades', flown in from Moscow, which will be cited briefly here just to underline the argument that Stalin's main political aim with regard to divided Austria was to use it as a source of economic exploitation, and as a bargaining chip at the international level, in part as a buffer state between the Western sphere of influence and countries of predominant Soviet interest, such as Czechoslovakia, Hungary and, to some extent, Yugoslavia.

Stalin and the Soviet nomenklatura wanted a traditional state and administration structure re-established in Austria using the same formal constitutional instruments as in the period from 1918 to 1933. Therefore, the Soviets explicitly turned down planning proposed by Communists like Ernst Fischer and the Austrian Communist Party for a new, more revolutionary constitution. Until early 1946 the Soviet administration was not interested in a thorough purge of the Nazi and Austro-Fascist elements in Austrian society, limiting these efforts to what was in the political interest of Austria (except for war criminals). On the other hand, the Communists prepared a thorough de-Nazification – and for some months they were backed by the left wing inside the Social democratic party. Only after the elections did 'Nazification' and the military leftovers (armament plants, soldiers, German refugees and so on) suddenly become issues of primary concern for the Soviet Union: then, because of the slowdown in de-Nazification, the militarization and the problems resulting from the separation of Germany, Allied control should continue. The 'security' problem – the code word for the raping and plundering by individual Soviet soldiers – turned out to be a decisive argument used against the Communists during the first elections, with more than 60 per cent of the voters being women, whereas the official Communist political propaganda was forced to suppress this theme.[39]

A further negative element of the Austrian Communist Party's total identification with the Soviet occupation forces was the kidnapping of Austrian citizens carried out after 1945 and as late as 1948. The media and public opinion reacted forcefully when senior officials like Anton

Marek (in charge of investigations against Communist activities in the Ministry of the Interior) and Margarete Ottilinger (head of the planning section in the Ministry of Property Control and responsible for ERP-planning)[40] were taken to the Soviet Union against their will and tried (both were returned after 1955). Obviously the Soviet Union wanted to signal its security concerns in Austria with shows of brute force, but the general image of the Soviets as a kidnapping occupation force destroyed any chance of broader support for the Austrian Communist Party. Austrian officials stated that from 1945 to March 1950 approximately 430 Austrians had been arrested and released, but nearly 780 Austrians were still in Soviet custody.[41] The *'Arbeiter Zeitung'*, the Social Democrat Party's daily, ensured popularity by putting these kidnap stories on the front page (*'die Zeitung, die sich was traut* – the newspaper which dares'). The editor-in-chief, Oscar Pollak, was denounced in confidential Soviet diplomatic dispatches as a Trotskyist.[42]

Conclusions

Today there is no doubt within Austrian historiography that Austria never became part of Stalin's strategic planning as far as overall and permanent political domination was concerned. When we look at de-classified Russian secret documents such as the Soviet Deputy Foreign Minister Litvinov's report as chairman of the foreign ministry special commission on postwar order and the preparation of peace treaties 'On the prospects and possible basis of Soviet–British co-operation (15 November 1944)', this policy becomes even more logical. Even 'the maximum Russian sphere of security' was to include Finland, Sweden, Poland, Hungary, Czechoslovakia, Romania, the Slav countries in the Balkans, as well as Turkey, while Austria and Italy were to constitute a neutral zone.[43]

Other new sources – declassified for the author of this chapter – from 25 May 1944 show that the Soviets' primary interest was to gain a foothold in those parts of Austria where their intelligence believed they could capture the largest war factories and at the same time maintain their lines of communication with Czechoslovakia, Yugoslavia and Hungary.[44] Stalin himself primarily feared that Austria would become part of a 'Catholic' *cordon sanitaire*, a bloc consisting of Spain, France, Italy, Austria, Bavaria and Poland.[45] Already in January 1945, it was evident to high level diplomats, like the Deputy Foreign Minister A. Losowskij, that the Western Allies were interested in gaining more influence and instituting tighter co-operation in Austria than in Romania and Hungary. Therefore, the option was discussed of strengthening Austrian sovereignty by giving South Tyrol back to Austria and changing the German border in favour of Austria. A Danubian federation, however, would never have been accepted by the Soviets, since from their point of view this represented again a 'Catholic anti-Soviet bloc'.[46]

Austria was to become a bargaining chip in the Cold War confrontation, but never really constituted a 'special case' since right from the early planning phase Stalin himself and his diplomatic and political nomenklatura wanted the small state in the centre of Europe to be re-established – possibly with a stronger Communist party, but within a strict three-party scheme and coalition. Therefore, the neutrality of Austria in 1955 corresponded, thanks to Khruschev's efforts at achieving détente,[47] with the 'neutral' status foreseen in the Soviet planning discussion of 1944.

At the same time the United States used a profoundly modified containment policy approach to Austria and carefully analyzed policy effects which might lead to a partition of the country along the lines of Allied occupation zones. Therefore, projects of an aggressive economic rollback policy, proposed by Eleanor Dulles (who worked as an economic expert in the US Legation in Vienna at that time) under the codename 'Neutralization plan',[48] were not carried out. A small part of Marshall Plan aid even reached the Soviet zone to maintain the unity of the country against any intervention from Capitol Hill. The rearmament of the Austrian police, carried out in top secret (not very effective by the way), was limited in the nature of the armaments and size, so that it did not constitute a real conventional military security risk for the Soviet forces in Austria.

Notes

1 M. Rauchensteiner, *Der Sonderfall. Die Besatzungszeit in Österreich 1945 bis 1955* (Graz: Verl. Styria, 1979); G. Stourzh, *Geschichte des Staatsvertrages 1945–1955. Österreichs Weg zur Neutralität, Studienausgabe* (Graz: Verl. Styria, 1985); a completely revised and enlarged edition of this book was published by Böhlau Verlag Wien-Köln-Weimar in 1998; G. Bischof, *Between Responsibility and Rehabilitation: Austria in International Politics, 1940–1950*, unpublished Ph.D. diss (Cambridge, Mass: Harvard University, 1989); published as *Austria in the First Cold War 1945–1955: the leverage of the Weak* (London: Macmillan, 1999).

2 R. Bollmus, 'Staatliche Einheit trotz Zonentrennung. Zur Politik des Staatskanzlers Karl Renner gegenüber den Besatzungsmächten in Österreich im Jahre 1945', *Festschrift Werner Conze. Soziale Bewegung und Politische Verfassung. Beiträge zur Geschichte der Modernen Welt* (Stuttgart: Klett, 1976), p. 688. Partly focusing on the same interpretation see A. K. Cronin, *Great Power Politics over Austria, 1945–1955* (Ithaca, NY: Cornell University Press, 1986).

3   H. Poitrowski, 'The Soviet Union and the Renner Government of Austria, April–November 1945', *Central European History* 20 (1987), pp. 246–79.

4   O. Rathkolb, *Politische Propaganda der Amerikanischen Besatzungsmacht in Österreich 1945 bis 1950. Ein Beitrag zur Geschichte des Kalten Krieges in der Presse-, Kultur-und Rundfunkpolitik,* (Vienna: unpublished Ph.D. Diss., 1981), pp. 124–30. This dissertation was published in 1998 by Studienverlag Innsbruck-Wien. Compare on the same subject R. Wagnleitner, *Coca-Colonization and the Cold War. The Cultural Mission of the United States in Austria after the Second World War* (Chapel Hill: University of North Carolina Press, 1994), pp. 69–75.

5   F. L. Hadsel, 'Reflections of the U.S. Commanders in Austria and Germany', H. A. Schmitt, ed., *U.S. Occupation in Europe after World War II: Papers and Reminiscences from the April 23–24, 1976, Conference Held at the George C. Marshall Research Foundation, Lexington, Virginia* (Lawrence: Kansas, 1978), p. 148 ff.

6   W. L. Stearman, *The Soviet Union and the Occupation of Austria. An Analysis of Soviet Policy in Austria, 1945–1955* (Bonn: 1961), p. 109.

7   Cronin *Great Power Politics* op. cit. p. 51.

8   P. B. Eggleston, *The Marshall Plan in Austria: A Study in American Containment of the Soviet Union in the Cold War* (unpublished Phil. Diss. University of Alabama: 1980) and W. Mähr, *Der Marshall-Plan in Österreich* (Graz: Verl. Styria, 1989).

9   G. Bischof, ' "Prag liegt westlich von Wien": Internationale Krisen im Jahre 1948 und ihr Einflu auf Österreich', in G. Bischof and J. Leidenfrost, eds, *Die bevormundete Nation. Österreich und die Alliierten 1945–1949* (Innsbruck: Haymon Verl., 1988), pp. 315–46.

10 National Archives, College Park, Maryland, Record Group 59, 711.637/3–846, p. 2.

11 Ibid., 863.108/3–1347.

12 H. Portisch and S. Riff, *Österreich II. Der lange Weg zur Freiheit* (Vienna: Kremayr & Scheriau, 1986), pp. 344–8.

13 For more details see Mähr *Der Marshall Plan* op. cit.

14 National Archives, College Park, Maryland, Record Group 319, Entry 154, Box 66, Plans & Operations Division, Trip to Europe, 24 June–19 July 1948.

15 G. Bischof, 'Karl Gruber and Austrian Foreign Policy', *Austrian History Yearbook* (XXVI) 1995, p. 115.

16 C. Stifter, *Die Wiederaufrüstung Österreichs. Die geheime Remilitarisierung der westlichen Besatzungszonen 1945–1955* (Innsbruck: Studien-Verl., 1996), pp. 87–119.

17 *Foreign Relations of the United States 1949. Volume III. Council of Foreign Ministers; Germany and Austria* (Washington DC: US Government Printing Office, 1974), pp. 1190–7.

18 Stifter *Die Wiederanfrustung Österreichs* op. cit. pp. 167–9.

19 National Archives, College Park, Maryland, Record Group 319, Entry 154, Box 150: memo for the Secretary of the Army, 7 January 1949, p. 1.

20 W. B. Bader, *Austria Between East and West* (Stanford CA: Stanford University Press, 1996) pp. 77–109.

21 Bischof, *Between Responsibility and Rehabilitation* op. cit. p. 336 ff.

22 O. Rathkolb, *Washington ruft Wien. US-Gromachtpolitik und Österreich 1953–1963* (Wien: Böhlau, 1997), p. 20.

23 National Archives, College Park, Maryland, Record Group 59, 863.108/3–29/ 47.
24 See more on this interpretation in the various articles edited by M. Ludwig, K. D. Mulley and R. Streibel, *Der Oktoberstreik 1950. Ein Wendepunkt der Zweiten Republik* (Wien: Picus-Verl., 1991).
25 G. Bischof, '"Austria looks to the West". Kommunistische Putschgefahr, geheime Wiederaufrüstung und Westorientierung am Anfang der fünfziger Jahre', in T. Albrich, K. Eisterer, M. Gehler and R. Steininger eds, *Österreich in den Fünfzigern* (Innsbruck: Österreich Studien-Verl., 1995), p. 188.
26 Ibid., pp. 187–90.
27 *Foreign Relations of the United States 1948. Volume II. Germany and Austria* (Washington DC: US Government Printing Office, 1973), pp. 1414–32.
28 Portisch and Riff, – *Österreich II* op. cit. pp. 344–6.
29 National Archives, College Park, Maryland, Record Group 59, 763.001/10–2650.
30 Stearman *The Soviet Union*, op. cit., 1961, p. 22.
31 A. Carew, *Labour under the Marshall Plan. The politics of productivity and the marketing of management science* (Manchester: Manchester University Press, 1987), p. 231.
32 Cited from Bischof 'Karl Gruber' op. cit., p. 112. with more details on Gruber's anti-Communism and pro-Western tendencies.
33 K. R. Stadler, *Adolf Schärf. Mensch, Politiker, Staatsmann* (Wien, 1982), p. 294.
34 R. Wagnleitner, 'Walter Wodak in London 1947 oder die Schwierigkeit, Sozialist und Diplomat zu sein', in G. Botz, H. Hautmann and H. Konrad (eds), *Bewegung und Klasse. Studien zur österreichischen Arbeitergeschichte* (Wien: Europa Verl., 1978), p. 236.
35 O. Rathkolb, ed., *Gesellschaft und Politik am Beginn der Zweiten Republik. Vertrauliche Berichte der US–Militäradministration 1945* in englischer Originalfassung (Graz-Wien-Köln: Böhlau, 1985), pp. 319–20.
36 Stadler *Adolf Schärf* op. cit., pp. 226–31.
37 Bader *Austria* op. cit., p. 120.
38 K. Ausch, *Licht und Irrlicht des österreichischen Wirtschaftswunders* (Wien: 1965), p. 100; Stearman, *The Soviet Union* op. cit., p. 156.
39 A number of these above-mentioned issues are covered in the document collections R. Wagnleitner, ed., *Understanding Austria. The Political Reports and Analyses of Martin F. Herz, Political Officer of the U.S. Legation in Vienna 1945–1948* (Salzburg, 1984) and also in English with German commentaries in Rathkolb, 1985.
40 S. Karner, ed., *Geheime Akten des KGB. 'Margarita Ottilinger'* (Graz: Leykam, 1992).
41 Archiv der Republik, Vienna, Bundeskanzleramt, Auswärtige Angelegenheiten, Box 114, Zl. 122.348/1950 and National Archives, College Park, Maryland, Record Group 59, 763.00/9–1751.
42 W. B. Bader, *Austria Between East and West* (Stanford CA: Stanford University Press, 1966), p. 24 ff.
43 V. O. Pechatnov, *The Big Three after World War II: New Documents on Soviet Thinking about Post War Relations with the United States and Great Britain* (Washington DC: Cold War International History Project, Working Paper 13, 1995), p. 12.

44   Bruno Kreisky Archives Foundation, Vienna: Copies from Records, stored in the Foreign Ministry Archives of the Russian Federation, Moscow, Chairman of the Commission for Armistice Negotiations to Molotow, 25 May 1944.
45   R. Badstüber, 'Beratungen bei J. W. Stalin', *Utopie kreativ* (1991), Number 7.
46   Bruno Kreisky Archives Foundation, Vienna: copies from records, stored in the Foreign Ministry Archives of the Russian Federation, Moscow, A. Losovskij, 'Plans With Regard to the Postwar Order of Austria', 23 January 1945.
47   V. Zubok and C. Pleshakov, *Inside the Kremlin's Cold War. From Stalin to Khrushchev* (Cambridge, Mass: Harvard University Press, 1996)
48   A. Einwitschläger, *Amerikanische Wirtschaftspolitik in Österreich 1945–1949* (Wien: Böhlau, 1986).

27
The Partition of Europe

René Girault

In contemporary history turning-points are so numerous that it is always difficult to point out the real moments during which global situations have moved on. However there is a general agreement among historians that the year 1947 was truly *the* year during which the Cold War began; that is the confrontation between the two superpowers and consequently the partition of Europe because of Europe's strategic, economic and political weight at that time.

Two separate events appear to be the main issues of that tremendous year: in June, the launching of the Marshall Plan pushed European states towards a decisive choice: linking them to American relief aid, which implied more or less adopting American views on foreign policy; accepting not only a liberal view of the world economy, but even the American way of life. In September, the creation of the Cominform marked a new set of relations within the Communist world: Moscow's predominance; and the assertion of a Communist faith. Thus two separate, antagonistic 'camps' came into existence: the first 'imperialistic and anti-democratic', the second 'anti-imperialistic and democratic' as A. A. Zhdanov said in his report, foreseeing a direct/indirect confrontation between them.

Hence we should ask ourselves two main questions: why the Marshall Plan? Why the creation of the Cominform?

Since the Marshall Plan was really decided and drafted in July–August 1947 – after the unsuccessful meeting in Paris between France, Britain and the USSR – and the creation of the Cominform followed in September, there is no difficulty in admitting that a close relation existed between these two events. The summer of 1947 was a genuine turning-point. So we are left with one question only: why did the two superpowers decide to launch a new policy for and in Europe?

Up until the last few years our knowledge of the decision-making process was limited to the Western camp and more precisely to the American choice: the rather rapid opening of the archives and the heated debates between the American historians or political scientists on the origins of the Cold War, have facilitated our understanding of American foreign policy. Then, after Gorbachev's *glasnost* and the collapse of Communism in Russia, the corresponding opening of the Soviet archives has led to a reappraisal of Soviet foreign policy, even if Stalin's personal views are still the subject of discussion and interpretation. One can add that the actions and choices of the European governments themselves are now better known, in particular what the so-called 'popular democracies' did in 1947. On the whole historians are now able to raise global issues or, as P. Renouvin would have said, they can now wonder about *'les forces profondes'* which actually determined those external policies. One must stress at once the importance of the European powers and of the situations in Europe in the progression of the events in 1947. After all the Cold War in Europe was first and foremost Europeans' business!

What were the main questions at stake in Europe in 1947?

1) a real economic crisis, which affected many countries;
2) related to this economic crisis, social difficulties which hardened the political life in many countries;
3) the impact of European nationalisms on both sides;
4) the difficulty of finding a solution to the German problem: what future for Germany?

In a well-known book, Alan Milward upheld the idea that in 1947 there was no economic crisis in Europe in a broad sense, but merely regional or local difficulties and a real shortage of dollars for European trade with America.[1] Therefore, he stressed that the Marshall Plan was not really necessary. In my view, not only did the Marshall Plan exist, which compels us to explain it, but it was a response to a real economic crisis in Europe. In his conclusion Milward wrote:

The first proposition of the book is that the economic crisis of 1947 which ended dollar–sterling convertibility and produced the European Recovery Programme was not caused by the deteriorating domestic economic situation of the western European economies. Even less was it attributable to an impeding political, moral or spiritual collapse. It was on the contrary attributable to the remarkable speed and success of western Europe's recovery.[2]

In fact, when looking at the statistics quoted by Milward himself, there is evidence to support the existence of a crisis: choosing the year 1938 as a year of reference, even though 1938 was not a 'good' year, could give the impression that recovery in Europe was well on the way, whereas this was not true; besides the index of European industrial production which was at 83 in the last quarter of 1946, fell to 78 in the spring of 1947 and was only 86 in the autumn of 1947.

But above all, the main thing is that during the spring of 1947 most Europeans living in continental Europe were struck by a pessimistic view of the whole situation; for them there was undoubtedly a crisis. I would just take one example to support that idea: when preparing the colloquium on 'Le Plan Marshall et le relèvement économique de l'Europe' (March 1991) a great number of French high commissioners were interviewed by the *Comité pour l'histoire économique et financière de la France*. In a synthesis of those testimonies, Florence Descamps wrote:

> When they evoke the economic and political situation of 1947 and the immediate context of the Marshall Plan, testimonies are all in agreement: a true unanimity emerges, this term is not too strong, for describing the state of dereliction, of economic and financial 'crack' in which France found itself on the eve of the Harvard speech. All the witnesses agreed on the ravages of the black market, the huge shortages and the financial bankruptcy – an aspect to which by reason of their functions they were particularly sensitive.[3]

History cannot be a mere reconstruction of the past using exact statistics, but it must first examine how contemporaries viewed the situation. Perhaps testimonies recorded years after the events are open to doubt; but when they are all in agreement, they can only be accepted as being truthful.

Anyway at the time, American diplomats in Europe had the same impression; for them Europe was in a crisis and they sent messages to Washington in that sense. It is possible to quote another witness, the former governor of the *Banque de France*, Emmanuel Mönick. In 1948 he met General Marshall at a dinner in Paris:[4]

> I told him that the preceding year I was in a good situation as Governor of the Bank of France to know that the economy of European countries was about to crash to the ground like an airplane losing speed [...]. There are – he told me in confidence – moments when the convergence of events is really extraordinary. Just before I

took the initiative you know, there was a fateful week when all the American ambassadors in Europe – I do say all of them and without consulting one another – sent cables on the continent's economic collapse.

Then General Marshall explained why he had decided to give a decisive answer to his ambassadors and to the distressed Europeans.

Among the huge difficulties which Europe had to face, was the growing dollar-gap. Trade between Europe and the USA almost had reached deadlock: the dollar shortage meant Europeans could not buy American goods at a time when only American means of production could satisfy European needs, chiefly for capital goods, for transport and for coal in some countries such as France and Italy after the Anglo-American decision to maintain German coal production for the Germans themselves as a priority.[5] On the other hand, at the time when American reconversion from a war economy to a peace economy was not complete, even if European customers could no longer buy in the US, it was considered safer to maintain close commercial transatlantic relations.

At the very end of the Second World War, in the Bretton Woods discussions, the American delegation thought that the reconstruction should follow regular laws inspired by liberalism, by the 'open-door policy', and by real free trade to avoid the bad old ways of the 1930s. They even thought that the transitory period during which Europe was to apply special measures due to the terrible destruction would not last more than three or four years. Significantly, when in December 1945 Great Britain obtained a huge loan for her reconstruction from her American ally, and former economic enemy, the American government dictated a speedy return to liberal laws, mainly in such questions as currencies, aimed at restoring the convertibility of the pound within the next 18 months (which was to become a disaster in the summer of 1947).

So, when the economic crisis occurred during the spring and summer of 1947, the time had come for realism after a time of illusions. The illusion of a rapid return to normality faded, just as did the practice of bilateral aid between the USA and single European countries. Undoubtedly the economic situation required a new global answer, which would take a rather longer time period (four years at least), ignore the traditional laws of the market, and apply to a united Europe. But here a choice had to be made: could American aid be extended to the whole European continent, including the eastern states? It seems to me that when Marshall delivered his speech in Harvard, stressing the correlation between the offer of American aid and a 'politically correct' moral attitude (that is anti-Communism) of European governments – apart from the fact that the American government still had to obtain the approval of the Senate and the House of Representatives – he knew that America only had sufficient economic capacity for western Europe. The testimonies of the former financial actors, on both sides of the Atlantic, prove that at the time American financial capacity could never have satisfied all European demands.

Therefore, the negative answer from the Soviet side and subsequently from the 'brother-countries', had been foreseen in Washington, though perhaps less so among western European governments such as France, and was of help to the American strategy. In the circumstances the questions and the doubts which arose among Communist leaders in the USSR and chiefly in some eastern European countries between the end of May and the beginning of June with regard to the American proposal, and so well described by Mikhaïl Narinskii in his study,[6] are of great interest. They prove that the fate of Europe – that is its partition – had not yet been fixed: but at the very moment when Stalin and his advisers – who were they in particular? – decided to rebuff the Marshall Plan the die was cast. At this point one must give a straightforward explanation of Stalin's motivations and calculations. We shall come back to this problem when looking at the explosion of nationalism in Eastern countries.

In 1947 the crisis was not only economic, but also social, and perhaps at a deeper level. Apart from the states which had remained neutral during the war, and Great Britain where a political change had taken place in 1945 with the victory of the Labour Party in the general election, everywhere in Europe there was a social turnover immediately after the war. The ancient élites were either out of the game or had been destroyed. When 'ordinary people' thought of their future, they hoped for a rapid return to prosperity, but also real profound social changes – a complete transformation from the old times. Reconstruction did not mean a return to the past, but a new departure in everyday life. In the political sphere this gave great weight to the Left and in particular to the Communist parties in France and Italy. In the spring and summer of 1947, in many countries people had the impression the situation was getting worse and worse; prices rose much faster than wages, rationing on essential goods remained, as did the black market; the only positive point was the permanent need for workers, which made strikes easier and more effective. On the whole, two years after the end of the war in Europe there was a widespread impatience with the many continuous difficulties in everyday life. This social unrest could give rise to revolutionary attitudes, or outbursts of revolt, which helped the Communist parties, according to American journalists and politicians; how then to solve the European social problem?

I think that we must stress the fact that the Marshall Plan had social aims, because the future effects of American aid on European states – which were developed countries suffering momentarily from a crisis – were to produce bigger and deeper effect than if they had been given to underdeveloped countries. They hastened the economic growth of western Europe whereas in the other half of Europe the development was to be much slower. In 1948, mainly after the Berlin crisis and after the so-called 'Prague coup', priority was given to military questions and the means for a common European defence: this tendency was even stronger in 1950, when the Korean war broke out. But such developments must not be allowed to conceal the social aims of the Marshall Plan. In the short term the action of the Marshall Plan was an answer to a political threat derived from social unrest; in the long term it was to affect western European society deeply, encouraging new trends in technology, productivity and marketing. Since the Marshall Plan paved the way towards European political construction, or at least towards co-operation among western European states, via the OEEC (Organization for European Economic Co-operation), one has the impression that nationalism was weak at that time in Europe. In fact the impact of 'nationalism' was strong in this period, in both halves of Europe.

In 1947–48 the effects of the war were still paramount in public opinion and often determined political behaviour. During the war patriotism was at its peak and at the end of the war 'patriotic fronts' were often used as a political umbrella for new governments. Of course they included intellectuals, politicians, even the rank and file who believed in the need to overcome nationalistic views or policies, but most people and decision makers thought priority must be given to national objectives. There were victorious and defeated countries, the first thinking that the second should pay both for the destruction and for their moral and physical responsibilities; the memories of occupation were still vivid, and Germany and Austria were still occupied, not to forget the presence of the military all over Europe, even if some were considered 'friends' or 'allies'. The peace treaties signed in February 1947 were greeted with much disapproval and even left unsolved many questions such as Trieste. Reconstruction was determined by national purposes in order to rebuild national power. The French case was quite clear from this point of view: French public opinion, and politicians as well, believed that German coal must support French reconstruction not only for domestic needs, but also to help the French to attain industrial leadership in western Europe. Under these conditions, the refusal of both the British and the Americans to allow France to exploit the Ruhr coal on a large scale was resented as a form of treachery. However, France needed American help too much and had to accept compromises and this was the origin of anti-American sentiment.

Even after the creation of the OEEC, the weight of national interest was predominant. In his *Mémoires*, the first general secretary Robert Marjolin, tells the truth: in referring to the results of the co-ordination among European industries through the OEEC, he wrote: 'Nous étions donc en gros satisfaits de la croissance de la production [.... Mais s'agissait-il vraiment d'un effort européen? Je devais reconnaître que le résultat global obtenu était dû à l'addition d'efforts nationaux distincts, sans coordination véritable et non à l'éxécution d'un programme européen tel qu'aurait pu l'appliquer un gouvernement central disposant à l'échelle du continent des pouvoirs que possédait chaque gouvernement national. Pour la première fois, et je devais retrouver le même problème quelque dix ans plus tard dans la Communauté Economique Européenne, il apparaissait clairement que *l'Europe n'existait pas* au moins dans le sens d'une économie européenne [...]. Sous l'égide des Américains, avec l'assentiment des Européens un système de coopération internationale se construisit après la fin de la guerre. L'OECE en fut le centre en Europe pendant quelques années. Nous n'avions pas l'illusion de penser que les différents gouvernements allaient désormais se déterminer en fonction d'un intérêt européen qu'il était difficile de définir. En fait, comme je l'ai déjà dit plus haut, l'égoïsme national était alors aussi fort que jamais.'[7] No comment!

The importance of national factors and interests in the European reconstruction was well understood by the American administration in charge of the European Recovery Programme. There I would agree with Ennio Di Nolfo's remark in his chapter, following C. Esposito: 'When the ERP is considered from such a point of view, one can no longer ignore the extreme difference of American intervention in different countries.'[8] In fact the local administration of the ERP, being of necessity in close touch with Italian, French, British and other individuals in charge of national economies, quickly understood that it would be a great mistake to enforce a global solution, at a European level, shaped by liberal principles everywhere in western Europe. Certainly, 'the time has come [...] to verify the interaction between the ERP, the ECA and national authorities.'[9]

Self interest was not limited to western Europe. It did exist in eastern Europe as well. At the end of the war, in almost all the eastern countries, governments were called 'Patriotic Fronts' giving echo to the Soviet expression used for Russia's resistance and struggle against Hitler: the 'Great Patriotic War'. Rather curiously Communist parties, who were internationalist in principle, used catchwords that stressed national aims and interests much more than proletarian solidarity or socialist brotherhood: in fact patriotism gave a sort of legitimacy to Communist parties and their allies. At least a new type of Communism emerged here and there, a 'national communism' which could follow the Soviet pattern in political, economic and social grounds, but whose roots were to be found in national histories and societies. The Comintern's disappearance during the war was a help to such a line; relations with Moscow became bilateral. The differences between the forms of reconstruction or the political systems seemed to assert a kind of national authority. In such a context some eastern states were able to play an independent role, even to the point of initiating separate negotiations with western European countries, such as the Franco-Czechoslovakian talks.

When General Marshall made his speech, naturally some eastern governments, who foresaw the many financial and industrial problems of their reconstruction, were eager to be associated with American aid just as they had received relief from UNRRA. What happened then is now well-known: after a while Stalin imposed a negative answer on his allies, notwithstanding their former positive responses. Was the creation of Cominform a broader and stronger response to the Marshall Plan? Anna Di Biagio's chapter, using quite a lot of new Russian archival material and some important new publications,[10] concludes that the available documentation is not yet sufficient to give a definite answer. She stresses that the idea of a new co-operation, or direction, among Communist parties existed before 1947, but had not yet been achieved. That during the conference in Poland in September 1947, some measures had been prepared and other were improvised and, indeed, 'one does get the impression that the aims pursued were often in contradiction with each other. In fact there is a glaringly inevitable incongruity between the request made by Zdhanov to the western parties to take heed of the values of patriotism and national pride in their opposition to the Marshall Plan and the beginning of the struggle against the "national limitedness" of the parties of the east envisaged as a phase of transition towards the forced integration of the eastern bloc promoted and led by Moscow.'

Although I quite agree with these conclusions, I should add that nationalism lay at the very root of the discussion between Communist leaders. Zhdanov's aggressiveness, mirrored by his two 'hounds' Djilas and Kardelj against the French and Italian representatives, proved anyhow that from then on attempts to participate in a coalition government with 'bourgeois parties' were strictly forbidden, since there now existed two opposite camps with only one leader – of the anti-imperialistic world – Stalin. It meant the end of 'national Communist parties'. Comrade Tito and the Yugoslavs, who should have been the first to understand the lesson, were first to suffer from Moscow's heavy-handedness, the following year, since they had not understood, or did not understand, the new line.

In fact, if the creation of Cominform was perhaps an answer to the Marshall Plan, it was certainly an answer to nationalism in eastern Europe. At the end of 1947, though Europe was divided into two camps (Czechoslovakia was forced to enter the 'Socialist camp' in February 1948), there remained a large indefinite zone in the very middle of the continent: Germany. The division of Germany into several occupation zones had been decided during the war as a temporary solution, but had not been foreseen as a durable solution. What was to be the future for the Germans? Was an agreement possible between the four victorious countries on Germany's boundaries, on its constitution (federation of *Länder* or a united state), on its industry, chiefly its coal, on reparations? At the end of 1947 Western diplomats had the same impression: after the failure of the conference in Moscow between the four (March–April), a political compromise on the German question proved very difficult, but it seemed impossible after the conference in London (December), even though some European politicians such as the French President, Vincent Auriol, thought that a compromise was still a necessity.[11]

Now Germany, a former great power, was a major stake in Europe for many reasons, but mainly for its geo-strategic position in the continent. Immediately after the end of the war, if the great powers had been able to agree on the fundamental idea of 'spheres of influence', then the German question would have been resolved; but under the system of two opposing hegemonies – which emerged in 1947 – such a compromise was a delusion. Had Charles Bohlen's prediction of 1945 become a reality: 'the Soviet mind is incapable of making a distinction between influence and domination or between a friendly government and a puppet government'?[12]

From now on political calculations were to be based on military force; and in this context Europe became a good place to test Western reactions from the Soviet point of view – especially Berlin! The Berlin crisis was prepared step by step by Stalin and a small group of advisers, including military officers in charge of Eastern Germany,[13] in order to avoid the creation of a Western Germany. It was based on the conviction that a Western military response was unlikely if not impossible: therein lay the Soviet mistake, for the Americans were able to build the air-bridge; in fact on both sides armed forces were taking precedence over diplomats in the shaping of foreign policy, even though at the top Stalin and Truman remained the decisive leaders.

An inability to find a solution to the German question moved the economic confrontation towards a semi-military confrontation, that is the use of local threats to force the other to agree on the need for negotiations. The Berlin crisis was the real signal of the beginning of the Cold War. It was also the signal of a long period of partition for Germany.

Notes

1   A. Milward, *The Reconstruction of Western Europe, 1945–1951*, (London: Methuen, 1984).
2   Ibid, p. 465.
3   F. Descamps, 'Une contribution à l'histoire du Plan Marshall: la mémoire des hauts fonctionnaires' in *Le Plan Marshall et le relèvement économique de l'Europe*, (Paris: CHEFF Imprimerie nationale, 1993), p. 788.
4   E. Mönick, *Pour mémoire* (Paris: Mesnil, impr. Firmin. Didot, 1970), p. 22.
5   On the coal market, see R. Perron, *Le marché du charbon, un enjeu entre l'Europe et les Etats Unis de 1945 à 1958*, (Paris: Publications de la Sorbonne, 1990).
6   M. Narinskii, 'The Marshall Plan and the Partition of Europe'. See also Milward, op. cit., and F. Gori and S. Pons eds, *The Soviet Union and Europe in the Cold War* (London and New York: Macmillan, 1996).
7   R. Marjolin, *Le travail d'une vie, mémoires 1911–1986* (Paris: Laffont, 1986), pp. 211, 234.

> We were more or less satisfied with the production growth.... But was it indeed a European effort? I had to admit that the global result was the sum of individual national efforts, without any true coordination; it did not result from a European programme implemented by a central government fully empowered as every single national government was. For the first time, and I would face the same problem ten years later in the European Economic Community, it was clear that Europe did not exist, at least in the meaning of a European economy.... Under the aegis of the Americans, with the Europeans' consent, after the end of the war a system for international cooperation was built. We did not have any illusion that the single governments would act in consideration of a European interest hard to define. Actually, as I said before, national egoism was then stronger than ever. (Editors' translation.)

8   E. Di Nolfo, 'The United States, Europe and the Marshall Plan' quoting C. Esposito, *America's feeble weapon. Funding the Marshall Plan in France and Italy 1948–1950* (Westport: Greenwood Press, 1994).

9   E. Di Nolfo, ibid, p. 11. G. Bossuat's work tends towards the same conclusions in his analysis of J. Monnet Reconstruction Plan for France: *La France, l'aide américaine et la construction européenne 1944–1954* (Paris: Comité pour l'histoire économique et financière de la France, 1992).

10   A. Di Biagio, *The Cominform as the Soviet response to the Marshall Plan.* See also *The Cominform Minutes of the three Conferences 1947/1948/2949*, Giulio Procacci ed. (Milano: Feltrinelli, 1994).

11   V. Auriol, *Mon septennat 1947–1954, notes de journal* (Paris: Gallimard, 1990) 9 February 1948.

12   'Bohlen's momerandum of October 1945', quoted in J. Gaddis, *The long peace: inquiries into the history of the cold war* (Oxford: Oxford University Press, 1987).

13   See M. Narinskii, 'The Soviet Union and the Berlin crisis 1948–1949', in *The Soviet Union and Europe in the cold war*, pp. 57–75.

Index